NEW YORK HISTORY

SPECIAL ISSUE

THE SUFFRAGE CENTENNIAL

VOLUME 101, NUMBER 2

WINTER 2020–2021

New York History (ISSN 0146-437x) is a peer reviewed journal published two times a year by Cornell University Press in partnership with The New York State Museum. Postage is paid at Ithaca, NY 14850 and additional mailing offices. POSTMASTER: Send all address changes to Cornell University Press, 512 East State Street, Ithaca NY 14850.

New York History is available in print and electronically Project Muse (http://muse.jhu.edu). Cornell University Press does not assume responsibility for statements of fact or opinions made by contributors. Unlicensed distribution of all materials (including figures, tables, and other content) is prohibited. Communications about subscriptions, back issues, reproductions and permissions, and other business matters should be sent to Cornell University Press (nyhjournal@cornell.edu). Digital and print subscriptions, for individuals and institutions, may be ordered via Project Muse (https://www.press.jhu .edu/cart/for-sale?oc=3729). Single print copies and print back issues are available for $20.00. For subscriptions and individual issues, inquiries and orders may be made by email, nyhjournal@cornell.edu, or by mail: *New York History* Journal, Cornell University Press, 512 East State Street, Ithaca NY 14850.

Submitted articles should address, in an original fashion, some aspect of New York State history. Articles that deal with the history of other areas or with general American history must have a direct bearing on New York State history. It is assumed that the article will have some new, previously unexploited material to offer or will present new insights or new interpretations. Editorial communications, including article submissions, should be sent to the Editorial Board via email (NYHJ @nysed.gov) Suggested length is 20-30 double spaced pages (or between 6,000 and 9,000 words), including footnotes. All submitted articles must include a 100-word abstract summarizing the article and providing keywords (no more than 10). Authors must submit articles electronically, with all text in Word and all tables, figures, and images in formats supported by Microsoft Windows. Provision of images in proper resolution (no less than 300 dpi at 5" x 7"), securing requisite permissions, and the payment of any fees associated with images for articles are all the responsibility of the author. *New York History* employs, with some modification, footnote forms suggested in the *Chicago Manual of Style*. More detailed submissions guidelines are to be found on the research and collections page of the New York State Museum: http://www.nysm.nysed.gov/research-collections/state-history/resources/new-york-history-journal

COVER ART: *Front*: Suffrage Parade in New York City, May 1912. Courtesy of Coline Jenkins, Elizabeth Cady Stanton Family. *Back*: Suffrage banner, 1917. A group of Orange County women carried this banner up 5th Avenue in New York City ten days before the 1917 suffrage referendum. New York State Museum Collections

CONTENTS

Volume 101, Number 2

vi   Letter from the Editors

viii   Contributors

ARTICLES

175   Love, Letters, and the Institutions of Gender
and Marriage in the Nineteenth Century:
The Marriage of William Henry and Frances Seward
SHELLIE CLARK

195   Doublespeak: Louisa Jacobs, the American Equal
Rights Association, and Complicating Racism in the
Early U.S. Women's Suffrage Movement
SUSAN GOODIER

212   "Moving Heaven and Earth": The Uses of Religion in
the New York Woman Suffrage Campaign
KAREN PASTORELLO

239   The Recovery of John Francis Rigaud's Portrait of
Joseph Brant
GILBERT L. GIGNAC

276   The Institute of Social Economics:
A Neglected Network in New York's
Progressive Community
STEPHEN LECCESE

297   The (Hydro)Power Broker: Robert Moses, PASNY,
and the Niagara and St. Lawrence Megaprojects
DANIEL MACFARLANE

319   Dutch Reformed Congregationalism in New
Netherland: The Case of Rev. Wilhelmus Grasmeer
KENNETH SHEFSIEK

343   Monuments, Legitimization Ceremonies,
and Haudenosaunee Rejection of Sullivan-Clinton
Markers

ANDREA LYNN SMITH AND NĚHDŌWES (RANDY A. JOHN)

FEATURES

366   Artifact NY: The Spirit of 1776 Suffrage Wagon

MARGUERITE KEARNS

372   Community NY: Historic Sites Relating to Women's
Suffrage in Central New York

JUDITH WELLMAN

377   Teach NY: Exploring Haudenosaunee Influence on
America's Suffrage Movement with Students

KATHRYN WELLER

BOOK REVIEWS

383   Michael W. Flamm's *In the Heat of the Summer:
The New York Riots of 1964 and the War on Crime*

ANN V. COLLINS

385   Joyce D. Goodfriend's *Who Should Rule at Home?
Confronting the Elite in British New York City*

CHRISTOPHER F. MINTY

387   Hinda Mandell's *Crafting Dissent: Handicraft as
Protest from the American Revolution to the Pussyhats*

ASHLEY HOPKINS-BENTON

390   Jerry Mikorenda's *America's First Freedom Rider:
Elizabeth Jennings, Chester A. Arthur, and the Early
Fight for Civil Rights*

KATHERINE PERROTTA

392   Timothy Miller's *Communes in America, 1975–2000*

DEVIN R. LANDER

394   Kara Murphy Schlichting's *New York Recentered:
Building the Metropolis from the Shore*

ROBERT CHILES

398   Steven A. Walton and Michael J. Armstrong's
       The Majestic Nature of the North: Thomas Kelah
       Wharton's Journeys in Antebellum America
       through the Hudson River Valley and New England
       PAUL G. SCHNEIDER JR.

       PUBLIC HISTORY REVIEW
401   #MuseumFromHome
       ERIKA SANGER

LETTER FROM THE EDITORS

Robert Chiles, Devin R. Lander, Jennifer Lemak, and Aaron Noble

New York State has always played a central role in American history. The pages of this journal are filled with New Yorkers whose creations and concepts, innovations, activism—and at times, errors—have changed the world. In fact, it was here in the Empire State that the women's rights movement was born in Seneca Falls in 1848.

This year marks the centennial anniversary of the ratification of the Nineteenth Amendment, which states, "The right of citizens of the United States to vote shall not be denied or abridged by the United States or by any State on account of sex." Historians recognize that this proved a hollow promise, as many African American women (and men) would not have the real opportunity to vote until passage of the 1965 Voting Rights Act. However, the Nineteenth Amendment was a fundamental step in the right direction, and it would not have happened without New York. Voter approval of the New York State women's suffrage referendum in 1917 was the national movement's first electoral win east of the Mississippi River. At a moment when the Empire State's political influence was approaching its zenith—including forty-three seats in the U.S. House of Representatives and forty-five electoral college votes—the New York suffrage victory semaphored the approaching national triumph; and beginning in August 1920, women's suffrage was constitutionally guaranteed.

Amid the COVID-19 pandemic, many of the planned celebrations in honor of the suffrage centennial have been curtailed or cancelled. However, by the time you receive this issue there will be a new statue in Central Park honoring women's rights pioneers Elizabeth Cady Stanton, Susan B. Anthony, and Sojourner Truth—New Yorkers all. This is the first statue in the park to depict real women. Other statues are in the works elsewhere in the state memorializing Congresswoman Shirley Chisholm (Brooklyn), as well as one in Seneca Falls depicting Sojourner Truth, Quaker and early activist Marth Coffin Wright, a Seneca Woman (Laura Cornelius Kellogg), and the abolitionist and women's rights activist Harriet Tubman. At a moment of intense public debate about statues and historical memory, the unveiling of these monuments is a crucial step toward a more realistic presentation of our state's past, for even in 2020, women's representation in history still lags far behind that of men.

In honor of the suffrage centennial, this issue of *New York History* celebrates new historical research about the women's movement produced by women historians. Susan Goodier's article chronicles the African American activist Louisa Jacobs and the challenge of racism within the women's movement. Karen Pastorello's article discusses the variety of ways religion was used in the New York women's suffrage movement. Shellie Clark's article investigates gender and marriage roles in the nineteenth century through the lives of New Yorkers William Henry and Frances Seward. Lastly, our features (Artifact NY, Community NY, and Teach NY) all reveal dynamic ways the suffrage movement's history is being presented to the public throughout the Empire State.

As we celebrate the long struggle of women's suffrage in New York State and across the nation, let us not forget the most important gift these women and men bestowed upon us—the right to vote. Be sure to exercise this right in November.

Excelsior!
The Editors

CONTRIBUTORS

SHELLIE CLARK

GILBERT L. GIGNAC

SUSAN GOODIER

Shellie Clark is a PhD candidate in the History Department at the University of Rochester, with research fields in nineteenth-century women's history and nineteenth-century history of the family. Her dissertation focuses on Frances Adeline Seward, the wife of prominent nineteenth-century politician William "Henry" Seward. Clark has previously served as an adjunct professor in the Humanities Department at the Eastman School of Music and as a teaching assistant at both the University of Rochester and SUNY Brockport, and currently works in the Seward Family Digital Archive in the University of Rochester's Rare Books, Special Collections, and Preservation Department, transcribing and annotating the letters of the Seward family and friends and making them available on a public website.

Gilbert L. Gignac was born in 1944 in Penetanguishene, Ontario, and attended Banff School of Fine Arts summer sessions in 1966, 1967, and 1968. He received his BFA in drawing/painting from the School of the Art Institute of Chicago in 1972, after a year of independent study at the Brooklyn Museum Art School and Hunter College at City University of New York. Gignac received his master's in history of Canadian art from Concordia University, Montreal, in 1992. He taught drawing in the Visual Arts Department at the University of Ottawa in 1972–73. He was the collections manager of documentary art at Library and Archives Canada from 1974 to 2004. Gignac has an abiding interest in the shared history of visual culture between Canada and the United States. He has published on the work of William George Richardson Hind (1833–89) and is presently examining the work of Peter Rindisbacher (1806–34). He is also studying the uses of the camera lucida in nineteenth-century Canadian art and researching the portrait prints of Joseph Brant.

Susan Goodier is an assistant professor of history at SUNY Oneonta. She studies women's activism, particularly woman suffrage activism, from 1840 to 1920. She earned a master's degree in gender history, a doctorate in public policy history, with subfields in international gender and culture and black women's studies, and a women's studies master's degree, all from the University at Albany. At SUNY Oneonta she teaches courses in women's history, New York State history, the Civil War and Reconstruction, and Progressivism.

Goodier is the coordinator for the Upstate New York Women's History Organization (UNYWHO). The University of Illinois published her first book, *No Votes for Women: The New York State Anti-Suffrage Movement*, in 2013. Her second book, coauthored with Karen Pastorello, is *Women Will Vote: Winning Suffrage in New York State* (Three Hills, 2017). In addition to working on a biography of Louisa M. Jacobs, the daughter of Harriet Jacobs, author of *Incidents in the Life of a Slave Girl*, she is writing a manuscript on black women in the New York State suffrage movement

MARGUERITE KEARNS

STEPHEN LECCESE

DANIEL MACFARLANE

Marguerite Kearns was raised in a family that valued equality, nonviolence, and the power of telling stories. She spent decades searching to understand her activist family's part in a much larger social and economic shift in the nation. In addition to being a freelance writer and family historian, she has been a teacher, a newspaper reporter and editor, and a Hudson River activist. Kearns writes about the joys and challenges of action and advocacy. Her award-winning blog, *Suffrage Wagon News Channel*, focuses on the early women's rights movement and the need to put a human face on American history.

The featured selection is from the memoir and family history *An Unfinished Revolution: Edna Buckman Kearns and the Struggle for Women's Rights*, which will be published by State University of New York Press in spring 2021. The work relies on research, family archives, photos, and memories spanning a lifetime.

Stephen Leccese is an independent scholar and educator with a PhD from Fordham University. He studies economic theory, reform, and policy in American history. His work has appeared in numerous popular and scholarly outlets, including the *Journal of the Gilded Age and Progressive Era.*

Daniel Macfarlane is an associate professor at Western Michigan University. He is the author or coeditor of four books, including *Fixing Niagara Falls: Environment, Energy, and Engineers at the World's Most Famous Waterfall* (2020) and *Negotiating a River: Canada, the US, and the Creation of the St. Lawrence Seaway* (2014).

NËHDÖWES

KAREN PASTORELLO

KENNETH SHEFSIEK

Nëhdöwes (Randy A. John) is from the Allegany Territory and a member of the Seneca Nation. He holds a PhD in social science from Syracuse University and currently publishes Seneca history and culture books and publishes other authors' Seneca works through RAJ Publications. He is a former director of the Seneca Nation Language Program, curator of the Seneca-Iroquois National Museum, assistant to the president of the Seneca Nation of Indians, director of the Seneca Nation Area Office for the Aging, and a retired sociology professor from St. Bonaventure University.

Karen Pastorello recently retired from her position as the chair of the Women and Gender Studies Program and professor of history at Tompkins Cortland Community College (State University of New York). Her publications include: *A Power among Them: Bessie Abramowitz Hillman and the Making of the Amalgamated Clothing Workers of America* (University of Illinois Press, 2008); *The Progressives: Activism and Reform in American Society, 1893–1917* (John Wiley and Sons, 2014); and *Women Will Vote: Winning Suffrage in New York State*, coauthored with Susan Goodier (Three Hills, 2017). She is a cocontributor with Susan Goodier to *Suffrage and Its Limits: the New York Story* (State University of New York Press, forthcoming) and has contributed several suffrage entries to *American National Biography* (Oxford University Press, forthcoming). She is dedicated to exploring the historical origins and implications of women's labor and political activism in the United States.

Kenneth Shefsiek is an associate professor of American history at the University of North Carolina Wilmington, where he also directs the graduate program in public history. He is the author of *Set in Stone: Creating and Commemorating a Hudson Valley Culture* (State University of New York Press, 2017), which received the 2017 Hendricks Award from the New Netherland Institute. He previously served as the curator of education at Historic Huguenot Street and director of the Geneva Historical Society in Geneva, New York. Shefsiek holds a PhD from the University of Georgia, and a Master's in heritage preservation from Georgia State University, as well as degrees in music from Ithaca College and the New England Conservatory.

ANDREA LYNN SMITH

KATHRYN WELLER

JUDITH WELLMAN

Andrea Lynn Smith is professor of anthropology in the Department of Anthropology and Sociology, Lafayette College, Easton, Pennsylvania. Her work centers on place-loss, settler colonialism, memory, and power. Her most recent project, *Celebrating Sullivan*, explores the public memory of the Sullivan Campaign (1779) in Pennsylvania and New York.

With an MA in museum studies, focusing on museum education, from the Cooperstown Graduate Program, Kathryn Weller is the director of education and visitor services for the New York State Museum. She oversees educational programming that serves over thirty thousand students a year, as well as over two thousand educators. Kathryn has worked in the museum field for fifteen years in a variety of educational, curatorial, and leadership roles. Prior to her work with the New York State Museum, she was the director of the Slate Valley Museum and curator of collections for the Schenectady County Historical Society. In these positions she worked to increase access to collections for visitors, researchers, and students, built new educational initiatives with community partners, and improved outreach efforts and public programming opportunities.

Judith Wellman, PhD, is principal investigator with Historical New York Research Associates, and professor emerita at State University of New York at Oswego. Her work focuses on historic sites relating to women's rights, the Underground Railroad, and African American life in New York State. She is the author of many scholarly articles, more than a dozen cultural resource surveys, more than thirty National Register nominations, thirty-five nominations to the National Park Service's Underground Railroad Network to Freedom, and four books: *Brooklyn's Promised Land: Weeksville, a Free Black Community* (New York University Press, 2014); *The Road to Seneca Falls: Elizabeth Cady Stanton and the Beginning of the Women's Rights Movement* (University of Illinois Press, 2004); *Grassroots Reform in the Burned-over District of Upstate New York: Religion, Abolitionism and Democracy* (Garland Press, 2000); and (as Editor) *Landmarks of Oswego County* (Syracuse University Press, 1988).

Love, Letters, and the Institutions of Gender and Marriage in the Nineteenth Century
The Marriage of William Henry and Frances Seward

Shellie Clark

Nineteenth-century marriages shared a universal definition of marriage as a lifelong con-tract with clear-cut expectations of each partner divided along gender lines, even as indi-viduals experienced marriage in their own ways. Gender determined not only the roles but also the perceptions, experiences, and behaviors of both partners in traditional nineteenth-century marriages, even when aspects of their gendered experience left them unhappy and powerless to make changes that would benefit them. Social and legal restrictions, deter-mined by gender, left many partners little recourse when marriages did not turn out as planned. The marriage of William "Henry" Seward and Frances Adeline Miller was a very traditional nineteenth-century arrangement experienced by two people who lived under exceptional circumstances. Henry Seward's business and political engagements kept him from home and family for a large portion of their married lives, leaving Frances home to raise their family and maintain their Auburn, New York, home in his absence. When they were together, particularly in Albany or Washington, DC, their marriage and behavior faced the scrutiny of the public spotlight, and Frances was required to fill the role of politi-cal wife in addition to the usual domestic roles of a married woman.

Though strained by distance, illness, and tragedy, the Sewards maintained a decades-long love story as they struggled to remain faithful to the vows they made to one another in 1824 and fulfill their obligations as husband and wife. The William H. Seward Collection at the University of Rochester documents more than forty years of this nineteenth-century marriage. The letters provide insight into Frances Seward's evolving views on gender roles as she and her husband navigated a maelstrom of politics, activism, and reform that in-cluded the burgeoning women's rights movement, abolition, and the Civil War. In spite of their exceptional circumstances and their challenges to other institutions of the time, the Sewards' marriage was defined by the institutions of gender and marriage in the nineteenth century.

To Have and To Hold

Law professor Hendrik Hartog explained, "All participants in the antebellum Anglo-American legal culture understood what marriage was. At least until the middle years of the nineteenth century, being married meant subjecting oneself to a known and coercive public relationship."[1] For Henry and Frances Seward, marriage would be more public than for most, as Henry's political ambitions resulted in him holding numerous high-profile political offices.

Gendered roles within marriage had legal and social implications, including the expectation that the wife submit to her husband in most matters. Historian Cassandra Good explained, "A husband's control over his wife had both public and private importance, as demonstrating domestic authority served as a basis for a man's political rights," leaving less room for individual negotiations of control than twentieth-century marriages eventually would.[2] Frances Seward, like the majority of wives in her time, sought her husband's approval in most things, from travel and finances to her own behavior. Visiting Henry's family in Florida, New York, early in their marriage, Frances wrote to Henry, "I shall be contented here as long as you desire me to stay and will try and be everything you wish."[3]

The potential to impact their husband's reputation as well as their own gave women a double-edged sword to wield in their unions. Henry once explained and defended his sister-in-law Lazette Worden's potentially damaging behavior: "Lazette has been unfortunate in her attachment and has become mellowed in a temper which bears sometimes too much of independence."[4] The Worden marriage was marred by physical abuse, financial difficulty, and an apparent lack of love that was only resolved with Alvah Worden's death in 1856. Shortly after, Lazette moved back to Auburn, writing, "I look back upon my life in Canandaigua as nineteen years of discipline which though perhaps necessary, is not pleasant to remember."[5] Henry also noted his sister-in-law Rachel Seward's suffering from his brother Polidore's alcoholism, writing to Frances in 1834, "Sister Lockey! I feel her misfortune—In that lonesome place with four infant children to provide for and the entire responsibility of conducting the concerns of the farm. I fear Polidore's case is hopeless. I should be willing he would go to sea on some long whaling voyage or board a Temperance ship. There can be little hope of his being reclaimed by any other means."[6]

---

1. Hendrik Hartog, "Marital Exits and Marital Expectations in Nineteenth Century America," Philip K. Hart Memorial Lecture, Georgetown University Law Center, April 10, 1991, published in *Georgetown Law Journal* 80 (1991), 96.
2. Cassandra A. Good, *Founding Friendship: Friendships between Men and Women in the Early American Republic* (New York: Oxford University Press, 2015), 100.
3. Frances Miller Seward to William Henry Seward, June 23, 1829, William H. Seward Collection, University of Rochester, Rochester, NY. Unless otherwise noted, all letters referenced in this article are housed in the Seward Collection.
4. William Henry Seward to Samuel Seward, June 21, 1824.
5. Lazette Worden to Sarah Hance, August 28, 1856.
6. William Henry Seward to Frances Miller Seward, December 5, 1834.

Henry's own attitudes toward wifely behavior and masculine control were revealed in a letter to his father describing his careful selection of a wife: "I would not unite myself to one who did not possess a strong mind together with a proper respect for me."[7] Henry also described a multigenerational display of patriarchal deference by Frances, proudly explaining, "My little girl when I told her of the communication I was to make to you upon the subject dropped a curtsy to her distant Father and Mother."[8] Frances's acceptance of the importance of patriarchal approval was still apparent after nearly thirty-five years of marriage when describing the union of Elizabeth Cady Stanton: "I should judge her own marriage not to be of the most fortunate kind—it was in opposition to the wishes of her Father, Judge Cady."[9]

Marriage for women in 1824 meant losing a legal identity as an individual and being subject to the legal doctrine of coverture, where a married woman was considered to be under the protection and authority of her husband, transferring to him the rights to her property and wages, and children in the event of separation or divorce, and making her, effectively, a part of his identity while stripping her of her own.

Born just a few years after Frances Seward, Mary Gove Nichols married Hiram Gove in 1831. Her loveless and abusive marriage illustrated the limitations faced by nineteenth-century women in bad marriages. Fleeing to her parents' home with her daughter in 1841, Mary was committing a crime in the eyes of the law.[10] Hiram's debt to Mary's father briefly protected her, but his death in 1842 left her vulnerable again, and when Hiram took their daughter in 1845, Mary and a friend stole her back. Hiram received damages from her accomplice for their interference with his family "property."[11] Although Mary finally escaped her abusive husband and retained her daughter, their situation was vulnerable and without legal protection, and she was unable to remarry until Hiram decided to divorce her for a remarriage of his own.[12] Mary and her second husband, Thomas Nichols, embraced a number of reform movements, writing and speaking on women's health and sexuality, and advocating legal reform that would allow women to leave bad marriages.

There is no evidence that the Seward marriage was marred by the kinds of abuse faced by Mary Gove Nichols or Lazette Worden, though Frances did live under her father's roof, and presumably his protection, for twenty-five years of her marriage. A condition of Judge Elijah Miller's approval of the Seward marriage was that Frances and Henry live in his home, which allowed Frances and her family use of the home while ensuring the house and property remained under his control. Had he given the property to Frances, control would

7. William Henry Seward to Samuel Seward, August 12, 1823.

8. William Henry Seward to Samuel Seward, August 12, 1823.

9. Frances Miller Seward to Augustus Henry Seward, November 12, 1857.

10. Philip Gura, *Man's Better Angels: Romantic Reformers and the Coming of the Civil War* (Cambridge, MA: Belknap Press of Harvard University Press, 2017), 174–75.

11. Gura, *Man's Better Angels*, 177.

12. Gura, *Man's Better Angels*, 187.

have gone directly to Henry on their marriage. Had he willed the property to Frances, it would have been under Henry's control if Miller had died prior to 1848. Judge Miller was no doubt aware of the New York Married Women's Property Act of 1848, which allowed married women to control their own property and protected it from their husbands' disposal and debt liability.[13] Miller deeded the house and property directly to Frances on his death in 1851, leaving Frances Seward the owner of the Auburn home until her death in 1865, when it passed to Henry.

It is hard to imagine this living requirement did not have an impact on Henry, forced to sacrifice his primary role as a husband, providing his family with a home. Henry defended his choice to remain in Miller's home to his father in terms that protected his masculinity, writing, "Now as to the support of my family, Mr. Miller says that our living shall cost us nothing. To this I object and say that we shall not be supported by any body and I insist on paying him $200 for our Board Lodging &c."[14] The living arrangements offered other challenges to his place at the head of his household. Miller maintained his preferred household servants, including John Butler and Peter Crosby, in spite of Frances's dislike for them, showing he retained some control of household operations. While it is doubtful that Henry's ambitions would have allowed for less travel or fewer distant offices if he and Frances had established a home of their own, living under Miller's roof likely provided additional incentive to stay away throughout much of his marriage. For Frances, however, the opportunity to remain in her childhood home and have the support and companionship of her family and friends during Henry's long and frequent absences provided critical survival networks in an otherwise lonely marriage

Judge Miller may have also tried to impose patriarchal control over his sister, Clara, as described in an 1834 letter written by Lazette's husband Alvah: "I have objected to Mrs. Worden's visiting at Judge Miller's house at this time. . . . I understand Clara is about to be married contrary to the Judge[']s wish and I have no doubt he will . . . identify Mrs W with . . . a wrong to himself if he thinks she has had any agency in the affair . . . if this objection is not regarded it will lead to unpleasant results."[15] Worden may have intended to impugn Henry's manhood with the reminder that it was Judge Miller's home, and while it is impossible to discern if his warning about "unpleasant results" related to Judge Miller or an implied a threat from himself, other letters suggest he was prone to manufacturing accusations. A letter from Henry to Alvah the previous year, defending himself from an epistolary attack, described Worden's false accusations, temper, and capriciousness and his tendency to lash out at those around him.[16]

13. New York State Married Women's Property Law, April 7, 1848, Law Library of Congress.
14. William Henry Seward to Samuel Seward, May 11, 1825.
15. Alvah Worden to William Henry Seward, October 9, 1834.
16. William Henry Seward to Alvah Worden, March 19, 1833.

For Better or Worse

Nineteenth-century married couples had to balance individual desires with shared fortunes, within relationships that prioritized male responsibilities and preferences. Within social constructs that placed men in the working world and women in subordinate domestic roles, it is unsurprising that more importance was generally placed on male desires in professional decisions, even when those decisions directly and sometimes negatively impacted their wives and children.

The marriage of John Quincy Adams (1767–1848) and Louisa Adams (1775–1852) was a stark example of the consequences of male political career decisions on families. Married in 1797, Louisa Adams was forced to leave her two young sons behind when her husband became Minister to Russia in 1809. Louisa, who suffered from headaches, miscarriages, and other illnesses similar to Frances, was not consulted in this arrangement. Her memoirs detail years of emotional distress as her sons grew up for five years without her, as she bore and lost a baby daughter far from her family and home, and as she undertook a harrowing journey to meet her husband in London during the tumultuous fall of Napoleon.[17]

Women who did not have children, as well as those in better physical health, often had more freedom to follow their husbands' careers without such heavy emotional and physical costs. First Lady Sarah Childress Polk (1803–91) gladly followed her husband James (1795–1849) to the Tennessee governor's mansion and the White House, enjoying the social life, hosting events that bolstered her husband's career, and providing insight and administrative help throughout his time in office. Like Henry, James valued and sought out his wife's opinion and assistance with editing, correspondence, and building and maintaining relationships with his social and political peers.[18]

Henry Seward's business and political aspirations left Frances increasingly alone and starved for the romance and affection she deeply craved. Frances began a long record of lonely nights and appeals to Henry's love for his children, writing, "I wish you were here this rainy night I am so lonely. . . . I should not know what to do with myself you are absent so much were it not for little Gus. . . . Little Gus has almost forgotten he has a pa,"[19] and "I am left quite alone with Gus. . . ."[20] Frances did not hesitate to encourage guilt in Henry for his absences, writing, "Augustus . . . says 'Pa gone leave Ma all alone'—Ma cry--cry--cry—."[21] In her lonely bed, Frances wished for Henry's companionship and comfort, writing, "I shall not see you so soon so you must not ask me to say I am glad—The wind blows hard and makes a most doleful noise to night—and then I have some frightful dreams—well I

17. Michael O'Brien, *Mrs. Adams in Winter: A Journey in the Last Days of Napoleon* (New York: Farrar, Straus and Giroux, 2010).

18. Amy Greenberg, *Lady First: The World of First Lady Sarah Polk* (New York: Alfred A. Knopf, 2019).

19. Frances Miller Seward to William Henry Seward, October 17, 1827.

20. Frances Miller Seward to William Henry Seward, February 24, 1829.

21. Frances Miller Seward to William Henry Seward, February 15, 1829.

won't talk about it, I know you will come home as soon as you can—and make light the heart of your own Frances."[22] A little over a week later, Frances expressed another wish for Henry's quick return: "I hope my dear Henry when you receive this letter you will be on your way home it seems a long-long-time since you left us."[23] Henry did not stay at home for long, as a letter from Frances in July revealed: "It will be nine weeks on Monday, dearest, since I parted with you—this is longer than we have been separated before in seven years—I shall be proportionably glad to see you when you do come."[24]

By this time, however, Frances realized that long separations would be a regular part of her marriage, needling Henry a bit when she wrote, "Your Ma and I laughed when I read the part of your letter where you anticipate having more leisure at some future day, five years has not much brightened the prospect. I have now become almost reconciled to that which the first years of our marriage seemed intolerable and marred much of my happiness. Your Ma says she imagines your leisure will be like your father[']s, constantly diminishing as you grow older."[25]

Frances and Henry's mother were closer to the truth than they might have realized—Henry was elected to the New York State Senate, serving in Albany from 1830 until 1834. Henry's sister-in-law Marcia Seward extended sympathy for Frances's loneliness and apprehensions in an 1833 letter, writing, "I am come to enquire after your widow-hood. . . . No I know too well, what my feelings are when Jen[nings] is absent . . . now that Father & Henry are away—where perils await them—among strangers, posting on from place to place we know not where, my mind has been singularly exercised & my sympathies & affections excited in a way new & strange to my bosom. A thousand times have I forayed to the Father of Mercies that He would preserve them & restore Henry to you and Father to the anxious bosom other his consort & both of them to us all."[26] These letters indicate that many of the women of the Seward family were regularly separated from their husbands, often without a say in the decision.

The Seward marriage went through a crisis in 1834 that led to numerous letters from Henry professing his love for Frances, and openly seeking her forgiveness for his shortcomings and absences.

> My dearest Frances. I have always loved you, as the best and chief of my affections. I have been led afar off by an ambition which has only this mitigation that it was neither sordid nor selfish. But depress that passion, break it or disappoint all its aspirings, and my heart turns to you possibly with less than its original force but still with all the energy that is left to it to exert toward any object. I now see clearly that I must not hope

22. Frances Miller Seward to William Henry Seward, March 3, 1829
23. Frances Miller Seward to William Henry Seward, March 12, 1829.
24. Frances Miller Seward to William Henry Seward, July 28, 1829.
25. Frances Miller Seward to William Henry Seward, July 9, 1829.
26. Marcia Seward to Frances Miller Seward, September 17, 1833.

to preserve your love in the measure necessary to my happiness, if my own heart and character grow more worldly while yours become more and more pure and heavenly.[27]

Henry attributed to Frances all the traditional feminine virtue, and to himself a masculine exposure to the chaos and degradation of the outside world, that was expected in their gendered spheres. Perhaps his frequent assurances and romantic introspections improved their relationship somewhat, but his contrition did nothing to stifle Henry's ambitions. After leaving Albany, he did not remain home to practice law as his wife and father-in-law urged, but took a position with the Holland Land Company, keeping him in Batavia, New York, for extended periods of time.

In 1838, Henry was elected governor of New York, sending him back to Albany for four years. He found maintaining an appropriate residence in Albany and entertaining lavishly an expected but expensive part of politics. Deeply in debt after his term, Seward went back to practicing law, yet still traveled frequently on legal business. An 1847 letter showed that Frances still shared the impact of Henry's absence on his family, writing, "Fanny and I had a sad walk in the garden the morning you left—'Where is father? Isn't he coming?' 'Shall I pick this for father?' were her frequent interrogations."[28]

Henry served as a U.S. senator from 1849 to 1861, immediately followed by the position of secretary of state for Abraham Lincoln in 1861, then for President Johnson from 1865 to 1869, keeping Henry at work in Washington, DC, for the better part of twenty years, and away from home for the vast majority of his marriage. While Frances did accompany him to Albany and Washington for short stays, most of her time was spent caring for their children in their Auburn home, along with her father Elijah Miller, until his death in 1851.

While historians have generally painted Frances Seward as an invalid and recluse, her letters provide a different perspective on her absence from Albany and Washington. As historian Karen Lystra described, "While marriage was supposed to be a voluntary act based upon personal choice, the obligations of husband and wife were conceived as prescribed duties, socially mandated."[29] Frances's primary duties were caring for her family and home, and her letters detail decades of illnesses and injuries that needed tending as well as the maintenance and renovation of the Auburn home, requiring Frances to direct, oversee, and pay construction workers, painters, and a staff of domestic helpers who were a regular source of dissatisfaction. Leaving the family home to unreliable household workers and putting her family and herself through long, treacherous, bone-rattling carriage and train journeys, packet boat trips, and questionable post houses to be with Henry could be seen as neglect of her gendered duties.

While it is true that Frances had a difficult time maintaining the demanding schedule of calling and receiving calls in Washington and did not always enjoy the social scene the way

---

27. William Henry Seward to Frances Miller Seward, December 8, 1834.
28. Frances Miller Seward to William Henry Seward, June 11, 1847.
29. Karen Lystra, *Searching the Heart: Women, Men, and Romantic Love in Nineteenth-Century America* (New York: Oxford University Press, 1989), 206

Sarah Polk had, her letters reveal a warm and social woman who loved to dance before her physical ailments made dancing and long social events painful and exhausting. Her decisions to remain in Auburn increasingly over the years were not solely the inward turning of an invalid and recluse but the result of the demands of her gendered sphere and the limitations placed on her by her own body. Frances's letters reveal her desperate need to be with her husband and her profound loneliness, indicating these decisions were not made lightly.

As Frances realized over time that her desire for a close, romantic relationship and regular companionship would not be met by Henry, her letters focused increasingly on domestic matters, including the family's health, the location and travel plans of the highly mobile Seward family, and politics. While Frances accepted the common nineteenth-century opinion that women did not belong in public politics, she did read a range of newspapers to keep abreast of current political issues, and wrote to Henry and other family members frequently about political issues. Like her contemporary Catherine Beecher, who "defined the parlor as a cultural podium and described the home not as the place isolating women from political and social influence, but as the base from which their influence on the rest of the culture was launched," according to historian Katherine Kish Sklar, Frances did not hesitate to exert influence on her husband and sons in her letters.[30] She was a firm abolitionist and often urged Henry to go further in speeches and efforts to achieve the end of slavery, explaining to Lazette, "Whatever my timid nature might prompt me to do I hope I shall never fail in the generosity which will enable me to encourage the actions of nobler spirits."[31] Marriage to Henry gave Frances's more stringent abolitionist views some access to powerful offices she could never hold as a woman.

By mid-century, Frances showed a clear shift toward favoring some forward movement for women in the political realm. While an 1846 letter to Lazette decried the inappropriate political involvements of a female author, "Mrs. Maury . . . was going back to Washington on some business which would better become the masculine gender," she struck a different tone three years later.[32] In 1849, she wrote to Lazette, "I have been reading a book entitled the Influence and Education of Women. . . . Although I cannot yet say that I think women ought to vote and be eligible for office holders yet I will say that if there is no other way of elevating them I would rather see them more masculine than to see them what they are now."[33] Her preference for seeing women lose some of their femininity by stepping into the world of politics revealed a moderate feminism that recognized the powerlessness of women in many legal and social matters, likely reinforced by witnessing many women, including her own sister, suffer through bad marriages with little real control over their financial, emotional, or physical worlds.

---

30. Kathryn Kish Sklar, *Catherine Beecher: A Study in American Domesticity* (New Haven, CT: Yale University Press, 1973), 137.
31. Frances Miller Seward to Lazette Worden, December 29, 1849.
32. Frances Miller Seward to Lazette Worden, June 7, 1846.
33. Frances Miller Seward to Lazette Worden, January 15, 1849.

Frances's attitude toward change was tempered by her expectations of femininity and womanly appearance, many taken from Alexis de Tocqueville's *Democracy in America* (1838), from which Frances painstakingly copied, "Hence it is that American women who often exhibit a masculine strength of understanding and manly energy generally preserve great delicacy of personal appearance, and retain the manners of women although they sometimes show that they have the hearts and minds of men."[34] In an 1857 letter describing her desire to meet woman suffrage advocate Elizabeth Cady Stanton, Frances wrote, "I have been long wishing to meet Mrs Stanton—She is a woman of great abilities—and now that she has laid aside the bloomer costume is womanly and attractive—though she still has some rather ultra notions on the subject of the education of women."[35] Her interest in politics also afforded Frances a way to stay connected with Henry by immersing herself in his world, providing topics of conversation as well as the knowledge to perform her role as political wife.

Frances relied heavily on Henry's advice in Washington as she tried to navigate her way through a complicated and heavily gendered social and political scene, where the slightest misstep could reflect poorly on both herself and Henry. In an 1850 letter to her sister, Frances described an extravagant Washington dinner where she was toasted, in French, by political guests, revealing her uncertainty about the proper reaction: "I looked at Henry to know what to do and ascertained that nothing was expected of me but to keep my seat and incline my head to the simultaneous bows of the whole company."[36]

For Richer or Poorer

Henry Seward, like the majority of men and women of his time, had to make financial considerations a large part of his decision in choosing a bride. His father had supported a union with Mary Ann Kellog, the daughter of a prominent lawyer and banker Henry did not respect and who had a number of other heirs. Henry explained his decision, writing

> I was resolved that I would not unite myself to any person where poverty would be the result of my union. I grant you in view of all these circumstances that Mr K[ellog] is rich and if he lives long will die very rich. But he has seven Children and may have a family increasing in the same proportion with his wealth. . . . There are men base enough to take away the bread even from their Children's mouths and me once in his power who shall assure me safety from his insatiable desire for lucre? . . . the dowry of Miss M[iller] cannot be much inferior if any to that of Miss K[ellog]. [Miller] has no host of children to pamper all the rest at the expense of one. His honesty and his

34. Alexis de Tocqueville, *Democracy in America*, Vol. 2 (London: Saunders and Ottley, 1838), 192.
35. Frances Miller Seward to Augustus Henry Seward, November 12, 1857.
36. Frances Miller Seward to Lazette Worden, January 26, 1850.

magnanimity are unsuspected. And if I should become his Son in Law he could not have any inducements to persecute me.[37]

Financial considerations were important for both parties. A bad choice could mean a life of poverty for a woman and her children or financial ruin for a man, putting an onus on women to choose husbands wisely and be frugal and deferential to them on money matters. Frances often asked Henry's advice or approval on spending. On a visit to Florida, New York, Frances wrote, "Your Pa gave me $20 dollars the morning after he received your letter— of course I do not want this money but you are determined to make me extravagant, you know the facility with which I part with it."[38] While Henry controlled major financial trans- actions, Frances ran the Auburn household for decades in Henry's absence, and oversaw daily operations and purchases, as well as coordinating household repairs and renovations with Henry. Once, when she received cash in the mail, she wrote to Henry, "H. C. Silsby sent you a letter from S. Falls containing $100—I kept the money and Clarence wrote him a receipt- I had occasion for some of the money the remainder I will keep for you. Was this right?"[39] After twenty-four years of marriage and household management, one must wonder if Frances continued asking for Henry's input or approval more as a matter of form than of genuine uncertainty.

Financial considerations sometimes caused extended separations even when political business did not, including those necessitated by Henry's legal career. He wrote to Frances in 1849, "We are taking testimony in Winslow's. . . . If I did not owe money I think I should not have spirit enough to contend with the crowd of Lawyers—I believe that the strongest and oldest are to be combined against me there day after day and for weeks."[40] Henry's letter illustrates how men, in their gendered role of breadwinner, had responsibilities that could limit their options, too, although they enjoyed considerably more options for generating income than women.

In spite of the $200,000 Henry owed after his term as governor, he appears to have been hardworking and conscientious in his financial affairs, and Frances appears to have been fairly frugal in her spending. For wives whose husbands were lazy, irresponsible, or simply unlucky, financial matters could be far more worrisome. Frances's sister Lazette of- ten turned to Henry for assistance finding her husband Alvah work and consulted with him rather than her husband sometimes in relation to her finances, writing Henry, "The bank account you send corresponds in every particular with the one I have kept. . . . I have been very sorry to present an overdrawn account but it was unavoidable—and I am glad it does not appear to you of as much consequence as I had considered it."[41]

37. William Henry Seward to Samuel Seward, August 12, 1823.
38. Frances Miller Seward to William Henry Seward, July 13, 1829.
39. Frances Miller Seward to William Henry Seward, September 28, 1848.
40. William Henry Seward to Frances Miller Seward, June 12, 1849.
41. Lazette Worden to William Henry Seward, November 23, 1853.

Other nineteenth-century marriages sometimes suffered from the financial misman-agement of the wife. Abraham Lincoln took on massive financial burdens when his wife Mary Todd Lincoln overspent financial allotments for redecorating the White House, re-portedly saying of the overage, "I shall pay it out of my own pocket . . . it would stink in the nostrils of the American people to have it said that the President of the United States had approved a bill over-running an appropriation of $20,000 for *flub-dubs* for this damned old house, when the soldiers cannot have blankets."[42] Mary also treated herself to lavish clothing, hats, jewelry, and accessories, telling her friend and seamstress Elizabeth Keckley in 1864 that she was $27,000 in debt, which her husband was unaware of.[43] Other hus-bands who lacked the ability to cover the charges of spendthrift wives could be ruined by their extravagant spouses, as coverture laws held them legally responsible for their wives' debts.

In Sickness and In Health

Illness, invalidism, and death were regular components of nineteenth-century life and mar-riage, and women were expected to care for their families' illnesses and maintain a healthy home. Frances regularly began her letters with descriptions of her illnesses or those of their children, and concerns for Henry's health. Responsibility for her family's health often placed Frances in the untenable position of treating her husband and children's illnesses from a distance, sending suggestions for treatment in letters, and balancing the needs of sick family with her own needs as she suffered from regular "sick-headaches," neuralgia, dental problems, depression, and heart issues that frequently left her confined to her bed.

Frances also experienced a number of health issues specific to women, although often misdiagnosed, misunderstood, or downplayed as feminine weakness or hysteria. Frances suffered at least one miscarriage early in her marriage, as an 1825 letter from Henry's sister-in-law Marcia appeared to chastise Henry for getting Frances pregnant, possibly against his own wish not to have children. "I should regret your loss very much were it not that I trust your happiness will be prolonged by what I should term a misfortune—did you not tell me Henry . . . that you sincerely believed that children would make you miserable? You are now safe, and remember that it depends entirely upon your own dear self whether you shall be happy or wretched. Take heed to your ways and lay no charge to your wife."[44] Since reliable contraception was difficult to obtain and highly controversial, Marcia appeared to advocate celibacy to protect Frances's health and Henry's happiness. Marcia included a message to Frances as well, writing, "My Dear Frances I am sorry to hear of your illness, but rejoice that you are so comfortable—keep good courage my dear, this is but a faint

---

42. Michael Burlingame, *The Inner World of Abraham Lincoln* (Chicago: University of Illinois Press, 1994), 299.

43. Margaret Leech, *Reveille in Washington, 1860–1865* (1941), chap. 14 (New York: New York Re-view of Books, 2011), 382–383 (originally published 1941).

44. Marcia Seward to William Henry Seward, January 29, 1825.

emblem of what married life will produce—I fear for your constitution, you are but delicate and such hopes are exceedingly destructive—Henry certainly ought to have taken better care of you."[45] Marcia discussed the topic much more boldly than Frances or Henry, and Henry's concern centered on Frances as well as the impact of her health on his business, writing his father, "Frances's health has become so delicate I cannot often with propriety keep my light burning at the Office so late at night as should be . . . [she] is still convalescent. She still remains weak however and the tone of her system is not nor soon will be restored. She rode out once about half a mile which has been the only time she has gone out since her confinement which is now a month since."[46] Horseback riding was one of the therapies recommended for depression, understood as melancholia, in the nineteenth century, which Henry may allude to here.[47]

There are signs of long-term depression and anxiety throughout Frances's life and letters, greatly exacerbated by childbirth in what we would now recognize as postpartum depression, and her miscarriage appears to have resulted in what we now might categorize as clinical depression. Without effective medical and psychological understanding and treatment, women like Frances Seward suffered often from depression throughout their lives, and social stigma attached to mental illness made it difficult for those afflicted to openly seek help. In more extreme cases, women such as Mary Todd Lincoln, whose profligate spending may have been a symptom of her depression or other mental illness, were involuntarily committed to institutions. The humiliating public trial required for her involuntary committal illustrates one of many reasons depressed patients and their families maintained an air of secrecy. The uncertainty of Mary Todd Lincoln's diagnosis, ranging from narcissism, clinical depression, and post-traumatic stress disorder, also illustrates the limitations of medical, psychological, and social understanding of mental illness in the nineteenth century.[48] Other, lower-profile married women, such as South Carolina's Charlotte Magee, sometimes willingly sought institutional treatment for "mental derangement," which Magee attributed to "'anxiety and fretting' about her husband and children." Charlotte Magee died just a few months later, "in spite of—or perhaps because of—her treatment, mainly a course of purgatives."[49] Given the options, it is easy to see why so many people, particularly high-profile women like Frances, did not seek treatment for mental illness and/or depression. The impact of untreated mental health issues on nineteenth-century marriages could be devastating.

---

45. Marcia Seward to William Henry Seward, January 29, 1825.
46. William Henry Seward to Samuel Seward, February 21, 1825.
47. Rashmi Nemade, Natalie Staats Reiss, and Mark Dombeck, "Historical Understandings of Depression," *Mental Help*, September 19, 2007, https://www.mentalhelp.net/articles/historical-understandings-of-depression-continued/.
48. Norbert Hirschhorn and Robert Feldman, "Mary Todd Lincoln's Final Illness: A Medical and Historical Reappraisal," *Journal of the History of Medicine and Allied Sciences* 54, no. 4 (October 1999): 511–42.
49. Peter McCandless, "A Female Malady? Women at the South Carolina Lunatic Asylum, 1828–1915," *Journal of the History of Medicine and Allied Sciences* 54, no. 4 (October 1999): 543–71.

Anxiety over family members' health was not limited to women, but the expectations of men's behavior made it more difficult for men to express, as Henry showed in an 1834 letter. He wrote Frances, "Your health is a subject of constant anxiety. I am growing womanish in fear for the safety of that little family with which Providence has blessed me. I feel that I have been so ungrateful that I shall be punished for my crime," portraying his reaction to a lack of letters from Frances as emasculating concern.[50]

In spite of her own struggles, Frances took her role as caregiver quite seriously, and once wrote her sister, "Henry thinks I will be a practicing physician myself presently but there is little danger of my going out of my own family for patients," highlighting her constant occupation caring for the sick as well as her diligent searches for treatments.[51] Her anxiety for her family's health and chronicling of the illnesses and deaths of family and friends is a constant theme throughout her lifetime of letters. Frances found fault with women less concerned about their female responsibilities. In an 1841 letter, she wrote, "Mrs [Eliza] Davis . . . is a plain woman in her personal appearance with a strong mind and manners rather masculine than coarse—Thought me very childish to be troubled about a boy 2 years old, said she left all 5 of hers five months at a time and never gave herself the least uneasiness about them."[52]

Frances had reason to be troubled. After the birth of a healthy baby girl in 1836, she wrote to Henry to assure him that her anxieties were under control, writing, "I endeavor to bear in mind constantly that all our treasures here are only lent us for a season and do not as I once did allow gloomy forebodings of the future to disturb my present tranquility."[53] Frances's uncharacteristic equanimity was sadly misplaced, and her worst nightmare came to pass in January of 1837, when their infant daughter Cornelia was struck with smallpox. Frances urged Henry to come home: "I have nothing to communicate which will lessen your apprehension about our darling babe. She had a very bad night and this morning exhibits an extremely violent case of small pox. . . . We can hardly hope she will survive it and sometimes I feel almost willing to resign her entirely rather than witness sufferings which are wearing away my heart. . . . I shall not write again for should you receive this I think you will not hesitate about coming home immediately."[54] Henry did come home, but the baby was by then blind and scarred. Cornelia passed away days later.

Frances's health issues, although shared by countless other women of her time, earned her a reputation as an invalid and a recluse, as she often remained at home and frequently in bed instead of attending social events. She wrote Lazette,

Visiting and receiving visits constantly is certainly not the kind of life adapted to my taste, feelings, or constitution, either physical or mental—When I dress at 12 to receive

50. William Henry Seward to Frances Miller Seward, December 5, 1834.
51. Frances Miller Seward to Lazette Worden, February 18, 1844.
52. Frances Miller Seward to Lazette Worden, June 20, 1841.
53. Frances Miller Seward to William Henry Seward, September 24, 1836.
54. Frances Miller Seward to William Henry Seward, January 8, 1837.

company and am thus occupied for four hours I am exhausted and unfit for any employment the remainder of the day and evening. . . . Yet this is life in Washington or at least the life to which I am doomed whenever I am in a large town—It is useless to complain although my unfitness for it must always give dissatisfaction. Other women differently constituted make these mornings only a prelude to a still gayer evening while I am too much exhausted to do any thing but go to bed. . . . I have fancied that with renovated health these duties might be less tiresome, but I am now compelled to admit that I am peculiarly, and considering my position, unfortunately constituted.[55]

Over the years, Frances's children and daughters-in-law began to spend more time with Henry in Washington, with Fred serving as Henry's secretary, and his wife Anna filling in for Frances as hostess. Fanny also spent time there, enjoying the parties, fashions, and intellectual and social stimulation not readily available in Auburn. Frances's hurt and resentment at a perceived abandonment by her family is revealed in an 1865 letter to Fanny, where she wrote, "I advise that your Father instead of building an addition to this house should unite with Fred and build somewhere on the Hudson or any other place they should prefer a house which will become a home for you all like that in Washington where you all seem so happy."[56] It is noteworthy that this letter ends without Frances's usual signature, "Your own, Mother," or any of the endearments and blessings she almost always signed off with when writing to her children. At this late date, so near the end of her life, Frances could have joined her family in Washington and joined in the social functions they attended, but her physical and mental illnesses kept her isolated in Auburn and fed into her loneliness, hurt, and disappointment, a stark contrast from her earlier romantic ideals.

To Love, Honor, and Obey

As popular literature created increasingly higher expectations that marriage be based on romantic love and companionship rather than business-like partnerships, couples considered more than dowries and social and business alliances. The psychologist Victor Karandashev explained, "[Nineteenth-century] Romantic literature greatly impacted relationships between men and women. . . . Romantics convinced people to follow their passion and portrayed love stories in romantic novels, plays, and poems."[57] The author Phyllis Rose,

---

55. Frances Miller Seward to Lazette Worden, December 29, 1849.
56. Frances Miller Seward to Frances Adeline Seward, March 1865.
57. Victor Karandashev, *Romantic Love in Cultural Contexts* (Switzerland: Springer International Publishing, 2018), 115.

noting the influence of romantic literature on nineteenth-century marriages, wondered, "Who can resist the thought that love is the ideological bone thrown to women to distract their attention from the powerlessness of their lives?"[58] Frances recognized the impact of romantic literature on her own attitudes toward love to some degree, writing, "I can easily imagine that such things might be as the love between Isabel and Mordaunt. But I suppose I should be called foolishly romantic should I say this to anyone else."[59]

While earlier marriages might have sometimes been coercive and restrictive of options for married people, changing expectations of marriage influenced by romantic literature could add their own pressures to marriage. Rose explained, "At least when marriages were frankly arrangements of property, no one expected them to float on an unceasing love-tide, whereas we and the Victorians have been in the same boat on that romantic flood."[60] People in nineteenth- century marriages also often understood that love is not the same as happiness, that love can indeed be a source of deepest pain as well as highest joy. Frances Seward certainly found this to be the case, and while she often chastised Henry for failing to express his love for her in a way that she wished, she as often chastised herself for her expectations.

Still, Frances insisted on the importance of love in marriage, though it cost her dearly. "I do think no home at all would be preferable to a home with a man I did not love of all others and even then I would be miserable were he not just such a man as my own Henry—it is fortunate that there are few people in the world that think and feel on this subject as I do were it otherwise it would occasion much misery."[61] A blend of old-fashioned pragmatism and newer romantic concepts regarding marriage was more common than rigid adherence to either. Historian Karen Lystra explained, "The nineteenth-century middle-class couple did not conflate romantic love with excitement and drama. They understood and generally accepted that marriage meant an exchange of some of the liveliness and fervor of courtship for a calmer, more predictable, even more boring relationship. This did not mean, however, that marital commitment was expected automatically to dispel romantic love. Nineteenth-century couples who married for love were not easily reconciled to its loss."[62]

For Frances, the realization that many of her romantic dreams would remain forever unfulfilled, even as her romantic love endured, was difficult. "I need not tell you how many and bitter were the tears I shed over the lines you sent me which contained so beautiful an expression of feelings I have long, and I trust not vainly, endeavored to smother. It is more

---

58. Phyllis Rose, *Parallel Lives; Five Victorian Marriages* (New York: Vintage, 1983), 8.
59. Frances Miller Seward to William Henry Seward, June 15, 1829.
60. Rose, *Parallel Lives*, 14.
61. Frances Miller Seward to William Henry Seward, October 17, 1827.
62. Lystra, *Searching the Heart*, 206.

than idle to indulge them now. The first two lines only will ever express my sentiments at least when you are so far away, 'I know that he loves me, I could not live on With the love of a thousand if his love were gone.'[63]

Henry also detailed his early expectations for love and affection when he laid out his considerations for marriage to his father:

My first principle was that I would never unite my fortune with another's unless there was a strong and devoted attachment mutually existing between us. . . . Frances M[iller] is a girl of strong mind and of an undissembling heart. She says she returns my affection. . . . Miss K[ellog] has pretended to love me when I know she did not. . . . I therefore think that if there be any one person to whom . . . you would be willing to join your errant son it is she . . . [who] has declared that she takes me to be her lawful wedded husband to love honor and obey for better for worse—for richer for poorer till death us do part.[64]

Henry clearly expected affection and happiness to constitute a large part of married life, and made his decision on a marriage partner accordingly. After years of difficulty and separations, an 1834 letter from Henry to Frances exposed his own insecurities and need for love and reassurance, asking Frances to "Tell me in your own dear way that I am loved and cherished in your heart as I used to be when I better deserved so happy a lot."[65] Through their letters Henry and Frances often expressed their most intimate thoughts—their fears and their sorrows, their hopes, joys, and accomplishments. As Lystra described, "Feelings and behaviors of love were deeply shaped by the idea that completely unfettered self-revelation should be reserved for intimates, and indeed defined intimacy. Thus the essential act of romantic love in nineteenth-century American culture . . . was free and open communication of the self to another."[66] This open, emotional communication is seen throughout the first decades of the Sewards' letters to one another, giving way to more mundane conversation in later years.

Forsaking All Others

While divorce was socially and legally difficult in the nineteenth century, infidelity was a factor in many marriages. Letters in the Seward collection reveal that Henry's friend and fellow politician Albert Tracy pursued some type of inappropriate relationship with Frances Seward in the 1830s. The exact nature of this relationship is unknown, as Henry burned the letters exchanged by Frances and Albert Tracy, but it appears there was, at a minimum,

---

63. Frances Miller Seward to William Henry Seward, September 15, 1831.
64. William Henry Seward to Samuel Seward, August 12, 1823.
65. William Henry Seward to Frances Miller Seward, December 5, 1834.
66. Lystra, *Searching the Heart,* 7.

an emotional exchange where letters crossed the acceptable b.
between a man and a married woman. As Lystra noted, howev
free and open communication first and foremost, so this does nov
there was ever any inappropriate physical contact. Frances's loneline.
absences left her vulnerable to the attractions of an attentive, sympath.
in an 1833 letter to her sister. "I spent the day Wednesday very 'unwisely' a.
weeping until I almost blinded my eyes—went to bed at eight oclock and .
morning feeling very much as if I had not a friend in the world—so much for the absence
of one warm heart."[67]

As time and distance provided the opportunity to work through their conflict over
Tracy, Frances and Henry began to assess their own contributions to the situation. In November of 1834, after Frances told Henry of the letters, she described her hurt over her
unmet expectations of marriage: "When I realized most forcibly that 'love is the whole
history of woman and but an episode in the life of man,' when I at last came to believe that
I had deceived myself from the beginning and that you were incapable of experiencing the
deep and enduring love which made me so miserable, even then I imputed it not to you as
a fault but reproached myself for wishing to exact a return for affections which I felt were
too intense."[68]

Henry admitted that he had thought Frances's expectations too much, and influenced
by the spirit of the age, writing,

> I have thought you the spoiled child of romance, for dreaming that love could be pre-
> served amid the complicated employments and passions of life. And I have listened
> unheeded—nay, turned from you with pity for your feminine weakness, when you
> reminded me 'this Henry is the anniversary of our marriage,' and 'do you remember
> loved one this is the birthday of our first born. . . .' Oh I have wasted time, and heart
> and happiness. And I have now awakened from my delusion with fears that it is too
> late to win back to me the love I have despised. I banished you from my heart, I made
> it so desolate so destitute of sympathy for you, of everything which you ought to have
> found there that you could no longer dwell in it, and when the wretched T[racy] took
> advantage of my madness and offered sympathies, and feelings and love such as I had
> sworn, and your expelled heart was half won by his falsehood, still I did not know and
> see that I was criminal.[69]

Perhaps finally feeling that Henry understood her and still blaming herself for her expectations, Frances reassured him, "You reproach yourself, dear Henry with too much se-
verity, never in those times when I have wept the most bitterly over the decay of my young

---

67. Frances Miller Seward to Lazette Worden, August 31, 1833.
68. Frances Miller Seward to William Henry Seward, November 30, 1834.
69. William Henry Seward to Frances Miller Seward, December 29, 1834.

.en my heart has been most oppressed with the want of sympathy have I thought
. otherwise than good and kind."[70]

Henry also wrote to Albert Tracy, directing his anger, disappointment, and betrayal toward Tracy and defending Frances as pure and virtuous, the victim of a man who considered turning her friendship into something dishonorable.[71] Their friendship was ultimately destroyed by the revelation of the letters between Albert and Frances.

Til Death Do Us Part

Death was a regular feature of nineteenth-century life. Tuberculosis, smallpox, death in childbirth or afterward from infection, among any number of other causes, took their toll on families and strained or ended many marriages prematurely. In some families, like that of Austin and Sue Dickinson, the death of a child could be the breaking point. The loss of their son Gib and Sue's subsequent mourning proved to be the excuse Austin needed to give in to the pursuit of an extramarital affair with Mabel Loomis Todd, asking, "Where is the wrong in preferring sunshine to shadow?"[72] For Mary Todd Lincoln, the deaths of three sons as well as the horror of her husband's assassination as she sat beside him contributed to her breakdowns, and regardless of other potential medical diagnoses that may have contributed to her challenging personality and spiraling decline, post-traumatic stress disorder would be a logical modern diagnosis.

For the Sewards, the loss of their infant daughter Cornelia to smallpox in 1837 might have created similar strains, and it did appear to assert more pressure on Henry to remain home more often. Henry's sister-in-law Marcia wrote Frances to express her sympathy along with her prayer that Henry might remain with Frances. "O that this might be the means of teaching brother Henry the perishableness of all created things. O tell him that this world and all things that are therein are to be burned up—tell him not to waste the precious talents which his creator has given him and the prime of life, in the pursuit of happiness and wealth, which will most assuredly take to themselves wings and fly away, when he comes to lie upon a dying pillow."[73] This was sadly not a realization that occurred to Henry, and he left home again days after Marica's letter and just weeks after Cornelia's death. Frances sought catharsis in her letters to Henry, writing to him in Batavia only four weeks after Cornelia's death. "The nights are . . . tedious, my sleep is troubled with all manner of hideous dreams—I awake almost every hour during the night, watch the window for

---

70. Frances Miller Seward to William Henry Seward, December 5, 1834.
71. William Henry Seward to Albert Haller Tracy, December 29, 1834.
72. Lyndall Gordon, *Lives Like Loaded Guns: Emily Dickinson and Her Family's Feuds* (London: Penguin Books, 2010), 44–46.
73. Marcia Seward to Frances Miller Seward, February 2, 1837.

the first beam of light and rise from my bed unrefreshed. O if I could only dream of my precious babe once as she was in health and beauty, that horrible disease does so haunt me. Do not allow this to distress you, time will make it all smooth again, but it is such a satisfaction to tell you just how I do feel."[74]

Nearly thirty years later, when Henry sustained serious injuries in an 1865 carriage accident, Frances raced to Washington to be with him. On April 14, Lewis Powell attempted to kill Henry Seward as he lay convalescing from his injuries, part of the plot that resulted in the assassination of Abraham Lincoln. During the attack, Powell also seriously injured the Sewards' son Fred, who tried to stop Powell from gaining access to Henry's room. Frances suffered an agony of physical and emotional strain as she waited to see if her son and husband would survive. Her death from heart failure nine weeks after the attack was largely attributed to this strain. Henry and Fred Seward survived, but Henry and Frances were finally parted by death rather than distance.

Frances Seward's obituaries regularly noted the gender-specific balance she tried to achieve throughout her marriage between illnesses, the responsibilities of nineteenth-century womanhood, her own values, and her duties as a political wife. The *New York Tribune* wrote, "Intellectually gifted and cultivated far beyond the average not merely of her sex but of her time, she gave much heed and thought to public affairs without neglecting or slighting any of the duties of a beloved, exemplary wife and mother. An invalid and sufferer for several years past . . . she has remained for the most part at home . . . but hastened to Washington . . . and the overtaxing of her impaired physical strength by that trying journey probably shortened her earthly career."[75]

For most people in the nineteenth century, marriage meant a lifetime together, fulfilling the gendered roles handed down to them from previous generations, even as they brought their own ideas about love and romance into the institution. Frances and Henry Seward closely followed their gendered marriage roles and held expectations of love and romance early in their relationship. Their experiences diverged from most in their long-term separations, necessitating a largely epistolary relationship that has left a unique record of their attitudes, challenges, and experiences, and in the high-profile nature of their marriage due to Henry's political offices, which put additional expectations on Frances that she was often unable to fulfill. Frances's expectations of love and romance conflicted with Henry's ambition and financial considerations, but their shared political views, particularly on abolition, provided common ground, and Henry's ambition gave Frances access to positions of power and influence she could never hold herself. Many modern marriages under such pressures end in divorce, lacking the institutionalized marriage and gender structures

---

74. Frances Miller Seward to William Henry Seward, February 11, 1837 (emphasis in original).
75. "Death of Mrs. Seward," *New York Tribune*, June 22, 1865, 4.

that locked most nineteenth-century partners together for life and dictated their roles. Without an acceptable alternative in the nineteenth century, Henry and Frances Seward found ways to forgive, to sacrifice, to accommodate, and to maintain a lifelong partnership, an imperfect and perhaps unromantic love story that nonetheless allowed Frances to address her husband as "My dearest Henry" right up to her death, and end nearly every letter over forty years with the dedication, "Your own, Frances."

Doublespeak

Louisa Jacobs, the American Equal Rights Association, and Complicating Racism in the Early U.S. Women's Suffrage Movement

Susan Goodier

Members of the U.S. women's suffrage movement, usually noted as being from the 1840s to the Nineteenth Amendment in 1920, faced many struggles related to race from the outset. Periods of close collaboration between Black and white activists have been punctuated by longer periods with virtually no cooperation between them. Turning our attention to Louisa Jacobs, the daughter of the once-enslaved Harriet Jacobs (author of *Incidents in the Life of a Slave Girl*), helps us unpack racial cooperation—and the lack thereof—in the years immediately following the Civil War. After establishing freedmen's schools in the South during the war, Louisa returned to the North and joined the American Equal Rights Association to promote universal suffrage as a speaker on the lecture circuit. This article, representing preliminary research into the topic, argues that while Black women criticized the women's suffrage movement for perpetuating racism, they maintained ongoing relations with members of the dominant movement as they sought to overcome that racism and win the right for women to vote.

Louisa Matilda Jacobs was born to Harriet Jacobs in Edenton, North Carolina, on October 19, 1833. Because her mother had been willed to the daughter of Dr. James Norcom, and children followed the condition of the mother, Louisa, too, was enslaved. Much of the knowledge we have of her is thanks to the extraordinary work of Jean Fagan Yellin, who, back in the 1970s, realized that a slave narrative, long dismissed as a fictional account written by Lydia Maria Child, a white woman, was instead an accurate "historical record" of the life of a woman born enslaved in a community in the South.[1] In addition to editing *Incidents* and writing a biography of Harriet Jacobs, Yellin has compiled the papers of the

---

1. Harriet A. Jacobs, *Incidents in the Life of a Slave Girl, Written by Herself*, edited by Jean Fagan Yellin (Cambridge, MA: Harvard University Press, 2000), vii.

Jacobs family in a two-volume set readily available in many libraries.[2] This article is indebted to and builds on the meticulous research of Yellin.[3]

From the time Harriet was fifteen, Norcom demanded she have sexual relations with him. She engaged in a close relationship with another elite member of the white community, Samuel Tredwell Sawyer, in an attempt to ward off the attentions of Norcom. She had two children with Sawyer: Joseph, born in 1829, and Louisa Matilda, born four years later. Despite this, Norcom persisted in his attentions. Fiercely determined that Norcom would not have his way with her, in 1835 Harriet went into hiding, spending a total of seven years in an attic space—measuring nine feet by seven feet, and three feet in height—above the woodshed at her grandmother's house.[4] Through tiny openings in the wall of the attic space she watched her children play and grow. Jacobs arranged for Sawyer, a newspaper editor and member of Congress, to purchase Louisa and her brother Joseph to keep Norcom from using them to blackmail her into sexual intercourse.[5] Sawyer also purchased Harriet's brother John, who ran away from Sawyer the next year, eventually making his way to Boston. A poignant passage in *Incidents* details the one night the mother spent with her daughter during that period, just before the father took her north in the spring of 1839. Apparently, the child had known of her mother's hiding place and deliberately kept in sight of her mother as much as possible. Louisa never told anyone about the hiding place.[6]

Sawyer took five-year-old Louisa to Washington to care for her infant half sister; six months later she moved in with relatives of her father in Brooklyn, New York. A Sawyer cousin had proposed adopting Louisa, or at least educating her. Neither plan came to fruition; Louisa seems to have been used by the family as a "waiting-maid."[7] When Louisa's mother Harriet left the hiding place in her grandmother's attic and arrived in New York in the fall of 1842, Harriet found work as a nursemaid in the family of Nathaniel Parker Willis, an author and editor of some note, and rescued her daughter from the Sawyers.[8] Eventually

---

2. See Jean Fagan Yellin, *Harriet Jacobs: A Life* (Cambridge, MA: Basic Civitas Books, 2004), and Jean Fagan Yellin, ed., *The Harriet Jacobs Family Papers*, 2 vols. (Chapel Hill: University of North Carolina Press, 2008).

3. This article is developed from a paper originally presented at the American Historical Association Annual Meeting, held in New York City in January 2020, and benefited from comments made by Cherisse Jones-Branch and Alison Parker. Mary Maillard, author of a volume of letters written by Louisa Jacobs, also read and commented on a draft of this article. I am grateful for the comments of two anonymous readers for the *New York History* journal.

4. Yellin, *Harriet Jacobs*, 27; Yellin, *Jacobs Family Papers*, Vol. 1, 37–38.

5. Yellin, *Harriet Jacobs*, 49.

6. Jacobs, *Incidents in the Life of a Slave Girl*, 139–41.

7. Yellin, *Jacobs Family Papers*, Vol. 1, lxxii–lxiii, 55.

8. The earliest biography of Nathaniel Parker Willis includes brief references to Harriet Jacobs, although they are not entirely accurate. Henry A. Beers, *Nathaniel Parker Willis* (Boston: Houghton Mifflin, 1885), 284–86.

the Willis family "purchased" Harriet in an effort to stop the former master's family from forcing Harriet to return to Edenton.[9]

Because members of Norcom's family continued harassing Harriet, in 1844 she and Louisa relocated to Boston to be near Harriet's brother John. Boston's African American community—about two thousand New England–born as well as formerly enslaved people—nestled at the base of Beacon Hill.[10] Harriet tutored the eleven-year-old Louisa to make up for the gaps in her education. Perhaps Louisa also attended classes at the Abiel Smith School, an institution for free African American students located in their community.[11] Through her relationship with John, already deeply engaged in antislavery work and well known to several prominent abolitionists, Harriet exposed her daughter to a thriving social justice activist environment. Some of the Black and white activists Louisa met during her years in Boston included William Cooper Nell, the African American historian, and antislavery activists Charles Lenox Rémond and his sister Sarah Parker Rémond of Salem, Massachusetts. She also met the white Maria Weston Chapman and her three sisters, all of whom worked closely with the radical abolitionist William Lloyd Garrison, as well as the abolitionist and women's rights activist Ednah Dow Cheney.[12] Louisa and her mother nurtured these important relationships through correspondence and personal visits all their lives.

By the time the Civil War erupted in 1861, Harriet Jacobs had published *Incidents in the Life of a Slave Girl*, and by the fall of 1862 she engaged in relief work in Washington, DC.[13] Louisa joined her in Alexandria, Virginia, the following year, and, with the support of New York and Philadelphia Quakers, the two women distributed clothing and supplies and provided nursing care in the city. They established and operated the Jacobs School, educating freed people in that city from January 1864 until the end of 1865.[14] Louisa Jacobs viewed Abraham Lincoln's body as it lay in state in the White House, writing of the heartrending

9. Both Harriet and Louisa kept in touch with the Willis family all their lives. Mary Maillard, ed., *Whispers of Cruel Wrongs: The Correspondence of Louisa Jacobs and Her Circle, 1879–1911* (Madison: University of Wisconsin Press, 2017). See also both volumes of Yellin, *Jacobs Family Papers* for examples of correspondence between the families.
10. Yellin, *Jacobs Family Papers*, Vol. 1, 55.
11. William Cooper Nell, a Black historian who befriended the family and eventually proposed marriage to Louisa, led the community in boycotting the school for its lack of resources. https://www.blackpast.org/african-american-history/abiel-smith-school-1798-1855/.
12. The Jacobs seem to have known everyone who was anyone in the Black and white activist communities of Boston, Philadelphia, Washington, DC, and Rochester and elsewhere in New York State. My database currently contains 168 recognizable names, including many prominent abolitionists and women's rights activists of the day.
13. A first edition of *Incidents in the Life of a Slave Girl* is held at the Library Company of Philadelphia, Philadelphia, PA. Harriet Jacobs signed and gifted the book to Mary Rebecca Darby Smith, who eventually donated her library to the Library Company. Harriet A. Jacobs, *Incidents in the Life of a Slave Girl* (Boston: Published for the Author, 1861).
14. Jacobs, *Incidents*, 247; Yellin, *Jacobs Family Papers*, Vol. 1, lix.

grief displayed by the thousands who viewed the Great Emancipator's body.[15] Following a visit to Richmond, Virginia, to drink tea at the home of Jefferson Davis and tour the city in November 1865, Louisa and Harriet relocated to Savannah, Georgia. Representing the New England Freedman's Aid Society, they began work with the Black community. After a year overseeing an orphanage and teaching school in the city, Louisa relocated to central New York. With no public speaking experience and little chance of receiving a salary, she agreed to become a lecturer for the American Equal Rights Association. According to Jean Fagan Yellin, she may have done so to fulfill a dream of her mother's.[16] It's also possible Charles Lenox Rémond urged her to join him in the movement.

Equal rights associations, founded by male abolitionists, both Black and white, had been springing up in places the Jacobs had lived and traveled to. Frederick Douglass, Robert Purvis, Henry Highland Garnet, and other prominent African American men founded a National Equal Rights League in Syracuse, New York, in 1864, and other men founded branches in states like Louisiana, Michigan, North Carolina, Pennsylvania, Massachusetts, Ohio, Georgia, and Missouri. Friends and coworkers in Savannah had established such an association during the Jacobs's time there.[17] These groups formed in response to the national debates, often marked by "bitter and often violent disagreements," about how the United States would reconstruct itself once the Civil War had ended.[18] Even people among those who vehemently opposed slavery often disagreed about how extensively citizenship rights should be expanded to those the war emancipated. Abraham Lincoln, in the last public speech of his life on April 11, 1865, had expressed his support for voting rights for the "very intelligent" Black man and those who had served as soldiers.[19] Many male African Americans and Republicans saw women's enfranchisement as a "distraction" to what they perceived as the more "urgent cause of black [male] rights."[20] Unless pressed, most activists

---

15. Louisa Jacobs, letter quoted in the Fourth Report of a Committee of the Representatives of the New York Yearly Meeting of Friends, upon the Condition and Wants of the Colored Refugees, reprinted in Yellin, *The Harriet Jacobs Family Papers*, Vol. 2, 628-30; Yellin, *Harriet Jacobs*, 187.

16. Yellin notes that this was a "surprising decision." Yellin, *Harriet Jacobs Family Papers*, Vol. 2, 682.

17. Yellin, *Harriet Jacobs*, 202; "Report on the National Convention of Colored Men held in Syracuse, NY," *Rutland Weekly Herald*, October 20, 1864, https://omeka.coloredconventions.org/items/show/1582.

18. Libby Garland, "'Irrespective of Race, Color or Sex': Susan B. Anthony and the New York State Constitutional Convention of 1867," *OAH Magazine of History* 19, no. 2 (March 1, 2005): 61; Stuart Galloway, "The American Equal Rights Association, 1866–1870: Gender, Race, and Universal Suffrage" (PhD diss., University of Leicester, 2014), 17. Galloway's recovery work is incredibly important to this study.

19. Faye E. Dudden, *Fighting Chance: The Struggle over Woman Suffrage and Black Suffrage in Reconstruction America* (New York: Oxford University Press, 2011), 61.

20. Garland, "'Irrespective of Race, Color or Sex,'" 61. Women who eventually joined the League included Mary Church Terrell and Ida B. Wells-Barnett. In 1914, Well-Barnett held office as vice-president. By 1921, the organization merged with the NAACP.

Louisa Jacobs. Courtesy Jean Fagan Yellin, Public domain.

did not think to include women even in discussions of universal suffrage.[21] While it is likely that these male-dominated groups did not connect to the American Equal Rights Association under examination here, the scattered existence of equal rights associations points to widespread interest in the issue.

The American Equal Rights Association Louisa Jacobs represented seems to have had a greater reach than the other, earlier organizations and reflected a more diverse membership. Founded at the conclusion of the first National Woman's Rights Convention held after the Civil War, activists met at the Church of the Puritans in New York City on May 10, 1866. Female and male attendees, drawn from both antislavery and women's rights organizations, joined forces in their opposition to the Fourteenth Amendment. The amendment

---

21. Dudden, *Fighting Chance*, 63.

passed both houses of Congress in June 1866 and was ratified by the necessary twenty-eight states in July 1868. But the amendment added the word "male" as a descriptor for "citizen," actually the first time the word was used in the Constitution.[22] This prompted activists to create their organization. At peak, the total membership of the American Equal Rights Association would rise to no more than five hundred. The majority of the membership was white and from the northeastern region of the United States. Reflecting the strong link with activists in Massachusetts, they scheduled the first meeting of the new organization for May 31, 1866, in Boston.[23]

Louisa and Harriet knew well many of the people who attended the founding meeting: the dedicated abolitionist Robert Purvis, Harriet Purvis, Sojourner Truth, Charles Lenox Rémond, and Sarah Rémond.[24] Lucretia Mott, well respected for her ability to mediate volatile meetings, served as president. Purvis, Frederick Douglass, and Elizabeth Cady Stanton became vice presidents. In addition to the speeches by Charles Rémond, Robert Purvis, Stanton, Reverend Henry Ward Beecher, Wendell Phillips, and others, Frances Ellen Watkins Harper spoke boldly about the racism she, as a free Black woman, had long experienced in the North.[25] Without documentary evidence for correspondence between them, it is not clear how well Louisa Jacobs knew Harper or Truth, but she would certainly have been aware of their activism.

Despite some disagreement, most activists believed that this point in the reconstruction of the United States offered the best opportunity of the century to advise the government on the "broad principle of equal rights to all," as Stanton put it.[26] Susan B. Anthony, in her resolutions to the body, claimed that the "solemn duty of Congress" must be to "see that there be no abridgement of suffrage among persons responsible to law, on account of color or sex."[27] She called upon the women of the several states represented at the meeting to petition their legislatures. Because all members hailed from a long reform tradition, their "collaboration" would "concentrate [their] forces for the practical application of . . . one

22. Akhil Reed Amar, "Women and the Constitution," *Harvard Journal of Law and Public Policy* 18, no. 2 (1995): 469.

23. Galloway, "The American Equal Rights Association," 14, 19.

24. "Proceedings of the First Anniversary of the American Equal Rights Association, held at the Church of the Puritans, New York, May 9 and 10, 1867. Phonographic report by H. M. Parkhurst," https://tile.loc.gov/storage-services/service/rbc/rbnawsa/n3542/n3542.pdf.

25. Carla L. Peterson, *"Doers of the Word": African American Women Speakers and Writers in the North (1830–1880)* (New Brunswick, NJ: Rutgers University Press, 1998), 119–24.

26. Elizabeth Cady Stanton, from "Woman's Rights Convention, New York City, May 10, 1866, including Address to Congress adopted by the Convention," quoted in *The Concise History of Woman Suffrage: Selections from History of Woman Suffrage, by Elizabeth Cady Stanton, Susan B. Anthony, Matilda Joslyn Gage, and the National American Woman Suffrage Association*, rev. ed., edited by Mary Jo Buhle and Paul Buhle (Urbana: University of Illinois Press, 2005), 223–31.

27. Susan B. Anthony, quoted in *Concise History of Woman Suffrage*, 225; Galloway, "The American Equal Rights Association," 71.

grand, distinctive, national idea—Universal Suffrage."[28] As Stuart Galloway points out, its "demand for equal citizenship rights was the most important intellectual definition" of the organization. Furthermore, the "most succinct definition [was] in relation to black women, who stood at the intersection of discrimination on race and sex lines."[29]

The organization's most radical idea, that citizens—irrespective of race or gender—should vote, thrilled attendees and prompted immediate action to win over the public more broadly.[30] Members of the newly established American Equal Rights Association agreed to make a thorough canvass of New York State in the months before the state held its fourth Constitutional Convention (June 4, 1867 to February 28, 1868) in Albany.[31] Reflecting national debates, delegates to the state convention would be considering the question of whether Black people and white women should have the right to vote. At the national level, for three days in December 1866, the U.S. Senate debated women's suffrage. Again, debates ensued regarding the advisability of linking Black and women's enfranchisement.[32] Members of the Equal Rights Association must have felt heartened by the discussions at the highest levels of government.

As soon as the founding meeting of the American Equal Rights Convention adjourned, Anthony began writing and distributing literature, raising money, and planning an ambitious door-to-door canvassing tour across upstate New York.[33] Anthony wrote to Wendell Phillips, longtime editor of the *National Anti-Slavery Standard*, despite their disagreement about the advisability of including women's rights with Black men's rights, to directly ask for funding from the Hovey Fund Committee, a fund Phillips oversaw.[34] Phil-

---

28. Elizabeth Cady Stanton, Susan B. Anthony, and Matilda Joslyn Gage, eds., "National Conventions in 1866–67," *History of Woman Suffrage*, Vol. 2 (Rochester, NY: Charles Mann, 1887), 152–78; Laura E. Free, *Suffrage Reconstructed: Gender, Race, and Voting Rights in the Civil War Era* (Ithaca, NY: Cornell University Press, 2015), 133.

29. Galloway, "The American Equal Rights Association," 78.

30. To date, virtually all scholars have focused on the American Equal Rights Association by studying its four national conventions and assessing the arguments that ultimately tore apart the organization in 1869. The 2014 dissertation written by Stuart Galloway expands that story. Galloway, "The American Equal Rights Association." Books that also serve as significant sources on the American Equal Rights Association include Free, *Suffrage Reconstructed*; Ellen Carol DuBois, *Feminism and Suffrage: The Emergence of an Independent Women's Movement in America, 1848–1869* (Ithaca, NY: Cornell University Press, 1978); and Dudden, *Fighting Chance*.

31. An 1847 provision in the state constitution required that every twenty years voters had to decide whether the New York State constitution would be amended by a convention.

32. Dudden, *Fighting Chance*, 90–91.

33. Stanton, Anthony, and Gage, *History of Woman Suffrage*, Vol. 2, 175; Galloway, "The American Equal Rights Association," 87; Yellin, *Harriet Jacobs Family Papers*, Vol. 2, 689–90. See also the finding aid for the New York State Secretary of State Proposed Constitution of the State of New York, A1806, New York State Archives, Albany, NY, http://iarchives.nysed.gov/xtf/view?docId=ead /findingaids/A1806.xml;chunk.id=fullfalink;brand=default#top.

34. Dudden, *Fighting Chance*, 89. The Hovey Fund had been created by a $50,000 bequest of Boston merchant Charles Fox Hovey (1807–59) to fund the abolition of slavery until Black men had the right to vote, women's rights, and other social reform movements. A committee of trustees oversaw the distribution of funds. Benjamin Quarles wrote about the response of Charles Hovey, a Boston merchant, to abolitionists who called for rich men to name antislavery societies as beneficiaries in their wills. He had left about $40,000 to be distributed at $8,000 per year for antislavery

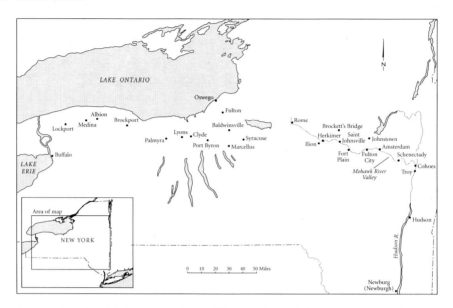

American Equal Rights Association, Tour of Upstate New York, Winter 1867. From The Harriet Jacobs Family Papers. Copyright © 2008 by Jean Fagan Yellin. Used by permission of the University of North Carolina Press. www.uncpress.org.

lips promised $3,000 to cover the costs of the American Equal Rights Association tour in New York. Reluctant to discontinue publication of the *Standard* until Black men won the right to vote, he agreed that a successful campaign in New York State to promote universal suffrage rights could help the cause of freed men.[35] Anthony also asked for money from a fund established by Francis Jackson, and she and Stanton wrote many fundraising letters to friends and colleagues, although with disappointing results.[36]

Jean Fagan Yellin has mapped the nearly thirty planned stops on the New York tour in the winter of 1866–67 in her invaluable two-volume *The Harriet Jacobs Family Papers* (see map above). The canvass of New York began after the November 1866 election. Upstate New York is still well known for its brutal winters and daunting travel in inclement weather. Average January temperatures in 1867 stayed around sixteen degrees, and we can

and other reforms. William Lloyd Garrison and Wendell Phillips served on the committee that determined where the money went. Benjamin Quarles, "Sources of Abolitionist Income," *Mississippi Valley Historical Review* 32, no. 1 (June 1945): 65. See Richard Abbott, *Cotton and Capital: Boston Businessmen and Anti-Slavery Reform, 1854–1868* (Amherst: University of Massachusetts Press, 1991).

35. William Lloyd Garrison ceased the publication of the *Liberator* in December 1865 after thirty-five years, but Phillips argued that the work of abolitionists would be incomplete until Black men had political rights. Lorenzo Sears, *Wendell Phillips: Orator and Agitator* (New York: Benjamin Blom [1909], 1967), 257–60.

36. A judge had ruled that women's rights did not constitute a "legal charity," so none of the Jackson money, once earmarked for abolition, could be used for the women's cause. Dudden, *Fighting Chance*, 90, 105.

only guess at the depth of the snow.[37] The American Equal Rights Association lecturers, wrapped in blankets or animal skins, would have had to travel over land by horse-drawn sleigh or across the frozen Erie Canal.

Charles Lenox Rémond (1810–73) represented the American Equal Rights Association as its first African American agent. He had a public speaking and social activism background that began in 1838 when the Massachusetts Anti-Slavery Society had first hired him, making him the most prominent African American speaker until Frederick Douglass entered the movement.[38] Born free in Salem, Massachusetts, in 1840 he traveled with William Lloyd Garrison to the World Anti-Slavery Convention in London, England. The first day of the convention found attendees arguing over whether women would be able to sit on the convention floor; they concluded that women could stay but had to be seated in the gallery. While women could observe the proceedings, they could not speak or otherwise participate in the proceedings. Consequently Rémond, William Lloyd Garrison, and Nathaniel Peabody Rodgers sat in the gallery with Elizabeth Cady Stanton, Lucretia Mott, and five other women, "glaring" at convention leaders and refusing to speak until the convention ended.[39] Although Rémond's primary commitment had long been suffrage for Black men, he argued that "principle dictated that he should support women's claim to the ballot at the same time as his own."[40]

In addition to Rémond, the upstate New York tour included Elizabeth Cady Stanton, Susan B. Anthony, Olympia Brown, Elizabeth Sophia Bisbee (a student of Theodore and Angelina Grimké Weld, well-known abolitionists and women's rights advocates then living in Hyde Park, Massachusetts[41]), Parker Pillsbury, and Louisa Jacobs.[42] Although it is not entirely clear how Jacobs became involved with the lecture tour, by December 9, 1866, Anthony could sing her praises in a letter to Amy Kirby Post: "she is everything proper & right in matter and

37. *Eighth Annual Report of the New York Weather Bureau, 1896* (New York: Wynkoop Hallenbeck Crawford Co., 1897), 439; James Rodger Fleming, *Meteorology in America, 1800–1870* (Baltimore, MD: Johns Hopkins University Press, 2000).

38. Yellin, *Harriet Jacobs*, 202.

39. Kathryn Kish Sklar, "'Women Who Speak for an Entire Nation': American and British Women Compared at the World Anti-Slavery Convention, London, 1840," *Pacific Historical Review* 59, no. 4 (November 1990): 473; Lisa Shawn Hogan, "A Time for Silence: William Lloyd Garrison and the 'Woman Question' at the 1840 World Anti-Slavery Convention," *Gender Issues* 25, no. 2 (June 2008): 75.

40. Rémond's speeches at the First Annual Meeting of the American Equal Rights Association, Stanton, Anthony, and Gage, eds., *History of Woman Suffrage*, Vol. 2, 215, 225; Galloway, "The American Equal Rights Association," 74.

41. Hyde Park was also the home of the all-Black 54th Massachusetts Infantry Regiment, depicted in the 1989 movie, *Glory*. Mark Perry, *Lift Up Thy Voice: The Grimké Family's Journey from Slaveholders to Civil Rights Leaders* (New York: Penguin Books, 2003), 221.

42. Ann D. Gordon, ed., *The Selected Papers of Elizabeth Cady Stanton and Susan B. Anthony: Against an Aristocracy of Sex, 1866–1873*, Vol. 2 (New Brunswick, NJ: Rutgers University Press, 2000), n4, 6.

manner—private and public."[43] It is also not clear that Louisa received a salary for lecturing. Anthony, in a March 6, 1867, letter to Gerrit Smith, complained that Wendell Phillips, in his role overseeing the Hovey fund, refused to pay the salaries of anyone on the tour except her own and that of Parker Pillsbury. Pillsbury and Anthony employed Rémond, Brown, and Stanton, but apparently paid only the travel expenses of Bisbee and Louisa Jacobs. According to Anthony, the money collected at the lecture halls paid travel expenses but could not cover printing or venue renting expenses.[44]

Several newspapers found the upstate New York tour newsworthy. The *Little Falls Journal and Courier* for January 17, 1867, published its local itinerary; the *National Anti-Slavery Standard* published regular reports.[45] Writing on February 3, 1867, from Johnstown, Rémond already considered the movement a success.[46] He said that he and Louisa Jacobs "suffer[ed] exceedingly for want of the current news." He also wrote of "severe storms and almost impassable roads." No matter the impediments, they refused to give up the tour: "the word *fail* finds no place in our vocabulary," he stated.[47] They spoke at venues in cities such as Buffalo, Rochester, and Syracuse; in towns such as Lockport, Palmyra, and Oswego; as well as in villages like Ilion, Brockett's Bridge, and Cohoes. They traveled nearly every day and spoke in a new community virtually every night, except when they held two- or three-day local conventions in Herkimer, Fulton, Troy, and Newburgh.[48]

Typically, Susan B. Anthony would contact someone in the community prior to the scheduled lectures. For example, when Rémond and Jacobs were scheduled to speak in Herkimer, Anthony contacted Ezra Graves, a local lawyer and reformer, asking him to secure either the Court House or Fox Hall for the event. She also sought "free" homes for the speakers, which may have been more challenging to find for African American speakers.[49] Sometimes the speakers themselves found overnight lodging with friends. For example, Jacobs and Rémond stayed with Jacobs's longtime friends, the Bricketts, who lived about sixteen miles northeast of Herkimer. John Jacobs had introduced Louisa and her mother to Zenas Brockett (1806–83), once a manager of the American Anti-Slavery Society in 1848 and, at least in 1867, a member of the American Equal Rights Association. The Brockett

---

43. Letter, Susan B. Anthony to Amy Kirby Post, February 17, 1867, Post Family Papers, https://rbscpexhibits.lib.rochester.edu/viewer/3886.
44. Yellin, *Harriet Jacobs Family Papers*, Vol. 2, 705–07.
45. Yellin, *Harriet Jacobs Family Papers*, Vol. 2, 682, 705.
46. Johnstown was Elizabeth Cady Stanton's hometown. Letter published in the *National Anti-Slavery Standard* (New York, NY), February 9, 1867, quoted in Yellin, *Harriet Jacobs Family Papers*, Vol. 2, 684.
47. Yellin, *Harriet Jacobs Family Papers*, Vol. 2, 684.
48. Yellin, *Harriet Jacobs Family Papers*, Vol. 2, 683.
49. Yellin, *Harriet Jacobs Family Papers*, Vol. 2, 685.

Dolgeville and the Civil War

Anti-Slavery Agitation Long Preceded War Between the States - Zenas Brockett Was a Leading Abolitionist

STATION ON UNDERGROUND RAILROAD, this original home of Zenas Brockett in the Town of Manheim, now the John Connors farm, was one of the hiding places for escaped slaves as they made their way to freedom in Canada.

(By ELEANOR FRANZ)

Johnstown had its final battle of | by night and hid in the woods by | while the Brocketts were at church

Louisa Jacobs and Charles Lenox Rémond stayed with the Brockett family in 1867. Louisa frequently visited the family and would spend summers there after the tour. "Station on Underground Railroad," unknown newspaper clipping, n.d. This image is in the Herkimer County Historical Society, Herkimer, NY.

home long served as a station on the Underground Railroad.[50] Louisa frequently stayed with the Brockett family, first between terms at school (1848–49), then during summers until 1880.[51] In February 1867, Louisa and Rémond stayed eight or ten days with the family.

Rémond's letter, dated February 10 and published in the *National Anti-Slavery Standard*, articulated the trials of lecturing in the Mohawk Valley: "To me it is a new ground, and not the less hard, harsh and malignant towards our race and their rights. If the sentiment of some of the towns and villages was indicative of things at large, I should indeed despair; but these rough influences cannot look us squarely in the face, much less . . . meet us in manly argument in the arena of manly and courteous debate."[52] Parker Pillsbury, writing of one local convention, put the challenges of winning support this way: "There is no real obstacle in the way of . . . speedy success, excepting the indifference growing out of a want of knowledge or reflection." The first day's speakers met "a whole winter of cold indifference," the second meeting met with "a thaw," and the next day of talks "broke up the frosts altogether."[53] Those on the tour seemed to keep up the spirits of each other.

Rémond and his colleagues, including Louisa Jacobs, moved on from the Herkimer area, giving talks at several stops along the way. Soon they reached Troy, New York, in time for a February 18 and 19 convention at Rand's Hall on the corner of Fourth and Congress Streets. They must have known that a Mr. Aldridge had read the American Equal Right Association's resolution "protesting against the legal or political distinction on account of color or sex" on the floor of the House of Representatives the previous week.[54] A reporter for the *Troy Daily Times* transcribed many of the speeches heard at the convention. He

---

50. John had earlier traveled with Jonathan Walker (the abolitionist whose hand carried the brand "SS" for slave stealer) to Brockett's Bridge. The modest home, built up against a hill, sheltered "freedom takers" in the root cellar, accessible from the downstairs kitchen. The term "freedom takers" belongs to Vanessa Johnson, a consultant at the Matilda Joslyn Gage Center, Fayetteville, NY. She argues that the more common term, "freedom seekers," is weak and inappropriate for people who overcame frightful odds and many dangers to make their way north for freedom. From the Brocketts' place, travelers would continue the still-unpaved Military Road on their way to Canada. Zenas Brockett confronted challenges from the community for his activities: one day he returned from church early, having a suspicion that people had gone to his home to see if he harbored any fugitives. He confronted them in his kitchen and bade them leave his home. Zenas Brockett folder, Herkimer County Historical Society, Herkimer, NY.

51. The Brockett home, much altered since the 1960s, still stands, although the New York State marker designating its importance is located inaccurately in front of a house further along the same road. Zenas Brockett folder, Herkimer County Historical Society, Herkimer, NY. https://www.findagrave.com/memorial/82180276/harriet-petrie.

52. Letter published in the *National Anti-Slavery Standard* (New York, NY), February 16, 1867; Yellin, *Harriet Jacobs Family Papers*, Vol. 2, 688. The region remains predominantly rural and white to the present day, making it all the more interesting that Louisa Jacobs stayed with the Brockett family most summers.

53. "The Equal Rights Enterprise," *National Anti-Slavery Standard*, January 26, 1867; Galloway, "The American Equal Rights Association," 92.

54. "XXXIXTH Congress: Second Session," *Buffalo Courier*, February 12, 1867, 1. Aldridge may have been an assistant to Thomas Estes Noell (1839–67), a Republican representative from Missouri, who initiated the reading.

described Louisa as tall, a brunette, under thirty years of age (she would have celebrated her thirty-fourth birthday the previous October), and a "fair speaker." The reporter noted that she spoke from a written document, unlike her colleagues who spoke extemporaneously, implying her lack of public speaking experience.

Perhaps this is the same speech Louisa Jacobs presented at other stops throughout upstate New York. Extrapolating from the reporter's comments, we know that Jacobs professed to be optimistic about the state of the country. She argued that the events of the Civil War had rendered the American people "one great family." After making points about the promise of the American Revolution and the "corruptions of the ballot box" without the influence of women, she continued:

> woman needs the ballot to enable her to work out her mission in life, to ensure her support and keep her from temptation. The nation needs woman's assistance and the support which her voice in its affairs would bring it. Full and large justice to the women of the land and to all the men is the only safety of the hour.[55]

Just what she means by the women's ballot "keep[ing] her from temptation" is not entirely clear. Presumably she meant that with the vote an independent woman would not be obligated to marry a man in order to exercise her political voice. At the conclusion of the convention, Louisa and other American Equal Rights Association speakers continued to lecture their way to Buffalo.[56] It must have been increasingly difficult for the members of the tour after Phillips cut off funding support.[57]

The record is silent on what Louisa Jacobs initially did after April 20, 1867. She may have tired of not receiving an income. Furthermore, there is some evidence that she faced a growing frustration with the lack of attention to universal rights in the speeches of her white colleagues.[58] Association members continued to argue about the connection of Black men's suffrage to women's suffrage; many prominent leaders believed that the two movements should be conducted separately. Since Black men had served as soldiers during the Civil War, the link between soldiering, citizenship, and voting rights had strengthened.[59]

---

55. *Troy Daily Times*, February 20, 1867; Yellin, *Harriet Jacobs Family Papers*, Vol. 2, 698.

56. "Personal," *National Anti-Slavery Standard*, April 20, 1867; Yellin, *Harriet Jacobs Family Papers*, Vol. 2, 710.

57. In addition, Kansas drew the attention of the association because it had scheduled debates on the proposal to remove both "white" and "male" from the definition of eligible voters for fall 1867, drawing members to that perhaps more obtainable "bellwether," in Dudden's view. Dudden, *Fighting Chance*, 89, 103.

58. Kate Culkin, "A Tale of Two Harriets: Working on Harriet Hosmer, Harriet Jacobs, and Their Complicated Nineteenth-Century World," 10-11; Papers of the Susan B. Anthony Conference, March 2006, https://urresearch.rochester.edu/institutionalPublicationPublicView.action;jsessionid=17ADAB95097CB6AF4FDCA3870F933EB0?institutionalItemId=2238.

59. For more on African American soldiers and citizenship, see William Gillette, *The Right to Vote: Politics and the Passage of the Fifteenth Amendment* (Baltimore: Johns Hopkins University Press, 1965), 40, 87–88, 162; Mary F. Berry, *Military Necessity and Civil Rights Policy: Black Citizenship*

Some activists feared agitation for women's voting rights would derail the goal of enfranchising African American men. Even Black women felt conflicted. In May 1867, at the first anniversary convention of the American Equal Rights Association, Frances Ellen Watkins Harper expressed her willingness to wait for women's enfranchisement as long as Black men won the right to vote.[60] Conversely, the outspoken Sojourner Truth called out members for ignoring women, Black or white: "There is a great stir about colored men getting their rights, but not a word about the colored women."[61] She, like many white women, supported a separation of the genders, calling for women's action: "I am glad to see that men are getting their rights, but I want women to get theirs. Now . . . is the time for women to step in."[62] Charles Rémond also spoke at the meeting.[63] Just two months later, on July 25, 1867, the New York State Constitutional Convention "voted 125 to 19 against the proposal to strike the word 'male' from New York's constitution."[64]

Louisa may have left the speaking tour for personal reasons. Harriet Jacobs had traveled to Edenton, North Carolina, in April. On April 25, Harriet wrote a letter to Ednah Dow Cheney, expressing her grief as she reflected on the seven long years she hid in her grandmother's attic as well as her gratitude that slavery had ended. Perhaps she also wrote to her daughter to ask that they be together. The record is otherwise silent for late spring, summer, and early fall of 1867. Then, in October Louisa and her mother set off for England where they spent the next year raising money for the orphanage and the old folks' home in Savannah where they had previously worked.[65]

The May 15, 1869, American Equal Rights Association convention, held at Steinway Hall in New York City, resulted in a cataclysmic split over the goals of the organization.[66] The Fifteenth Amendment granting Black men—but not Black or white women—the right to vote had passed in the U.S. House of Representatives February 25, 1869, and in the Senate the day after. By the May association meeting, fourteen of the necessary twenty-eight states

---

and the Constitution, 1861–1868 (Port Washington, NY: National University Publications, 1977), 41–57; Eric Foner, Reconstruction: America's Unfinished Revolution, 1863–1877 (New York: Harper & Row, 1988), 278–79.

60. Galloway, "The American Equal Rights Association," 74.

61. Quoted in Garland, "'Irrespective of Race, Color or Sex,'" 61. Black conventions, dominated by men, had increasingly ignored the rights of Black women. See Dudden, Fighting Chance, 18–19.

62. Nell Irvin Painter, Sojourner Truth: A Life, a Symbol (New York: W. W. Norton, 1996), 220.

63. Proceedings of the First Anniversary of the American Equal Rights Association, held at the Church of the Puritans, New York, May 9 and 10 (New York: Robert J. Johnston, Printer, 1867), https://www.loc.gov/item/ca10003542/, 2.

64. Garland, "'Irrespective of Race, Color or Sex,'" 62. Garland points out that New York State voters rejected the measure to enfranchise all Black males in 1868.

65. Interestingly, this April 25 letter is the very letter that proved to be the key to discovering the truth of Harriet Jacobs's account of her life in slavery. See Yellin, Harriet Jacobs Family Papers, Vol. 2, 711–16. Culkin, "A Tale of Two Harriets," 11.

66. There is no record of Louisa Jacobs attending the American Equal Rights Association meeting May 9–10, 1867 in New York City, although it is, of course, possible that she did so. Stanton, Anthony, and Gage, eds., History of Woman Suffrage, 182–228.

had already ratified the amendment.[67] In favor of the amendment, Lucy Stone and Henry Blackwell of Boston, among others, argued that the enfranchisement of any group signified a step in the right direction. Ernestine L. Rose, a strong advocate for women's rights, expressed her frustration that so many members of the American Equal Rights Association advocated for "manhood suffrage," leaving women out entirely. She demanded that those who supported her point of view establish a separate women's suffrage organization.[68]

That evening Elizabeth Cady Stanton and Susan B. Anthony founded the National Woman Suffrage Association, based in New York and focused on winning an amendment to the U.S. Constitution. Within a couple of months, Stanton and Anthony, lured by the promise of financial security for their cause, had cast their lot with the wealthy, but eccentric and racist, George Francis Train and took the campaign for women's rights to Kansas. By September, Stone and Blackwell retaliated by establishing the American Woman Suffrage Association to support women's enfranchisement on a state-by-state basis. The women's rights leadership seemed less inclined to support Black women's right to the vote as time passed, sometimes becoming virulently racist. Despite this, a few Black women joined each organization. Although Louisa Jacobs knew women who were connected to both organizations, perhaps because of her acquaintance with Susan B. Anthony she stayed loosely aligned with the National Woman Suffrage Association.[69]

For another year, members of the American Equal Rights Association tried to revive the organization and maintain its collaboration across race and gender lines. Margaret Winchester of New York City hosted the final meeting at her mansion on May 14, 1870. Most of those who attended the meeting supported the National Woman Suffrage Association, and despite the passionate opposition of Lucy Stone and Henry Blackwell, the membership voted to merge the American Equal Rights Association with the National Woman Suffrage Association.[70] Some of the relationships between the activists never recovered although other relationships endured, or time eventually healed their rifts. The cross-race potential of the American Equal Rights Association rarely found purchase in the women's rights movement again. While working within a broad suffrage movement that caused no

---

67. For more on the Reconstruction amendments, see Foner, *Reconstruction*.

68. "Debates at the American Equal Rights Association Meeting, New York City, May 12–14, 1869," in *Concise History of Woman Suffrage*, 272–73.

69. As conflicted as the movement became, Black women did not automatically join the American Woman Suffrage Association. Rosalyn Terborg-Penn identifies Charlotte Forten, Frances Ellen Watkins Harper, Mrs. K. Harris, Caroline Rémond Putnam, Charlotta (Lottie) Rollin, Louisa Rollin, Josephine St. Pierre Ruffin, Sojourner Truth, and Frances Rollin Whipper as joining the American Woman Suffrage Association. Those who joined the National Woman Suffrage Association include Naomi Talbert Anderson, Mrs. Beatty, Mary Ann Shadd Cary, Harriet Purvis, Hattie Purvis, and Charlotte E. Ray. Rosalyn Terborg-Penn, *African American Women in the Struggle for the Vote, 1850–1920* (Bloomington: Indiana University Press, 1998), 42; Susan Goodier and Karen Pastorello, *Women Will Vote: Winning Suffrage in New York State* (Ithaca, NY: Cornell University Press, 2017), 74.

70. Galloway, "The American Equal Rights Association," 138.

end of difficulties and frustrations, Black women persisted in demanding their rights with or without the collaborative relationships with white women. Racism on the part of white suffragists did not stop Black women from wanting the right to vote or from working toward female enfranchisement. Louisa Jacobs and other Black women continued to engage with white women in the suffrage movement, despite the myriad, sometimes hurtful, challenges of doing so.

Louisa Jacobs, like many of the other Black women of her era, never lost interest in voting rights for women, although evidence of her involvement is scant for the period after the tour of upstate New York in the winter of 1867. Charlotte Forten Grimké, a friend of Jacobs from Philadelphia, articulated her perspective on the heightened racism of the mainstream suffrage movement, observing that it "strengthen[ed] a most unjust and cruel prejudice," yet Grimké, closely connected with Black and white friends in Boston, held membership in the American Woman Suffrage Association.[71] Despite her discomfort with the racism she encountered, Jacobs renewed her relationship with Susan B. Anthony in 1884 at the home of their mutual friend, Julia Wilbur, a white woman who knew the Jacobs during their time in Alexandria, Virginia.[72] Two years later the Jacobs attended the National Woman Suffrage Association convention in Washington, DC, held February 17–19, 1886.[73] During Anthony's Sunday afternoon visit to Wilbur, Louisa Jacobs agreed to distribute suffrage literature for the National Association.[74] Expressing her annoyance with the racism apparent in the movement, Wilbur said that she could not blame Black women for staying away from the National Association. Furthermore, she wrote, African American women "can hardly think that Mrs. Stanton and Miss Anthony are their friends from the way they speak of the Negro." Wilbur also confronted Anthony directly about this issue.[75]

Depending on where we mark the origin of the suffrage movement, it took seven or eight decades for women to extend their constitutional rights and win the right to vote. We today find that movement for women's enfranchisement marred by its lack of broadminded thinking in terms of race. Certainly in the century since women won the right to

71. Charlotte Forten Grimké, quoted in *African American Women and the Vote, 1837–1965*, edited by Ann Dexter Gordon, Bettye Collier-Thomas, John H. Bracey, Arlene Voski Avakian, and Joyce Avrech Berkman (Amherst: University of Massachusetts Press, 1997), 5.

72. Culkin, "A Tale of Two Harriets," 11.

73. "Program for the 18th Annual Washington Convention of the National Woman's Suffrage Association, 1886," Amy C. Ransome Collection on Women's Suffrage, collection number 0001, folder 63, box 5, University of Southern California, Los Angeles, CA. See also Ellen Carol DuBois, *Woman Suffrage & Women's Rights* (New York: New York University Press, 1998), 92–94.

74. Diary of Julia A. Wilbur, entry dated March 7, 1886, quoted in Yellin, *Harriet Jacobs Family Papers*, Vol. 2, 789. See also the entry dated February 19, 1886, and Culkin, "A Tale of Two Harriets," 10–11.

75. Julia Wilber Pocket Diary, entries dated January 17 and 18, 1874, MC.1158, Quaker & Special Collections, Haverford College, Haverford, PA; Paula Tarnapol Whitacre, *A Civil Life in an Uncivil Time: Julia Wilbur's Struggle for Purpose* (Lincoln: University of Nebraska Press, 2017), 220.

vote, many women and men have been disenfranchised or prevented from voting at all. The existence of the short-lived American Equal Rights Association nonetheless highlights the point that the power to change the world lies in interracial and cross-gender collaboration. As long as members of the organization refused to commit to true universal rights, they would fail. Yet, clearly, even as long ago as the 1860s and as fraught with disagreement as the organization was, for a time, people did cross race and gender lines to work for those rights for all people.

"Moving Heaven and Earth"
The Uses of Religion in the New York Woman Suffrage Campaign

Karen Pastorello

On November 2, 1915, all eyes focused on New York. Election Day marked the culmination of more than a half century of relentless work by thousands of suffrage supporters to win the elective franchise for women in the country's most populous state. Trained female poll watchers, who had volunteered their time to guarantee an orderly election, paid close attention to the 1.3 million men who turned out to vote. The ballot included Amendment Number 2 on woman suffrage. One of five "Amendments to Be Submitted to the People in 1915," the amendment proposed eliminating the word "male" from the New York State constitution to enable women to vote on an equal basis with men.[1] Along with four other measures on the ballot involving constitutional language, state debt, legislative apportionment, and taxation, Amendment Number 2 failed. Deeply disappointed with the results, suffragists headed for their homes and sleep.[2]

Press coverage of the vote on woman suffrage varied considerably. For example, several prominent New York City newspapers broadcasted the defeat of the woman suffrage amendment with banner headlines the day after the election.[3] However, in small town newspapers across the state, including the Seneca County *Courier-Journal*, the election results appeared in a single paragraph buried deep in the paper, days after the election.[4] Few,

1. The New York State Constitutional Convention Commission, "New York State Constitution Annotated Part 2, Amendments Adopted and Proposed, 1895–1914, 'Amendment to Be Submitted to the People in 1915,' Article II, Section 1 'Woman Suffrage,'" 40–41.
2. Other states holding votes on suffrage in 1915 were Massachusetts, New Jersey, and Pennsylvania, and as in New York, the woman suffrage propositions were defeated. Illinois women won partial suffrage in 1913. They could vote for presidential electors and local officials, but not governors, state representatives, or congressmen.
3. "New Constitution Beaten by 398,000; Massachusetts and Pennsylvania also Deny Women Vote; Swann and Smith Win; Republican Gains in Country," *The Sun*, November 3, 1915, 1.
4. "Tuesday's Election," *Courier-Journal*, November 4, 1915, 4. Other representative examples of small town reporting: "New York Defeats Constitution," *Westfield Republican*, November 3, 1915, 3; "Constitution Lost," (Watertown) *Herald*, November 6, 1915, 4.

if any, newspapers speculated on the reason(s) for the defeat of the suffrage proposition. Perhaps some people had assumed all along that the woman suffrage referendum would fail. After all, it was a midterm election year, and this was the first time the woman suffrage question had come before New York voters. The vocabulary relating to the term "woman suffrage" could be perplexing. The possibility that men might have to share the political process, or worse yet political power, with women loomed ominously for many voters. In the weeks leading to the election, Tammany Hall's leaders reaffirmed their staunch antisuffrage stance, casting their influence over multitudes of city voters. For many New Yorkers preoccupied with the possibility of the country stepping into the Great War, the defeat of women's bid for enfranchisement did not rise to the level of a newsworthy item.

While some suffragists privately pondered viable explanations for the defeat of the women's suffrage amendment, Empire State Campaign Committee Chairman Carrie Chapman Catt quickly announced what she considered to be the definitive reason for the defeat. In a letter written to her district chairmen three days after the election, Catt emphatically stated: "I believe that we failed to work enough with the orthodox churches of all religions."[5] She argued that to effectively direct the next stage of the New York campaign, activists must acknowledge and overcome the sheer force of pious opposition to suffrage. What Elizabeth Cady Stanton had recognized in 1860 as the equivalent of trying to "move heaven and earth"—surmounting unwavering opposition to suffrage for men and women of faith—remained over a half century later one of the greatest obstacles to women's enfranchisement.[6]

Suffragists in New York had a complicated history of dealing with issues concerning the intersections of religion and suffrage, however the question of how suffrage leaders appropriated religion to advance the suffrage movement has not yet been thoroughly addressed by scholars of women's history.[7] Questions that demand a detailed analysis concern

---

5. Carrie Chapman Catt to "My dear Chairman," November 5, 1915. Carrie Chapman Catt Papers, box 1, folder 17, Bryn Mawr College.

6. "Elizabeth Cady Stanton to Susan B. Anthony, January 25, 1860," in *Elizabeth Cady Stanton as Revealed in Her Letters, Diary and Reminiscences*, Vol. 2, edited by Theodore Stanton and Harriot Stanton Blatch (New York: Harper and Brothers, 1922), 76.

7. Historiography lacks synthesis from scholars of women's history addressing intersections of American religions and woman suffrage in the late nineteenth and early twentieth century. This is a particularly difficult proposition, in part because of the necessity to recognize each religion has its own historiography. The work that has been done thus far is by scholars of religion and/or has focused on a specific religion or on regions outside New York. Examples include: Evelyn A. Kirkley, "'This Work is God's Cause': Religion in the Southern Woman Suffrage Movement, 1880–1920," *Church History: Studies in Christianity and Culture* 59 (December 1990): 507–22; James J. Kenneally, "Catholicism and Woman Suffrage in Massachusetts," *Catholic Historical Review* (April 1967): 617–33. In her study of Catholic women, Kathleen Sprows Cummings recognizes scholars' attempts to study religion as to promote the understanding of gender systems, however, she concludes that "most historians of U.S. women and gender continue to show little interest in religion, leaving the field to those who identify themselves as religious historians." See Kathleen Sprows Cummings, *New Women of the Old Faith: Gender and American Catholicism in the Progressive Era* (Chapel Hill: University of North Carolina Press, 2009), 14. Although she concentrates her study on the second women's movement, Ann Braude of Harvard Divinity School suggests that the

the suffrage leaders' own religious beliefs (or lack thereof), the strategies suffragists used to appeal to the clergy and their followers, and how relationships between suffrage organizations and religious institutions played a vital part in building the 1917 woman suffrage coalition that made victory in New York possible. To fully understand the women's suffrage movement in New York, it is imperative to recognize religion as an essential component of the campaign.

Suffrage and Religion in New York State

In the decades before the inception of the formal suffrage movement, religion had come to occupy an important place in Americans' lives. A proliferation of steepled churches dotted the landscape even in the tiniest hamlets. Along the Erie Canal, echoes of the Great Awakening's revivalist preachers could still be heard in mill villages as they grew into manufacturing centers.[8] Until the late decades of the nineteenth century, New York State remained predominately rural and the majority of residents affiliated with Protestant sects. Belonging to a congregation and attending church on Sunday fed the soul, offered comfort, and strengthened kinship and community ties. Upstate women marked their daily lives with holiday rituals that coincided with church calendars. Women coordinated and cooked for church suppers, raised money with bake sales and bazaars, and dispensed charity through church-related benevolent associations and ladies' aid societies. Church-sponsored social functions directed by women and open to all regardless of congregational affiliation, contributed to a sense of mutuality in the lives of rural residents.[9] On warm summer nights after their work was done, townspeople gathered on village greens or in town squares to take part in tent-covered revival meetings or to listen to dynamic Chautauqua lecturers speaking on popular topics.

New York churches and meetinghouses regularly hosted meetings for antislavery

---

scarcity of works that offer combined treatments of religion and feminism may be a consequence of the assumption that religion and feminism are "inherently incompatible." See Ann Braude, "A Religious Feminist—Who Can Find Her? Historiographical Challenges from the National Organization for Women," *Journal of Religion* 84, no. 4 (October 2004): 557.

8. Whitney R. Cross, *The Burned-Over District: The Social and Intellectual History of Enthusiastic Religion in Western New York, 1800–1850* (New York: Octagon Books, 1981), 55–77. The term "burned-over" refers to the towns and cities along the Erie Canal where the fires of evangelical preachers had a profound influence on area residents. See also Paul E. Johnson, *A Shopkeeper's Millennium: Society and Revivals in Rochester, New York, 1815–1837* (New York: Hill and Wang, 1978), 137–38; and Carol Sheriff, *The Artificial River: The Erie Canal and the Paradox of Progress, 1817–1862* (New York: Hill and Wang, 1996). In cities, especially during suffrage conventions, churches often charged rental fees for the use of their buildings. By the late nineteenth century, rural towns and villages tended to be "overchurched," meaning they had more churches than one place could support. See Paula Baker, *The Moral Frameworks of Public Life: Gender, Politics, and the State in Rural New York, 1870–1930* (New York: Oxford University Press, 1991), 129.

9. Nancy Grey Osterud, *Bonds of Community: The Lives of Farm Women in Nineteenth-Century New York* (Ithaca, NY: Cornell University Press, 1991), 263.

activists and temperance advocates. In 1848 Lucretia Mott and Elizabeth Cady Stanton held the Seneca Falls women's rights convention in the Wesleyan Methodist Chapel. Despite the Declaration of Sentiments' criticism of men for women's subordination, including exclusion from the ministry and public participation in church affairs, the convention set a precedent for a host of similar conventions.[10] Religion so predominated American life that even the Seneca Falls Resolutions contained a religious reference in the suffrage clause: "It is the duty of the women of this country to secure to themselves their sacred right to the elective franchise." In many rural areas, when suffragists spoke to mixed audiences of women and men, they combined abolition or temperance with women's rights advocacy because of the unlikelihood of finding a venue for the sole promotion of women's rights. (Unitarian and some Baptist churches proved to be exceptions.) Pastors in urban areas did not always welcome suffrage activity either, often charging rental fees for the use of their buildings during suffrage conventions.[11]

Although women congregants outnumbered men, women and men held unequal positions in New York churches.[12] Bolstered by societal norms that viewed women's proper place as the domestic realm, clergymen refused to relinquish even the slightest degree of authority to women. Until the mid-nineteenth century, male religious leaders consistently pointed to biblical texts to justify the subordination of women. Even for Americans not affiliated with any organized religion, the clergy's religious canon influenced mainstream culture beyond church and synagogue walls, molding public opinion and prohibiting women from gaining full social, economic, legal, or political rights.

By the late nineteenth century, increasing numbers of women began to react against their oppression. In some cases, suffrage sentiments motivated their resistance. In New York State after 1848 married women could own land and were required to pay taxes but had no voice in local, state, or national government. On October 12, 1887, ten Allegany County women, all members of the Seventh Day Baptist Church, presented a prime example of resistance when they cast their ballots in the Alfred Centre municipal election. According to a local newspaper, the election inspectors accepted the ballots "declar[ing] that the legal opinions gathered and published by counsel for the woman's suffrage party

---

10. National in scope, women's rights conventions were held almost every year beginning in 1850.
11. See Ann D. Gordon, ed., *The Selected Papers of Elizabeth Cady Stanton and Susan B. Anthony: An Awful Hush, 1895–1906*, Vol. 6 (New Brunswick, NJ: Rutgers University Press, 2013), 233. On May 27, 1898, Susan B. Anthony reported to members of the Business Committee that at the National American Woman Suffrage Association meeting in Des Moines in 1897, the association paid $120 to rent the Central Christian Church for three days.
12. For statistics regarding church membership, see Department of Commerce and Labor, Bureau of the Census, E. Dana Durand, Director, *1906 Report of Religious Bodies*, Bulletin 103, 2nd ed. (Washington, DC: Government Printing Office, 1910), 51. See also Osterud, *Bonds of Community*, 266–67. In her study of Nanticoke Valley, Osterud finds that in the evangelical Glen Aubrey Church, women "gained a legitimate and integral place within the church."

had convinced them of the legal right of women to vote."[13] Yet within two weeks an Allegany County grand jury indicted the women, mostly faculty or farmers' wives, who represented "the very best of Alfred citizenship." At a well-attended trial in November the judge dropped the charges of illegal voting and disturbing the peace against nine of the women. The jury however chose to make an example of the group's leader, Lucy Sweet Barber, who had "escaped punishment" already once before when she voted in a prior election.[14] This time the judge charged Barber with illegal voting and sentenced her to confinement in the Allegany County jail for one day.[15] Barber's sentence took the other defendants by surprise, and she immediately rose to prominence as a martyr for the suffrage cause.

Educated in leadership practices through experiences in women's clubs, temperance meetings, and the Granges, women like those in Alfred Centre mounted a quest for political agency. Following Matilda Joslyn Gage's founding of the New York State Woman Suffrage Association in 1869, women organized political equality clubs in hundreds of communities. By 1891 thousands of Chautauqua County women, proud of having the most highly organized county in the state, celebrated the first Political Equality Day in the state.[16] At the same time women confronted challenges in the religious realm. Ministers routinely sought to limit women's autonomy in their churches, but some women refused to cooperate. Building on the success of their political activities they mounted a fight to assume greater equality in the church. Church women overoptimistically reasoned that making financial contributions toward church mortgages or a minister's salary would afford them a voice in policymaking decisions.[17]

Upstate women pinned their hopes on the cause of women's rights, creating a version of radical feminism that went beyond recognizing women's contributions to their families and churches.[18] In making a transition from moral suasion to political activism, women realized that if they wanted to move beyond their ascribed duties as the guardians of moral order and community piety, they would need the vote.[19] Early suffrage leaders realized this first. In fact, they envisioned women's full equality with men.

---

13. *Wellsville Daily Reporter*, October 13, 1887. It is highly likely that at least some of these women belonged to the Alfred Centre Women's Christian Temperance Union. See Baker, *Moral Frameworks*, 205.

14. *Wellsville Daily Reporter*, October 25, 1887.

15. "Minor Items," *The Cultivator and Country Gentleman*, vol. 52 (1887): 975.

16. Susan Goodier and Karen Pastorello, *Women Will Vote: Winning Suffrage in New York State* (Ithaca, NY: Cornell University Press, 2017), 35–36.

17. Osterud, *Bonds of Community*, 217–74.

18. Osterud, *Bonds of Community*, 286.

19. Carolyn DeSwarte Gifford, "Nineteenth- and Twentieth-Century Protestant Social Reform Movements in the United States," in *Encyclopedia of Women and Religion in North America*, Vol. 3, edited by Rosemary Skinner Keller, Rosemary Radford Ruether, and Marie Cantlon (Bloomington: Indiana University Press, 2006), 1023–24.

Early Suffrage Leaders and Religion

From the initial stages of the women's suffrage movement, suffragists recognized the importance of religion in women's lives.[20] Some early suffrage leaders—Quaker Lucretia Mott is one—had been born into families whose religious beliefs compelled them to enlist in the cause of women's rights. Others, including Matilda Joslyn Gage, whose family attended the Baptist Church in Cicero, and Elizabeth Cady Stanton, who grew up in a strict Presbyterian household in Johnstown, felt confined by religious doctrines and expectations as they matured.[21] By the time they reached young adulthood, both Gage's and Stanton's paths had diverged from their natal churches. Although Susan B. Anthony was raised in a Quaker household, as an adult she regularly attended the services in Rochester's First Unitarian Church where her friend and women's right's activist William Channing Gannett, a staunch supporter of women's rights, served as pastor. Several prominent suffragists including Carrie Chapman Catt never belonged to any church.[22] As the suffragists grew into mature adults, their circumstances enabled them to develop their own philosophies regarding religion.

As the only child of activist parents who had advocated for abolition, temperance, and woman suffrage, Matilda Joslyn Gage believed that the Christian church, rather than religion itself, was the major barrier to the suffragists' demand for full personhood. Gage contended that as long as women believed in its misogynist Christian dogma, they could never be free. Centering the issue of woman's religious freedom on the woman suffrage platform, Gage believed in the complete separation of church and state contending they served as dual barriers conspiring to limit basic human rights.[23] A prolific writer, Gage made significant intellectual contributions to the woman suffrage and women's rights movement, despite the strong resistance from within and outside the movement.

Gage made her speaking debut on the platform at the National Woman's Rights Convention in Syracuse in 1852, held near her Fayetteville, New York, home. The mother of four surviving children, Gage centered her activism at the state and local levels, founding the New York State Association for Woman suffrage in 1869 and encouraged women

---

20. On the necessity of connecting religious orientation of individuals to the public policies historical actors advocated, see Maureen Fitzgerald, "Losing Their Religion," in *Women and Twentieth-Century Protest*, edited by Margaret Lamberts Bendroth and Virginia Lieson Brereton (Urbana: University of Illinois Press, 2002), n16, 300.

21. Sue Boland, "Matilda Joslyn Gage," in *American Radical Reform Writers*, 2nd ser., edited by Hester Lee Furney (New York: Gale Cengage Learning), 145; Elisabeth Griffith, *In Her Own Right: The Life of Elizabeth Cady Stanton* (New York: Oxford University Press, 1984), 19, 45.

22. Jacqueline Van Voris, *Carrie Chapman Catt: A Public Life* (New York: Feminist Press, 1996), 9.

23. Sally Roesch Wagner, "Introduction," *Woman, Church, and State* (Watertown, MA: Persephone Press, 1980), xxix–xxxi. According to Wagner, Gage was in fact "deeply religious."

to organize suffrage clubs in their own communities.[24] Despite her sometimes precarious health, Gage wrote extensively and contributed numerous articles to woman suffrage publications while serving as president of both the state and national suffrage associations. At the National Woman Suffrage Association convention in Rochester in 1878, celebrating the thirtieth anniversary of the Seneca Falls convention, Gage introduced a series of resolutions outlining her criticisms of the Christian church for "dwarfing and degrading" women.[25] Convention delegates adopted Gage's resolutions, an action that provoked outrage from the clergy and the press.

After a lifetime of fighting for women's rights and speaking out against women's "complete subjugation by the priest-craft," sixty-seven-year-old Matilda Joslyn Gage published the deeply researched *Woman, Church and State: The Original Expose of Male Collaboration against the Female Sex* in 1893 extolling the perfection of the ancient Matriarchate where women ruled. Gage went on to devote scores of pages recounting the horrors endured by women under Judaic-Christian patriarchy. Gage's eloquent radical anticlericalism cost her her rightful place in suffrage history.[26] Although some suffrage leaders feared that Gage's ideology would alienate some hard-won supporters, her teachings exerted a profound influence on select suffragists, including Elizabeth Cady Stanton.[27] Although they never lived in the same town as one another, Gage and Stanton managed to work together on multiple occasions.

Married seven years to fellow abolitionist and circuit court judge Henry Brewster Stanton, with three little boys in tow, Elizabeth Cady Stanton relocated from Johnstown to Seneca Falls in 1847. Appearing to exemplify Christian motherhood, she escorted her growing family to Trinity Episcopal Church "more or less regularly." Despite being "in the good graces of the parsons," including the Episcopal preacher Mr. Guyon, Stanton never officially joined a Seneca Falls church due to their failure to support women's rights.[28] Although she coauthored the Declaration of Sentiments replete with its criticism of the Christian church's treatment of women, throughout her life, Stanton counted numerous

---

24. David Kevin McDonald, "Organizing Womanhood: Women's Culture and the Politics of Woman's Suffrage in New York State, 1865–1917" (PhD diss., State University of New York at Stony Brook, 1987), 51, 187. Early membership in Rochester's Political Equality Club was mainly Unitarian.

25. Susan B. Anthony, Matilda Joslyn Gage, and Elizabeth Cady Stanton, "1878 Convention," *History of Woman Suffrage*, Vol. 3 (Rochester, NY: Susan B. Anthony, 1886), 124–26.

26. Wagner, "Introduction," xv; Boland, "Matilda Joslyn Gage," 145, 148, 153; Kathi Kern, *Mrs. Stanton's Bible* (Ithaca, NY: Cornell University Press, 2001), 144.

27. Wagner, "Introduction," xv; Boland, "Matilda Joslyn Gage," 151.

28. Elizabeth Cady Stanton, *Elizabeth Cady Stanton as Revealed in Her Diary, Letters, and Reminiscences*, Vol. 2 (New York: Harper, 1922), entry for January 5, 1886, 254–55. For more on the conflicts in Stanton's life between her upbringing and her "more optimistic religious ideas," see Judith Wellman, *The Road to Seneca Falls: Elizabeth Cady Stanton and the First Women's Rights Convention* (Urbana: University of Illinois Press, 2004), 163–64, and Elizabeth Cady Stanton, *Eighty Years and More: Reminiscences 1815–1897* (Boston: Northeastern University Press, 1993), 14, 17, 41–45.

ministers among her close friends. Stanton remembered thinking that, "not withstanding my very pronounced opinions concerning woman and the church, I must after all appear very gentle to these gentlemen of the cloth, since I have always been on friendly terms with so many of them." Although she often spoke in churches, she was careful not to offend churchgoers or the clergy and "sow[ed] as much good seed as possible" to win support for suffrage.[29]

Perhaps because of her close connection to the clergy, Stanton realized that the place to change public opinion regarding women's rights was in the churches. In a letter to Unitarian minister John Pierpont, Stanton claimed, "If I were a clergyman, I could easily reach the ear of slumbering womanhood." Whereas Gage held the clergy and their clerical authority responsible for women's oppression, initially Stanton placed part of the blame on women themselves, "who had no absorbing interest in life, nothing to take their minds off the little domestic troubles, real or imaginary."[30] A few years later, growing increasingly frustrated by the political conservatism of the temperance and abolitionist movements, Stanton complained to Anthony, "The Church is a terrible engine of oppression, especially as it concerns woman."[31]

The women's movement lost some ground when in 1881 the Methodist Church abandoned its liberal policy of ordaining women as ministers, joining Baptists, Episcopalians, Presbyterians, and Congregationalists in refusing to officially ordain women.[32] Stanton consulted with Antoinette Brown Blackwell, one of the first ordained female preachers. Blackwell resented being bound by masculine laws. Expelled from a national temperance convention because of her sex, "Nettie" Brown had a long history of advocacy for women.[33] Born in Henrietta, near Rochester, New York, she completed her theological education at Oberlin, but had to fight for her ordination in 1853.[34] Blackwell spoke at numerous women's rights conventions and, along with another female pastor, Olympia Brown (no relation), would be one of the few early suffragists to live long enough to see the passage of the Nineteenth Amendment. As female preachers joined the suffrage movement, they offered

---

29. Stanton, *Elizabeth Cady Stanton as Revealed*, Vol. 2, entry for January 5, 1886, 254–55. List of ministers included "Beecher, Frothingham, Bellows, Channing, Conway, Cheever, Couyer, Tying, Parker, May, Hinckley, and Furness."

30. Stanton, *Elizabeth Cady Stanton as Revealed*, Vol. 2, entry for September 30, 1849, 23.

31. Elizabeth Cady Stanton to Susan B. Anthony, April 2, 1852, Stanton, *Elizabeth Cady Stanton as Revealed*, Vol. 2, 39–40. Stanton warns Anthony that Amelia Bloomer is too conservative and in her paper she fails to speak out against the fugitive slave law or the church's position on intemperance. Abolitionists, too, compromise to "draw in numbers and bring over to them a large and respectable body of priests and rabbis."

32. Lois Banner, *Elizabeth Cady Stanton: A Radical for Women's Rights* (Boston: Little, Brown and Company, 1980), 160.

33. Elizabeth Battelle Clark, "The Politics of God and Woman's Vote: Religion and the American Woman Suffrage Movement, 1848–1895" (PhD diss., Princeton University, 1989), 44.

34. Elizabeth Cazden, *Antoinette Blackwell Brown: A Biography* (New York: Feminist Press, 1983), 80.

a rationale for the suffrage argument on religious grounds.[35] Most would-be female preach-ers, however, had to win recognition in their respective churches before they could fight for their formal ordination.

In 1885 at the suffrage convention in Washington, DC, after pointing out that women were licensed to preach in Unitarian, Universalist, and some branches of Baptist denom-inations, Stanton declared, "Now we intend to demand equal rights in the church."[36] This demand went unfulfilled for decades. In September 1893 Stanton spoke for two hours in a "drawing room full of ladies" in Peterboro, New York. She had learned that the village's Methodist Church had two men and fifty women communicants but only the women sup-ported the church with "fairs, donation parties, and constant begging," while the men spent all the money. Stanton reminded the women that it was "their duty to assert themselves and demand equality in the church."[37] A prolific writer, Stanton marshalled her efforts toward motivating women and informing clergy of their responsibilities tied to women's political rights.[38]

Stanton was equally direct when addressing clergymen. While visiting Bristol, En-gland, someone in a crowded parlor inquired about the situation of woman suffrage in the United States. According to Stanton, several clergymen present "made the mistake of asking me if the Bible was not opposed to woman suffrage." She responded by seizing upon the opportunity to "give them a piece of my mind."[39] Despite her strong opinions rebuking the church, Stanton, like Gage, was not entirely antireligious. Temporarily residing in John-stown while working on the *History of Woman Suffrage* with Susan B. Anthony, Stanton went to church every Sunday evening finding inspiration in the organ music.[40] Neverthe-less, as she put it, "I am most truly a protestant, for I protest indifferently against all systems and all sects."[41]

Henry Stanton's death in 1887 unleashed Elizabeth Cady Stanton's anticlerical senti-ments. Freed from the responsibilities of maintaining a house, she published the *Woman's Bible* in 1895, lamenting that women were "the chief support of the church and clergy; the

---

35.The earliest women preachers with ties to New York State came out of the abolitionist move-ment. A sampling of female New York preachers also known for their commitment to suffrage includes: Lucretia Mott (1793–1880), Sojourner Truth (1797–1883), Antoinette Brown Blackwell (1825–1921), Frances Ellen Watkins Harper (1825–1911), Phebe Coffin Hanaford (1829–1921), Olympia Brown (1835--926), Augusta Jane Chapin (1836–1905), Annis F. Eastman (1852–1910), Marie Jenney Howe (1870–1934), and Anna Howard Shaw (1847–1919).
36. "National Suffrage Convention, January 20–22, 1885," in Susan B. Anthony and Ida Husted Harper, *History of Woman Suffrage*, Vol. 4 (Bloomington, IN: Hollenbeck Press, 1902), 59.
37. Stanton, *Elizabeth Cady Stanton as Revealed*, Vol. 2, entry September 8, 1893, 287–88.
38. For example, see Elizabeth Cady Stanton, "The Duty of the Church to Women at this Hour," *Boston Investigator*, May 4, 1901, and Elizabeth Cady Stanton, "The Duty of the Church," *Free Thought* 189 (April 1902).
39. Stanton, *Elizabeth Cady Stanton as Revealed*, Vol. 2, entry May 21, 1883, 206.
40. Stanton, *Elizabeth Cady Stanton as Revealed*, Vol. 2, entry May 27, 1883, 217.
41. Stanton, *Elizabeth Cady Stanton as Revealed*, Vol. 2, entry January 5, 1886, 254–55.

very powers that make her emancipation impossible."[42] In 1898 Stanton published "Bible and Church Degrade Women," a sixteen-page pamphlet, accompanied by a reprint of the *Woman's Bible*, informing readers that "the Christian Church "interprets Christianity as to make it the basis of all religious and political disqualifications for woman, sustaining the rights of man alone."[43] In the end both Stanton and Gage first confronted and then reacted to their Protestant roots, eventually concluding that enfranchisement provided the only route possible if women wanted true social and political change.[44]

Occasionally the intersection of religious women and support for woman suffrage provoked controversy among the suffragists themselves. The Women's Rights Convention in Syracuse in 1852 erupted into the site of a "somewhat bitter discussion" incited by a confrontation between Protestant theologian Antoinette Brown Blackwell and Russian Polish immigrant Ernestine Rose. The suffragist Rose disagreed with Blackwell's strict adherence to religious doctrine. The debate raged on for two days and included a "coarse speech" by Reverend Junius Hatch and shouts of "Sit down! Shut up!" until convention president Lucretia Mott ended the meeting.[45] This episode marked one of many between orthodox Christians and those, like freethinker Rose, who fell outside the fold of traditional Christianity.

While including Frances Willard and Woman's Christian Temperance Union members in the suffrage coalition potentially drew large numbers of evangelical women to the cause of enfranchisement in the late 1800s, it led to a rift between Anthony on the side of Willard and an outraged Gage and Stanton on the other. While Anthony welcomed any alliance that would forward the cause of woman suffrage, the prospect of an alliance with conservative church women, who would certainly prioritize religion over suffrage, frightened Stanton and Gage. Referring to the union's penchant for religious opinions as the "great danger of the hour," Gage feared a conservative Christian takeover of public office.[46] Warning that the possibility of prohibition imposed by female voters would increase anti-suffrage sentiment among men, Stanton observed that, "Frances Willard needs watching."[47]

The merger of the National Woman Suffrage Association and the American Woman Suffrage Association in 1890, much to Gage's consternation, included Willard's organization. Condemning the merger, committed to maintaining the separation of church and

---

42. Kern, *Mrs. Stanton's Bible*, 12. Gage was one of the collaborators on the *Woman's Bible*.

43. Elizabeth Cady Stanton, *The Bible and Church Degrade Women* (Chicago: H. L. Green, 1898), 14. Library of Congress, cdn.loc.gov/service/rbc/rbnawsa/n8346/n8346.pdf.

44. For a detailed analysis of Protestantism's complex relationship to feminist ideology, see Carolyn Haynes, "Women in the Divine Republic: Feminism and Protestantism in English and American Literature" (PhD diss., University of California, San Diego, 1993), 13–37.

45. Susan B. Anthony, Matilda Joslyn Gage, and Elizabeth Cady Stanton, *History of Woman Suffrage*, Vol. 1, 2nd ed. (Rochester, NY: Charles Mann, 1889), 518, 540.

46. Matilda Joslyn Gage, "The Dangers of the Hour," Reprint of the speech of Matilda Joslyn Gage at the Woman's National Liberal Union Convention, February 24, 1890 (Fayetteville, NY: The Matilda Joslyn Gage Foundation, 2004). See also Wagner, "Introduction," xxxi.

47. Griffith, *In Her Own Right*, 200.

state and determined to wage war against religious fundamentalism, Gage founded her own Woman's National Liberal Union.[48] Such action strained relations between suffrage leaders and threatened the women's movement itself.[49] With Willard's death in 1898, the union quietly returned to its narrowly focused goal of prohibition.[50] Gage died that same year, just as the more radical women's rights leaders began to perceive the Woman's Christian Temperance Union as less of a threat. With the dispute behind them, suffragists could now make a more concerted effort to shift public opinion by persuading men, namely religious leaders and their followers, to enfranchise women.

Clergymen and Woman Suffrage

Since pastors, priests, and rabbis wielded significant influence on their members' political opinions on issues, their support of suffrage was crucial. While many nineteenth-century clergymen certainly opposed the idea of women's enfranchisement, the more egalitarian Quakers, Universalists, and Unitarians provided avenues for women to enter the public domain of American politics fighting for humanitarian causes, including abolition and women's rights.

Samuel J. May, Unitarian minister at Church of the Messiah in Syracuse, is one of the earliest and most prominent examples of men who declared his support for women's political rights. Initially an abolitionist, May saw the plight of women as similar to that of black people. In his widely published November 1845 sermon on "the Rights and Condition of Women," May asserted that women had the same right as men to participate in the government under which they lived.[51] May countered all the popular arguments clergy employed to denounce suffrage—that women were too delicate, that they would neglect their families, and that the political process was too grueling or complicated for politically uninformed women. May frequently attended women's suffrage conventions and worked closely with Susan B. Anthony and Elizabeth Cady Stanton among others.[52]

Throughout the nineteenth century, however, mainstream Christianity continued to represent the most vocal opposition to women's equality. In their sermons, ministers and priests maintained that women's suffrage would disrupt the family and upset the balance of society as ordained by God. Reverent Christians justified women's subordination by claiming that the Bible supported the notion of separate spheres, repeating Paul's command for

---

48. Boland, "Matilda Joslyn Gage," 151.

49. Baker, *Moral Frameworks*, 70–71; Gage, "Introduction," xxxi.

50. Susan Hill Lindley, *"You have Stept out of your Place": A History of Woman and Religion in America* (Louisville, KY: Westminster John Knox Press, 1996), 106.

51. Samuel J. May, "The Rights and Conditions of Women: A Sermon, Preached in Syracuse, Nov., 1845," Library of Congress, loc.gov/item/09002749/. The sermon was published as a tract in 1853 after he attended the Syracuse Convention in 1852.

52. Anthony, Gage, and Stanton, *History of Woman Suffrage*, Vol. 1, 518; "Samuel Joseph May," *Dictionary of Unitarian and Universalist Biography*, uudb.org/articles/samueljmay.html.

"women to keep silent." For most clergy, suffragists—particularly organized suffragists—posed a threat to a divine plan by overstepping the traditional boundaries of the male-over-female hierarchy.[53]

Even prior to formal antisuffrage opposition, the clergy and the press accused suffragists of being antireligious heretics. Antisuffrage propaganda relied heavily on religious mandates rooted in the defense of home and family.[54] Male and female suffrage opponents believed that women did not belong in the corrupt world of politics and that home life as they knew it would be destroyed if women won the right to vote. Consequently, the patriarchy of the dominant churches, the persistence of the separate spheres ideology, the reluctance of most men to relinquish social, legal, economic, and political power to women, and the notion that voting would interfere with their womanly responsibilities, discouraged many women from joining the suffrage movement. In 1895 antisuffragist women organized the New York State Association Opposed to Woman Suffrage to coordinate their efforts.[55]

Despite the growing organized opposition to the movement, some suffrage leaders optimistically observed that in the cases where clergymen supported suffrage, they often seemed "much more liberal than their people."[56] This sentiment rang true even in the most remote rural areas where various congregations did not always agree with one another. By the late nineteenth century, Protestant churches began to experience "consequential transformations" in their doctrines and worship practices. Once seemingly stable denominations employed ministers who publicly altered their religious convictions often influencing many middle-class women. The notion of progressivism embodied not just the revival of the church but the reconstituting of the individual and the nation.[57]

Making the Commitment to Woman Suffrage

Since the organization's inception, the National American Woman Suffrage Association had been cognizant of the need to recruit supporters in churches. Nineteenth-century suffrage leaders made sporadic attempts to attract churchgoers, but as a new century dawned, a new generation of suffrage leaders reformulated their campaign strategies in the interest of a more cohesive approach. By the early 1900s, the new generation of national and state leaders, led by Carrie Chapman Catt who served two terms as president of the National American Woman Suffrage Association (1900–04 and 1916–20), adopted tactics previously used only by men, modelling the political aspects of her organization after the major political parties. In addition to dividing locales into districts, suffragists began to attend

---

53. Boland, "Matilda Joslyn Gage," 150.

54. Kirkley, "This Work Is God's Cause," 511.

55. Susan Goodier, *No Votes for Women: The New York State Anti-Suffrage Movement* (Urbana: University of Illinois Press, 2013), 4–6.

56. Stanton, *Elizabeth Cady Stanton as Revealed*, Vol. 2, entry January 5, 1889, 255.

57. Haynes, "Women in the Divine Republic," 10–11.

political party conventions, hold mass meetings and rallies, and canvass Christian homes.[58] Through frequent correspondence with local organizers, Catt provided detailed instructions for starting and maintaining suffrage clubs that included questionnaires regarding suffrage activity in churches. She asked workers if they had held any meetings in churches, and she also asked how many churches held suffrage sermons.[59]

Furthermore, with anticlerical arguments all but silenced by Elizabeth Cady Stanton's death, religion and the issues surrounding it warranted renewed attention from the emerging group of younger leaders as they worked to advance the woman suffrage campaign. National suffrage leaders requested that all ministers devote at least one sermon a year to speak favorably on women's suffrage.[60] In 1902, the National American Woman Suffrage Association formed a special three-person Committee on Church Work. The first committee included future National American Woman Suffrage Association president Reverend Anna Howard Shaw from Pennsylvania, Laura DeMerritt from Maine, and Laura Clay from Kentucky. At the close of the annual convention, President Carrie Chapman Catt charged the committee with exploring "ways and means of interesting conservative church women" and winning public endorsements from ministers.[61] By 1904 under the direction of national president Anna Howard Shaw, the church work committee recommended each state form its own committee to appeal to women and men including those in New York State churches where over three million or approximately 60 percent of all New Yorkers professed to regularly attending a church or synagogue.[62]

As more men allied with the suffragists, the names of clergymen became more common on the rosters of the state and local men's leagues for woman suffrage founded in the

58. Elisabeth Israels Perry, *After the Vote: Feminist Politics in LaGuardia's New York* (New York: Oxford University Press), 22. House-to-house canvassing was previously used as a tactic by the Women's Christian Temperance Union in their "white ribbon" campaign to win converts to temperance.

59. Carrie Chapman Catt to "My dear Chairman," November 5, 1915. Carrie Chapman Catt Papers, box 1 folder 17, Bryn Mawr College.

60. "Convention Minutes," *Proceedings of the* Thirty-Third Annual Convention of the National American Woman Suffrage Association, May 30–June 5, 1901 in Minneapolis, 49, https://catalog .hathitrust.org/Search/SearchExport?handpicked=100565995&method=ris

61. "Closing Meeting," Proceedings of the Thirty-Fourth Convention of the National American Woman Suffrage Association, February 12–18, 1902 in Washington, DC, 61, 118, https://catalog .hathitrust.org/Search/SearchExport?handpicked=100565995&method=ris

62. "Convention Minutes," *Proceedings of the Thirty-*Sixth Annual Convention of the National American Woman Suffrage Association, February 11–17, 1904 in Washington, DC, 40, https:// catalog.hathitrust.org/Search/SearchExport?handpicked=100565999&method=ris Department of Commerce and Labor, Bureau of the Census, E. Dana Durand, Director, *1906 Report of Religious Bodies*, Bulletin 103, 2nd ed. (Washington, DC: Government Printing Office, 1910), 75–77. Upstate New Yorkers tended to affiliate with Protestant denominations while downstate residents, particularly those who lived in New York City, were increasingly Catholic or Jewish. There is no mention of a separate church work committee in New York State until 1914. The assumption is that since the national league was headquartered in New York, the state work was subsumed at the national level.

early twentieth century. Along with Dr. Anna Howard Shaw, Congregationalist minister Annis Ford Eastman and Reform Rabbi Stephen Wise assisted in the founding of the New York Men's League for Woman Suffrage in 1909.[63] By 1912, indicating the growing support for woman suffrage, at least twelve prominent Christian and Jewish religious leaders had joined the New York League.[64] Increasing men's visibility in the woman suffrage forces promised to temper antisuffrage sentiments. The movement became more respectable after men's league members marched in the 1911 and 1912 suffrage parades in New York City.

More upstate men also joined the movement, sometimes by starting their own men's leagues or participating in woman suffrage events. Suffragist publications and local papers reported on the New York State Woman's Suffrage Association convention held in 1911 at the First Baptist Church in Ithaca where Reverend R. T. Jones gave the opening day prayer.[65] The following year, Reverend Cyrus W. Heizer preached a sermon in support of suffrage, entitled "Let Woman Live Out Her Own Life," in Ithaca's Unitarian Church. Womanhood suffrage, as Heizer saw it, was a complement of manhood suffrage.[66] A vocal suffrage supporter since 1894, Heizer maintained close connections to Ithaca's Political Study Club and to Cornell University. With the aid of male supporters, women suffragists in Ithaca and across New York persuaded more men to join their campaign.

In 1909 efforts to attract worshipers into the suffrage fold intensified when National American Woman Suffrage Association leaders appointed Mary E. Craigie to head the newly created Committee on Church Work. Craigie founded the first public library in Brooklyn in 1896 and helped to establish ten branches in her first two years as library director. Arbitrarily dismissed in 1902, the assertive Craigie successfully sued the City of New York for wrongful termination and the financial losses that she suffered.[67] During this time, she emerged as an important figure in state and national suffrage work. Craigie, whose

---

63. Annis Ford Eastman was the mother of two suffrage activists. Crystal Eastman was a lawyer and noted member of Heterodoxy, a radical group of intellectual women based in Greenwich Village. Max Eastman became a popular speaker on the college campus suffrage circuit as well as the editor of the *Masses*, a leading Socialist publication. On the founding of the men's league, see Goodier and Pastorello, *Women Will Vote*, 93–98.
64. "Men's League for Woman Suffrage," sixteen-page pamphlet by Executive Secretary New York City, 1912, League of Woman Voters Records, Box 13, Rare Book and Manuscript Library, Butler Library, Columbia University, New York, NY.
65. Reverend Jones had hosted the 1894 New York State Woman Suffrage Association convention at his Baptist church in Ithaca. New York State Woman Suffrage Party, Forty-Third Annual Convention of the New York State Woman Suffrage Association, October 31–November 3, 1911, Division of Rare Books and Manuscript Collections, Carl A. Kroch Library, Cornell University, Ithaca, NY, Rmc.library.cornell.edu/suffrage/exhibit/new century/index.html.
66. "Let Woman Live Out Her Own Life," in *Sermons by C. W. Heizer of the First Unitarian Society Ithaca, New York*, compiled by his daughter (Cambridge, MA: Andover-Harvard Theological Library, 1915), 17–24. Heizer also spoke at the February 1914 New York State Woman Suffrage Association on "How to Reach the Voter." Woman Suffrage Conference and School Ithaca, New York, Woman Suffrage Collection, 1914–1915, Collection 8041, Division of Rare and Manuscript Collections, Carl A. Kroch Library, Cornell University, Ithaca, NY.
67. "Mrs. Mary E. Craigie," *New York Times*, December 28, 1928, 16.

father had been a pastor in the Dutch Reform Church in upstate New York and in Michigan, concentrated her work on reacting against religiously charged antisuffrage propaganda.[68]

In 1911 working in conjunction with the committees on church work, Carrie Catt insisted that suffrage sermons be preached in all churches all over the country on Mother's Day. If a minister refused, Catt instructed suffragists to stand at church doors to distribute suffrage leaflets as congregants left the services. In New York City the highly organized Woman Suffrage Party carried out Catt's directive requiring the chairman of the church work committee in each borough to attempt to have every minister in their district preach a prosuffrage sermon.[69] In the meantime, some women who belonged to church groups such as the Woman's Association of the Presbyterian Church in Penn Yan began to voluntarily discuss coming to the aid of the suffrage cause.[70]

While working in Buffalo in 1912, Mary Craigie published "Christian Citizenship," addressing the questions, "Would the Extension of Suffrage to Women Raise the Standard of Christian Citizenship? If so, should not our Clergy and the Church Give their Support to this Reform Movement?" In the opening statement of the booklet, Craigie extolled the "Power of the Christian Religion" as a great redemptive force and argued that the church should support women in their struggle to secure political rights and in doing so raise the standard of Christian citizenship. Then she tapped into a portion of the long-standing expediency argument to convince the clergy of the advantages of woman suffrage. According to Craigie, if women won suffrage, the power of church would be greatly extended in the pursuit of "civic betterment."[71] Suffragists hoped that by working through the churches, they would be less likely to be labelled dangerous atheists or lunatics.

In the first decade of the new century, other states, especially those with approaching votes on suffrage, started their own church work committees.[72] Reporting that U.S. church membership totaled 34,517,317 persons by 1911, Craigie remarked, "It would mean a great deal to the Woman Suffrage cause if this great organized force, representing the most thoughtful and most influential of every community, could be brought to endorse suffrage and to work for it." In keeping with the prevailing progressive climate, she hoped that others would join her in seeing suffrage as a much-needed reform to curb drinking, white

68. "Mary E. Whitbeck Craigie," *Woman's Who's Who of America: A Biographical Dictionary of Contemporary Women in the United States and Canada, 1914–1915* (New York: American Commonwealth Company, 1914), 213.
69. "Church Work," *Woman Voter* 5, no. 5 (May 1914): 25; Lillian Faderman, *To Believe in Women: What Lesbians Have Done for America, A History* (New York: Houghton Mifflin, 1999), 66.
70. "Church Notes," *Penn-Yan Democrat*, March 1, 1912, 4. The article notes that women would be discussing suffrage at the upcoming regular meeting.
71. Mary Craigie, "Christian Citizenship," fourteen-page pamphlet (New York: National American Woman Suffrage Association, 1912), 11, 14.
72. States with recorded church work committees included: Nebraska (1903), Georgia (1907), Massachusetts (1907), Maine (1907), Washington (1909), and New Jersey (1910). Ida Husted Harper, *History of Woman Suffrage*, Vol. 6 (New York: National American Woman Suffrage Association), 87, 123, 237, 370, 418, 686.

slavery, and child labor. She believed that the vote was "an indispensable tool" without which women had no voice at all.[73] Craigie's call was answered when in March 1913, following an address by Dr. Anna Howard Shaw, the Methodist Episcopal Church in America passed a resolution at their Philadelphia conference stating "the Methodist Church stands for equal rights and complete justice for all men in all stations of life."[74] Influential female religious leaders, whose number the National American Woman Suffrage Association estimated to be approximately four thousand, could play a vital part in helping to make the cause of suffrage more acceptable.[75] Throughout the Empire State Campaign (1913–15), Carrie Chapman Catt and Anna Howard Shaw traveled across the state to promote woman suffrage in hundreds of churches.[76]

While Craigie astutely couched suffrage arguments in religious rhetoric, Empire State Campaign press department chair Rose Young and publicity chair Vira Boarman Whitehouse worked hard to keep women's suffrage in the news. In 1915 Mary Craigie's "Woman Suffrage and the Church" appeared in *Literary Digest*. Deeming her church work successful, she acknowledged that even though in the past suffragists may have avoided alliances, they now associated themselves with the highest moral and religious enterprises without dividing their ranks. Craigie reflected, "It is gratifying to observe that the movement for woman suffrage is taking on a more distinctly moral or religious aspect." Attempting to appeal to the churches, she ended the article by urging church leaders and their congregants to use the vote to their advantage once suffrage was won by controlling the vote instead of waiting to accept the outcome.[77]

As condemnation of the cause dissipated, more church leaders than ever before readied to cast their votes for women as a compromise in the spirit of the times. A wire service article, "There are No Sects in Woman Suffrage," appeared in papers across New York State in June 1915, reporting that virtually all of the major Protestant denominations, including the Baptists and Episcopalians, had adopted resolutions favoring the ballot for women.[78]

73. *Forty-Third Annual Report of the National American Woman Suffrage Association, in Louisville, Kentucky October 19–25, 1911* (New York: National American Woman Suffrage Association Headquarters, 1911), 58.

74. "Forty-Fifth Annual Report of National American Woman Suffrage Association," December 1913, 55–56, https://catalog.hathitrust.org/Search/SearchExport?handpicked=100566004 &method=ris; "Odds and Ends of Suffrage News," Post-Star (Glens Falls, New York), April 22, 1914, 10.

75. Mary Craigie, "Report of Church Work Committee," National American Woman Suffrage Association Forty-Fifth Annual Convention Proceedings, 1913 (New York: National American Woman Suffrage Association, 1913), 55, https://catalog.hathitrust.org/Search/SearchExport ?handpicked=100566004&method=ris

76. "Forty-Seventh Annual Convention Report of the New York State Woman Suffrage Association," New York City November 30–December 2, 1915, https://catalog.hathitrust.org/Search /SearchExport?handpicked=009793006&method=ris

77. Mary Craigie, "Woman Suffrage and the Church," *Literary Digest* 50 (May 1915): 1156.

78. "No Sects in Woman Suffrage," *Portville Review* (Cattaraugus County), June 24, 1915, 4; "No Sects in Woman Suffrage," *Allegany County News,* June 3, 1915, 7.

Catt also reported that, "In one meeting lately held, a Presbyterian clergyman, a Jewish rabbi, a priest of the largest Catholic church and several local politicians sat upon the platform!—with the result that a tremendous push forward for the movement in that town was given." Catt's last word on the subject on the eve of the election was that "Men ought to regard Election Day and the vote they cast as the holiest and most religious service they ever perform."[79]

On the Sunday before Election Day in 1915, in New York City alone more than one hundred churches had suffrage sermons preached by their ministers or held special suffrage meetings where suffragists spoke from the pulpit. Members of the Catholic Committee systematically distributed a barrage of literature at the Catholic churches. Members of the Protestant Committee at the Protestant churches imitated the Catholics' example. Although the suffragists had high hopes, on November 2, 1915 a disappointed Catt learned that the New York suffrage referendum had failed. Heaven and earth remained unmoved.

Examining the 1915 loss in New York State through a religious lens, it becomes clear that large numbers of Catholic and Jewish immigrant men did not vote at all.[80] Perhaps the lack of citizenship precluded some from voting. Others may have avoided the polls because they did not know what suffrage meant. Those who voted and lived in New York City probably followed their church's or synagogue's directives and/or Tammany Hall's instructions to vote no on women's suffrage. Furthermore, in the upstate towns where the Roman Catholic priest was against suffrage, he wielded great influence, as in Clinton County where suffrage was defeated by a wide margin.[81] One notable exception came in Susan B. Anthony's adopted hometown of Rochester where social worker Florence Kitchelt ran the Housekeeping Center (later renamed the Lewis Street Center) in the heavily populated Italian Catholic Sixteenth Ward. The Sixteenth Ward was the only ward in that city that approved suffrage.[82]

Religious Immigrants and the Referenda

A key priority for suffragists in decades prior to 1917 was to win the support of foreign-born and working-class voters.[83] Working women came late to the cause of suffrage in part because of the reluctance on the part of suffrage leaders to recruit immigrants. Suffragists' speeches and writings contain a myriad of examples of xenophobic insults directed

79. "Mrs. Catt Says a Million Women in New York Want the Vote," Press Release dated October 1915, Carrie Chapman Catt papers, box 1 folder 17, Bryn Mawr College.
80. National American Woman Suffrage Association, *Victory: How Women Won It* (New York: H. W. Wilson, 1940), 115.
81. Baker, *Moral Frameworks*, 144–45.
82. Kitchelt unsuccessfully ran for secretary of state in New York in 1914 under the Socialist Party ticket.
83. McDonald, "Organizing Womanhood," 97–120.

at foreign-born women and men. Even Universalist minister Olympia Brown echoed the concerns of many white middle-class suffrage women when she proclaimed that "we are in danger in this country of Catholic domination" because of the threat of Catholic foreigners who voted when women make up the majority in Protestant churches.[84] Suffragists' sensitivity to accusations of radicalism minimized the roles of Jews in the suffrage movement.[85] However, given the growing cultural, ethnic, and religious diversity at the turn of the century, the effort to draw church and synagogue members into the woman suffrage movement became imperative.

In the wake of the 1915 defeat, Mary Craigie's observation that "With great Catholic Church on the side of Woman Suffrage and the Protestant and Jewish churches also committed to it, our battle would be speedily won" assumed a new meaning.[86] New York City's immigrant population had grown exponentially, and by 1910, numbered approximately 37 percent Roman Catholic and 31 percent Jewish people in its densely settled neighborhoods.[87] Recently arrived immigrant women and men migrated to jobs in the city's sweatshops and clothing factories. By 1915 many of these immigrants began to relocate upstate to the rapidly industrializing cities of Buffalo, Rochester, Syracuse, and Albany. Smaller cities like Troy and Utica had also evolved into manufacturing hubs, attracting large numbers of immigrant workers.

Jewish Involvement in the Campaign

Eastern European Jewish women and men carried a long tradition of radical labor and political activism with them to the United States.[88] Immigrants from Tsarist Russian Poland like Ernestine Rose, who anticipated a new world replete with political rights including woman suffrage, met with a disheartening reality after settling in the new country. Yet Rose and others like her saw the opportunity to fight for political rights in the suffrage movement. Even the native-born such as Maud Nathan, whose "Judaism was the source of her philanthropy," became committed suffrage activists. Serving as the president of the

84. Susan B. Anthony and Ida Husted Harper, *History of Woman Suffrage*, Vol. 4 (Bloomington, IN: Hollenbeck Press, 1902), 148–49.

85. Elinor Lerner, "Jewish Involvement in the New York City Woman Suffrage Movement," *Jewish History* 70, no. 4 (June 1, 1981): 460.

86. Mary Craigie, "Report of Church Work Committee," *National American Woman Suffrage Association Forty-Fifth Annual Convention Proceedings, 1913* (New York: National American Woman Suffrage Association, 1913), 56.

87. In keeping with the prevailing progressive climate, she hoped that others would join her in seeing suffrage as a much-needed reform to curb drinking, white slavery, and child labor. She believed that the vote was "an indispensable tool" without which women had no voice at all.

88. Karen Pastorello, *A Power Among Them: Bessie Abramowitz Hillman and the Making of the Amalgamated Clothing Workers of America* (Urbana: University of Illinois Press, 2008), 8–9; Lerner, "Jewish Involvement," 456–57. Jewish women reasserted their activism soon after their arrival in the kosher meat boycott on the Lower East Side.

New York Consumers' League, Nathan traveled to Rochester to address the local political equality club in 1906.[89] Originally from Hungary, Reform Rabbi Stephen Wise represented a male supporter who offered unconditional suffrage support to New York City residents. Wise believed that woman suffrage was a human right inevitable in a democracy.[90] While helping to found the New York State Men's League for Woman Suffrage, Wise joined forces with Elizabeth Cady Stanton's daughter, Harriot Stanton Blatch, to take the campaign out of the parlors and instead reach out to working-class women on the streets and at their workplaces.[91]

In late March 1911, banner headlines across the nation reported the loss of 146 mostly Jewish and Italian women and children's lives in the Triangle Factory Fire. With workplace safety their paramount concern, working women demanded a political voice to improve their economic circumstances. The Wage Earners' League formed when leaders from the Women's Trade Union League and the Woman Suffrage Party tried to recruit women workers to march in a 1911 suffrage parade on the Lower East Side. Two young Jewish women, garment worker Clara Lemlich and glove worker and union organizer Rose Schneiderman, assumed leadership roles in the league and worked to bridge the gap between middle-class suffragists and working women and, ultimately, to achieve women's suffrage.[92]

Before it disappeared, the Wage Earners' League gave rise to a suffrage club at Lillian Wald's Henry Street Settlement House. Henry Street Settlement House did not have any official religious affiliation and was popular among labor reformers because unions held meetings there.[93] For immigrants in general, settlements offered a respite from the hardships of work and family life, interesting programs and events, citizenship and English classes, and the opportunity to become politically active. By 1912 the Henry Street suffrage club claimed a membership list numbering into the hundreds. The suffrage club sponsored dances and other social events in the evenings so that working people could attend. The suffragists' torchlight parades were especially popular.[94] Organizers distributed

---

89. Johanna Neuman, *Gilded Suffragists: The New York Socialites who Fought for Women's Right to Vote* (New York: New York University Press, 2017), 119–20; Goodier and Pastorello, *Women Will Vote*, 59–60.

90. Randi Storch, "More than a 'Trophy for Womankind': Rabbi Stephen S. Wise and the Paradox of Citizenship in the Struggle for Suffrage in New York State," *New York History* 98, no. 3–4 (Summer/Fall 2017): 397–421.

91. Brooke Kroeger, *The Suffragents: How Women Used Men to Get the Vote* (Albany: State University of New York Press, 2017), n20, 264.

92. Lerner, "Jewish Involvement," 445–48; *Woman Voter* 3, no. 9 (September 1912): 5.

93. Kathryn Kish Sklar, "The Historical Foundations of Women's Power in the Creation of the American Welfare State, 1830–1930," in *Mothers of a New World: Maternalist Politics and the Origins of the Welfare State*, edited by Seth Koven and Sonya Michel (New York: Routledge, 1993), 66. See also Karen Pastorello, "The Transfigured Few: Jane Addams, Bessie Abramowitz Hillman and Immigrant Women Workers in Chicago, 1905–1915," in *Jane Addams and the Practice of Democracy: Multidisciplinary Perspectives on Theory and Practice*, edited by Marilyn Fischer, Carol Nackenoff, and Wendy Chmielewski (Urbana: University of Illinois Press, 2009), 98–118.

94. Lerner, "Jewish Involvement," 452, 455.

pamphlets and posters printed in Hebrew and Italian at suffrage meetings in Manhattan's ethnic Second and Eighth districts. Henry Street Settlement worker Lavinia Dock visited editors of Italian and Jewish papers to garner their support for suffrage. Other settlement houses in immigrant neighborhoods such as the College Settlement on Rivington Street on the Lower East Side also held suffrage meetings.[95]

In New York City working women frequented settlement houses and held dual membership in the Socialist Party and the Women's Trade Union League, both organizations that worked closely with the Woman Suffrage Party. Interorganizational community connections facilitated suffrage organizing and provided established networks through which to communicate the suffrage message.[96] Members of the Jewish community also helped forge important cross-class and cross-ethnic connections. As one of the most popular suffrage speakers in the city, Rabbi Wise sustained ties to the labor movement and the settlements through his work with Rose Schneiderman, Lillian Wald, and others.[97]

By 1914 Rose Schneiderman and Jewish garment union activist Pauline Newman combined their efforts to establish an Industrial Section of New York City's Woman Suffrage Party. Putting the goal of suffrage above all else, Carrie Catt prepared to overlook tensions between New York City's working-class women and middle-class "allies" over ethnicity and Socialist politics.[98] When residents of the heavily populated Jewish Lower East Side were canvassed in 1915, 75 percent of them articulated their support for woman suffrage.[99] As indicated by the Italian ward's passage of the suffrage referendum, Rochester's ethnic support of suffrage based at the settlements differed from New York City's. Despite the ethnic diversity of their respective membership, Rochester's Italian Housekeeping Center and the Jewish Baden Street Settlement were intertwined from the start; many of the Unitarians and Reform Jews who helped found these two Rochester settlements already belonged to the city's political equality club. Contrary to the situation in New York City, however, only a few middle-class Rochester suffrage leaders reached outside their inner circle to attract new members. Those who made any effort at all found it difficult to attract working women from the rapidly growing population of Eastern European Jewish immigrants probably due to the lack of a Women's Trade Union League branch and the overarching political conservatism of the city's bosses, including George Eastman, the founder of Eastman Kodak.[100]

---

95. "The Woman Suffrage Party," *Woman Voter* 4, no. 2 (February 1913): 33; "The Woman Suffrage Party," *Woman Voter* 6, no. 4 (April 1915): 20.

96. Lerner, "Jewish Women," 453–54.

97. Lerner, "Jewish Women," 453–59.

98. Annelise Orleck, *Common Sense and a Little Fire: Women and Working-Class Politics in the United States, 1900–1965* (Chapel Hill: University of North Carolina Press, 1995), 106.

99. *Woman Voter* 2, no. 3 (March 1911): 3; *Woman Voter* 6, no. 5 (May 1915): 14; *Woman Voter* 6, no. 8 (August 1915): 22.

100. McDonald, "Organizing Womanhood," 104–05, 167.

Catholics and the Suffrage Connection

While many Reform and secular Jews appeared to be receptive to suffrage, Catholics had an unearned reputation for opposing the measure. In 1900 only a handful of Catholic leaders openly voiced their support of suffrage, but by 1917 the tide had shifted dramatically. For most of his career, Cardinal James Gibbons, the leader of the Catholic Church in the United States, opposed women's suffrage. In February 1900, acting as representatives of the Catholic Church, Cardinal James Gibbons and Bishop William Doane gave speeches "against the exercise of the right of suffrage by women," at a Washington, DC convention. Elizabeth Cady Stanton, who also spoke at the convention, had no tolerance for such sentiments declaring, "Such men should be ashamed of themselves."[101] Although Stanton did not live to see it, in the last years of the New York campaign, woman suffrage leaders finally made inroads into the Catholic churches.

As the campaign progressed, Cardinal Gibbons explained his perspective on suffrage. Admittedly "depreciate[ing] suffrage," he felt becoming politically active would undoubtedly "rob women of all that is amiable and gentle." He reasoned that they already exercised the right of suffrage by proxy through their husbands and sons.[102] Antisuffragists strategically quoted from Gibbons's addresses in their publications.[103] As the 1917 New York referendum approached, however, Gibbons's opposition of woman suffrage waned considerably.

Other church leaders also clarified their opposition to woman suffrage carefully noting that they were offering their individual opinions rather than official church policy. In March 1914 Cardinal James Gibbons authored a letter stating that the church has no official position on suffrage and "leaves the matter to the good judgement of her children, as to what they think is best."[104] The same letter appeared at the beginning of a book written by actress turned suffragist Margaret Hayden Rorke, "prompted by the desire to correct the prevalent impression that the Catholic Church is officially opposed to Woman Suffrage. . . ."[105] Like certain clergymen, Rorke emphasized that suffrage presented a political rather than a moral question that gave voters the latitude to decide the issue for themselves. Contrary to popular belief, the Catholic hierarchy never issued a blanket policy opposing women's suffrage.

Some Catholic clergy, such as Bernard McQuaid of the Rochester diocese, had been

---

101. Elizabeth Cady Stanton, *Elizabeth Cady Stanton as Revealed* , Vol. 2, entry February 16, 1900, 347.

102. Gibbons, James, 1834–1921, "Letter: Cardinal Gibbons to the Maryland Association Opposed to Woman Suffrage. April 22, 1913," *Ann Lewis Women's Suffrage Collection*, https://lewissuffrage collection.omeka.net/items/show/1273.

103. Woman's Anti-Suffrage Association pamphlet, "The Case Against Woman Suffrage," 1917. By February 1917 Cardinal James Gibbons who was quoted on the back cover, had withdrawn his opposition to suffrage. Antisuffragists, however, continued to quote his prior views.

104. Margaret H. Rorke, *Letters and Addresses on Woman Suffrage by Catholic Ecclesiastics* (New York: National American Woman Suffrage Publication Company, 1914), 2.

105. Rorke, *Letters and Addresses on Woman Suffrage*, foreword.

promoting woman suffrage since the late 1800s. According to the Catholic press, the idea that the church "declined to favor woman suffrage or refused to preach suffrage" was "absolutely false."[106] Reverend Joseph McMahon, rector of Our Lady of Lourdes Church in New York City, "bitterly resented" the leaders of "the feminist movement" attacking the Catholic Church and "construing it as being opposed to women." In fact, McMahon cited the church as "the defender of women through the ages" and insisted that when it came to moral questions, the church had always treated men and women as equals.[107]

McMahon saw no reason that women should not have the right to vote and pointed to several instances where members of the clergy supported women's enfranchisement. He praised his colleague Father John H. Dooley for being the first Catholic priest to open the doors of his Corpus Christi Church to a suffrage meeting. Dooley attended the meeting held by the Women's Auxiliary of the St. Vincent DePaul Society where Harriot Stanton Blatch was the featured speaker. At the end of the meeting he wished the suffragists, "Godspeed."[108] Some priests, like Reverend John H. O. O'Rourke, agreed that granting suffrage to women would result in economic benefits. In short, he favored giving women the vote so that working women would enjoy equal pay with men, shorter hours, and safer workplace conditions.[109] Church leaders who attended the Catholic prohibition conference at Niagara Falls on August 5, 1914, also endorsed equal suffrage.[110]

Despite the increasing Catholic and Jewish support for women's enfranchisement, however, the defeat of the suffrage referendum in November 1915 prompted New York suffrage leaders to reexamine their campaign strategy. Given the low rates of affirmative votes in urban areas in the 1915 election, suffragists decided to pay extra attention not only to religious leaders but to the urban immigrants themselves.[111] New York State and National American Woman Suffrage Association officials realized that sweeping prosuffrage declarations aimed at the general public proved woefully inefficient. To win votes for women, the suffrage message needed to be fine-tuned to sway distinct groups including the military, labor, farmers, and especially immigrants of varied religious persuasions.

In January 1917, the *Woman Voter* advertised an essay contest to address the question: "Why Should Churches Help Women Get the Ballot?" The contest recognized "those who do the humdrum work for the support of the church without which no church of any denomination would survive" while reiterating the importance of religious vote. Rochester

---

106. Glen Janus, "Bishop Bernard McQuaid: On 'True' and 'False' Americanism," *U.S. Catholic Historian* 11, no. 3 (Summer 1993): 53–76. Apparently, Bishop McQuaid had voiced prosuffrage sentiments as early as the 1870s. See also Anthony and Harper, *History of Woman Suffrage*, Vol. 4, 367.
107. "Not Correct," *The Catholic Journal* (Monroe Co.), June 25, 1915, 4.
108. "Catholics for Equal Suffrage," *Oswego Palladium*, February 22, 1913, 3; Rorke, *Letters and Addresses*, 21.
109. "Reverend John H. O. O'Rourke, S. J. Says," *Catholic Journal*, October 29, 1915, 3.
110. Cummings, *New Women of the Old Faith*, 172.
111. Carrie Chapman Catt to "My dear Chairman," November 5, 1915. Carrie Chapman Catt Papers, box 1, folder 17, Bryn Mawr College.

Baptist and suffragist Helen Barrett Montgomery served as one of the contest judges.[112] Montgomery and her progressive suffragist colleagues hoped to develop a stronger rapport with the city's immigrant working women by working with local reform organizations such as the Women's Educational and Industrial Union to address the problems of newly arriving Jewish and Italian women.

.Contrary to what many believed, Italian Catholic women had a history of radical activism in Italy.[113] Yet, in part because the men immigrated before the women of the family, the male-dominated culture they established in their homes and ethnic churches after settling in the United States reached deep into women's daily lives, restricting their mobility and curbing even the slightest activist impulse. Finding themselves in unfamiliar circumstances and with little choice to do otherwise, Italian wives abided by male entreaties to stay at home and tend to the family and any borders that the family took in to help with the rent. As a rule, only the daughters of Italian families went into the workforce with the expectation that their pay envelopes would be placed in parental hands on payday.[114] Consequently, with a reputation for being under the control of their male relatives and discouraged from personal autonomy under any circumstances, Italian Catholic women workers were not initially recruited by the Women's Trade Union League, the Socialist Party, or by any other organizations at same rate Jewish women were. Some young Italian women, often daughters of immigrants, gradually became politicized after they became members of the garment workers' unions. In New York and in Rochester, suffragists who came to the aid of striking clothing workers began to earn their trust.[115] Women workers began to realize that once they gained the right to vote, their working conditions would improve.

Witnessing the success of these independent women suffrage reformers, some felt threatened. Several Catholic writers linked the New Woman who departed from the supposed domestic tradition to liberalism and the Protestant Reformation, both of which were considered anti-Catholic.[116] Sensing skepticism, the suffragists treaded lightly. One "New Woman" organizer for the Eighth District in Buffalo, the attractive and unpretentious Mary Elizabeth Pidgeon, used innovative tactics such as attending union meetings to draw Polish

---

112. *Woman Voter* 8, no. 1 (January 1917). "Why Churches Should Help," *Woman Citizen*, October 20, 1917, 401–02.

113. On Italian women's activism, see Jennifer Guglielmo, *Living the Revolution: Italian Women's Resistance and Radicalism in New York City, 1880–1945* (Chapel Hill: University of North Carolina Press, 2010), 179–97. Italian men often immigrated as individuals, thus leaving their female relatives behind in Italy. Women used this opportunity to organize numerous peasant uprisings over collective land rights in Southern Italy and Sicily in the late nineteenth and early twentieth centuries.

114. For a detailed account of Italian women's lives in Progressive Era New York, see Elizabeth Ewen, *Immigrant Women in the Land of Dollars: Life and Culture on the Lower East Side, 1890–1925* (New York: Monthly Review Press, 1985), and Virginia Yans-McLaughlin, *Family and Community: Italian Immigrants in Buffalo, New York, 1880–1930* (Urbana: University of Illinois Press, 1982).

115. Goodier and Pastorello, *Women Will Vote*, 64.

116. Cummings, *New Women of the Old Faith*, 19.

and Italian Catholic immigrants into the suffrage fold. The campaign's success in Buffalo could be partially attributed to the presence of a strong teachers' union organized by the American Federation of Labor.[117] Across the state, the effort to appeal to immigrant workers had mixed results. In the North Country, for example, the large number of French-Canadian Catholics who were often staunchly opposed to suffrage hindered organizing efforts.[118] Since Catholic immigrants often associated suffrage with Protestantism and the Woman's Christian Temperance Union, they, too, were hesitant to join the movement.

Along with the advocacy on the part of suffrage organizers and speakers, the press department secured space "in the Catholic press and leaflets of opinions favorable to woman suffrage by Catholic clergy were widely distributed to priests, educators, and laymen."[119] A leaflet entitled "Catholic Opinions," with quotes from seven church officials who supported suffrage, such as John Talbot Smith of Watertown who argued that, "From the day suffrage entered the world it became inevitable that women should enjoy it as well as men," was widely used from 1913 until 1917. Toward the end of the campaign, the leaflet went into multiple printings so that it could be widely distributed among worshippers of all faiths.[120]

Undoubtedly, the most influential factor in winning the clergy and the parishioners to the side of suffrage was the activism of the suffragists themselves. With the assistance of Bostonian Margaret Foley, the St. Catherine's Welfare Association of Catholic women organized a branch in New York in 1911.[121] New York branch founders Sara McPike, an executive secretary at the General Electric Corporation, and Winifred Sullivan, a Manhattan lawyer, made it their mission "to better social and economic conditions for women and the extension of suffrage as a means to this end."[122] The two women linked the association directly to needs of working women calling for equal pay for equal work, an eight-hour day for working women, a living wage, and strict enforcement of child labor laws. Association organizers held Votes for Women meetings in Catholic communities throughout New York City. Unique among Catholic suffrage organizations for its combination of labor advocacy with a suffrage agenda, within a few years the organization grew to include ten thousand women.

---

117. McDonald, "Organizing Womanhood," 355, 358–59. For more on Mary Elizabeth Pidgeon's suffrage career, see Mary Elizabeth Pidgeon Papers, Friends Historical Library, Swarthmore College Archives, Swarthmore, PA.
118. McDonald, "Organizing Womanhood," 319, 393.
119. Harper, *History of Woman Suffrage*, Vol. 6, 488.
120. "Catholic Opinions," box 5, folder 13, S-469, Lindseth Collection 8002, Division of Rare Books and Manuscripts, Carl A. Kroch Library, Cornell University, Ithaca, NY; "Catholic Opinions," *Woman Voter* 8, no. 24 (April 1917): 24. Originally published for the New York Woman Suffrage Association for the Empire State Campaign and later published by the National American Woman Suffrage Association.
121. James J. Kenneally, "Catholicism and Woman Suffrage in Massachusetts," *Catholic Historical Review* (April 1967): 617–33. Modeled after a similar organization in Boston, in 1893 at the Catholic Congress, women founded the Catholic Women's League, which would also join suffrage forces. See also Rorke, *Letters and Addresses on Woman Suffrage*, 159. In addition to New York and Massachusetts, similar organizations were founded in Pennsylvania, New Jersey, and other states.
122. Harper, *History of Woman Suffrage*, Vol. 6, 487.

In a single year, the especially active Brooklyn branch of the welfare association held eighteen hearings before Catholic officials, three large mass meetings, and a well-publicized debate between suffrage author Margaret Rorke and antisuffragist E. J. Hoffman.[123]

In 1914 Ella Hastings, a Catholic and member of the executive committee of the New York County Democratic Committee, took the helm as the Chair of Church Work in the New York State Woman State Suffrage Association.[124] Under Hastings's direction, local suffragists established specific Catholic or Protestant committees to work within churches.[125] Suffrage organizers took advantage of every opportunity to advertise votes for women. Anna O'Shea, a special captain for Catholic work in the city, rode in a decorated car from headquarters on 34th Street and passed literature out to crowds along the St. Patrick's Day parade route.[126] In June 1916 the *Woman Voter*, the official publication of the Woman Suffrage Party, reported hundreds in attendance at the third annual St. Catherine's Welfare Association dance, euchre, and bridge party at Hotel McAlpin.[127]

Suffragists had learned a hard lesson in the 1915 election—merely planting the suffrage message in workplaces and in churches was not enough. Suffragists need to follow up with in-person contacts to educate potential male voters and to enlist them in local suffrage organizations. Catholic woman suffrage leaders also carried their message to church-affiliated organizations, including Catholic summer schools and conventions. Suffragists interviewed bishops and priests and persuaded them to speak at parish school halls throughout New York City. As the St. Catherine's Welfare Association's political activity accelerated, members worked closely with the Woman Suffrage Party evident when the Catholic Committee of the party, also led by McPike, began to address church societies and women's clubs.[128] The *Woman Voter* reported that on March 12, 1917, at a regular meeting of the Rector's Aid Society of All Saints Church, Miss Eva Potter and Miss Adele Frank made suffrage addresses, and as a result three-quarters of those present endorsed suffrage. The article carefully noted that the remainder of the group had previously enrolled.[129]

Catholic women worked especially hard to change Cardinal James Gibbons's mind. In March 1917, following a meeting between the cardinal and suffrage delegates from cities in four states including New York, the *Woman Voter* reported that Cardinal Gibbons was willing to consider woman suffrage. The cardinal had been surprised that a number of women

123. "Catholic Committee of the Woman Suffrage Party," *Brooklyn Daily Eagle*, September 16, 1915, 21.

124. "Ella Hastings," *Who's Who in America, 1914–1915*, Vol. 8 (New York: A. N. Marquis and Company, 1914), 371.

125. Proceedings of the Forty-Seventh National American Woman Suffrage Association, New York City, November 30–December 2, 1915, 31, https://catalog.hathitrust.org/Search/SearchExport ?handpicked=009793006&method=ris

126. "The Woman Suffrage Party," *Woman Voter* 7, no. 4 (April 1915): 20.

127. "St. Catherine Welfare Association," *Woman Voter* 7, no. 6 (June 1916): 24.

128. *Woman Voter* 8, no. 4 (April 1917): 24; "Miss Sara McPike Suffrage Leader," *New York Times*, February 27, 1943, 13.

129. "Woman Suffrage Party of New York City," *Woman Voter* 8, no. 4 (April 1917): 24.

from his own congregation in attendance at the meeting also wanted suffrage.[130] Catholics, including the most prominent Catholic leader in the country who had opposed suffrage his entire life, came around to the side of the suffragists once they realized it was inevitable.[131] Within a few months, women suffrage advocates had even persuaded Catholic clergymen to march in the last New York City suffrage parade. In October 1917, five hundred Catholics marched under the banner of St. Catherine's Welfare Association.[132]

On the eve of the 1917 election, endorsements from religious officials crowded women's suffrage publications. The final issue of the *Woman Voter* in May 1917 reported that "literature to Catholic clergy has been sent out."[133] In 1917 suffragists printed over sixteen million pieces of prosuffrage propaganda to distribute throughout New York State. Five million pieces of suffrage literature went to New York City alone. The Woman Suffrage Party's Church Section under the direction of Miss Adella Potter received a commendation from suffrage leaders who noted that the efforts were "very successful with specially prepared literature and the churches were an active force."[134]

The October 20, 1917, issue of the *Woman Citizen*, billed as "the Official Organ of the National American Woman Suffrage Association," dedicated the last thirteen pages to a series of short articles on religion in New York State. The articles indicated that, in addition to all Protestant denominations, Catholics and Jews stood poised to support the woman suffrage referendum. "Justice, and No Compromise" featured images of rabbis Louis Kupold of Buffalo, Horace Wolf of Rochester, and Stephen Wise of New York City, all of whom had been present at the Central Conference of American Rabbis in July 4, 1917, when Jewish leaders declared their unequivocal support for suffrage.[135] The articles, including coverage of Gibbons's suffrage conversion in "For Righteousness' Sake," elaborated on the prosuffrage influence of religious leaders on urban populations.[136] Resolute prosuffrage views had disseminated well beyond New York City to smaller cities upstate.

On November 6, 1917, men in New York State approved woman suffrage with unprecedented numbers of immigrant men casting their ballots in favor of woman suffrage. Suffragists made the New York victory possible in part by convincing most religious leaders of the inevitably of woman suffrage. Some Catholic and Jewish religious leaders swung to the side of suffrage once they realized it was imminent so that they could position themselves to command an influential political voice once women won the vote. The sixty-nine-year-long campaign came to fruition just as readers' responses to the essay prompt, "Why

---

130. "Suffragists to Meet Cardinal," *Yonkers Herald*, February 14, 1917, 7; "The Cardinal Will Consider," *Woman Voter* 8, no. 3 (March 1917): 13.

131. "For Righteousness Sake," *Woman Citizen*, October 20, 1917, 389.

132. Harper, *History of Woman Suffrage*, Vol. 6, 487–88.

133. *Woman Voter* 8, no. 5 (May 1917): 26.

134. Harper, *History of Woman Suffrage*, Vol. 6, 480. Potter also wrote articles for the *Woman Citizen*.

135. "Justice, and No Compromise," *Woman Citizen*, October 20, 1917, 391.

136. "For Righteousness Sake," *Woman Citizen*, October 20, 1917, 389.

Churches Should Help Women Get the Ballot," appeared in the *Woman Citizen*. Mrs. H. E. Jones, a member of Presbyterian Manse, in Ovid, New York, won the contest with her answer that stated churches should help with woman suffrage because woman suffrage rendered democracy complete and "in harmony with the spirit of democracy."[137]

Initially the clergy's condemnation of suffrage may have deterred some worshipers from supporting women's enfranchisement. However, as suffrage support from religious officials increased, it seemed to dilute the mainstream opposition. In the immigrant-rich New York City area, the suffrage amendment passed in 1917 with more than 53 percent of the vote with the metropolitan counties of New York, Kings, Bronx, Westchester, Nassau, and Richmond carrying the referendum.[138] Tammany Hall's lack of a strong voting recommendation regarding women's suffrage this time around translated to Democratic boss Charlie Murphy's support for woman suffrage. The *New York Times* gave one group of religious women a preponderance of credit for the suffrage victory when less than a week after the election, the paper ran a telling article entitled, "Debt of Suffrage to Catholic Women."[139] Jewish communities and, ultimately, Jewish Reform rabbis played a crucial part in New York's suffrage victory.[140] Upstate, Rochestarians in the Jewish Eighth Ward including Baden Street passed the suffrage referendum with 55 percent of vote, marking the suffragists' lone success in that city.[141] Although there are a number of factors that help explain the suffragists' decisive victory, a reinvigorated strategy entailing special attention to religious groups in the 1917 campaign and advanced by thousands of women suffrage workers ultimately won for women in New York what Carrie Chapman Catt proudly proclaimed "The Very Greatest Victory."

137. "Why Churches Should Help," *Woman Citizen*, October 20, 1917, 401–02.
138. Lauren Santangelo, *Suffrage and the City: New York Women Battle for the Ballot* (New York: Oxford University Press, 2019), 146–47. Baker, *Moral Frameworks*, 146. See also Lerner, "Jewish Involvement," 442. Lerner states that by 1920 approximately 80 percent of Manhattan's residents were either foreign-born or children of foreign-born parents.
139. "Debt of Suffrage to Catholic Women," *New York Times*, November 11, 1917, 11.
140. Lerner, "Jewish Involvement," 459–60. Lerner maintains that part of the reason the Jewish contribution to the suffrage movement is not credited is because the politically astute suffrage leaders, including Carrie Chapman Catt, may have considered Jewish allies a liability especially when it came to securing a federal amendment, which would require broad support including in the American South.
141. McDonald, "Organizing Womanhood," 231.

The Recovery of John Francis Rigaud's Portrait of Joseph Brant

Gilbert L. Gignac

The many portraits of Mohawk leader Thayendanegea (also known as Joseph Brant (1743–1807)) demonstrate how Brant used portraiture as a tool for public purposes and how portraiture acted as a virtual avatar for this important figure.[1] These portraits constitute his personal portrait gallery and continue to captivate our imagination due to the robust character of their sitter and to the significant and controversial role that he undertook on behalf of both Indigenous and colonial settler loyalists before, during, and after the American War of Independence (1775–83).[2]

This article will reexamine the known existing portraits of Joseph Brant painted in oil on canvas and present new information that led to the recovery of the lost oil portrait of Brant painted by the Royal Academician, John Francis Rigaud (1742–1810), for public

I owe a debt of gratitude to James (Jim) Burant (a member of the Algonquins of Pikwakanagan First Nation, historian of Canadian art, adjunct research professor of art history at Carleton University, and former director of the documentary art and photography collections of Library and Archives Canada (LAC), Ottawa), who read and much improved this article's overall structure and legibility; and for the support of Brian Foss, director of the School for Studies of Art and Culture at Carleton University, Ottawa, who also read and helped shape its final form. I also thank art archivists Shane McCord and Mary Margaret Johnston-Miller at LAC for access to works of art and research files available on site, and Annie Arsenault, assistant librarian at the National Gallery of Canada Library, for providing copies of pertinent articles and previous sale catalogs.

1. In Mohawk today his name is written and pronounced Kanyen'kahaka. For his 1776 *London Magazine* article, James Boswell interviewed Joseph Brant and received and recorded the eighteenth-century spelling and pronunciation of his Mohawk name: "Upon his tomahawk is carved the first letter of his Christian name, Joseph, and his Mohock [sic] appellation thus, Thayendaneken (pronounced Theandenaigen) the g being sounded hard as in get." Joseph Brant's Christian surname was often spelled Brandt, at a time when orthography was not yet fixed. In all pertinent eighteenth-century English publications, including his translation of the Gospel of Saint Mark, Brant's Mohawk name appears in italics consistently as Thayendanegea and is cited as such in this study for consistent historiographical purposes. See also Isabel Thompson Kelsay, *Joseph Brant, 1743–1807, Man of Two Worlds* (Syracuse: Syracuse University Press, 1984). For Joseph Brant origins, see chaps. 2 and 3, 38–46.

2. Gloria Lesser, "Iconography in the Portraiture of Joseph Brant (1743–1807)" (Master's thesis, Concordia University, Montreal, 1983).

display in London at the annual Royal Academy of Arts Exhibition in 1786.[3] A succinct overview of the various known oil portraits of Brant lets us discern three distinct phases of Brant's portraiture: (a) works painted in England between 1776 and 1786 as tributes honoring his military exploits during his lifetime; (b) portraits produced as historical chronicles during his lifetime after the American War, in both Canada and the United States, from 1786 until his death in 1807; and (c) works painted as commemorations contrived after his death and based on earlier lifetime portraits. These three distinct phases define the order and transformative evolution of Brant's portraiture over time, and also provide a precise framework to better reference and articulate their function, intent, and purposes, the circumstances of their conception and creation, and the structure of their form, which together reveal their underlying meanings and historical influences and uses.

The first oil portraits of Joseph Brant were painted during his two short visits to London, England: first in 1776, to assess the benefits and to negotiate the engagement of North American Indigenous peoples as allies of Great Britain at the beginning of the American War, and second in 1786, to seek compensations for the human, material, and territorial losses, and to seek redress for the exile that his people had incurred at the conclusion of the war. Though the human and territorial rights of North American Indigenous peoples were totally ignored in the Treaty of Paris of 1783, Brant arrived in London not only as a peacemaker, but also as a founding member of a new Indian Confederacy that was ready to confront the new U.S. government's further territorial encroachment on unceded Indigenous lands.[4]

The only tribute portrait of Brant painted in oil during his first visit to London in 1776 was a life-size, three-quarter length composition by George Romney (1734–1802). It was commissioned by and for the private use of George Greville, second Earl of Warwick (1746–1816). This portrait has hung in the National Gallery of Canada in Ottawa since 1922, and was the first English portrait of Brant to be publicly displayed in North America.[5] During Brant's second sojourn in London in 1786, Brant sat again for three additional tribute portraits. The first was commissioned and painted by John Francis Rigaud, which became the first oil portrait of Brant to be publicly exhibited in Britain, but it vanished after the artist's death in 1811 and has never been traced since. That spring, Brant also sat for two privately commissioned, smaller, half-length oil portraits, both painted by Gilbert Stuart (1755–1828).[6] The first (figure 9) was done at the behest of Francis Rawdon, second

3. L. H. Cust and Martin Myrone, "John Francis Rigaud, " *Oxford Dictionary of National Biography* (Oxford: Oxford University Press, 2004).

4. Kelsay, *Joseph Brant*, 379–94.

5. Jennifer C. Watson, *George Romney in Canada* (Kitchener: Kitchener-Waterloo Art Gallery, 1985), See also, Elizabeth Hutchinson "The Dress of His Nation: Romney's Portrait of Joseph Brant," *Winterthur Portfolio* 45, no. 2/3 (Summer / Autumn 2011): 209–28.

6. Dorinda Evans, *The Genius of Gilbert Stuart* (Princeton, NJ: Princeton University Press, 1999). See also, Carrie Ribora Barratt and Ellen G. Miles, *Gilbert Stuart* (New Haven, CT, and London: The Metropolitan Museum of Art, Yale University Press, 2014).

Earl of Moira (1754–1826), and is now in the Fenimore Art Museum, Cooperstown, New York,[7] of which two anonymous early copies are known to exist: one at the British Museum, London (figure 10) since ca. 1896,[8] and another in the Olive Blake-Lloyd collection in England, about which little is known.[9] The second (figure 8), commissioned by Sir Hugh Percy (1742–1817), the future second Duke of Northumberland, remained in his family until it was sold to an anonymous private collector at Sotheby's in London in 2014.[10]

Joseph Brant never returned to Europe after 1786. A decade later, American and Canadian artists also painted lifetime oil portraits of Brant, no longer as a tribute to the warrior, but purposely as a chronicle of the leader of his people for historical exhibition and for biographic and historical publications. In 1786, the American portraitist Charles Willson Peale (1741–1827) founded the Peale Museum in Philadelphia. In 1797 Peale painted a half-length oil portrait of Brant (figure 6) to display in his historical gallery of notables, making it the second oil portrait of Brant to be publicly exhibited during his lifetime and the first in North America, which now hangs in Independence National Historical Park in Philadelphia. In 1799, the Canadian artist William Berczy (1744–1813) painted a small, oval, half-length portrait sketch of Brant in oil on paper, now in the Canadiana Collection at the Royal Ontario Museum, Toronto. Berczy had intended to use the portrait to illustrate his chapter on local Indian Nations in his planned History of Upper and Lower Canada, for which he had also recorded a vivid textual description of Brant.[11] The last known lifetime chronicle portrait of Brant was a half-length composition painted in oil on canvas in 1806 by Ezra Ames (1768–1836) as a private commission for James Caldwell (c. 1747–1829), a wealthy merchant from Albany, New York, that also hangs in the Fenimore Art Museum. Ames's oil portrait served as a model for a hand-colored, lithographic portrait print, published in 1830 at Philadelphia, in Thomas McKenney and James Hall's History of the Indian Tribes of North America.

After Joseph Brant's death in 1807, the third phase of commemorative portraits of Brant painted in oil on canvas was initiated to satisfy the growing needs of nineteenth-century historical publications about Brant. William Berczy produced two posthumous, oil portraits after his earlier oil sketch: the first was a small neoclassical, whole-length oil portrait painted around 1807, now in the National Gallery of Canada, Ottawa, while the second

7. Lawrence Park, *Gilbert Stuart: An Illustrated Descriptive List of His Works* (New York: William Edwin Rudge, 1926), 4 Vols. See Vol. II, 947 - Past Owners. Park identifies Dr. Hayes as having owned four portraits by Stuart: Chevalier d'Éon, Francis Rawdon-Earl of Moira, Duke of Manchester, and Thayendanegea-Joseph Brant.
8. British Museum Number, Am2006, Ptg. 1.
9. Lesser, "Iconography."
10. Sotheby's London. Old Masters and British Paintings Evening Sale, July 9, 2014, No 21. Gilbert Stuart.
11. Mary Macaulay-Allodi, Peter N. Moogk, and Beate Stock, *Berczy*, edited by Rosemarie L. Tovell (Ottawa: National Gallery of Canada, 1991).

was a small half-length figure of Brant set in a tondo, now at the Art Gallery of Ontario, Toronto. The last commemorative portrait of Brant (figure 13) painted in oil on canvas, which was copied after an enamel portrait miniature of Brant (figure 14) now in the Joseph Brant Museum at Burlington, Ontario, hangs today in the Johnson Hall Historic Site at Johnstown, New York.

In the introduction to his biography of Brant published in 1838, William Leete Stone (1792–1844) detailed how he had selected and reproduced the printed illustrations published in his book.[12] The lawyer and historian William Clement Bryant (1830–98) would reference Stone's publication in his 1873 article, which was illustrated with a wood-engraved portrait of Brant related to Rigaud's portrait.[13] The complex history of Brant's posthumous portraits after lifetime portraits that were subsequently printed on paper and published will not be fully discussed in this study, as their convoluted circumstances merit an in-depth study that would far exceed the focus and space of this article.

Of the seven known tribute and chronicle lifetime oil portraits of Joseph Brant listed above, the second, painted in 1786 by Rigaud, stands out, both for its prominence and unique grandeur and paradoxically for its conspicuous absence. Though it eventually faded from human memory, seemingly without any pictorial or textual descriptions, the portrait has cast a shadow that can be dimly discerned by historians through numerous historical records that mention it, or that relate to its original commissioning, its timely completion for public display, its subsequent exhibition and studio sightings, its pictorial influences, its public sale, and its final disappearance. These records provide the basis for much of what follows.

Two types of historical documents intertwine to chronicle the creation and life cycle of Rigaud's portrait of Joseph Brant: personal eyewitness accounts and published records. The first record (and first eyewitness account) relating to a possible Rigaud portrait is from the Private Diary (1786–90) of the former governor general of Quebec, Sir Frederick Haldimand (1718–91), who unexpectedly became instrumental in the portrait's conception and manufacture.[14] His concise diary entries provide important contextual information and a fairly detailed timeline for the portrait's creation. The second record (and first published account) that identified Rigaud's portrait of Brant appeared in the catalog of the 1786 Royal

---

12. William Leete Stone, *Life of Joseph Brant-Thayendanegea*, 2 Volumes (New York: G. Dearborn & co., 1838).

13. William Clement Bryant, "Joseph Brant, Thayendanegea, and His Posterity," *The American Historical Record* 2, no. 19 (July 1873).

14. British Library Manuscripts, Haldimand Papers 21890-92 - Private Diary. See also Douglas Brymner, "Private Diary of Gen. Haldimand," *Report on Canadian Archives* (Ottawa: Brown Chamberlin, 1889 (1890)), 126–299. The original diary was written in French and was published in French with an English translation (henceforth: Haldimand, *Diary*).

Academy Exhibition, London.[15] A third record (and second eyewitness account) is from the diary of the German novelist Sophie von La Roche (1730–1807), who, while in London as a tourist, noted her chance sighting of the large portrait of Brant during her visit to Rigaud's studio in September 1786, soon after the portrait had returned from the Royal Academy Exhibition.[16] The fourth record (and second published account) of the portrait appeared two decades later, in the 1806 catalog of the first exhibition of the British Institution, where the portrait was dusted off, retitled, and publicly exhibited in London for a second time.[17] A fifth record (and third published account) appeared soon after John Francis Rigaud's death on December 6, 1810, when Brant's portrait was listed in the catalog published by the London auctioneer Peter Coxe (d. 1844), for the posthumous sale[18] of the contents of Rigaud's studio on April 4 and 5, 1811, when the portrait was sold to an unknown bidder for £10, and soon after vanished.[19]

However, since none of the above evidence provided a visual record or textual description of the portrait's physical characteristics and iconographic composition, the nature of the portrait and its later influences remained obscure for over two hundred years. That remained the situation, until February 2014, when I recognized that a watercolor painting in the documentary art collections of Library and Archives Canada (LAC) in Ottawa had to be a sketch of the lost oil portrait of Joseph Brant painted by John Francis Rigaud in London in 1786 (figure 1). I was able to immediately validate my conclusion by consulting John Francis Rigaud's memoir, the sixth record (and third eyewitness account), which his son and artist, Stephen Francis Dutilh Rigaud (1777–1861), had conflated into a family history titled "Facts and Recollections of the XVIIIth Century in a Memoir of John Francis Rigaud Esq., R.A." that included John Francis Rigaud's exact description of his portrait of Joseph Brant and its symbolic meanings:

> This year [1786] my father had (six) seven pictures in the [RA] Exhibition—No. 1 A very interesting large size (Historical) Whole length Portrait of Captain Joseph

15. Algernon Graves, *The Royal Academy of Arts. A complete dictionary of contributors and their works from its foundation in 1769 to 1904* (London: H. Graves and Co. Ltd., 1905–6), Vol. 6, 299. Listed as no. 11 Portrait of Captain Joseph Brant, alias Thayendanegea, of the Mohawks.

16. Claire Williams, trans., *Sophie in London, 1786. Being the Diary of Sophie v. La Roche* (London: J. Cape, 1933).

17. Algernon Graves, *The British Institution. A Complete Dictionary of Contributors and Their Work From the Foundation of the Institution* (Bath: Kingsmead Reprints, 1969), 455.

18. Algernon Graves, *Art Sales from Early Nineteenth Century to Early in the Twentieth Century (Mostly Old Masters and Early English Pictures [oil paintings])*, 3 Vols. (London: Published by Algernon Graves, 1921). See Vol. 3, 71–72.

19. Peter Coxe, *The Catalogue of All the Genuine and Valuable Collection of Ancient and Modern Paintings of the Late John Francis Rigaud, Esq. R.A.* (London: J. Moyes, Printer, 1811), 1–15, annotated; Frits Lugt, *Art Sales Catalogues Online* (Leiden and Boston: Brill, 2000), http://primarysources.brillonline.com'browse/art-sales-catalogues-online. To promote the sale, the portrait of Brant was also listed on the front cover.

Brandt, the Mowhawk Chief thus described, "Joseph Brandt, alias Thayendenega of the Mohawks, a principal chief and warrior of the five Nations, as he appeared in the great Council in 1783, when he informed them it was the King of England's desire that hostilities should cease between them and the Americans. He holds in his right hand the calumet or pipe of Peace, with the wampum belt, on which are delineated two figures, representing two nations, who have made a road of communication between each other in token of Peace. On his spear are marked each of his various expeditions, one (only) of which is crossed, as having been unsuccessful. On his tomahawk, which lies at his feet, are marks for every person he had either slain in battle or made his prisoner. The tortoise is introduced as emblematic of his tribe; and in the background is represented the manner in which the Indians make their fires, and fish with the spear.[20]

LAC acquired this watercolor sketch in 1981 from the David I. Bushnell Jr. Collection of American Art at the Peabody Museum of Archaeology and Ethnology of Harvard University.[21] Though the artist of the sketch remains unknown, the subject had always been correctly identified as Thayendanegea-Joseph Brant and was published in color as such by the Smithsonian Institute in 1929.[22] Yet the nature of the original portrait was so obscured from human memory that no one had associated this sketch with Rigaud's lost 1786 oil portrait of Brant.

The undated and unsigned sketch was painted in watercolors with brush and pen on laid paper and framed in wash borders and three black ink outlines, the whole measuring 27.8 x 17.3 cm. In the lower margin, a capitalized title is inscribed in brown watercolor, in Italian, CAPO Ẋ X AMERICANO (American Chieftain). Between these two words, inscribed by an informed hand in pen and brown ink, is a North American Indigenous pictograph in the minimal form of two Xs, representing two human figures standing side by side, which symbolized equality, communication, harmony, and peace, similar to those depicted in the white wampum belt held by Brant in the portrait. The Italian title suggests the artist may have been Rigaud himself, who had studied and worked in Italy for a decade

---

20. Stephen Francis Dutilh Rigaud, "Facts and Recollections of the XVIIIth Century in a Memoir of John Francis Rigaud Esq., R.A.," edited by William L. Pressly, *The Volume of the Walpole Society* 50 (1984): 120. (henceforth: Rigaud, "Facts and Recollections") Rigaud's convenient but erroneous use of the word "Chief" to designate Brant's identity and authority is incorrect, as Brant was not a hereditary chief or sachem, but rather a military leader and spokesperson for Indigenous peoples allied with the British in the American War.

21. David Ives Bushnell (1875–1941) was an independently wealthy American anthropologist, who studied and collected works of art documenting North American Indigenous cultures, which he had given to the Peabody Museum, Harvard University. James R. Glenn, "David Ives Bushnell Jr.," in *International Dictionary of Anthropologists*, edited by Christopher Winters (New York: Garland Publishing, 1991). See complete LAC's Bushnell Collection of Canadiana, acquisition file MIKAN-98142. Earlier provenance of this watercolor sketch has not been traced.

22. Rose A. Palmer, *The North American Indians*, Smithsonian Scientific Series, Vol. 4 (New York: Smithsonian Institution Series Inc., 1929), plate 31.

Figure 1. Joseph Brant, unknown artist, after John Francis Rigaud's 1786 oil portrait, watercolor, 27.8 x 17.3 cm. LIBRARY AND ARCHIVES CANADA, ACC. NO. 1981-55-78R.

and was fluent in Italian.[23] To secure design and color accuracy, the sketch was likely taken in front of the original picture, sometime before its disappearance in 1811.

Beyond all doubt, Rigaud's own textual description of his portrait of Joseph Brant perfectly mirrors the LAC watercolor sketch. Using both textual and pictorial evidence, we can now substantiate and restore a true similitude of Rigaud's grand portrait of Brant. Rigaud's description vivifies the iconographic elements of his composition with such specificity of time and place as to evoke the very oration that Brant had declaimed at the 1783

---

23. Rigaud, "Facts and Recollections," 36. Rigaud's son described his father as such: "his disposition was naturally warm and very lively; he spoke French and Italian perfectly . . . , and . . . conversed in English better than I have ever known a foreigner to do; it was the language always spoken in the family." Rigaud's new translation after Leonardo's original Italian manuscript, *A Treatise on Painting, by Leonardo Da Vinci* (London: John Taylor, 1802), endures to this day.

Council (Council of the Western Indian Confederacy at Sandusky).[24] This documentary evidence reinstates the work within the context of Brant's personal portrait gallery and within Rigaud's still too little known body of work, while validating its legitimacy within the history of eighteenth-century portraiture in England, Canada, and the United States.

The Haldimand diary records the time, place, and circumstances of the portrait's gestation and identifies the three individuals who collaborated to create Brant's portrait: the artist and patron, John Francis Rigaud, the sitter, Joseph Brant, and the facilitator, Haldimand himself. On January 10, 1786, Haldimand noted that Rigaud had expressed his desire to paint a portrait of the general's friend, Captain Joseph Brant, who had just arrived in London from Canada in December of 1785. Haldimand instantly obliged and invited both Rigaud and Brant to meet and discuss the matter over dinner that evening at his residence on Curzon Street, in the exclusive Mayfair district of London. Though no record of their conversation exists, the evening's singular purpose lets us imagine some of the more practical issues they would likely have considered. Though the portrait was Rigaud's personal commission, each of the three men could bring to the discussion his considerable personal experience with the concepts of portraiture that helped shape the parameters of Rigaud's portrait of Joseph Brant. Haldimand's chronicle of the painting's progress from January 10 to March 7, 1786, sheds light on various aspects of each individual's participation and contribution, motives, and ambitions regarding the picture.

Though Haldimand's involvement in the production of Rigaud's portrait of Brant may surprise many, his participation was as natural and sophisticated as it was expedient. After the conclusion of the American War of Independence in 1783, Haldimand left Quebec in November of 1784 and retired to London where he continued to advise the British government on American and Canadian military and administrative matters. He was acclaimed and celebrated for his distinguished North American military career and was invested a Knight of the Order of the Bath, Grand Cross, by the king.[25] Haldimand and Rigaud's cordial relationship in London had been shaped earlier, through their successful family business relations in the textile trade in Switzerland. Haldimand resettled in Mayfair with the assistance of his wealthy nephew, Anthony Francis Haldimand (1741–1817), who had successfully extended the family business in London and had his own portrait painted by Rigaud in 1779.

Sir Frederick Haldimand attended court regularly and enjoyed London's rich cultural

---

24. "Letter from Sir John Johnson to General Frederick Haldimand, Sept. 8, 1783 – Transactions with Indians at Sandusky," in *Michigan Historical Collections*, Vol. 20, edited by Michigan Pioneering and Historical Society (Lansing, MI: Robert Smith & Co., 1892), 174–85. This letter includes the text of Brant's oration and presentation of three wampum belts and several strings at the Council of September 6, 1783.

25. Jean N. McIlwraith, *Sir Frederick Haldimand* (Toronto: Morang & Co. Ltd., 1906), 323, 324; see also Stuart R. J. Sutherland, Pierre Tousignant, and Madeleine Dionne-Tousignant, "Haldimand, Sir Frederick," in *Dictionary of Canadian Biography*, Vol. 5 (Toronto: University of Toronto/ Université Laval, 2003).

and social life, becoming known for the soundness of his military and administrative judgment. His London diary provides some of the minutia of his daily life that reflects his elegant personality and complex human character. We learn of his artistic discernment and of his awareness of London's contemporary art scene, as he made visits to the annual Royal Academy of Arts exhibitions and to other art galleries around the city, as well as viewing private art collections with a critical eye.[26] His building activities reveal his affinity with the new neoclassical style of design, and that he particularly enjoyed visiting the celebrated Townley Museum of Classical Antiquities, which was an intellectual and aesthetic interest that he shared with John Francis Rigaud.[27] Haldimand had built two private country houses in the fashionable Palladian style: one at Montmorency Falls near Quebec City[28] and another on his domain of Champ-Pittet overlooking Lake Neuchatel near his native village of Yverdon in Switzerland.[29] On April 14, 1786, he noted his critical appreciation of a new house that had recently been designed and built in London by the architect Robert Adams (1728–92), a strong proponent of the neoclassical style.

Haldimand had also assembled modest collections of pictures at his residences in Quebec and later in London. In Quebec he collected large watercolors and hand-colored outline etchings of Canadian views by a young military surveyor and draftsman under his command, Lt. James Peachey (c. 1773–97), who had become acquainted with Brant in Canada and with Rigaud in London through his professional and artistic association with Haldimand.[30] In pursuing his personal printmaking practice, Peachey had produced the first known landscape prints in Canada with Haldimand's assistance.[31]

While in London in 1786, Peachey had painted large watercolor views of Montreal and Quebec that were exhibited in the same 1786 Royal Academy Exhibition in which Rigaud

---

26. Haldimand, *Diary*, February 10, 1787. Haldimand notes having viewed and assessed Dr. Adair's "excellent" collection of pictures: "I did not find a single poor one among them."
27. Haldimand, *Diary*, May 31, 1787.
28. Nathalie Clerk, *Palladian Style in Canadian Architecture* (Ottawa: National Historic Parks and Site Branch, Parks Canada, Environment Canada, 1984). A published 1785 inventory of a subscription library in Quebec included Palladio's *The Four Books of Architecture*. Haldimand's Manoire Montmorency was a Palladian-style villa with a central building flanked by pavilions based on a design published in Robert Morris, *Rural Architecture Consisting of Regular Designs of Plans and Elevations for Buildings in the Country* (London: Printed for the author, 1750). Haldimand's manor house was built of wood and destroyed by fire on May 13, 1993.
29. Chateau de Champ-Pittet was built of stone and still stands today as the Centre Pro Natura that supports an important nature reserve.
30. W. Martha E. Cooke, *W. H. Coverdale Collection of Paintings, Watercolours and Drawings* (Ottawa: Public Archives of Canada, 1983), 158–61. See also W. Martha E. Cooke and Bruce G. Wilson, "Peachey James," in the *Dictionary of Canadian Biography*, Vol. 4 (Toronto: University of Toronto/Université Laval, 2003). See also British Library Manuscripts, Haldimand Papers, Additional 21736, 230–32.
31. Mary Macaulay-Allodi, *Printmaking in Canada: The Earliest Views and Portraits* (Toronto: Royal Ontario Museum, 1980), 2–3, No. 1.

Figure 2-A. (*above, left*) Detail of figure 1.

Figure 2-B. (*above, middle*) Joseph Brant, unknown artist, after John Francis Rigaud, ca. 1786, graphite, color chalks, 11.7 x 7.5 cm. LIBRARY AND ARCHIVES CANADA, C-114468.

Figure 2-C. (*above, right*) Joseph Brant, by James Peachey, 1786, after John Francis Rigaud, 1786, line and stipple etching, 12.7 x 8.0 cm. NATIONAL PORTRAIT GALLERY, LONDON, NPG D23311.

had exhibited his portrait of Brant.[32] He also created a small bust portrait etching[33] of Joseph Brant after Rigaud's portrait (figure 2-C), similar in scale and composition to the fine "miniature-like" color chalk drawing[34] of Brant by a yet unidentified artist, also part of the Bushnell Collection at LAC (figure 2-B). Though the relationship between the National Portrait Gallery (NPG) print and the LAC drawing remains under study, there is no doubt that both compositions derived from Rigaud's lost oil portrait of Brant (figure 2-A, detail) rather than after those painted by Gilbert Stuart around the same time. For his investiture into the Order of the Bath, Haldimand had also used Rigaud's portrait of Brant for the design of a North American Indigenous figure, at left, supporting his personal arms on his stall plate (figure 3) still affixed on the south range of stalls in Henry VII Chapel in Westminster Abbey.[35] After his investiture, Haldimand sat for his portrait wearing his scarlet army tunic and Bath ribband and star, for London's renowned portraitist Sir Joshua

---

32. Graves, *Royal Academy*.

33. Portrait of Capt. Joseph Brant, National Portrait Gallery, London, NPG D23311, etching, 127 x 80 mm sheet; signed and dated on the image: J. Peachey Sculpt. 1786 / Capt. Joseph Brandt. The only other known impression of this very rare print is preserved in the Print Collection of the Miriam and Ira D. Wallach Division of Art, Prints and Photographs, New York Public Library, ID: 438930.

34. Joseph Brant by unknown artist, ca. 1786, LAC, Acc. no.: 1981-055-57, graphite and colored chalks on laid paper, formerly attributed to Samuel Wale (1721–86). Also acquired in 1981 from the David I. Bushnell Jr. Collection of American Art, in the Peabody Museum of Archeology and Ethnology at Harvard University.

35. Westminster Abbey Library maintains records of the copper plate. See also McIlwraith, *Sir Frederick Haldimand*, chap. 16, 346.

Figure 3. Arms of Sir Frederick Haldimand (detail), engraved and painted gilded copper, 22.8 x 16.5 cm. PHOTO COPYRIGHT: DEAN AND CHAPTER OF WESTMINSTER, LONDON.

Reynolds (1723–92).[36] When Sir Frederick was next greeted by Queen Charlotte at court, she mentioned having seen his portrait and thought it a very fine and true likeness. A few years later, before Haldimand's death in 1791, Rigaud painted another portrait of the general wearing his Bath insignia, which the artist exhibited posthumously at the Royal Academy Exhibition of 1793.[37] In short, Haldimand brought to the discussion that evening a fair appreciation of contemporary British portraiture, and considerable insight into its capacity to negotiate personal and social values and its ability to convey political nuances of power within different classes of British society. Along with Haldimand's investiture as a Knight of the Bath, his portraits symbolized the gratitude and recognition of the British Empire for his distinguished military service in North America and demonstrated to us the level of his social eminence in London.

In facilitating the production of Rigaud's portrait of Brant, Haldimand favored the opportunity to have a large celebratory portrait of Brant publicly exhibited at the heart of the Empire, which could draw attention and support for the successful outcome of Joseph Brant's claims before the British government. During and after the American War, Haldimand had continually urged government ministers to maintain the vital support of their North American Indigenous allies to strengthen the defense of what remained of British North America. Canada, as well as Britain's maritime colonies and territories in the north

---

36. Portrait of Sir Frederick Haldimand, by Sir Joshua Reynolds, c. 1788, oil on canvas, National Portrait Gallery, London, NPG 4874. Reynolds's studio also produced several copies of Haldimand's portrait.
37. Rigaud, "Facts and Recollections," 88. See also Graves, *Royal Academy*, Vol. 5, No. 222 Portrait of a General officer and Knight of the Bath. The portrait is now at the Musée du Château de Morges, Morges, Switzerland, Acc. no. MMV 1005007.

and west, continued to be under threat of invasion by the rebellious new American Republic to the south. Haldimand also had the responsibility of resettling loyal American colonists and loyal Indigenous peoples seeking refuge in Canada.[38] Upon his arrival in London, Joseph Brant had solicited Haldimand's further support in dealing with issues of redress from the British government in the aftermath of the lost American War. Haldimand's support for the execution of Brant's portrait and his convivial dinner invitation disposed him to openly share with Rigaud some of his North American military experiences and his relationship with Joseph Brant. Rigaud's unexpected request to paint a portrait of Brant came at an optimal time for both Haldimand and Brant.

John Francis Rigaud was born (Jean-François) in 1742 near Turin, Italy, where his Protestant and wealthy merchant family had recently arrived from France to escape religious persecution and where they established and maintained business relations with Haldimand's family.[39] Rigaud's evident artistic talents blossomed under the tutelage of the history painter Claudio Francesco Beaumont (1694–1766) of Turin, who was also history painter to the king of Sardinia. Over the next decade Rigaud further developed his artistic talents in Rome and other major artistic centers in Italy, studying the best of contemporary art, as well as that of the great masters of the past, including the sculpture and architecture of antiquity. Upon his arrival in London via Paris in 1771, at age twenty-nine, his membership in the Academia Clementina in Bologna resulted in his immediate election as an associate of the newly formed Royal Academy of Arts in London, being later elected a full Academician on February 10, 1784. His embrace of the new neoclassical style is evidenced by his various collections and his artistic activities including history painting, portraiture, reproductive printmaking, restoring damaged pictures, finishing pictures left incomplete by others, and the design and execution of interior architectural decoration, the latter becoming a major source of income. He also renewed ties with members of the prosperous Haldimand family who were now successfully established in London. Though he was a reluctant portraitist, Rigaud is perhaps best known today for his group portraits of prominent fellow Academicians.[40] He also designed several scenes published in John Boydell's Shakespeare gallery and published prints after his own works, including portraits, for the London print trade.[41]

Over dinner on January 10, 1786, one can reasonably expect that Rigaud likely shared

---

38. This land grant, known as the Haldimand Treaty of 1784, remains a key document today to support Six Nations Land and Resources litigation against injustices by the Ontario and Canadian governments.

39. Rigaud, "Facts and Recollections." See also Coxe, *The Catalogue*, for a concise biography of J. F. Rigaud.

40. Arlene Leis, "Jean-François Rigaud: Portraying the Royal Academy of the Arts," *Life Writing* 8, no. 3 (2011): 257–71.

41. John Boydell, *The Boydell Gallery: A Collection of Engravings Illustrating the Dramatic Works of Shakespeare* (London: Bickers and Son, 1874), three designs by Rigaud for *Comedy of Errors, King Henry IV, Part I,* and *Romeo and Juliet,* and also seven illustrations for *The Life of Mary Queen of Scots.*

with Brant and Haldimand his vision for Brant's portrait and his intention to exhibit the painting in three months' time at the annual Royal Academy of Arts Exhibition, between May 1 and June 10, 1786. He may have also imparted that the portrait he wished to submit to the academy's selection committee needed to transcend mere likeness and express a significant historical theme, just as Sir Joshua Reynolds had promoted in his published Discourses.[42] Establishing the subtle parameters of this critical issue would determine the portrait's composition, and Rigaud needed to draw out a suitable historical theme from Brant and Haldimand's experiences in the American War. After gaining Brant's consent to pose for a portrait and establishing the portrait's historical theme, which he later described in his memoir, Rigaud could not leave Curzon Street that evening without also securing Brant's commitment to a schedule of urgent studio sittings to meet the academy's April submission deadline.

Well before his first visit to London, Joseph Brant had witnessed and experienced the social and political uses of portraiture in North America. In his youth, Brant had glimpsed the persuasive potency of portraiture through his personal association with Sir William Johnson (1715–74), the British government's superintendent of Northern Indians.[43] After the death of his first wife in 1759, Johnson had maintained an intimate and discrete relationship with Molly Brant (1736–96), Joseph's older sister. He had also taken young Joseph under his wing and enabled his formal education, seeing the boy's potential as a translator of Indigenous languages that could help bridge Indigenous and colonial settler cultures.[44] As a young man Brant had often visited Sir William's great manor house, Johndon Hall, occupied by Johnson's family from 1763 to 1779,[45] whose parlors and dining room walls were lined with large oil paintings, including portraits, in gilt frames. Three "Indian pictures" had hung in the front hall, while other rooms were ornamented with numerous portrait prints framed under glass, including portraits of George III and Queen Charlotte, to whom Joseph Brant would later be presented at court.[46] Brant understood that even portraits of him could be disseminated to a wider public as smaller paper prints through the print trade and the popular press.[47]

---

42. Sir Joshua Reynolds, *Seven Discourses on Art*, edited by R. Wark (New Haven, CT, and London: Paul Mellon Centre, 1975 [1771]).

43. Kelsay, *Joseph Brant*, chap. 5, 77.

44. While in London in 1786, Brant saw to the publication of his translation of The Gospel of Saint Mark in an illustrated bilingual edition in English and Mohawk of a *Book of Common Prayer* as well as a bilingual educational primer, both of which were illustrated by James Peachey.

45. Kelsay, Joseph Brant, chaps.5-7

46. Milton W. Hamilton, ed., Daniel Claus, *Inventory, The Papers of Sir William Johnson*, Vol. 13 (Albany: The University of the State of New York, 1962), Vol. 13, 647–65 (addenda). After Sir William Johnson's death in 1774, his son-in-law, Christian Daniel Claus (1727–87), drew up an inventory of articles in Johnson Hall that included twelve large oil paintings in gilt frames and twenty-four framed prints. The nature of the "3 Indian Pictures" has not yet been established.

47. Julian Gwyn, "Johnson, Sir William," in *Dictionary of Canadian Biography*, Vol. 4 (Toronto: University of Toronto/Université Laval, 2003). Johnson sat several times for his portrait painted in oils and in miniature, some of which were reproduced in print form. Brant had experienced the manifestation of Johnson portraiture; Brant's portraiture followed a similar production pattern and dissemination process.

Posing for another portrait in London in 1786 was not a novel experience for Brant; however, collaborating to devise an historical theme for his portrait was likely quite unexpected. At dinner Rigaud likely listened attentively to Brant and Haldimand recall significant events they had lived through during the American War and which brought them together again in London. Rigaud's detailed description of his portrait of Brant, cited above, informs us that the historical theme agreed upon had been the momentous event of "the great Council in 1783" (Council of the Western Indian Confederacy at Sandusky) when at the conclusion of the American War, Brant had pleaded for the cessation of hostilities and appealed to his brothers to now "lay down the hatchet."[48] Nevertheless, Brant had also urged all Indigenous peoples to remain united and be prepared to "take up the hatchet" again if need be, to defend their unceded ancestral lands against further encroachment by the new and aggressive United States. These historical circumstances defined Brant as a leader and peacemaker. Haldimand evidently concurred, having always stressed to the British government Brant's crucial leadership role in preventing further bloodshed at the end of the War of Independence.

Joseph Brant's understanding of the expressive powers of portraiture in British society and his fluency with patronage and the artistic production of portraiture were further shaped through his own portrait sittings to some of London's most prestigious portraitists. He could also be confident in the knowledge that for millennia the cultural values of his own North American Indigenous civilization were richly suffused with expressive symbolism, some of which he manifested when he purposely donned his Indigenous dress in European and colonial society.[49] He could appreciate that here was a propitious opportunity to publicly assert his presence to advance his London agenda on one of the grandest stages in the heart of the British Empire. Brant likely agreed to pose only if the artist consented to paint him in his Indigenous dress and would also have reassured Rigaud of his commitment to the schedule of required sittings.

Sir Frederick Haldimand recorded making at least fifteen visits to Rigaud's studio, sometimes twice weekly, between January and April 1786, revealing that his collaboration was more than a token gesture of support. Rigaud was the only artist to have painted Joseph Brant from life in a whole-length, life-size figure as the central axis of his composition, with many detailed North American Indigenous artifacts filling the left foreground, while a river flowed through a wooded mountainous landscape dotted with Indigenous encampments

---

48. See *Michigan Historical Collections*, with numerous historical symbolic phrases—"taking up the hatchet," "placing the hatchet in our hand," "laying down the hatchet," and "sharpen the hatchet"—used in councils by both Indigenous allies and British officers, discussing committing, preparing, engaging, or ceasing battle with an enemy.

49. Josephine Paterek, *Encyclopedia of American Indian Costume* (New York: W. W. Norton, 1994). Wearing of national dress was universally adopted by most Indigenous peoples under colonialism in order to affirm inherent values of identity and sovereignty. To Europeans and colonial observers, they expressed otherness and barbarism.

in the background on the right. The landscape's conventional low horizon enhanced the vertical elongation of the figure, which was further extended by a tall feathered headdress against a cloud-filled sky. Rigaud's design expanded the picture beyond a mere descriptive likeness into the realm of the historical and symbolic, a form of portraiture embraced by the Royal Academy that prioritized history painting above all.

To achieve greater exactitude in further comparative studies, it is important to account for Brant's characteristic dress, as much as the reduced LAC sketch (figure 1) will allow.[50] The foundation of Brant's headdress is a cloth cap with a fur headband ornamented with silver buckles, which supports a spray of white, black, and red feathers bound at the front. He wears a light pink, cotton shirt that hangs over his hips and is cinched at the waist with a woven red sash with a long fringe. Above his open shirt collar he sports a choker made of fur tied with a ribbon high around his neck. The right shoulder of his shirt is also ornamented with rows of small silver buckles, and his right sleeve is gathered just above the elbow with a wide silver armlet. A large, white shell gorget is suspended on his chest from a wide blue ribbon tied around his neck, below which hangs an embossed silver medal framed in brass depicting George III. He wears a bandoleer strap with diamond shape designs over his right shoulder, across his chest, and down to his left hip. A red and black blanket, also ornamented with buckles, is draped over his left shoulder like a classical Roman toga. It falls to his feet at the back, but is gathered at the front with his left arm that crosses at his waist to grasp the opposite edge. He also wore leggings buttoned all along the sides, with garters trimmed in red with fringes and tied just below the knees. At his hips hangs a black breech cloth ornamented with buckles, which is worn over his long shirt. His feet are dressed in ornamented yellow moccasins.

Brant's right arm extends down along his right side and his right hand grasps a ceremonial pipe elaborately ornamented with beaded designs and long white feathers, as well as a white wampum Friendship Belt, on which Rigaud noted "are delineated two figures representing two nations, who have made a road of communication between each other in token of Peace," the symbolic meaning which was likely conveyed by Brant.[51] In the foreground at lower left, a ceremonial pipe tomahawk with visible markings on its handle

---

50. Some details, textures, and materials of Brant's dress can be better discerned in the closer, half-length portraits painted by Gilbert Stuart that same year in 1786.

51. The Friendship Belt, representing the Covenant Chain, is known to the Confederacy Council of Chiefs, Grand River Territory, as Thontatenentsonterontahkhwa (the thing by which they link arms). The common symbol of peace and unity in wampum diplomacy is two figures holding hands, or interlocking their arms, thereby making a human chain. This Chain of Friendship was employed many times to obligate the Hodinohson:ni to defend the interests of the Crown. The imagery shows two figures, one of the king and the other of the Hodinohson:ni. They hold the chain, which represents clear and honest communications between them, as well as the open path of peace that connects the two. To the Grand River Hodinohson:ni, the Covenant Chain obligated them to defend the king's interest. In Native tradition, the white color of the wampum belt denotes peace. Six Nations Public Library, Digital Archives, Local identifier SNPL000068v00i - The Friendship Belt.

lies on a cloth at his feet, the placement of which may have been intended to imply the cessation of hostilities. Brant's authoritative clan symbol, the turtle, is depicted near his foot in
the lower right corner of the picture.[52] Traces of two indented parallel lines in the trees on
the left represent his spear, while the landscape suggests Brant's North American ancestral
lands along the banks of the Mohawk River in today's New York State.

However, before the end of the first week of sittings, Haldimand unexpectedly intervened in the progress of the portrait, bluntly noting in his diary, "1786 Tuesday, January 17, . . .
I went to Rigaud's and had him change some thing in Joseph's portrait, which I hope will be
very good," with no further explanation. This bold intervention expresses the collaborative
spirit of the portrait's enterprise and the high degree of trust that Rigaud had in Haldimand's discernment.[53] There is no record of the proposed change, but a closer examination
of the portrait's parameters will help narrow probabilities. We know that Brant controlled
his manner of dress, which was unassailable, and that Rigaud commanded the integrity of
his art and personal style of painting.[54] The type of landscape representing Brant's homeland and the inclusion of Brant's turtle clan symbol were likely made in consultation with
Brant. We are left with the specificity of the prominent artifacts represented in the picture,
some of which are not integral to Brant's manner of dress, yet are pertinent to the spiritual,
symbolic, and circumstantial uses in commemoration and communications within North
American Indigenous cultures, aspects of which both Brant and Haldimand had far greater
knowledge than Rigaud. It is reasonable to consider that the change proposed by Haldimand likely related to the artifacts that surrounded Brant, specifically the sacred ceremonial pipe and white wampum belt held in his right hand. Both were deployed as significant
diplomatic symbols of communication, friendship, and peace and also represented Brant's
influential role at the important Council of 1783, which Rigaud described in his memoir as
being the very essence of this historical portrait. A more overt representation of the sacred
symbols of peace would exemplify Brant not only as the valiant warrior, as depicted in
Romney's previous tribute portrait and subsequent print, but also now more emphatically

---

52. Brant was born a Mohawk of the Wolf Clan (his mother's clan). He married Catherine Adonwentishon Croghan in the winter of 1780, who was the daughter of the prominent American col-
onist and Indian agent George Croghan and a Mohawk mother, Catharine Tekarihoga. Through
her mother, Brant's wife, Catharine Adonwentishon, was head of the turtle clan, the first in rank
in the Mohawk Nation. Her birthright was to name the Tekarihoga, the principal sachem of the
Mohawk Nation.
53. Haldimand, *Diary*, March 27, 1786. During one of Haldimand's regular studio visits, Rigaud
had shown Haldimand his recent design for a painted ceiling, which Haldimand thought very
good.
54. C. James Taylor, et al., eds., *The Adams Papers, Adams Family Correspondence, Vol. 7, January
1786–February 1787* (Cambridge, MA: Harvard University Press, 2005), 33–46. Letter from
Abigail Adams to her brother John Quincy Adams, February 9, 1786, with her observation while
attending court at St. James Palace: "I was, struck with the appearance of . . . Joseph Brant. . . . He
has been presented to the King and Queen and has appeared at the drawing Room, in the dress of
his Nation with that pretty plaything his Tommy Hawk in his hand. The Ladies admired his figure
and saw in his Countenance something Good."

Figure 4-A. Apollo Belvedere, Vatican Museums, photo by Darafsh - Own work, CC BY-SA 3.0, https://commons.wikimedia.org/w/index.php?curid=50909284.
Figure 4-B. See figure 1.
Figure 4-C. Emperor Hadrian, Archeological Museum, Istanbul. Wikimedia, photo by Dr. Carl Rasmussen, courtesy of www.HolyLandPhotos.org. These works show the neoclassical influences.

as the heroic peacemaker. Rigaud was likely enthusiastic in augmenting the portrait's historical symbolism, which would further enhance its acceptance for exhibition. Both Rigaud and Brant seemed to have concurred with the change proposed by Haldimand, who three days later dutifully noted in his diary, "1786, Friday, January 20, . . . I went to Rigaud's and was pleased with Joseph's portrait." Haldimand's last recorded studio visit was at the end of March 1786, as the portrait was being finished.

Comparisons reveal that Rigaud modeled Brant's pose (figure 4-B) in the neoclassical style after antique Greco-Roman sculpture (figure 4-C) and in particular after the Apollo Belvedere (figure 4-A), which Rigaud had certainly seen and studied at the Vatican while in Rome, a plaster cast of which then stood in London's Royal Academy, which Rigaud had represented symbolically in the background of his triple portrait of the founders.[55] Since its discovery in Rome early in the sixteenth century, the sculpture had been a symbol of male beauty and grace.[56] Its complex stance, showing the figure both frontally and in profile, had lent its quintessential poise to various schools of European portraiture. For display at the Vatican the sculpture was raised on a pedestal that provided a view from below, which remained the characteristic viewpoint of Rigaud's composition, suggesting the artist may have had Brant pose on an elevated stand in his studio.

This lower viewpoint provided the unique structure and angle of Brant's head, tilted

---

55. Soon after its discovery, numerous plaster casts of the Apollo Belvedere could be found (often restored) in art academies and in public and private collections throughout Europe, including the Royal Academy of Arts, London. See Arlene Leis, "Jean-François Rigaud: Portraying the Royal Academy of the Arts," *Life Writing* 8, no. 3 (2011): 257–71
56. Joseph Alsop, *The Rare Art Traditions* (New York: Harper & Row, 1982), chap. 1.

up and slightly backward, which created the specific angle that reveals the underside of Brant's facial features—jaw, chin, nose, lips, and eye sockets—the details of which become critical in subsequent comparative studies with later portraits of Brant, particularly the two painted by Gilbert Stuart around the same time, but taken at a much closer range to capture an eye-level likeness. The discovery of the LAC sketch of Rigaud's portrait allows us to correct many previous erroneous attributions with greater clarity and discernment.

Referencing an image of Brant to the renowned sculpture of the Apollo Belvedere from Greco-Roman antiquity had a precedent of which Rigaud was likely highly aware, which came from his fellow Royal Academician, the American-born Benjamin West (1738–1820). Rigaud's composition evokes West's well-recorded declamation when he first viewed the Apollo in the Belvedere at the Vatican while studying classical antiquities in Rome in 1760: "My God, how like it is to a young Mohawk warrior. . . . I have seen them often, standing in that very attitude, and pursuing, with an intense eye, the arrow which they had just discharged from the bow."[57] West's comment so shocked the delegation of connoisseurs in attendance that West had to further explaine that the sculpture, representing the Greek god Apollo as a standing archer, having just released from his silver bow a golden arrow that killed the mythic serpent Python, had evoked memories from his childhood in North America of seeing Mohawk hunters skillfully drawing their bows and gazing in the same manner.[58] Rigaud, who then had a living, breathing North American Mohawk warrior in his Indigenous dress standing before him, endeavored to suffuse his portrait of Brant with the historian Johan Winckelmann's (1717–1768) aesthetic perception of the Apollo's "noble simplicity and quiet grandeur."

When completed by mid-April 1786, the finished portrait was transported to the Royal Academy of Arts at Somerset House on the Strand. Rigaud had described the picture as "a large size, whole length portrait." Given Brant's impressive physical height and allowing for the tall headdress, with additional compositional space all around the figure, we can estimate that the stretched canvas measured approximately 2 meters (9 feet) in height by 1.50 meters (5 feet) in width. The picture's subject and large scale would have secured an advantageous hanging placement "above the line" in the Great Room (figure 5),[59] which David H. Solkin aptly described as "the centre of the London art world. . . . Although contemporary art could be found in numerous other venues, there was only one official showcase for the achievements of modern British painters. . . . The exhibition also provided a glamorous

57. John Galt, *The Life and Studies of Benjamin West, Esq.* (London: Cadell & Davies, 1816), chap. 6, section VII, 105–06. The account of West's notorious encounter with the Apollo Belvedere no doubt echoed through the Royal Academy School, where West taught, long before it was first published in 1816.

58. Ovid, *The Metamorphosis*, Book I, translated by Horace Gregory (New York: Viking Press, 1958), 43.

59. David H. Solkin, ed., *Art on the Line: The Royal Academy Exhibitions at Somerset House, 1780–1836* (New Haven, CT, and London: Yale University Press, 2001).

Figure 5. Portraits of Their Majesty's [George III and Queen Charlotte] and The Royal Family Viewing The Royal Academy Exhibition, 1788, by Pietro Antonio Martini, after Johan Heinrich Ramberg, published 1789, etching, 39.0 x 52.8 cm (plate). NATIONAL PORTRAIT GALLERY, LONDON, NPG D21303.

social occasion, where everyone who was anyone had to see and be seen."[60] For forty days, between May 1 and June 10, 1786, the exhibition was attended by 55,404 visitors who, with catalog in hand, had the opportunity to gaze upon Brant's portrait by Rigaud.[61]

The picture was listed on the first page as "No. 11 Portrait of Captain Joseph Brandt, alias, Thayeadanegea, of the Mohawks. J. F. Rigaud R.A."[62] This descriptive title itself was quite exceptional, as Royal Academy Exhibition rules at the time stipulated that no sitter could be identified by name, except members of the royal family. Other sitters were referred to by a general descriptor of their social class, gender, age, action, occupation, etc.[63] Listing the portrait with Brant's Indigenous name and that of his Nation demonstrated that the sitter's elevated status as the representative of allied North American Indigenous Nations had gained a respectful consideration from the hanging committee.

As patron of the Royal Academy, George III and the royal family attended a preview of the exhibition (figure 5), while the lavish celebratory dinner and boisterous public opening

---

60. Solkin, *Art on the Line.*

61. Information from Andrew Potter, research assistant, Collections Department, Royal Academy Library, London.

62. Graves, *Royal Academy.* See also 1786 RA exhibition catalogue online at https://www.royal academy.org.uk/art-artists/exhibition-catalogue/ra-sec-vol18-1786.

63. Marcia Pointon, "Portrait! Portrait! Portrait!" in Solkin, *Art on the Line*, chap. 7.

was later presided over by the Prince of Wales.[64] However, given the mood of the nation at this time, George III likely viewed the grand portrait of his courageous friend, Captain Joseph Brant, with mixed feelings of admiration and personal affection, and of anger and bitter disappointment at the disastrous failure and humiliating defeat suffered by the English in the American War, of which no Englishman, above all the king, ever wished to be reminded. Professor Holger Hoock has explained that "since British Artists had precious little to commemorate during the American War, only military portraiture offered the opportunity for 'an edifying conflatory style of historical portrait' and the 'only form of encomiastic image making open to painters."[65] Sensitive to this issue, Rigaud had seized the opportunity to create an historical military portrait of Captain Joseph Brant that could rise above that ignoble military defeat. The depiction of Brant as leader of his people, loyal British ally, heroic warrior, and distinguished peacemaker was one of the few English pictures at the time to underscore a noble and strategic military alliance, which remained critically relevant to continued British sovereignty over Canada.

Though the portrait's deeper political virtues could be read by some, the portrait, in such dismal political climes, was received with detached public indifference and with slights against the artist by a mostly hostile English press. The war in America had pitted British colonial loyalists against British colonial rebels, whose enduring family ties and financial interests instigated hatred in Britain against even allied warring Indians.[66] To many, there was nothing heroically "English" about the picture or its production that could then help heal such deep personal wounds and uphold national pride. Though the portrait might have helped sustain and support Brant's postwar claims, this was surely not the overall result that the three portrait collaborators had hoped for. The picture's subsequent disappearance for over two centuries had prevented future art historians from establishing its merits within the artist's oeuvre and British visual culture. It was only by the mid-twentieth century that the mystery of its disappearance was revisited.[67]

---

64. Peter Pindar (alias for John Wolcot), "Academical Diner," *The New London Magazine: Being a Universal and Complete Monthly Repository*, May 14, 1786, 326. "On Saturday last the Royal Academy gave their usual grand dinner, at Somerset House, to the nobility and patrons of the arts, previous to the exhibition being opened to the public. The Prince of Wales . . . accompanied by the Dukes of Orleans, Fitz-James, and Lauzun . . . dined in the exhibition room . . . till near nine o'clock, when the Prince retired, and the company soon after broke up, delighted with the highest entertainment a refined mind is capable of enjoying."

65. Holger Hoock, *The King's Artists: The Royal Academy of Arts and the Politics of British Culture 1760–1840* (Oxford: Clarendon Press, 2003), 155.

66. Troy O. Brickham, *Savages within the Empire: Representations of American Indians in Eighteenth-Century Britain* (Oxford: Oxford University Press, 2005). The author amply demonstrates the British public's hostility toward American Indians during the War of Independence, and how and why little mention was made of any North American Indigenous peoples in the British press after the end of the American War of Independence and their total exclusion from the Treaty of Paris in 1783.

67. Milton W. Hamilton, "Joseph Brant painted by Rigaud," *New York History* 40, no. 3 (July 1959): 247–54.

Figure 6. Joseph Brant, by Charles Willson Peale, 1797, oil on canvas, 25 1/2 x 21 3/8 in. INDEPENDENCE NATIONAL HISTORICAL PARK, PHILADELPHIA, MUSEUM NO. INDE 11880.

By the close of the exhibition on June 10, the portrait had not sold and was returned to the artist's studio, where it was subsequently viewed on September 29 by visiting German author Sophie V. de LaRoche, who noted aspects of the portrait in her travel journal: "We also saw … still more interesting, a picture of the American Joseph Brant, who became eminent as the leader of a party of natives, and came to London some years back, when Rigaud painted him full-length in national costume. The dress, strong colours and flame red which the native Americans paint their cheeks in battle gives him quite a grim and fearsome look. . . ."[68] She had observed the picture's scale and format, but also the vibrant colors of Brant's "national costume" and "flame red" paint on his cheeks. The small LAC watercolor sketch does not reveal any red paint on Brant's cheeks, and none appear in the close-up portraits by Stuart. However, three stripes painted on each of Brant's cheeks do appear in Peachey's 1786 etched print after Rigaud's portrait and in the related color chalk drawing, as well as in Charles Willson Peale's 1797 oil portrait of Brant (figure 6). Before Rigaud's portrait was completed, Haldimand tersely jotted in his diary, "1786, Feb, Saturday 4, Was at Rigaud's respecting the engraving [print] of Joseph's portrait," again with no further explanation. No print by Rigaud of his portrait of Brant has yet been located, and we cannot say whether Haldimand was referring to Peachey's print. Rigaud's involvement in the London print trade and the publicity from the forthcoming Royal Academy Exhibition might have

---

68. Williams, *Sophie in London*, 245.

Figure 7-A. (*above, left*) Joseph Brant, etching by James Peachey, 1786 (detail of figure 2-C).
Figure 7-B. (*above, middle*) Joseph Brant drawing, by unknown artist, c. 1786 (detail of figure 2-B).
Figure 7-C. (*above, right*) Joseph Brant, by Charles Willson Peale, 1797 (detail of figure 6).

inspired a print, but the portrait's poor public reception in such unfavorable times would likely have revealed the project to be a futile investment.

All exhibiting artists hoped to sell their work and secure further commissions, the business of which was conducted privately. Haldimand noted in his diary that during one of his regular studio visits while Brant was sitting, he had heard Rigaud speculate boastfully that his grand portrait of Brant could command an astounding top price of 50 guineas. Haldimand also noted Brant's instant riposte, that if it did not sell, he would purchase the picture himself and have it sent to America. Here we see Brant suddenly transformed from sitter to collector, a transition that expressed his evolving sense of the social and political significance of portraiture. In the past Brant had been gifted portraits of himself, which made him an inadvertent collector, but in this instance, he would be a collector by intent. Haldimand later stated in his diary, "1788, March, Tuesday 23, I sent a case containing the portrait of Joseph Brant . . . to the care of Craigie [at Quebec]."[69] Brant received a large copy of Rigaud's portrait, which both Stone and Bryant later saw and described as still hanging in Brant's house that was later occupied by his descendants, and to date it has not been traced.

While Rigaud was creating his grand portrait of Brant for public display, Gilbert Stuart had also quietly painted two private and more intimate half-length oil portraits of Joseph Brant, who was already preparing to leave London and return to Canada by mid-May 1786.[70] Yet one could not imagine more dissimilar portraits of a same sitter, painted by the same artist, in the same studio, within days of each other. One portrait (figure 9) was commissioned by Francis Rawdon, second Earl of Moira, and the other (figure 8) by Sir Hugh Percy, future

---

69. John Craigie (1757–1813) was appointed by Haldimand as commissary general of the British Army in Canada at Quebec in 1784. The portrait sent to Canada in 1788 was a copy of Rigaud's 1786 full-length portrait of Brant, which Rigaud would exhibit for a second time in London in 1806 at the British Institution.
70. Kelsay, *Joseph Brant*, chap. 18.

Figure 8. Joseph Brant, by Gilbert Stuart, 1786, oil on canvas, 76.2 x 61.0 cm. The following three images of Brant by Gilbert Stuart reveal dissimilarities. PRIVATE COLLECTION © SOTHEBY'S.

Figure 9. Joseph Brant, by Gilbert Stuart, unfinished in 1786, completed by John Francis Rigaud in 1789, oil on canvas, 76.2 x 61 cm. FENIMORE ART MUSEUM, COOPERSTOWN, NY. MUSEUM NUMBER: N0199.1961.

Figure 10. Joseph Brant,
copy after Gilbert Stuart
and John Francis Rigaud,
by unknown artist, after
1789, oil on canvas, 80.5 x
70.2 cm. BRITISH MUSEUM,
NO. AM2006, PTG. 1.

second Duke of Northumberland, both of whom were well acquainted with Stuart, as they had recently sat for their portraits by him. Though both portraits of Brant have been well scrutinized by scholars, newly discovered information concerning the circumstances surrounding their creation allows us to readjust our previous perceptions of them.[71]

The provenance of Stuart's portrait of Joseph Brant for the Earl of Moira was documented by Lawrence Park and by J. R. Fawcet Thompson, stating that the portrait was commissioned by the Earl of Moira in 1786, who soon after gifted the portrait to Doctor, Sir John Macnamara Hayes (c. 1750–1809), an army surgeon who had served under Moira during the American War, and soon after became physician to the Prince of Wales and was created a baronet.[72] John Simonds, a Hayes family descendant by marriage, had brought the portrait to the United States when he emigrated in 1939. Eventually the portrait was acquired from a private collector by the Fenimore Art Museum in 1961.[73] However, when perusing Rigaud's memoir, I discovered that in 1789, John Francis Rigaud had completed Gilbert Stuart's "unfinished" portrait of Brant at the persistence of Dr. Hayes:

71. Evans, *The Genius of Gilbert Stuart.*
72. Park, *Gilbert Stuart,* Vol. 2, 746, No. 830; see also J. R. Fawcett Thompson, "Thayendanegea the Mohawk and his Seven Portraits . . . ," *The Connoisseur* 170, no. 683 (January 1969): 49–53.
73. I thank Ann H. Cannon, assistant curator, Collections Department, Fenimore Art Museum and The Farmers' Museum, for diligently providing a most comprehensive summary of the FAM provenance records.

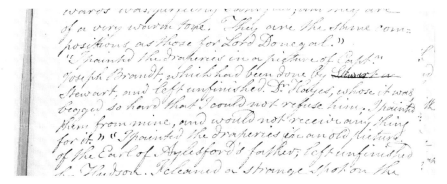

Figure 11. Stephen Francis Dutilh Rigaud (1777–1861). "Facts and Recollections of the XVIIIth Century in a Memoir of John Francis Rigaud Esq., R.A.," BEINECKE RARE BOOKS & MANUSCRIPTS LIBRARY, YALE UNIVERSITY, ID NO. 2033993, CALL NO. OSBORN D76, FOLIO 182 (DETAIL).

I painted the draperies in a picture of Capt.n / Joseph Brandt, which had been done by [James] / Stewart, and left unfinished. Dr. Hayes, whose it was, / begged so hard that I could not refuse him; I painted / them from mine and would not receive anything / for it.[74]

When comparing the above transcription published by the Walpole Society in 1984 to the original manuscript text, we see that the editor misinterpreted the artist's name as "[James] Stewart," suggesting the existence of another yet unknown portrait of Joseph Brant, but the editor also inadvertently mistranscribed the troublesome and ambivalent overlaid names of the artist from the original manuscript text (figure 11). The art historian Adrienne Leigh Sharpe at Beinecke Library accurately described the layers of text and marks (in quotation) from the original manuscript as: " . . . which had been done by Stuart or . . . ," which "Stuart or" was then overlaid with the name "Stewart," then the whole was crossed out and the text resumes with the name "Stewart."[75]

Thus we are faced with the well-worn debate on the correct spelling of Gilbert Stuart's surname, which like all similar names, could be spelled and written differently, as Stuart and Stewart, but pronounced phonetically the same. This confusion stems from early family legal documents and personal correspondence in which the family name is written both ways, at a time when orthography was not as fixed. The artist never signed his work, but had identified himself and achieved his fame under the name Stuart, which scholars have since respected. That Gilbert Stuart had left the Earl of Moira an "unfinished"

---

74. Rigaud, "Facts and Recollections," 80. Though Pressley did not transcribe the exact, if somewhat confusing manuscript text, it is nevertheless the mention of Dr. Hayes' ownership that clearly determines the identity of the artist to be Gilbert Stuart.

75. I am grateful to Adrienne Leigh Sharpe at Beinecke Library for her diligent verification of Pressley's transcription of Stuart's name published in Rigaud, "Facts and Recollections," against the 1789 original Rigaud memoir manuscript.

portrait of Joseph Brant should not surprise, as Stuart was notorious throughout his career for suddenly abandoning commissions and leaving many portraits unfinished for a variety reasons.[76]

Rigaud's consequential 1789 statement identifying Dr. Hayes as the owner of the "unfinished" portrait firmly establishes its attribution to Gilbert Stuart and provides the exact date for its completion by John Francis Rigaud. Since Gilbert Stuart fled England permanently in October of 1787, he could not have painted copies of a portrait that by 1789 still remained "unfinished."[77] Stuart's portrait of Brant for Moira (figure 9) can now be assuredly attributed to both Gilbert Stuart and John Francis Rigaud with attendant dates of execution, while the copy at the British Museum (figure 10) and the Olive Blake-Lloyd collection can now be dated as "after 1789" and attributed to an artist yet unidentified.[78] This new information will also help painting conservators reexamine Stuart's portrait of Brant for Moira to assist art historians to better appreciate the discrepancies of the dual and uneven energies of Stuart's "unfinished" original completed by Rigaud, compared to the seamlessness of the later polished copy (figure 10). Furthermore, Peachey's 1786 portrait etching of Brant at the National Portrait Gallery, London (figure 2-C) and the related anonymous chalk portrait drawing at LAC (figure 2-B) are now firmly established as being after John Francis Rigaud and not Gilbert Stuart. This new information also sheds light on the production of a rarely seen posthumous portrait miniature of Brant, presently under study, which was commissioned to illustrate Stone's 1838 biography of Brant.

Having abandoned Brant's portrait being done for the Earl of Moira, Stuart persisted and successfully completed the portrait of Joseph Brant for Sir Hugh Percy (figure 9) just before Brant returned to Canada. In previous portraits by Romney and Rigaud, including Stuart's portrait finished by Rigaud, the bright colors of Brant's dress remain consistent. Comparison between the two Brant portraits by Stuart reveals that the most blatant and dramatic dissimilarity is in the extreme painterly difference of the colors of Brant's dress and of the cloud-filled backgrounds; the color key establishes the distinctly different tone and mood of each portrait. Given Brant's insistence on being depicted in his national dress, the somber "blackness" that washes over Brant's identical dress in Stuart's portrait for Percy is strikingly incongruous and has never been addressed nor clearly understood.

Appreciating the portrait within eighteenth-century British society reveals the much overlooked context. Sober black dress was then the symbol of deep grief and was worn

---

76. Park, *Gilbert Stuart*, Vol. 1, 15, 16.

77. Evans, *The Genius of Gilbert Stuart*, chap. 3, 135, note 3. The distinct painterly discrepancies between the Fenimore Art Museum portrait and British Museum copy were astutely noted by Evans, whose reasonable doubts led her to suggest the possibility that neither was likely painted by Gilbert Stuart, as cited in Park, *Gilbert Stuart*, Vol. 2, 747. However, Rigaud's 1789 statement identifying Dr. Hayes as the owner now clarifies their attributions and dates.

78. The tone of Rigaud's statement implies his earlier refusal of Hayes's request, but relinquished only to rid himself of the annoyance. Though Rigaud finished and repaired damaged paintings by other artists, there is no mention in his memoir of his providing copies of this picture.

during prescribed periods of mourning, with protocols that marked profound social transitions and succession in personal and family life, as well as in national life. Such protocols were strictly adhered to at court and by the aristocracy.[79] Consequently, the wearing of mourning black permeated the detail of all aspects of aristocratic daily life, including mourning portraiture.[80] I argue that the emphatic presence of somber black dress in Stuart's portrait of Brant for Sir Hugh Percy was occasioned through the close personal relationships between patron, sitter, and artist, but obligated through momentous extraneous circumstances.

Sir Hugh Percy, who came from one of the most prestigious and wealthiest families of the British aristocracy, with a long tradition of social philanthropy and art patronage, had by this time become one of Gilbert Stuart's most faithful patrons.[81] When he had commissioned Brant's portrait from Stuart, Percy had not yet acceded to the dukedom. When received at Syon House, Brant was likely respectfully informed of the elderly first duke's serious decline, signifying an impending period of deep grief and of momentous hereditary transition. Indeed, just as Stuart was painting Brant's portrait in London, the first Duke and Earl of Northumberland died at age seventy-four, on June 6, 1786, at Syon House, the sad event thus elevating his son as second Duke of Northumberland.[82] The nation, including Gilbert Stuart, would have been made aware of the first duke's passing and of the succession, along with the prescribed periods of mourning to be strictly observed. Joseph Brant had sailed from England just days earlier and would receive the sad news in Canada only weeks later. The first duke's passing was considered a "truly public loss and will cause it to be long and sincerely lamented."[83] On June 21, after the first duke lay in state for two days at Northumberland House (today Trafalgar Square), the pageant of an extravagant cortege draped in black, with numerous dignitaries in horse-drawn carriages, solemnly conveyed his body to be interred in the Northumberland family vault in Saint Nicholas Chapel in Westminster Abbey.

---

79. Lou Taylor, *Mourning Dress: A Costume and Social History [Britain 1600–1950]* (Abingdon: George Allen & Unwin Ltd., 1983). See also Fred Davis, *Fashion Culture and Identity* (Chicago: University of Chicago Press, 1992). Mourning protocols at the English court are still strictly adhered to, as their expression extend beyond personal grief to legal entitlements and even to royal succession. Even today, given Queen Elizabeth II's advanced age, mourning protocols require that immediate members of the royal family travel abroad prepared with a minimum of suitable mourning attire.

80. Paul S. Fritz, "The Trade in Death: The Royal Funerals in England, 1685–1830," *Eighteenth-Century Studies* 15, no. 3 (Spring 1982): 291–316.

81. Carrie Rebora Barratt and Ellen G. Miles, *Gilbert Stuart* No. 17, Joseph Brant, 68–73.

82. Hugh Percy, First Duke of Northumberland (ca. 1712-14–1786), *Dictionary of National Biography London.*

83. "Obituaries of Considerable Persons with Biographical Annecdotes, number 6," *Gentleman's Magazine* 56, pt. 1 (1786): 529–30. The two-page obituary stated the duke's aristocratic ascendance, his interests, and his accomplishments, and describes the elaborate cortege on June 21, 1786, from Northumberland House to the Abbey. A view of Northumberland House had been painted by Canaletto in 1752. After a devastating fire in 1874, the ruins were cleared to establish Trafalgar Square.

The higher status of Stuart's aristocratic patronage in London at this time no doubt informed his dutiful social response, and the seriousness of the prescribed period of mourning to be strictly observed cannot be underestimated. On this occasion Stuart could not make a misstep, for completing this portrait of Percy's much-admired friend, Captain Joseph Brant, during this sad period of transition was nonetheless lucrative for the artist who was again being strangled by choking debts. Successfully fulfilling this commission could secure other forthcoming commissions for portraits required to mark the elevation of the new second duke and duchess. Given Northumberland's social rank and the mourning rituals prescribed, the resulting portrait of Brant being painted and delivered at that hour speaks eloquently. The dress historian Susan North observed that "Stuart's modification of Brant's characteristic dress was quite creative, aesthetically pleasing and deeply respectful."[84] Brant's usual light pink cotton shirt was colored a somber grey-black to harmonize with the silver-trimmed black blanket draped over his shoulder, the whole contrasting starkly against the restless clouds of a cheerless grey sky. The following year, in 1787, at the conclusion of the prescribed period of mourning, the new second Duke of Northumberland commissioned family portraits from Gilbert Stuart and had even extended to the artist the rare privilege of living and working at Syon House, in order to facilitate his access to the duke and duchess, including their many children of whom a large group portrait by Stuart still hangs at Syon House. But by the fall of 1787, Stuart's perilous debts forced him to suddenly flee England permanently for Ireland and to return to America in 1793.

Stuart's portrait of Brant for Northumberland was thus invested with layers of meaning, for it celebrated their enduring friendship and acknowledged Brant's visit and mission, it conveyed his likeness while describing the dress of his nation and his military rank, but also marked the passing of the first duke, as well as Percy's elevation. In his letter to Joseph Brant, September 3, 1791, the second duke had expressed in rare personal detail his attachment to the portrait of his friend, stating, "I preserve with great care your picture, which is hung up in the Duchess's own room . . . ,"[85] revealing that the portrait was displayed in their more intimate and private quarters rather than being hung for show in the formal rooms or great hall. The duke's comment also implied that Brant understood the various uses of portraiture at his residence. Much later, in 1857, Stuart's portrait of Brant for Northumberland was publicly exhibited for the first time in London at the British Institution, where Rigaud had earlier exhibited his grand portrait of Brant in 1806. The portrait was known to have remained in the family and was again loaned for exhibitions, until the present and twelfth Duke of Northumberland sold the picture through Sotheby's on July 9, 2014.[86] The

---

84. I thank Doctor Susan North, curator of fashion 1550–1800, Victoria and Albert Museum, whose discussions with the author shed light on the strict protocols of mourning dress observed by the English court and aristocracy at that time.

85. Dr. B. Read. *The Life and Times of Gen. John Graves Simcoe.* (Toronto: George Virtue Publisher, 1891). 132. Transcription of letter.

86. Sotheby's London. Old Masters and British Paintings Evening Sale, July 9, 2014, No 21. Gilbert Stuart. Exhibition History.

portrait was acquired by an enlightened anonymous collector, who made the portrait available to the public, through a generous promised gift to the Metropolitan Museum of Art in New York.[87]

To provide additional perspective on the circumstances of ritual mourning that occasioned Brant's somber portrait of 1786, we briefly note that these social conditions are historically reminiscent of those encountered earlier during the London visit in 1710 of the four North American Iroquois Chiefs, known as the Four Indian Kings (figure 12).[88] They had attended the court of Queen Anne (r. 1702–14) respectfully attired in black English mourning dress, as the court remained in official mourning at the death of the queen's husband, Prince George of Denmark (1653–1708).[89] To commemorate their visit to London just before they returned to America, Queen Anne ordered a set of four portraits from her court painter, Jan Verelst (1648–1734), who painted similar small portraits of each of the chiefs attired in their red and white reimagined Indigenous dress, except for one, Chief Tejonihokarawa (figure 12-C), who was depicted wearing his red English cloak and also holding a sacred wampum belt, but still fully attired in black English mourning dress.[90] Though these portraits honored the visit of the chiefs at court, this singular pictorial dissimilarity encoded the circumstances that had disrupted the life of the grieving monarch and of the nation. The historical coincidence of somber black mourning dress adjusted in both portraits of visiting North American Indigenous leaders in 1710 and again in 1786 is exceptional and expresses the social gravitas with which prescribed mourning protocols were then strictly observed at the English court and by the aristocracy.

Little was known about the last significant commemorative portrait of Joseph Brant painted in oil on canvas that hangs today at Johnson Hall, in Johnstown, New York (figure 13). New research on the portrait's historical and artistic circumstances sheds light on its artistic patronage and creation and reveals the intricacies of its social function and purpose, including its formal presentation and display in England and later sale in London, and its subsequent return to North America.

This small half-length oil portrait was an enlarged replica of the small enamel portrait miniature of Joseph Brant (figure 14) attributed to Henry Bone (1755–1834) that was gifted to Brant in London in 1786 by Francis Rawdon, the second Earl of Moira. Brant had the verso of the locket engraved with the year and a personal dedication to his wife, "Katerine,+Rones, 1786" (Catherine-Wife), which had been treasured by her descendants

---

87. *Metropolitan Museum of Art, Annual Report for the year 2015–2016, Promised Gifts,* 56, Gilbert Stuart, American; Mohawk Chief Thayendanegea, Known as Joseph Brant; oil on canvas, 1786; Anonymous, in honor of Annette de la Renta.

88. John G. Garratt and Bruce Robertson, *The Four Indian Kings* (Ottawa: Public Archives of Canada, 1985).

89. Fritz, "The Trade in Death."

90. Portrait of Tejonihokarawa (baptized Hendrick), Named Tee Yee Neen Ho Ga Row, Emperor of the Six Nations, LAC, Acc. no. 1977-35-4.

Figure 12. The Four Indian Kings, by Jan Verelst (1648–1734), painted in 1710, oil on canvas, 91.5 x 64.5 cm. LIBRARY AND ARCHIVES CANADA, NO. 1977-035. (A) SAGAYENKWARATON, NO.1977-35-2, MIKAN 2836995; (B) ETOWAUCUM, NO.1977-35-1, MIKAN – 2836996; (C) TEJONIHOKARAWA, NO.1977-35-4, MIKAN 2836993; (D) ONIGOHERIAGO, NO.1977-35-3, MIKAN 2894503.

Figure 13. Joseph Brant, by William Daniel Edy, oil on canvas, 1874, 12 x 9 in. Courtesy of Johnson Hall State Historic Site, New York State Office of Parks, Recreation and Historic Preservation, ID No. JH.1971.160.

Figure 14. Joseph Brant, attributed to Henry Bone, before 1789, enamel on copper, 6.0 x 4.3 cm (locket). Courtesy of Joseph Brant Museum, Burlington, Ontario, Acc. No. 969.071.7.

until it was acquired by the Joseph Brant Museum.[91] The picture at Johnson Hall was commissioned in 1874 by the Council of Chiefs of the Grand River Six Nations at Ohsweken, Ontario, from local Canadian amateur painter and photographer William Daniel Edy (1832–1916) (figure 14-A) and mentioned in his biography published in 1891:

> He [William Daniel Edy] then joined his brother, the late J. [James] M. Edy, in the business of photography in the city of Brantford. . . . They were the first in Ontario to adopt the practice of retouching negatives, which brought them into prominence. During their stay at Brantford they produced an oil painting from a miniature on ivory made in England of Capt. Joseph Brant, which was presented to Prince Arthur through Lord Dufferin. . . . [92]

---

91. The words of dedication are separated by a small Greek cross, likely to mark their Christian betrothal. The date, 1786, refers to when the gift was made and not to when the miniature was executed. The attribution remains under study.
92. Before entering his brother's photographic studio, William Edy was a farmer and also an amateur painter in oil and watercolors and could provide and apply that specialty. He later became a member of the Photographic Association of Canada, organized on January 24, 1884, and appointed secretary and treasurer in August 1891.

Figure14-A. William Daniel Edy Offset book illustration, from John Castell Hopkins and W. J. Hunter, *Men of Canada: Or Success by Example*, Vol. 1 (Brantford, ON: iBradley Garretson & co, 1891), 429. LIBRARY AND ARCHIVES CANADA, OCLC NO.:1032858620 / LCCN:04020336.

The chiefs intended the commission of the oil portrait of Brant from Edy to be a gift to His Royal Highness, Prince Arthur (1850–1942) (figure 15), third son of Queen Victoria, to mark his earlier visit among them in 1869, at age nineteen.[93] The chiefs chose to make their gift an enlarged replica of a unique original oval portrait miniature of their ancestral leader, Captain Joseph Brant, in appreciation for the three oval lithographic portraits by John Alfred Vintner (1828–1905) after large oil portraits by Franz Winterhalter (1805–73) of the prince's mother and late father, Queen Victoria and Prince Albert, and one of himself, which he had gifted to the chiefs during his visit.[94] The significance of their attachment to these three portrait prints was later noted in their 1874 address to Prince Arthur:

> to convey to your Royal Highness their grateful thanks of the kindness which placed in their possession the highly prized portraits of their no less illustrious than good

93. E. Pauline Johnson, *Legends of Vancouver* (Vancouver, BC: David Spencer, Limited, 1911), 157–65.

94. The Royal Collection Trust maintains impressions of the oval bust portrait lithograph of Queen Victoria, RCIN 60568, and of Prince Albert, RCIN 605865, that were drawn on stone in 1859 by John Alfred Vintner (1828–1905), after detail of Franz Xaver Winterhalter's (1805–1873) full-length oil portraits of Queen Victoria, RCIN 405131, and Prince Albert, RCIN 405130, painted in 1859, that hang today at Buckingham Palace, London.

Figure 15. His Royal Highness Prince Arthur, photograph by William Notman, Montreal, 1869, silver albumen print, 14.2 x 10.1 cm. LIBRARY AND ARCHIVES CANADA, C-006377 (DETAIL)

Queen, your royal mother, of your no less distinguished than justly lamented father, and of yourself, all of which now grace and adorn the walls of their Council House. . . . They would also be permitted to beg the acceptance of your Royal Highness of a likeness of their said lamented chief [Joseph Brant], made from a portrait of him taken on the occasion of his visit to England in the year 1786. . . . [95]

A rare interior photograph (figure 16) of a meeting of the Council of Chiefs, taken around 1910, captured the framed oval lithographic portraits still hanging in a row above a draped Union Jack in the Old Council House in Ohsweken.[96] The display's expression of royal allegiance and succession was accentuated by the hanging of additional photographs of Queen Victoria alongside that of her successors, King Edward VII and Queen Alexandra (both in black mourning dress), and of their son Prince George, later King George V, and of Princess Mary, his wife and future queen and grandmother of the present Queen Elizabeth II. We cannot overlook hanging at the far right another oval portrait of Joseph Brant in its original frame, similar to the painting at Johnson Hall (figure 13).

When William joined Edy & Co. photography studio around 1870, they promoted

95. *The History of the County of Brant, Ontario* (Toronto: Beer & Co., 1883), Part II—Indian History, 41–142. Council of Chiefs 1874 address to H. R. H.

96. I am grateful to Feather Maracle, CEO, Six Nations Public Library, Ohsweken, Ontario, for our discussions of the important significance of the appearance of the gifted portraits in this group photograph.

Figure 16. Six Nations Confederacy Council, Council House, c. 1910. Six Nations Legacy Consortium Collection, No. SNPL000091v00i. See at upper-right corner the portrait of Joseph Brandt in its original frame, similar to figure 13 from the Johnson Hall State Historic Site. COURTESY OF SIX NATIONS PUBLIC LIBRARY, OHSWEKEN, ONTARIO.

a variety of photographic products in any size, including portraits in oil (figure 17). It is very significant that the artist chosen to produce the oil portrait was not only an amateur painter but also a professional photographer.[97] The use of photography was expedient, but also perceived at the time as the ultimate recorder of truth.[98] Late nineteenth-century photographic methods could enlarge any image to any required size, and allowed Edy to overcome the inherent constraints of the tiny 6.0 x 4.3 cm miniature, by enlarging its scale to a 25.87 x 20.64 cm photographic format that could be more easily copied with a minimum loss of details.[99] The encased miniature was photographed, not as a flat two-dimensional picture, but rather as a three-dimensional object, including incidental light reflections and optical distortions from the glazing and the shadows cast by the rim of the locket over parts of painted surface. True to what the photograph had captured, we can see that Edy had also

97. Ann Thomas, *Fact and Fiction: Canadian Painting and Photography 1860–1900* (Montreal: McCord Museum, Montreal, and Plow & Watters Ltd., 1979).
98. Jenifer L. Mnookin, "The Image of Truth: Photographic Evidence and the Power of Analogy," *Yale Journal of Law and Humanities* 10, no. 1, article 1.
99. I thank Michele Phillips, supervising conservator, New York State Parks, Recreation & Historic Preservation, for authorizing the examination of the painting, and oil painting conservator, Mary Betlejeski, who analyzed the painting in June 2015, that determined the picture was not an overpainted photograph.

EDY & Co

ARTISTIC PHOTOGRPAHERS,
COLBORN ST, BRANTFORD,
Portraits of any size in India Ink, Crayon,
Water colours or Oil, made a Specialty.

Figure 17. Label transcribed from verso of Edy & Co. photograph of an anonymous sitter, ca. 1870.

painted the shadow effects (see figure 13, lower left) cast by the locket along the lower edge of the painting. In their address, the chiefs had stressed the authenticity of the oil portrait's provenance as an enlarged replica of the oval lifetime portrait miniature that Brant had received in London in 1786.

When Lord Dufferin (1826–1902),[100] then governor general of Canada (1872–1878), visited the peoples of the Six Nations of the Grand River Reserve, on August 25, 1874,[101] he was entrusted with the oil portrait, along with other gifts, to convey to Prince Arthur on their behalf.[102] The prince received the picture and eventually had it hung at his royal residence of Bagshot Park,[103] until it was sold through Christie's auction house after his death in 1942. Its listing in the sale catalog continued to faithfully assert its unique origin, "No. 587, . . . Portrait of Captain Joseph Brant (Thayendanegea), painted from a miniature, 1786."[104] It is not yet known who next acquired the oil portrait, or how the painting came to the United States during or after World War II. In 1959, the historian Milton Hamilton (1907–89) stated that the portrait had been acquired in 1958 by the New York State Education Department from Mrs. Gertrude Bryant, widow of William Letchworth Bryant, the

---

100. Ben Forster, "Blackwood, Frederick Temple, 1st Marquess of Dufferin and Ava," *Dictionary of Canadian Biography*, Vol. 13. (Toronto: University of Toronto/Université Laval, 2003).

101. "The Vice-Regal Tour, Brantford, August 25," *Globe and Mail*, August 26, 1874, 4. The *Globe and Mail* published regular accounts of Dufferin's vice-regal tour of southern Ontario in the summer of 1784. See LAC, Acc. No. 1978-49-190, to view three ornamented addresses from Six Nations to Lord Dufferin, presented during his visit, August 24, 1874.

102. Jasper Tough Gilkison, *Narrative. Visit of the Governor General and Countess of Dufferin to the Six Nations Indians, August 25, 1874* (Brantford: Indian Office, 1874). The gifts to the prince also included an ornamented address and a copy of Stone's biography of Joseph Brant.

103. The Crown Estate of Bagshot Park is west of London, in Surrey, just south of Windsor, and remains a royal residence, rented since 1998 by Queen Elizabeth II's third son, Prince Edward, Earl of Wessex, and family.

104. Christie's, Manson & Woods, LTD, London, *Catalogue of the Remaining Contents of Bagshot Park Surrey the Property of H.R.H. the Duke of Connaught, K. G. Deceased (Sold by order of the Executors) and of Lady Patricia Ramsay [his daughter]*, 43, lot 587; annotated copy from Christie's archives. The auction took place at Bagshot Park over four days, July 27–30, 1942.

son of the previously mentioned William Clement Bryant.[105] In the 1960s, the portrait was transferred to New York State Historic Parks, and was officially accessioned in 1971 as part of the collections of the Johnson Hall Historic Site.[106]

This study demonstrates that the tribute portraits of Joseph Brant painted in England in 1776 and in 1786, and the commemorative portraits painted later in Canada, were emblematic of the historical relationship between the Indigenous peoples of the Grand River Six Nations and the British Crown and Government, as articulated by the chiefs in their 1874 address to Prince Arthur:

> to convey to your Royal Highness their grateful thanks of the kindness placed in their possession the highly prized portraits . . . all of which now grace and adorn the walls of their Council House, animating and inspiring them with that zeal for and loyal attachment to the Crown and Empire which characterized their fathers in troublous times. . . . [107]

This reference is perhaps the first inscribed record and public expression of the social and political values that the Indigenous peoples of the Grand River Six Nations invested in portraits and their exchange by the end of the nineteenth century. Though the institution of the British monarchy had been repudiated by the new American Republic, it was cherished by both loyal Indigenous nations and British colonial settlers who had sought refuge in Canada where the British monarchy was respected, maintained, and eventually enshrined constitutionally in 1867 as Canada's head of state, which remains one of Canada's distinctive national characteristics. The chiefs' gift of a commemorative portrait of Joseph Brant to Prince Arthur in 1874 reasserted their loyalty and demonstrated their enduring fealty to Queen Victoria and all her successors and representatives.[108]

The presentation of these new findings revitalizes the portrait of Joseph Brant painted by John Francis Rigaud in 1786, and it is hoped that it will spur a reexamination of various aspects of other portraits of Brant, including their patronage and purpose, the nature of their form and interrelationships, their intended viewers, and the nature of the cultural exchanges between two worlds. In addition to time and place and the identity of all of the actors involved in the production of Brant's portraiture, it is the circumstances surrounding the creation, function, and uses of these portraits that shape their coherent history and

---

105. Hamilton, "Joseph Brant," 252.

106. Portrait of Joseph Brant (Acc. no. JH1971.160) information provided by curators at New York State Archives, New York State Museum, and Johnson Hall Historic Site.

107. *The History of the County of Brant, Ontario* (Toronto: Beer & Co., 1883), Part II—Indian History, 41–142. Council of Chiefs 1874 address to H. R. H.

108. Today Queen Victoria's great-great-granddaughter, Queen Elizabeth II, is the sovereign of the parliamentary democracy and constitutional monarchy of Canada, through an appointed vice-regal Canadian representative as governor general of Canada, selected by the government of Canada and appointed by the sovereign. Canada is a member of the British Commonwealth of Nations, comprising fifty-four nations over which Queen Elizabeth II is sovereign.

reveal their deeper meaning. A closer scrutiny of their form has revealed new aspects of their function and ownership. In turn, their intent and form shed light on their uses, accessibility, and dissemination.

The significance of Brant's portraiture to the peoples of the Six Nations evolved over time and will continue to change, as will their perceptions of former British imperial colonialism, of the present-day British monarchy, and of both Canadian and United States governments. Debates about Joseph Brant's political and social legacy have also shaped contemporary perceptions of his many portraits. Historical records attest that not all North American Indigenous peoples agreed with Joseph Brant's position in the American War, the aftermath of which continues to shape their future. This study demonstrates that both historical and contemporary attitudes toward Joseph Brant's portraiture were also never static, and will continue to evolve over time through the inquiring gaze of new observers.

Our heightened awareness of the ever-shifting perceptions of Brant's portraiture reveals a fundamental core element that Brant himself contributed to each of his many portraits. When facing the unanticipated and unsolicited requests for numerous portraits during his lifetime, Joseph Brant actively participated in sittings with the immutable proviso to always be depicted in his distinctive Indigenous dress, as a visible manifestation of his personal identity and that of his nation. At all times, he remembered and asserted who he was. While proudly acknowledging and respecting the truth and integrity of his Mohawk identity, he stood throughout those exceptionally troubled times for what he perceived to be the just path forward for himself and for his people. It is a testimony that reverberates through his portraits and invests them with the inestimable values of his truth and human dignity.

The Institute of Social Economics
A Neglected Network in New York's Progressive Community

Stephen Leccese

"The School of Social Economics," declared the *New York Times* in 1893, "while only in the third year of its existence, promises to be one of the successful educational institutions of the day."[1] This school, the Institute of Social Economics, was indeed on its way to prominence. The Institute's president, economist and former labor activist George Gunton, was building his school into a central link in New York City's economic reform network, leading to a position of considerable prestige and political influence for himself. During its existence from 1891 to 1904, the Institute hosted countless intellectuals, social workers, and civil servants for free lectures, exposing audiences to the latest reform ideas. The Institute also spread these ideas far beyond the city, as local chapters formed throughout the country and the YMCA adopted its course program. Such efforts received consistent press attention, making Gunton a household name among reform circles. By the turn of the century, Gunton had translated this power into political influence, having fostered a relationship with Theodore Roosevelt and provided input for state and federal labor policy. In just a decade, the Institute grew from a loose series of public lectures to one of the key institutions in New York's progressive community.

Why, then, does the Institute receive such little attention from historians? It is certainly well known that New York City was an epicenter of progressive reform, and that economists operated as social reformers within this community.[2] Yet the Institute of Social Economics is virtually unknown. This neglect likely relates to the checkered historiography of Gunton himself, whose prestige suffered due to his unapologetic advocacy of big

---

1. *New York Times* [*NYT*], June 29, 1893.
2. See, for example, Kevin Mattson, *Creating a Democratic Public: The Struggle for Urban Participatory Democracy during the Progressive Era* (University Park: University of Pennsylvania Press, 1998); John Recchiuti, *Civic Engagement: Social Science and Progressive-Era Reform in New York City* (Philadelphia: University of Pennsylvania Press, 2007).

New York History, 101.2, Winter 2020–2021

business. His defense of trusts, coupled with news in 1908 that he had accepted substantial subsidies from the Standard Oil Company, led to his long-standing reputation among the labor movement as a mere corporate shill and sellout. After this news broke, *The Independent* declared that whenever Gunton said anything about big business, "we should consider it as an advertisement paid for at a high rate."[3]

For some time, historians responded similarly by either ignoring Gunton or writing off his work as mere propaganda.[4] Labor historians often ignore him as well, though a few have rediscovered Gunton's early labor activism and proven that he was an important figure in the eight-hour movement. However, their analyses stop before he transitioned into a trust-defending political economist, leaving us with only part of his story.[5] Gunton is more popular among historians of economic thought. Several have analyzed his unique and unorthodox ideas on political economy, which advocated widespread working-class consumption as an essential economic boost. This viewpoint absolves Gunton somewhat, as it shows that his praise of business was closely related to his particular vision of working-class uplift.[6] Yet these historians only explore his theoretical work and neglect

---

3. *Independent*, November 5, 1908, 1076.

4. Pioneering labor historians pay him little mind. See George E. McNeill, *The Labor Movement: The Problem of Today* (New York: M. W. Hazen Co., 1887); Foster Rhea Dulles, *Labor in America: A History*, 2nd ed. (New York: T. Y. Crowell, 1955); Philip S. Foner, *History of the Labor Movement in the United States*, Vol. 3 (New York: International Publishers, 1972), 224; John B. Andrews, "Nationalisation (1860–1877)," in *History of Labor in the United States*, Vol. 2, edited by John R. Commons, 2nd ed. (New York: Macmillan, 1926), 302. For critical assessments, see John T. Flynn, *God's Gold: The Story of Rockefeller and His Times* (New York: Harcourt, Brace, 1932), 329; Matthew Josephson, *The Robber Barons: The Great American Capitalists, 1861–1901* (New York: Harcourt, 1934), 324; Chester McArthur Destler, "The Opposition of American Businessmen to Social Control During the 'Gilded Age,'" *Mississippi Valley Historical Review* 39 (March 1953): 652–58; Hans B. Thorelli, *The Federal Antitrust Policy: Origination of an American Tradition* (Baltimore: Johns Hopkins University Press, 1955), 129. Some newer work shows the same opinion, like T. J. Jackson Lears, *Rebirth of a Nation: The Making of Modern America, 1877–1920* (New York: HarperCollins, 2009), 166.

5. Philip T. Silvia Jr., "The Spindle City: Labor, Politics, and Religion in Fall River, Massachusetts, 1870–1905" (PhD diss., Fordham University, 1973); Mary H. Blewett, *Constant Turmoil: The Politics of Industrial Life in Nineteenth-Century New England* (Amherst: University of Massachusetts Press, 2000).

6. Joseph Dorfman, *The Economic Mind in American Civilization Vol 3: 1865–1918* (New York: Viking Press, 1949), 47, 127–28, 209; Sidney Fine, "The Eight-Hour Day Movement in the United States, 1888–1891," *Mississippi Valley Historical Review* 40 (December 1953): 441–62; Jack Blicksilver, "George Gunton: Pioneer Spokesman for a Labor-Big Business Entente," *Business History Review* 31 (Spring 1957): 1–22; Daniel Horowitz, "Consumption and Its Discontents: Simon N. Patten, Thorstein Veblen, and George Gunton," *Journal of American History* 67 (September 1980): 301–17; Daniel Horowitz, *The Morality of Spending: Attitudes toward the Consumer Society in America, 1875–1940* (Baltimore: Johns Hopkins University Press, 1985), 41–49; David Roediger, "Ira Steward and the Anti-Slavery Origins of American Eight-Hour Theory," *Labor History* 27 (Summer 1986): 410–26; Lawrence Glickman, "Workers of the World, Consume: Ira Steward and the Origins of Labor Consumerism," *International Labor and Working-Class History* 52 (Fall 1997): 72–86; Rosanne Currarino, "The Politics of 'More': The Labor Question and the Idea of Economic Liberty in Industrial America," *Journal of American History* 93 (June 2006): 17–36; Rosanne Currarino, "The 'Revolution Now in Progress': Social Economics and the Labor

his reform activities, only noting the institute as a brief biographical introduction, leaving readers with little indication of how popular Gunton actually was.[7] The historian of consumerism Daniel Horowitz made the logical conclusion that Gunton was simply not very influential in his time, despite producing some fascinating and forward-looking theories.[8]

Gunton only seems unknown, however, when we focus on his minimal impact on contemporary economists. When we step beyond theory and look at him as a reformer within New York's progressive community, we see a much greater influence. Gunton was not simply an obscure figure. He was among the most active reformer-economists of the time, delivering thousands of lectures to clubs all over New York. As a result, he received consistent press coverage as a prominent New Yorker. The *New-York Tribune* even considered him famous enough to report on when he fell from his horse and broke his leg.[9] His educational techniques spread nationally and were adopted by institutions like the YMCA. From the level of press coverage alone, Gunton was certainly not an obscure figure.

Furthermore, he was a well-known political actor of the time, a fact hidden by mere quick mentions as Roosevelt's labor adviser.[10] While never holding an official government position, he used his Institute lectures as a bullhorn for Republican policies. His Institute accordingly drew support from powerful Republican politicians, including Theodore Roosevelt, House Speaker Thomas Brackett Reed, Henry Cabot Lodge, and tens of other senators, representatives, and civil servants at the federal and local level. His relationship with Roosevelt specifically led to political influence when Roosevelt was elected governor of New York in 1898. Clearly then, many people, some of whom were quite powerful, did in fact consider Gunton an important actor, despite historians' doubts. There is accordingly a significant historiographical gap to fill that reveals the operations and spread of New York's progressive reform network.

This article reconstructs that history in three sections. The first introduces Gunton, his economic theories, and his foundation of the Institute of Social Economics in 1891. The second reconstructs the Institute's activities within New York, and then its expansion into

---

Question," *Labor History* 50 (February 2009): 1–17; Jack High, "Economic Theory and the Rise of Big Business in America, 1870–1910," *Business History Review* 85 (Spring 2011): 85–112; Stephen R. Leccese, "Economic Inequality and the New School of American Economics," *Religions* 8, no. 6 (2017): 99–110.

7. For example, Joseph Dorfman, "The Seligman Correspondence I," *Political Science Quarterly* 56 (March 1941): 113; Destler, "The Opposition of American Businessmen," 652; Sidney Fine, *Laissez Faire and the General Welfare State* (Ann Arbor: University of Michigan Press, 1956), 318; Rosanne Currarino, *The Labor Question in America: Economic Democracy in the Gilded Age* (Urbana: University of Illinois Press, 2011), 8.

8. Horowitz, "Consumption and Its Discontents," 315.

9. "George Gunton Injured," *New-York Tribune* [*Tribune*], September 25, 1895.

10. G. Wallace Chessman, *Governor Theodore Roosevelt: The Albany Apprenticeship, 1898–1900* (Cambridge, MA: Harvard University Press, 1965), 220; Howard L. Hurwitz, *Theodore Roosevelt and Labor in New York State, 1880–1900*, 2nd ed. (New York: AMS Press, 1968), 217, 225, 259; Kathleen Dalton, *Theodore Roosevelt: A Strenuous Life* (New York: Alfred A. Knopf, 2002), 180.

a nationwide movement. The third demonstrates how Gunton used the Institute to gain a position of political influence, resulting in a policy impact during Theodore Roosevelt's 1899–1900 gubernatorial term.

Reconstructing this network is difficult. While Gunton was a prolific author and speaker, he left no collection of personal papers that would allow a look below the surface into his organizational activities. Nonetheless, with some archival sleuthing and examination of contemporary newspapers, uncovering the Institute's inner workings is possible. Such examination of the Institute of Social Economics and its president demonstrates that both deserve a place in the story of New York progressivism.

George Gunton and the Institute's Foundation, 1874–1891

By the time George Gunton opened his Institute of Social Economics in 1891, he'd lived a roller coaster of a life.[11] Born in England in 1845, he started working in a Lancashire textile mill at age eleven. With a mother active in the radical Chartist movement, he grew up steeped in proletarian politics and fought for working-class suffrage as a young man. In 1874, he joined a wave of Lancashire men who headed to industrial New England in search of higher wages. Like many of them, he settled in the manufacturing town of Fall River, Massachusetts.[12]

Fall River was a hotbed of labor organizing, and Gunton jumped right into the eight-hour movement with activists like Ira Steward and George McNeill.[13] Steward was an originator of the view that leisure time and higher wages for laborers would boost working-class consumption and stimulate the economy, a principle that greatly influenced Gunton's later economic thinking.[14] Steward was evidently impressed with Gunton's enthusiasm, quoted as saying, "Years ago Mr. McNeill and I used to pray for the third helper. Finally he came in Mr. George Gunton."[15] Gunton indeed threw himself into the movement. Shortly after his arrival, he was blacklisted from local factories for participating in an 1875 strike. Afterward he became a full-time organizer and traveled the country in support of the National Labor Union. In contrast to his later probusiness views, his rhetoric at the time utilized radical working-class republicanism. He told a Chicago crowd that "The tendency of the industrial system . . . was to abolish the republic," and the usage of sweatshops and child

---

11. For biographical details, see "Professor Gunton's Work," *Tribune*, March 13, 1892. The best source on his early life and labor career is Blewett, *Constant Turmoil*, 131, 193–208, 246–52, 280–91. His obituary, *NYT*, September 13, 1919, contains several factual inaccuracies, as does his Wikipedia page.
12. Blewett, *Constant Turmoil*, 131.
13. On Fall River activism, see Blewett, *Constant Turmoil*; McNeill, *The Labor Movement*, chap. 9.
14. On Steward's theory, see Ira Steward, *The Eight Hour Movement: A Reduction of Hours Is an Increase of Wages* (Boston: Boston Labor Reform Association, 1865); Roediger, "Ira Steward"; Glickman, "Workers of the World, Consume."
15. Quoted in Andrews, "Nationalisation (1860–1877)," 88.

labor was "one of the groundworks by which the capitalists were trying to build up a monarchy in America."[16] He also took over editing the Massachusetts *Labor Standard*, the local labor organ. By all measures, he was a key operative in the fight for labor protections in Massachusetts.[17]

Despite his organizational skills, Gunton had a well-known temper and ego. He sought more influence and power for himself in the Fall River labor scene, and used his *Labor Standard* to publicly vilify rivals in the movement. His attacks caused discord among other activists and made him several enemies. The public bullying even earned Gunton a physical assault from one of his targets, rival labor activist Sandy Harrison. With tensions high in Fall River, coupled with a messy public divorce trial from his first wife, Gunton had to flee Massachusetts in 1884. With his career as a labor organizer finished, he settled in New York City and focused on building a career as an economist.[18]

However, Gunton's transition from an activist to a political economist was not especially smooth. That transition began in 1883, when Ira Steward died. Steward had been planning a monograph on his economic theories, but Gunton agreed to finish the work when Steward's health deteriorated. Gunton accepted the project "with the expectation that the work was far advanced towards completion." But to his surprise, Gunton found nothing more than notes when he started looking at Steward's papers.[19] Now, "instead of a book to finish I had one to write," he complained to Parke Godwin, a supporter who eventually became chairman of the Institute. Producing a full monograph of economic theory nearly overwhelmed him. After a bit more than a year of work, Gunton was in despair. He considered giving up on the manuscript altogether and returning the advance payment he'd received from Steward's estate.[20] However, moral support from two leaders among the emerging school of academic economists, Richmond Mayo-Smith and Edwin R. A. Seligman of Columbia University, alleviated his doubts. Gunton had sent them chapter drafts, and Gunton told Godwin that they "make a most flattering report upon my book," a welcome confidence boost.[21] With this encouragement and feedback, Gunton completed and published *Wealth and Progress* in 1887. This book is the opening statement in a theory that remained consistent over the course of Gunton's career.

The guiding theme for Gunton's economic doctrine was essentially a "harmony of interests" principle—that economic growth would remedy class conflict and inequality. He

---

16. "Ten-hour Movement in New-England," *Tribune*, August 17, 1875; quoted in *Chicago Daily Tribune*, July 1, 1878.
17. Blewett, *Constant Turmoil*, 312.
18. Blewett, *Constant Turmoil*, 280–91.
19. George Gunton, *Wealth and Progress* (New York: D. Appleton, 1887), v–vi.
20. Gunton to Parke Godwin, September 19, 1885, Box 7, Bryant-Godwin Papers, New York Public Library, New York, NY.
21. Gunton to Seligman, n.d. (ca. spring/summer 1886), Box C13, Edwin R. A. Seligman Papers, Columbia University, Rare Book and Manuscript Library [RBML], New York, NY; Gunton to Godwin, n.d. (ca. 1887), Box 7, Bryant-Godwin Papers.

took influence from Steward's general line of thought, but had a much different goal. Steward was a labor radical who argued that steadily increasing wages would, eventually, make the wage system unprofitable. As he wrote in 1865, "wages will continue to increase until the capitalist and laborer are one." Taken to its logical conclusion, Steward's system was an anticapitalist one.[22] Gunton, however, had shed any anticapitalist leanings that he may have held in the past. In stark contrast, he presented his system as one that would strengthen and reinforce capitalism by focusing on working-class uplift and economic growth.

For Gunton, the key to economic progress was the well-being of the working class. But rather than a redistribution of wealth, as some anticapitalists advocated, he called for an increase in overall wealth. The key was turning workers into consumers. "Consumption is always productive," he asserted, attacking classical economics for dividing consumption between productive and unproductive.[23] His two consistent goals were an eight-hour day and wage increases. The combination would boost working-class consumption, pacify laborers, and stabilize the economy. Gunton advocated cross-class cooperation, as his goal required organization of both labor and capital. Unions would push for higher wages and fewer working hours, while trusts would maximize production and provide cheap goods.[24] This line of argument remained consistent throughout his career and he advocated policies that would bring this goal about.

One of Gunton's most notable principles was his "living standards" wage theory. Following Steward, Gunton denied that supply and demand determined wages. Treating wages as a mere commodity subject to market forces left no remedy for low wages besides a cut in labor supply—"a convenient way of telling the laborer to go and die, in order to improve his condition," as Gunton saw it.[25] Gunton accepted that workers were entirely separated from the means of production. Unlike labor republicans who interpreted workplace control as a loss of independence, Gunton saw this separation as a position of bargaining power for the working class.[26] Since laborers owned no part of the final product, wages were not determined by a proportional share of that product, but an entirely different calculation. Wages were in fact the cost of a worker providing his labor power. "Obviously," he explained, "the cost of labor power to the laborer is the cost of his maintenance or living."[27]

---

22. Steward, *Eight Hour Movement*, 6; Roediger, "Ira Steward."
23. Gunton quoted in John Bates Clark to Members of Committee on Terminology, March 17, 1890, Joseph Dorfman Papers, RBML.
24. Gunton, *Wealth and Progress*, 1–10, 278–83; Blicksilver, "George Gunton."
25. Gunton, "Our Economic Creed," *Institute of Social Economics Lecture Bulletin* [*Lecture Bulletin*], December 18, 1897, 67.
26. Leon Fink, *Workingmen's Democracy: The Knights of Labor and American Politics* (Urbana: University of Illinois Press, 1983); Currarino, *Labor Question in America*, chap. 5; Richard White, *The Republic for Which It Stands: The United States during Reconstruction and the Gilded Age, 1865–1896* (New York: Oxford University Press, 2017), 674–90.
27. George Gunton, *Principles of Social Economics: Inductively Considered and Practically Applied, with Criticisms on Correct Theories* (New York: G. P. Putnam's Sons, 1891), 200–05.

Wages, then, are not determined by the productivity, skill, or supply of labor, but what laborers will consent to. Workers with a high standard of living will demand greater pay, just as workers with a low standard of living will consent to lower pay.

Gunton's novel ideas on political economy put him in good company with the emerging "New School" of American economists.[28] These economist-reformers like Mayo-Smith, Seligman, Richard T. Ely, John Bates Clark, and Henry Carter Adams challenged classical economic principles and sought to update economic policy for the industrial era. This group organized the American Economic Association in 1885 and eventually influenced public policy in the Progressive Era.[29] Unlike his university-trained counterparts, Gunton was a self-taught economist. Though the New School sometimes distanced themselves from such amateurs, Gunton enjoyed acceptance within the group. He was an early member of the American Economic Association (AEA) and served on its Committees of Questions on Economic Theory and Economic Terminology.[30] Gunton's wage theory, while controversial, enjoyed some influence in the 1890s. Richard Ely and John R. Commons cited Gunton's views and accepted that working-class living standards played at least some role in the wage rate.[31] Clark, Seligman, and Commons positively reviewed Gunton's monographs. All mentioned disagreements, but praised Gunton for making some welcome updates to economic theory.[32]

Gunton's wage theory proved particularly influential on discussions around immigration restriction. Unfortunately, like many progressives, he took influence from race science and eugenics, viewing most immigrants as members of lower races with lower standards of living.[33] If working-class living standards determined wages, then workers with lower wants would demand less and depress wages for everyone. This wage theory dominated the conversation over immigration more so than simple job competition from an expanded labor pool. Degraded immigrants from lower civilizations could subsist on much less than

---

28. On this movement, see Mary O. Furner, *Advocacy and Objectivity: A Crisis in the Professionalization of American Social Science, 1865–1905* (Lexington: University Press of Kentucky, 1975); Dorothy Ross, *The Origins of American Social Science* (New York: Cambridge University Press, 1991), chap. 4; Daniel T. Rodgers, *Atlantic Crossings* (Cambridge, MA: Belknap Press of Harvard University Press, 1998), chap. 3; Nancy Cohen, *The Reconstruction of American Liberalism, 1865–1914* (Chapel Hill: University of North Carolina Press, 2002), chap. 5; Currarino, *Labor Question in America*, chap. 3; White, *The Republic for Which It Stands*, chap. 12.

29. For one case study on tax policy, see Ajay K. Mehrotra, *Making the Modern American Fiscal State: Law, Politics, and the Rise of Progressive Taxation, 1877–1929* (New York: Cambridge University Press, 2013).

30. *Publications of the American Economic Association* 3 (July 1888): 74.

31. Richard T. Ely, *Outlines of Economics* (New York: Hunt and Eaton, 1893), 184; John R. Commons, *The Distribution of Wealth* (Macmillan & Co., 1893), 174–76.

32. John Bates Clark, "Review," *Political Science Quarterly* 3 (September 1891): 574; John R. Commons, "Review," *Annals of the American Academy of Political and Social Science* 2 (September 1891): 122–24; Edwin R. A. Seligman, "Review," *Political Science Quarterly* 2 (December 1887): 696.

33. For a clear statement, see "What to Do For the Slums," *Gunton's*, May 1898, 318–24.

American workers. The resulting "race to the bottom" would pull American standards of living down with it, degrading the entire American workforce.[34]

These arguments coincided perfectly with the period of "New Immigration" in American history, as older stock Western European immigrants gradually gave way to Hungarians, Italians, Greeks, Lithuanians, and other seemingly exotic peoples from Eastern Europe and Asia.[35] While this change took place over decades and was only just beginning in the 1880s, observers quickly noted the development. By 1888, Richmond Mayo-Smith argued that recent immigrants "are coming more and more from the destitute and dependent classes rather than from the more enterprising and wealthier."[36] Richard Ely concurred that the "poorer quality of a large proportion of European emigrants in recent years" was because migrants came from more depressed and degraded regions of their home countries.[37] The influx of immigrants led to nearly hysterical "racial displacement" or "race suicide" theories. The fear that lower races would outbreed white Americans spread widely among intellectuals, policymakers, and the general public at the time.[38]

Gunton and others concluded that undesirable elements should therefore be locked out of the workforce to protect American living standards. As he lectured, "For the next five years we ought to have practically no immigration at all," and afterward there should still be strict limitations.[39] Gunton's wage theory in particular had legs in this period of immigration. The economist Edward Bemis, in one of the earliest arguments for exclusionary literacy tests, cited *Wealth and Progress*, writing that "Mr. George Gunton has clearly shown how important it is to maintain a high standard of living among wage-earners." "If, then," he continued, "a new class of workmen can be introduced, whether Chinese, Hungarians, or Italians, content or at least used to a cheaper mode of life, less comforts and decencies

34. Thomas C. Leonard, *Illiberal Reformers: Race, Eugenics, and American Economics in the Progressive Era* (Princeton, NJ: Princeton University Press, 2016), 133–35. For the conversation about Chinese immigration, see Currarino, *Labor Question in America*, chap. 2.

35. For general overviews, see Sean Dennis Cashman, *America in the Gilded Age*, 3rd ed. (New York: New York University Press, 1993), chap. 3; Roger Daniels, "The Immigrant Experience in the Gilded Age," in *The Gilded Age: Perspectives on the Origins of Modern America*, edited by Charles W. Calhoun, 2nd ed. (New York: Rowman & Littlefield, 2007), 75–100; White, *The Republic for Which It Stands*, chap. 19. For individual ethnic experiences, see Eric L. Goldstein, *The Price of Whiteness: Jews, Race, and American Identity* (Princeton, NJ: Princeton University Press, 2006); Thomas Guglielmo, *White on Arrival: Italians, Race, Color, and Power in Chicago, 1890–1945* (New York: Oxford University Press, 2003); Matthew Frye Jacobson, *Whiteness of a Different Color: European Immigrants and the Alchemy of Race* (Cambridge, MA: Harvard University Press, 1998); Beth Lew-Williams, *The Chinese Must Go: Violence, Exclusion, and the Making of the Alien in America* (Cambridge, MA: Harvard University Press, 2018).

36. Richmond Mayo-Smith, "The Control of Immigration I," *Political Science Quarterly* 3 (March 1888): 71–73.

37. Richard T. Ely, *Problems of To-day: A Discussion of Protective Tariffs, Taxation, and Monopolies* (New York: T. Y. Crowell & Co., 1890), 77–78.

38. Thomas G. Dyer, *Theodore Roosevelt and the Idea of Race* (Baton Rouge: Louisiana State University Press, 1992); White, *The Republic for Which It Stands*, 698–709.

39. "Will Protection Always Be Necessary?" *Lecture Bulletin*, January 8, 1898, 90.

than our American workmen, wages will tend to fall."[40] While he certainly did not invent xenophobia, Gunton's work provided an economic language for restrictionists as they provided scientific rationale for their policies. He wholly endorsed this usage.

Clearly, then, Gunton's theories were making a splash in the economic scene. Yet it was his participation in New York's vibrant lecture circuit that established his name among the city's general public. Lacking a university or government appointment, Gunton required other sources of income. Self-promotion was his only choice for publicizing his work. Tapping into this popular form of public entertainment, he became a regular on the city's lecture circuit shortly after his arrival. By 1889, he attracted paying crowds for lectures throughout New York and Brooklyn.[41] Gunton had bigger plans than these side lectures, however. Almost immediately he began planning his own lecture series, the origins of the Institute of Social Economics.

In 1887, Gunton advertised "a class for the systematic study of social economics" to meet weekly for free lectures. He invited all those interested in the "social problem" to "ascertain in what direction social and industrial reform can most wisely and safely be undertaken."[42] Just like in his writing of *Wealth and Progress*, Gunton received crucial help from Edwin Seligman. From a wealthy and philanthropic banking family, Seligman often funded causes he deemed important. He believed in Gunton's work enough that he made donations helping get the lecture series off the ground.[43] With financial support like this, Gunton's lectures formalized into the Social Economic Society, centered at All Soul's Church on Sixty-Sixth Street. Primarily, Gunton used the society to publicize his economic views. R. Heber Newton, social gospel activist and rector of All Soul's, later remembered the society as "founded upon your [Gunton's] own doctrine and committed to their inculcation."[44] As the primary lecturer, Gunton gave regular presentations on politics, economics, and municipal government. He claimed that within a year, the lecture series had two hundred regular attendees.[45] Gunton remained with this group until 1891, when he decided it was time to expand. Leaving the group in the hands of a former student, he established an entire school around his theories, the Institute of Social Economics.[46]

---

40. Edward Bemis, "Restriction of Immigration," *Andover Review* 9 (March 1888): 253.

41. "Answering Henry George," *New York Herald,* June 11, 1887; "What Brooklyn Talks of," October 13, 1889, *Tribune; Brooklyn Daily Eagle,* January 29, 1889. Remember before 1898 New York City only consisted of Manhattan and parts of the Bronx.

42. *NYT,* January 7, 1887.

43. Gunton to Seligman, December 8, 1886, and March 11, 1889, Box C13, Seligman Papers.

44. "Correspondence," *Social Economist* (March 1891): 61.

45. George Gunton and Washington Gladden, *A Lecture and Debate on Trusts* (Akron, OH: Beacon Publishing Co., 1889), 120.

46. *NYT,* January 15, 1888, February 5, 1890; *Christian Union,* January 8, 1891.

The Institute's Operations, 1891–1904

The Institute formally opened in January of 1891 on Twenty-Third Street. "Our object," Gunton advertised, "is to teach nothing that is useless, but to give a thorough education in those branches most essential to a useful and important career." The school's first term ran from January to June, meeting twice weekly on Tuesday and Friday evenings. Students received instruction on "social economics with history and government," paired with free weekly lectures from Gunton, just like at the Social Economic Society. Gunton considered this first session such a success that he soon expanded the Institute's services and offered both day and evening sessions.[47] He was also a relentless promoter, founding a monthly magazine, *The Social Economist* (later *Gunton's Magazine*), "to discuss public questions from the economic point of view represented by the Institute."[48] Gunton's efforts were evidently successful, as within one year the Institute outgrew its original location and relocated to a larger building at 34 Union Square.[49]

The Institute's April 27 opening at Union Square was celebrated as a grand opening, despite its operation for a year before. The event attracted some leaders of the new economics movement that Gunton had allied himself with. Edwin Seligman, whose personal and financial support had helped Gunton forge his career, gave a speech, as did commissioner of labor and fellow AEA member Carroll D. Wright. Both praised Gunton and the "new economics" in general for critiquing past economic dogma and proposing much-needed updates to economic theory. Two Institute students, Mollie B. Luck and George A. Pace, also spoke, praising the opportunities that the Institute provided them. As Luck said, "What Social Economics has done for us it shall do for *all*."[50] Doubtless, then, hopes were high for what Gunton's Institute would accomplish.

What, then, did a program look like for an average student at the Institute? The school's standards were similar to a college. Gunton required grammar school graduation and desired that students have some high school experience as well. Potential applicants who presented a grammar school diploma were eligible for admission. Those without credentials could gain admission by passing an entrance exam in arithmetic, grammar and spelling, geography, and history. Upon admission, students had two options of study. Daytime classes met in twenty-week sessions, from September to February and February to June. Completion of both terms, one year of study, would constitute graduation from the Institute.

While courses were in session, classes met on weekdays from 9 a.m. to 2:30 p.m. During the Junior Term, the curriculum consisted of accounts and bookkeeping, penmanship, arithmetic, language (meaning "rhetoric and business correspondence," not foreign

---

47. *Social Economist* (July 1891): 325.
48. "Economics as Party Politics," *Social Economist* (March 1892): 257.
49. *Tribune*, April 28, 1892.
50. "A New College of Economics," *Tribune*, April 28, 1892. For text of speeches, see *Social Economist* (May 1892): 22–45.

language), commercial law, and, of course, Gunton's specialty, social economics. The Senior Term replaced arithmetic with literature and language with civil government. Tuition was one hundred dollars for the year.[51] For working people unavailable during the day, the Institute offered a second program of evening classes. For a more affordable twenty dollars annually, applicants could attend classes four nights a week from 7:30 to 9:30 p.m. These sessions lasted from October to May. The curriculum remained the same, but the program stretched over two years rather than one.[52] As time went on, admission fees for the Institute fell, likely as Gunton secured more funding. By 1896, he advertised annual tuition at fifty dollars, and local papers praised the Institute as an affordable educational opportunity for New Yorkers.[53]

The Institute prided itself on being "open to both sexes on equal conditions."[54] Gunton, possibly influenced by his Chartist mother, had a history of supporting women's causes when he was a labor activist. Even before the Institute formally opened, Gunton noted that women regularly attended his lectures and on examinations often did better than the men. The Institute's *Lecture Bulletin* proudly noted that almost half its enrollees were women.[55] Gunton wholly supported female education, and his magazine stated that women should be educated in civics and political science because suffrage was expanding and would likely expand further.[56] But that was not exactly an endorsement of suffrage, and Gunton also entertained views to the contrary. Another article stated that women would suffer upon gaining voting rights. "Gone will be the 'might of her gentleness,' and a man's reverence for woman's womanliness," the author warned. "Only the office-holding, lobbying, mannish-woman will really welcome the day of this newfound 'emancipation.'"[57]

Gunton's own views on female education were not exactly liberating, but rather well within the framework of contemporary gender relations.[58] The women who participate in Institute classes "realize the importance of the work in the home making and society making of the country," and attend classes "not so much with a view to participating in public

---

51. "Institute of Social Economics," *Social Economist* (July 1891): 325.

52. "Institute of Social Economics," *Social Economist* (July 1891): 325.

53. *Tribune*, September 8, 1896.

54. *Social Economist* (July 1891): 325.

55. Blewett, *Constant Turmoil*, 198–99; Gunton and Gladden, *A Lecture and Debate on Trusts*, 120; *Lecture Bulletin*, November 20, 1897, 15.

56. "Political Education for Young Women," *Gunton's*, June 1902, 560. For the gradual trend of women's suffrage, see Alexander Keyssar, *The Right to Vote: The Contested History of Democracy in the United States*, revised ed. (New York: Basic Books, 2009), chap. 6.

57. Alden Bell, "Shall the Ballot be Given to Women?" *Gunton's*, December 1899, 43.

58. See Glenna Matthews, *"Just a Housewife": The Rise and Fall of Domesticity in America* (New York: Oxford University Press, 1989); Ellen Garvey, *The Adman in the Parlor: Magazines and the Gendering of Consumer Culture, 1880s to 1910s* (New York: Oxford University Press, 1996); White, *The Republic for Which It Stands*, chap. 4. Of course, there was tension between the ideal and reality of gender relations, and women frequently did not conform to expectations. See, for example, Kathy Peiss, *Cheap Amusements: Working Women and Leisure in Turn-of-the-Century New York* (Philadelphia: Temple University Press, 1986).

affairs, as with a view to directing the education of their families."[59] The aim of female education, then, was uplifting the family through women's domestic roles. Gunton's economic doctrine dictated that workers cultivating greater wants would lead to higher wages and consumption. Women would cultivate those higher wants with instruction in the home. Undoubtedly this was an important role as far as Gunton conceived it, but not one that questioned overall gender roles. However, while Gunton's own views were well within gender norms of the time, the Institute did admit women on an equal basis with men and many women evidently took the opportunity.

While formal classes enjoyed adequate enrollment, Gunton's weekly lectures were the Institute's major draw. They were so popular that local newspapers announced them ahead of time and sometimes printed transcripts.[60] To keep up the publicity, Gunton kept Institute secretaries consistently busy with taking dictation and recording all the questions and answers at every lecture.[61] In terms of content, Gunton's lecture program differed little from his past work. While there was little new material in Gunton's lectures, they exposed new audiences to Gunton's theories who otherwise would likely not have read his books. The lectures also provided a forum for other reformers with whom Gunton shared the stage. Many other economists supported using public education to promote "proper" economic principles. As Richard T. Ely wrote to Edwin Seligman, he hoped the AEA would "exercise an influence on public opinion" and challenge the prevailing laissez-faire doctrine in economics.[62] Gunton built a platform for these new economic principles, and many welcomed the opportunity he offered. Commissioner of Labor Carroll D. Wright became a regular contributor to Gunton's publications and served as an Institute lecturer for a course on statistics.[63] Edwin Seligman also published articles in *Gunton's* and lectured occasionally.[64] Both became counselors for the Institute. Additionally, Gunton had other notable guest lecturers at the school like Columbia economist John Bates Clark and Seth Low, Columbia University president and future New York mayor.[65] Between hosting these speakers at the Institute and commissioning their articles in his magazines, Gunton provided something

---

59. *Lecture Bulletin*, November 20, 1897, 15; March 5, 1898, 221.

60. "Evolution and Socialism," *NYT*, February 6, 1896.

61. Alberta Crampton Dufva, who worked as an Institute secretary from January to March 1900, describes taking dictation for many hours straight as her main daily task. Entries January 1–March 31, Alberta Crampton Dufva Diaries, 1893–1913, Box 1, Rubenstein Library, Duke University (Durham, NC).

62. Ely to Seligman, June 9, 1885, Box C9, Seligman Papers.

63. For some of Wright's articles, see "The Unemployed," *Social Economist* (December 1891): 71; "Social and Industrial Statistics" *Gunton's Magazine of American Economics and Political Science* (April 1896), 289; "Industrial Arbitration in Congress," *Gunton's Magazine of American Economics and Political Science* (April 1898), 20; "Hand and Machine Labor," *Gunton's*, March 1900, 209. For his lectureship, see *Tribune*, September 6, 1895.

64. Edwin Seligman, "Government Ownership of Quasi-Public Corporations" *Gunton's* (April 1901), 305; "The Taxation of Franchise Values," *Gunton's*, June 1903, 505.

65. Gunton to John Bates Clark, March 4, 1890, Folder 6, Box 2, Clark Papers; Gunton to Seth Low, November 3, 1893, Box "G," Seth Low Papers, RBML; *NYT*, November 26, 1893.

of a nerve center for the city's economic reformers. In doing so, the Institute exposed the general public to economic ideas they likely would not have experienced elsewhere.

All of these initiatives—a school building, a magazine and lecture bulletin, free weekly lectures—naturally required money. With relatively low tuition fees, the Institute needed a steady stream of funding. This need led to the most controversial aspect of Gunton's career, his relationship with big business, particularly the Standard Oil Company. As one of the most hated trusts in the country, Standard Oil was eager for good publicity, and Gunton's vehemently pro-big business views attracted the company's attention.[66] John D. Rockefeller Jr. complimented Gunton's book *Principles of Social Economics* in 1891, indicating a relationship by this point.[67] Before long, Standard Oil subsidized Gunton's work to the tune of $15,000 annually.[68] Gunton also actively courted other corporate donors, sometimes using his political influence. For instance, he enlisted Theodore Roosevelt's help in encouraging (unsuccessfully) J. P. Morgan to fund a new Institute building in 1901, demonstrating the extent to which Gunton would lobby for corporate funding.[69] While some accused Gunton of tailoring his opinions to please Standard Oil, official company historians Ralph and Muriel Hidy concluded that Gunton's already pro-trust views attracted Standard Oil, not vice versa.[70] Nonetheless, this news tarnished Gunton's reputation when exposed.

Gunton's corporate funding, however, was not out of the ordinary. When challenged about relying on rich donors, Gunton answered that "Outside of the common schools practically all educational work of any importance is mainly supported by the rich."[71] In an era where new institutes of higher learning regularly sported the names of their megarich donors—Vanderbilt (1873), Johns Hopkins (1876), Wharton (1881), Carnegie (1900), Rockefeller (1901), to name a few—Gunton had a point. Such funding reveals the sometimes uncomfortably close relationship between business and progressive reformers, especially in a city like New York.

Of course, the ambitious Gunton ultimately hoped that his Institute would spread. He wanted distant followers to feel as if they were attending his New York classrooms. By the mid-1890s, he provided means for his followers to set up local chapters across the nation. Feeling that a monthly magazine was insufficient for this purpose, in 1897, he began publishing the *Lecture Bulletin*. For just one dollar annually, subscribers received a weekly

---

66. On this trend, see Stephen R. Leccese, "John D. Rockefeller, Standard Oil, and the Rise of Corporate Public Relations in Progressive America, 1902–1908," *Journal of the Gilded Age and Progressive Era* 16 (July 2017): 245–63.

67. John D. Rockefeller Jr. to Gunton, February 1891, Series L: Letterbooks, FA431, John D. Rockefeller Papers, Rockefeller Archive Center [RAC], Sleepy Hollow, NY.

68. Ralph Willard Hidy and Muriel E. Hidy, *Pioneering in Big Business, 1882–1911* (New York: Harper, 1955), 660.

69. Gunton to Theodore Roosevelt, April 1 and April 5, Reel 12, 1901; TR to Gunton, March 27 and April 8, 1901, Reel 325, Theodore Roosevelt Papers [TR Papers] (Library of Congress); TR to JP Morgan, April 6, 1901, *The Letters of Theodore Roosevelt*, 8 vols., edited by Elting Morrison (Cambridge, MA: Harvard University Press, 1951–54) [TR Letters], 3: 42.

70. Hidy and Hidy, *Pioneering in Big Business, 1882–1911*, 660.

71. *Lecture Bulletin*, May 6, 1899, 723.

printout of Gunton's entire Wednesday-night lecture, including questions and answers, providing the most accessible source of his doctrines. Yet the plan was not merely to spread Gunton's ideas, but also to actively "extend the work of the school all over the country."[72] The *Bulletin* provided a working syllabus for the Institute's social economics courses, complete with required reading and discussion suggestions. Those starting local Institute chapters could use the *Bulletin* as a teaching aid and acquire textbooks directly from the New York office. Instructors would receive an honorarium for their services based on the size of the local group. Gunton advertised that subscribers to the *Bulletin* would complete the normal instruction on social economics within two years.[73]

Shortly after its founding, the *Bulletin's* pages began sharing stories of successful local chapters, like that of a "young friend of the Institute in Indiana" who started a local and nurtured it into a regular group of twenty-one attendees.[74] Since the Institute's records are unavailable, knowing the true extent of its reach is difficult. There is no doubt, however, that Gunton was a national figure, as reports from newspapers across the states demonstrate. Several Indiana papers, where the Institute's "young friend" set up his small local, praised Gunton. The *Crawfordsville Daily Journal* endorsed Gunton's high wages doctrine, while the *Indianapolis Journal* appreciated that his program was "designed to bring labor and capital into harmony."[75] Not all the coverage was positive. The *Greencastle Democrat*, unsurprisingly given Gunton's Republican activism, maligned him as a defender of trusts who authored "dreary protection rubbish."[76] Such coverage, both positive and critical, shows that Gunton and his doctrines were known nationwide. It is feasible that local chapters were indeed forming, especially given the *Bulletin's* low subscription fees and textbooks only costing a few dollars. The *Bulletin* even claimed that its programs had gone international and reported that locals had opened in Nova Scotia and Sydney, Australia.[77] Further investigation into local communities may reveal more on the true extent of the Institute's spread and add to our understanding of the dissemination of reform ideas during the Progressive Era.

The popularity of social economics and Gunton specifically is evident in the Institute's partnership with the YMCA. Around the turn of the century, the YMCA grew interested in solving industrial and labor issues, adopting programs that would assist this goal.[78] The field of social economics offered some promising possibilities, and the YMCA announced in 1894 that it would begin hosting lectures on the subject.[79] In 1899, the organization formally added "Social Economics" to its official prospectus. As the country's foremost social

72. *Lecture Bulletin*, November 20, 1897, 13.

73. *Lecture Bulletin*, November 27, 1897, 13–15; December 4, 1897, 46.

74. *Lecture Bulletin*, December 11, 1897, 61.

75. *Crawfordsville Daily Journal*, August 23, 1894; *Indianapolis Journal*, February 6, 1896.

76. *Greencastle Democrat*, July 20, 1895.

77. *Lecture Bulletin*, November 15, 1900, 50.

78. Thomas Winter, *Making Men, Making Class: The YMCA and Workingmen, 1877–1920* (Chicago: University of Chicago Press, 2002), 1–3.

79. "Around the Campfire," *Brooklyn Daily Eagle*, September 13, 1894.

economist, Gunton naturally got involved. The YMCA enlisted his aid in organizing its social economics and political science courses, appointing him as the examiner in those subjects. Students and instructors were encouraged to correspond with Gunton directly and read his two most famous monographs, *Wealth and Progress* and *Principles of Social Economics.* Becoming a fulltime YMCA secretary was an enormous commitment of time that Gunton did not have, so he instead worked on organizing the social economics programs and finding a suitable full-time instructor.[80] This included his guarantee to provide a salary for that instructor. He tried using his pull with the Rockefeller family to fund these efforts, though John Rockefeller declined because he felt he already made enough contributions to the YMCA.[81] Gunton evidently secured the funding elsewhere, however, and by October 1900 a suitable instructor was organizing social economics classes at YMCA centers around the country.[82]

Gunton never neglected a publicity opportunity. Afterward, Institute ads contained the sidebar, "Its courses have been officially adopted by the International YMCA for evening class work."[83] The *Brooklyn Daily Eagle* reported that "The adoption of these courses by the International Young Men's Christian Association has made the opening this fall the busiest in the history of the institution."[84] Through relentless promotion, Gunton successfully brought social economics to one of the premiere educational institutions in the country. The Institute's work had gained national legitimacy.

Gunton and Republican Politics

Gunton's educational work, while interesting in its own right, is doubly intriguing for the way he used the Institute to gain political influence. Though his early labor activism linked him with Democratic politicians in Massachusetts, by the time the Institute formed, Gunton was an unapologetic Republican partisan.[85] His lecture topics, sometimes in front of the New York Republican Club, consistently praised Republican economic policies, especially protective tariffs, and lambasted Democrats as antimodern demagogues.[86] His network of followers and publications made him an attractive political partner, explaining the Institute's numerous political patrons.

Despite telling Theodore Roosevelt that, "I never flatter," Gunton was in fact skilled

---

80. On the workload of a secretary, see Winter, *Making Men, Making Class*, 91–93.
81. Rockefeller Jr. to Gunton, March 2, 1900, RAC.
82. *Lecture Bulletin*, May 13, 1899, 744; November 8, 1900, 25; YMCA Research Librarian to David Siskind, September 5, 1946, Box 76, YMCA Biographical Files, Kautz Family YMCA Archives, University of Minnesota Libraries, Minneapolis, MN.
83. *Lecture Bulletin*, March 2, 1902.
84. "Social Economics," *Brooklyn Daily Eagle*, October 4, 1900.
85. Blewett, *Constant Turmoil*, 246–52.
86. For an early speech, see *Tribune*, March 19, 1892.

at flattery and fostering relationships with potential supporters.[87] His lectures and publications gave him a sizable audience, and he threw this weight behind politicians that he liked. In 1894, for instance, he wrote a whole *Social Economist* article complimenting the former Speaker of the House, Rep. Thomas Brackett Reed's (R-ME) "great speech" for marking "the advent of sound economic discussion into the United States Congress."[88] Reed must have taken note of the compliment because by 1897, two years after regaining the speakership, he was listed as a counselor for the Institute.[89]

Reed was only one of many powerful politicians and civil servants that Gunton counted among his supporters. In 1898, when Gunton appeared in front of the Senate Finance Committee, the *Lecture Bulletin* predicted he would "enjoy his sojourn in Washington, since the presence of a number of Institute Counselors there can hardly bring about a different result." Gunton would indeed be in familiar company. At the time, counselors included Speaker Reed, Vice President Garret Hobart, Treasury Secretary Lyman Gage, Commissioner of Labor Carroll Wright, at least eight senators, the secretary of the interior, the postmaster general, and the interstate commerce commissioner. He also counted then-assistant secretary of the Navy as a supporter, Theodore Roosevelt.[90] Their relationship gave Gunton his greatest level of political influence.

It is difficult to say when Gunton and Roosevelt first met. Both were active in the city's Republican organizations and may have encountered each other through these networks. They had definitely met by 1896, when both attended the Political Science Club for Roosevelt's talk on the Monroe Doctrine.[91] Their relationship obviously blossomed from there. By 1897, Gunton was on the small guest list for a dinner with Roosevelt and some of his closest personal advisers—Nicholas Murray Butler, Seth Low, and Elihu Root.[92] Shortly after, Gunton started commissioning Roosevelt's articles in *Gunton's*. Evidently the support was mutual, as Roosevelt became an Institute counselor and one of its "most ardent well-wishers."[93] During the war fever that swept the nation after the *USS Maine* exploded in Havana Harbor, Gunton declared that Roosevelt's views were prescient: "The tragic disaster to the *Maine* has given additional significance to Assistant Secretary Roosevelt's strong plea for an adequate navy."[94]

Gunton was therefore a well-positioned booster for Roosevelt when he returned from the Spanish-American War and sought the Republican nomination for New York's 1898 gubernatorial election. While complimenting incumbent Governor Frank Black for his

87. Gunton to TR, June 12, 1900, Reel 5, TR Papers.
88. "Sound Economics in Congress," *Social Economist* (March 1894): 129.
89. *Lecture Bulletin*, November 27, 1897.
90. *Lecture Bulletin*, January 8, 1898, 95–96.
91. *NYT*, January 31, 1896.
92. TR to Seth Low, February 16, 1897, Box "Roosevelt," Seth Low Papers.
93. Gunton to TR, December 15, 1897, Reel 315, TR Papers; Roosevelt, "The Need for a Navy," *Gunton's*, January 1898, 1; *Lecture Bulletin*, January 8, 1898, 95.
94. *Lecture Bulletin*, February 26, 1898, 205.

efficiency, he noted Roosevelt's undeniable position as a "public favorite." This was not merely because of his successful war record, but his status as a "reformer who shows political sense." Gunton praised Roosevelt's work in civil service reform and as New York police commissioner. If Roosevelt were elected, "New York will be sure of an active, efficient, progressive Governor."[95] Roosevelt did indeed secure nomination and election, and Gunton had a new, high-ranking supporter in Albany.

With Roosevelt's inauguration, Gunton took on an unofficial advisory role in the administration. Given Gunton's reputation and relationship with the new governor, some speculated that Roosevelt would appoint him state commissioner of labor statistics. Ultimately, however, the position went to a Republican machine pick. Nonetheless, Gunton met with Roosevelt shortly after the election with a delegation of labor advocates, including Jacob Riis and several union leaders.[96] Gunton, encouraged from this meeting, praised Roosevelt for "his willingness to confer with level-headed labor leaders" and predicted labor-friendly legislation from his administration.[97]

While lacking an official appointment, Gunton became something of a confidante with whom Roosevelt would consult and discuss ideas. His most common role was reviewing and editing the labor portions of Roosevelt's annual addresses.[98] But Roosevelt also took Gunton's input as he developed his own ideas on government and political economy. He read Gunton's *Trusts and the Public* (1899) and credited the work for giving him insight on approaching the issue of big business. When Roosevelt was considering New York's corporate franchise taxation law, Gunton was one of the advisers he consulted. He also credited Gunton for "showing the good that has been accomplished by the unions," at a time when Roosevelt felt frustrated by some intransigent labor leaders.[99] We could not say how much Gunton's input actually swayed Roosevelt, because as Lewis Gould writes, Roosevelt "preferred those who told him to follow a course he had already decided to pursue."[100] Still, investigation of some legislation demonstrates that Gunton provided input that shaped New York policy.

Gunton likely shaped the two labor laws Roosevelt signed on April 1, 1899. The first placed firmer restrictions on sweatshop production in tenement houses, requiring licenses to manufacture garments or cigarettes within tenement buildings. The second, among other provisions, dictated that children under eighteen and women were not permitted to

---

95. "Economics and Public Affairs Growing Political Sense," *Gunton's*, October 1898, 241.

96. *NYT*, November 27 and 28, 1899; Hurwitz, *Theodore Roosevelt and Labor*, 211.

97. *Gunton's*, December 1898, 436.

98. TR to Gunton, December 20, 1899, Reel 317; TR to Gunton, September 17, 1901, Reel 327, TR Papers.

99. TR to Gunton, May 26, 1899, Reel 317; TR to Gunton, March 23, 1900, Reel 323; TR to Gunton, August 27, 1901, Reel 327, TR Papers; *TR Letters*, 2: 981.

100. Lewis L. Gould, *The Presidency of Theodore Roosevelt*, 2nd ed. (Lawrence: University Press of Kansas, 2011), 9.

work more than ten hours per day or a total of sixty hours per week.[101] During the preceding month, Gunton and Roosevelt discussed these bills several times, starting with Roosevelt inviting Gunton to Albany for a meeting.[102] Two days later, on March 4, Gunton gave his usual lecture at the Institute. During the talk he mentioned that he had copies of two bills currently before the legislature that addressed sweatshops, and rejoiced that New York had a governor willing to attack this issue.[103] The following week, Roosevelt requested that Gunton provide proposed amendments for "these two laws." Additionally, Roosevelt hoped he could "get the other bills the amendments you suggested."[104] At month's end, just before signing the sweatshop bill, Roosevelt reported that he was unable to get one amendment added, a proposition increasing the amount of factory inspectors.[105] Regardless, Roosevelt received the other amendments he had hoped for, and was satisfied enough to sign both bills.

While correspondence does not reveal the specific amendments Gunton proposed, the two bills contained elements that Gunton had long advocated. Of course, the key to Gunton's theory was an eight-hour law, so he would approve of the reduction of hours amendment. He had also supported improving tenement houses, a key aspect of which was ending the tenement sweatshop system. Finally, he was a consistent opponent of child labor. He had once advocated a law banning any child under sixteen from working more than half-time and requiring children to spend the remaining time in school.[106] These two laws clearly put measures in place that Gunton had long supported, and even based his economic theories around.

Gunton's relationship with Roosevelt also had a material impact on national matters with his suggestions for the Republican national platform in 1900. In June, just before the Republican National Convention, Gunton sent Roosevelt six items for the party platform: (1) restrictions on immigration, (2) education for working children and raising the age restriction for child labor, (3) protections against contract and convict labor, as well as a system of labor insurance, (4) reduction of working hours, (5) granting labor organizations the same rights as business organizations, and (6) anti-sweatshop legislation. Roosevelt liked these suggestions and passed them along to Henry Cabot Lodge.[107] At Roosevelt's direction, Gunton sent the planks to New York's Lemuel Quigg, who sat on the Committee of Resolutions. According to Elting Morison, Quigg took these suggestions to the convention

---

101. Chap. 191 and 192, *Laws of the State of New York* (1899), 1: 345–55.
102. TR to Gunton, March 2, 1899, Reel 320, TR Papers.
103. "Consumers' Leagues and Sweatshops," *Lecture Bulletin*, March 4, 1899, 508–09.
104. TR to Gunton, March 10 and March 14, 1899, Reel 316, TR Papers.
105. TR to Gunton, March 31, 1899, *TR Letters*, 2: 974.
106. *Gunton's*, May 1898, 318; September 1898, 194; "Our Economic Creed," *Lecture Bulletin*, December 18, 1897, 73.
107. Gunton to TR, June 6, 1900; TR to Lodge, June 11, 1900, *TR Letters*, 2: 1324–25, 1327. Elting Morison compiled this list in the first letter's footnote.

and got the first three into the party platform.[108] Gunton, however, publicly asserted that the Republicans were still committed to all six propositions, even though only the first three were included.[109] He was either making a rash assumption, or he was trying to attract the labor vote for Republicans. As Gunton was an experienced Republican promoter and had previously argued that the Republicans should become the nation's labor party, the latter seems more likely.[110] Despite Gunton's unfounded assertion, his suggestions clearly made an impact. While the 1896 Republican platform called for immigration and contract labor restrictions, it made no mention of education, labor insurance, or child labor.[111] Gunton effectively introduced these planks into the party's position. His role as Roosevelt's labor adviser allowed him to insert his ideas into the party's national platform.

As Roosevelt's governorship wrapped up, it was clear that his reform agenda had annoyed elements within the state Republican machine. Boss Thomas C. Platt expressed interest in getting Roosevelt nominated for vice president in 1900, "kicking him upstairs" and out of his hair in New York politics.[112] Gunton was attuned to these plans, warning Roosevelt that he was "afraid that they are going to stampede for the Vice-Presidency, but I hope you will resist it. You must not permit the machine to shelve you that way." He thought Roosevelt should instead prepare for "still greater responsibilities."[113] Those greater responsibilities came in a way that neither could have expected with William McKinley's assassination in September 1901. Two days after Roosevelt assumed the presidency, Gunton wrote encouraging him that "in the trying ordeal to which you have been called we shall all stand ready to hold up your hands." He assured Roosevelt that "whenever I can be of service to you I shall be at your command."[114]

Unfortunately for Gunton, his influence with the president was fleeting. The two maintained their relationship for a while, but Gunton caused a personal falling-out in 1903. Gunton, who happily used his influence to support politicians he liked, could be equally vicious in using that influence to vilify opponents—the same habit that caused his expulsion from the Fall River labor movement.[115] Soon he turned this ire on Roosevelt. In May of that year, Gunton, a near-fanatical protectionist, wrote a scathing editorial criticizing Roosevelt for hinting that he may abandon protective tariffs. Further, in a personal insult,

---

108. TR to Gunton, June 12, 1900, Reel 324, TR Papers; Footnote 1, *TR Letters*, 2: 1325. For the whole platform, see http://www.presidency.ucsb.edu/ws/index.php?pid=29630. Gunton's amendments are in paragraphs eight and nine.
109. *Gunton's*, August 1900, 126.
110. *NYT*, November 26, 1896.
111. See Republican Party Platform of 1896, https://www.presidency.ucsb.edu/documents /republican-party-platform-1896.
112. Edmund Morris, *The Rise of Theodore Roosevelt*, 2nd ed. (New York: Modern Library, 2001), 755–57.
113. Gunton to TR, June 12, 1900, Reel 5, TR Papers.
114. Gunton to TR, September 16, 1901, Reel 19; Gunton to TR, October 5, 1901, Reel 20, TR Papers.
115. Blewett, *Constant Turmoil*, 288–89.

Gunton suggested that William Jennings Bryan goaded Roosevelt into an antitrust stance during the campaign. If Roosevelt continued on this path, "his administration will be more disastrous to the country than was that of [Grover] Cleveland, and he will justly deserve retirement from public life."[116] Of course Roosevelt would not ignore this personal attack. "In the past I have liked him," he wrote, but with these articles "He lies, and he knows he lies."[117] Correspondence between the two ceased after this. Though years later Roosevelt still professed support for Gunton's theories, it appears their personal relationship had ended.[118]

Conclusion

The end of the Institute of Social Economics came with more of a fizzle than a bang. The *Lecture Bulletin* ceased publication in 1903, and the last issue of *Gunton's Magazine* was published in December 1904. This sudden end could be partially related to Standard Oil cutting off Gunton's funding in 1904 for uncertain reasons.[119] A more likely culprit is Gunton's personal life. That same year, he married Rebecca Lowe, a wealthy Southerner who claimed lineage from John C. Calhoun. After this point, he spent most of his time at their estate in Hot Springs, Virginia, rather than New York, and no longer managed the Institute's activities.[120] This marriage was furthermore wrapped up in controversy because he had married Rebecca without legally divorcing his previous wife, Amelia, whom he had abandoned and left destitute. Amelia sued the couple, and Gunton's minor celebrity status made this news a juicy press story that reemerged from time to time.[121] After this point, Gunton became reclusive. He spoke and published very little, living until 1919 in relative obscurity.[122]

Despite its inauspicious end, the Institute of Social Economics' thirteen years of activity made it a nerve center of New York's progressive community. Under Gunton's direction, the Institute hosted reformers from around the city and country. The combination of affordable educational opportunities and free lectures exposed countless New Yorkers to progressive ideas. Further, the Institute's university extension efforts spread such ideas nationally, further reinforcing New York's place as an epicenter of progressivism. Contemporary politicians accordingly gave the Institute their support, translating into considerable

---

116. *Gunton's*, May 1903, 377.

117. TR to James Clarkson, May 27, 1903, *TR Letters*, 3: 482–83.

118. Frank Harper (TR Secretary) to James M. Finlay, July 22, 1912, Theodore Roosevelt Digital Library, Dickinson State University, http://theodorerooseveltcenter.org/Research/Digital-Library/Record/ImageViewer?libID=o229689.

119. Hidy and Hidy, *Pioneering in Big Business, 1882–1911*, 660.

120. *NYT*, February 14, 1904; *Washington Post*, January 15, 1906; May 22, 1901.

121. *NYT*, January 12, January 15, August 10, 1906. For the divorce story, see Stephen Leccese, "Labor Reformer George Gunton and a Progressive Era Divorce Scandal," *Society for Historians of the Gilded Age and Progressive Era Blog*, March 20, 2019.

122. Horowitz, *Morality of Spending*, 48–49.

influence for Gunton. For this relatively brief moment, then, the Institute was an important component in the New York reform community.

Moreover, the Institute's activities serve as a case study for ground-up reform efforts during the Progressive Era. Gunton lacked any esteemed pedigree and arrived in New York with few friends or funds. Through relentless networking, self-promotion, and fundraising, he made himself an influential operative for the Republican Party. In doing so, he impacted both state and federal policy. This process is revealing for Progressive Era politics more broadly. It provides an institutional model for how reformers could shape policy from the bottom up, jumping from the local, to state, and finally federal level through their political connections. For all its undeniable impact, the Institute of Social Economics is truly a neglected network in New York's progressive community.

The (Hydro)Power Broker
Robert Moses, PASNY, and the Niagara and St. Lawrence Megaprojects

Daniel Macfarlane

From 1954 to 1962 famed urban planner Robert Moses was chairman of the Power Authority of the State of New York (PASNY), now known as the New York Power Authority (NYPA). Moses was headhunted for the PASNY position chiefly to see through the transborder St. Lawrence and Niagara hydropower projects undertaken in tandem with Canada. On both of these rivers, in the late 1950s and early 1960s New York State built major powerhouses that bore Moses's name. Moses had relatively little interest or background in hydropower—but he had extensive experience in planning the parkland and parkways that were part of these power developments.[1] And, of course, Moses had extensive experience when it came to moving people out of the way for large infrastructure projects.

Moses's PASNY tenure is arguably the most neglected phase of his storied career, particularly since he held the power authority position while still holding many of his other state and New York City posts. Granted, very little academic historical scholarship has been produced on PASNY/NYPA in general.[2] Robert Caro's Pulitzer Prize-winning *The Power Broker,* the voluminous 1974 biography of Moses, accords but a handful of pages to Moses's years as head of PASNY.[3] The Moses historiography is still largely defined by Caro's work,

---

1. Caro reports that Moses also hoped to bring atomic energy development in the state under the aegis of PASNY. Robert Caro, *The Power Broker: Robert Moses and the Fall of New York* (New York: Vintage, 1974), 1062.
2. Recent exceptions include: Robert Lifset, *Power on the Hudson: Storm King Mountain and the Emergence of Modern Environmentalism* (Pittsburgh: University of Pittsburgh Press, 2014); Rock Brynner, *Natural Power: The New York Power Authority's Origins and Path to Clean Energy* (New York: Cosimo, 2016). See also Raymond Edward Petersen, "Public Power and Private Planning: The Power Authority of the State of New York" (PhD diss., City University of New York, 1990).
3. NYPA granted me access to a smattering of PASNY meeting records, which I was able to supplement with files from other archives, such as those of the Canadian federal government, Ontario Hydro, International Joint Commission, and the Robert Moses Papers at the Syracuse University Library.

New York History, 101.2, Winter 2020–2021

which paints a decidedly negative portrait of the man.[4] However, a revisionist perspective has been obvious since the 1980s. This approach offers more sympathetic assessments of Moses, contending that the good outweighed the bad.[5] For example, Phillip Lopate and Kenneth T. Jackson have argued that, though Moses had many faults, Caro exaggerates the extent to which Moses was an "evil genius."[6] Jackson suggests that it was Moses's efficiency that was unparalleled, rather than his vision or ideas. Lopate argues that the master builder was, in fact, "one of the greatest heroes of the twentieth century, and one of our greatest Americans." Both invoke a "man of his times" defense for Moses, arguing that his accomplishments have served New York City, especially the middle class, better than Caro allows; though Moses sought power and influence, he was not corrupt; though Moses was prejudiced against other races and the poor, these views were not defining aspects of his character or undertakings.

Drawing from my research on the environmental, technological, and transnational history of remaking Niagara Falls and the St. Lawrence River, this article provides a selective history of PASNY's first two megaprojects, with the emphasis on Moses's approach to acquiring property and reconfiguring iconic environments. I contend that assessments of Moses should take into account what he built outside of New York City; at the same time, assessments of NYPA's history need to recognize the influence of Moses during the power authority's formative years. As others have pointed out, Moses's reputation seems to be tied to the fortunes of the Big Apple.[7] Caro's biography of Moses was published when the metropolis was at its reputational nadir. But, just as New York City's post-1970s rebound led scholars to cast Moses's accomplishments in a better light, contemporary twenty-first-century concerns about ecological impacts, climate change, and environmental justice frame Moses's legacy in a different way.

My view of Moses—based on his time heading PASNY—falls between the two poles represented by Caro and the revisionists. Moses subscribed to a high modernist logic that relied on large-scale technological and engineering solutions that have bequeathed a mixed, and often unsustainable, legacy of concrete, auto dependency, ravaged ecosystems, and other negative path dependencies. High modernist plans, according to James C. Scott,

---

4. Of course, Moses had many critics in the 1950s and 1960s, with Jane Jacobs's critique of Moses's technocratic and modernist planning likely the most prominent: Jane Jacobs, *The Death and Life of Great American Cities* (New York: Random House, 1961).

5. The range of revisionist perspectives is captured in two edited collections: Joann P. Kreig, ed., *Robert Moses: Single-Minded Genius* (New York: Heart of the Lakes Publishing, 1989); Hilary Ballon and Kenneth T. Jackson, eds., *Robert Moses and the Modern City* (New York: W. W. Norton & Company, 2007).

6. Kenneth T. Jackson, "Robert Moses and the Rise of New York: The Power Broker in Perspective," in Ballon and Jackson, *Robert Moses and the Modern City;* Phillip Lopate, "Rethinking Robert Moses: What if New York's Master Builder Wasn't Such a Bad Guy After All?" *Metropolis*, August/September 2002; Phillip Lopate, *Waterfront: A Walk Around Manhattan* (New York: Anchor, 2004).

7. Jackson, "Robert Moses and the Rise of New York"; Phillip Lopate, "A Town Revived, a Villain Redeemed," *New York Times*, February 11, 2007.

rely on a synoptic view informed by bureaucratic and technocratic expertise, and involve large-scale attempts to make "legible" social and natural environments through simplification, standardization, and ordering so as to control them and prescribe utilitarian plans for their betterment.[8] The huge generating stations and allied infrastructure Moses constructed along the New York-Ontario border were built efficiently but with autocratic and high modernist methods. That said, though Moses could be flexible about the means to his ends, he was at times inefficient precisely because of his arrogance and need to thwart all opposition. Moses's racism and disdain for lower classes did clearly manifest themselves in his PASNY projects, cumulatively revealing a pattern of environmental injustice, most obviously in his interactions with Haudenosaunee (Iroquois) peoples.

St. Lawrence

The public development of St. Lawrence power had been the chief reason that Governor Franklin D. Roosevelt created PASNY in 1931. But decades of delay on a transborder St. Lawrence agreement left PASNY with nothing to do in the meantime.[9] The St. Lawrence Seaway and Power Project was eventually built between 1954 and 1959.[10] It involved two separate but interrelated components that reconfigured the second largest river in North America: a hydroelectric project (dams and generating stations) and a navigation project (locks and canals). New York State and Ontario were responsible for the hydropower aspects, to be approved by the International Joint Commission (IJC), and delegated responsibility to their respective power utilities: PASNY and the Hydro-Electric Power Authority of Ontario (HEPCO or Ontario Hydro). The combined St. Lawrence project cost more than $1 billion, with Ontario and New York each spending $300 million on the hydro works. For its portion of the work, PASNY sold revenue bonds, at an interest rate of 3.18 percent.

---

8. James C. Scott, *Seeing like a State: How Certain Schemes to Improve the Human Condition Have Failed* (New Haven, CT: Yale University Press, 1998), 89. However, given that Scott argued that high modernism was not possible in liberal democracies, I have previously suggested that these megaprojects be considered an example of *negotiated* high modernism: Daniel Macfarlane, "Negotiated High Modernism: The St. Lawrence Seaway and Power Project," in *Made Modern: Science and Technology in Canadian History*, edited by Edward Jones-Imhotep and Tina Adcock (Vancouver: University of British Columbia Press, 2018).

9. PASNY was very much modeled on HEPCO, which was established in 1906, and its creation also owed much to Alfred Smith. PASNY, in turn, would prove to be a formative influence on Roosevelt's presidential creation of the Tennessee Valley Authority and Bonneville Power Administration. See Mark Sholdice, "The Ontario Experiment: Hydroelectricity, Public Ownership, and Transnational Progressivism, 1906–1939" (PhD diss., University of Guelph, 2019); Robert Chiles, "Working-Class Conservationism in New York: Alfred E. Smith and 'The Property of the People of the State,'" *Environmental History* 18, no. 1 (January 2013): 157–83.

10. For a detailed history of the St. Lawrence Seaway and Power Project, see Daniel Macfarlane, *Negotiating a River: Canada, the US, and the Creation of the St. Lawrence Seaway* (Vancouver: University of British Columbia Press, 2014).

Lake St. Lawrence

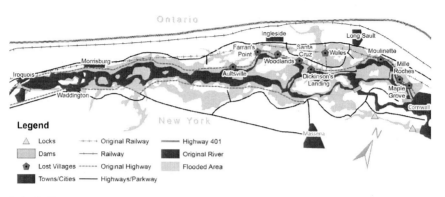

Lake St. Lawrence. CREATED BY THE AUTHOR.

The major new power dam, initially called the Moses-Saunders generating station, would have a generating capacity of 1,880,000 kilowatts. It was built by both New York and Ontario, with the two halves meeting in the middle where they were bisected by the international border; for several decades it was the world's largest transborder dam. But the aspect of the St. Lawrence power project that would prove more politically challenging was all the "rehabilitation" involving the forty thousand acres that would be flooded out by the new reservoir, with about eighteen thousand acres of that in American territory. On the south side of the river there were less communities astride the water in the affected area, and thus considerably less people had to be moved in New York State (1,100) than in Ontario (6,500).

Not everyone was thrilled about Moses's appointment to head PASNY. David Cort, writing in *The Nation*, called him a "dictator" and said that "[t]he prospect of Moses, unsupervised, unchecked and unaudited, running wild with Niagara Falls and the great Saint Lawrence River is, to put it quickly, disquieting."[11] Moses's temperament and legendary ripostes raised the hackles of some, while heartening others. Indeed, by this point in his career, it is questionable whether Moses had any ideological commitments beyond amassing power—of the political and social variety—and quashing any opposition. It was about winning and getting his way; the actual issue up for debate was secondary. Indeed, Moses was not particularly interested in, or knowledgeable about, hydropower. What he really cared about was the opportunity to develop recreational and tourism amenities, which he called "conservation in the truest sense."[12] One gets the sense that if Moses had been hired

---

11. David Cort, "Robert Moses: King of Babylon," *The Nation*, March 31, 1956.
12. Syracuse University Library (SUL), Robert Moses Papers, Box 8: Remarks of Robert Moses at a Luncheon of the New York State Society of Newspaper Editors, Treadway Inn, Niagara Falls, June 20, 1960.

by a private electrical utility, he would have railed just as vociferously against PASNY and government-controlled hydropower. Of course, a private firm did not offer access to the levers of power in quite the same way as government positions, and accountability to share-holders or boards of directors might have limited his executive decision making. Indeed, PASNY records indicate that Moses was given a wide latitude to run the public utility as he saw fit and faced little internal opposition.

PASNY was responsible for acquiring New York property affected by the power com-ponent of the St. Lawrence Seaway and Power Project. In a publication intended for public consumption, Moses outlined the land acquisition process in New York. He stated that a "sacrifice" had to be made "for the common good," while warning that PASNY would not "be cajoled, threatened, intimidated or pressured into modifying sound engineering plans to suit selfish private interests."[13] In Moses's mind, anyone who did not willingly give over their land was a speculator, and those who did not agree with all aspects of his plans were part of the selfish private interests. PASNY adopted a blanket expropriation plan, but without a bonus for inconvenience, with the goal of having title to all necessary land by the end of 1955. The necessary Federal Power Commission (FPC) license had stipulated that PASNY would need the St. Lawrence shoreline up to a measurement of 249 feet above sea level; this was revised to 246 feet, and PASNY generally also took the 100 feet above this line, though it claimed that it did not "propose to prevent the reasonable use" of this area by the public once the project was complete.[14] This meant that the amount of land taken was a little less than what had been envisioned in earlier plans based on 249 feet.

Easements were generally rejected in New York. PASNY needed to possess the land outright (i.e., "fee title"). PASNY agents were accused of first targeting the vulnerable or un-aware by getting them to agree to deals that would deflate values in the area. Homeowners were usually offered a market value price with little room for negotiations, though many did not know what constituted a fair market value anyway. Residents were made to feel that the first offer was the best they could expect. If they refused, property owners were forced off their land and told that they could argue about compensation afterward. Internally, PASNY admitted that "in some cases" during the first year of property acquisition, the au-thority had been "unable to give much notice of intent to acquire as desirable and had to move in to construct immediately after filing maps to acquire and before negotiations for purchase have been undertaken."[15] However, PASNY showed little public remorse and took measures to simplify and accelerate its land procurement program, which including hiring an outside appraisal company. The private utility Niagara Mohawk challenged PASNY's

---

13. St. Lawrence University Archives, St. Lawrence Seaway Series, box 66, Power Authority of the State of New York, "Land Acquisition on the American Side of the St. Lawrence Seaway and Power Projects," July 18, 1955.
14. Power Authority of the State of New York (PASNY), Minutes of Trustee Meetings, May 26, 1955.
15. PASNY, Minutes of Trustee Meetings, July 18, 1955.

Robert Moses at the St. Lawrence generating station. COURTESY OF NYPA.

valuation of its property, and eventually received a $2 million settlement for its 4,500 acres of land and a small generating station.[16]

In response to public feedback, Ontario authorities adopted the idea of moving houses, an option that Moses had used in some of his previous New York City projects. Unlike in Ontario, PASNY generally did not help people relocate. Numerous houses and buildings were moved on the American side, though these relocations were arranged privately.[17] At Waddington, spoil and backfilling meant that only the street fronting the river was flooded. An old power dam and mill site, the Ogden Mansion, and several other homes on an island were lost to the project.[18] A stretch of Waddington houses were raised up and allowed to remain on the new waterfront because it was cheaper than relocating them, plus PASNY developed a new waterfront recreation area.[19] Unlike on the Ontario side, PASNY

16. Heather M. Cox et al., "Drowning Voices and Drowning Shoreline: A Riverside View of the Social and Ecological Impacts of the St. Lawrence Seaway and Power Project," *Rural History* (1999): 242–43.
17. Group interview by author with Grace McBath, Kathy Dupray, Donna Dunn, Alice Dumas, Nancy Badlam, and Helen Badlam, Waddington, NY, December 6, 2012.
18. "Historic Waddington Island House Must Give Way to St. Lawrence Seaway Work," *Massena Observer*, August 8, 1955, 5; Group interview by author with Grace McBath, Kathy Dupray, Donna Dunn, Alice Dumas, Nancy Badlam, and Helen Badlam, Waddington, NY, December 6, 2012.
19. Interview by author with Russell Strait, Norfolk, NY, May 21, 2012.

did not build barracks for workers or an employee hospital, or provide some financial support for municipal services. Moses did not think such assistance was necessary, and PASNY limited itself to building 133 houses near Massena for its engineers.[20]

Some property owners at other places on the south shore of the international section of the St. Lawrence were granted rights-of-way to the water. But there were strict limitations on what could be done with this land, since the river was now a power reservoir, and PASNY's permission was needed to build even docks and boathouses. Many who lost waterfront property were promised that they would eventually have the option of reacquiring it, though this rarely proved to be the case.

The Wilson Hill development was likely the only instance in New York where local opposition forced PASNY to substantially modify its St. Lawrence plans.[21] In this area, which had been part of the mainland but became an island connected by causeways after the raising of the reservoir, PASNY initially allowed quasi-waterfront property on twenty-year leases. But the power authority technically retained control of the land directly abutting the water. An unsuccessful lawsuit was brought against this appropriation of land on Wilson Hill, though PASNY ended up paying approximately 25 percent more than the appraised value, and let the claimants buy back some of their unnecessarily expropriated land.[22] PASNY had hoped that as many as two hundred owners might relocate there; only forty-two had done so by mid-1956. Apparently, many were dissuaded by the cost of the new water supply and sanitation works, which was being passed on to the new residents.[23] As a result, PASNY returned the lot deposits that had already been made, scaled back considerably the upgrades and services it planned for the area, and then reopened the area for cottages under new terms.[24]

Given that a new lake was flooding out an enormous river, much of the preexisting transportation infrastructure had to be changed, relocated, or removed. One of the most controversial issues in this regard was the location of a bridge for the New York Central Railroad line across Cornwall Island. The St. Lawrence project displaced that railway's bridge, and the two countries were legally obligated to provide a replacement. Moses planned for a traffic and rail tunnel that would pass under the easternmost lock in the new canal near Massena. But in 1956 the railway was persuaded to abandon its whole line from New York to Ottawa. Without railway grade to worry about, a high-level traffic bridge could be built directly from Cornwall to Cornwall Island, and then another to the U.S. mainland. But this led to cost overruns for PASNY because of the planning and preparation that had already

20. Trailer parks sprouted up in Massena, and in 1957, 10 percent of Massena lived in trailer courts. Carleton Mabee, *The Seaway Story* (New York: Macmillan, 1961), 242.
21. PASNY, Minutes of Trustee Meetings, February 17, 1958; PASNY, Minutes of Trustee Meetings, July 19, 1956.
22. PASNY, Minutes of Trustee Meetings, February 17, 1958.
23. PASNY, Minutes of Trustee Meetings, July 19, 1956.
24. PASNY, Minutes of Trustee Meetings, December 19, 1956.

gone into the initial scheme (a traffic tunnel was instead installed under the Eisenhower Lock), and the late start on the new bridge threatened schedules and deadlines.

The bridge relocation infuriated Moses. He fired off his trademark letters, protesting that this new bridge siting would not allow traffic to wind through the expansive parkland system he was creating in conjunction with the St. Lawrence project. Moses himself oversaw the planning of an extensive park system on Barnhart Island featuring beaches, campsites, and a marina, and communicated these plans to the public via reports and pamphlets. PASNY also paid for other recreation areas along the St. Lawrence.[25] But the recreational facilities were not developed to the level promised, and the expropriated land required for these parks was taken from the communities without compensation. Massena alone claimed that it would lose about $4 million in assessed valuation for the taken land.[26]

Courts in the United States generally upheld appeals about PASNY's property payouts.[27] The complaints about land acquisition offers and techniques were noticeable enough that New York Governor W. Averell Harriman brought them up with Moses, and President Eisenhower inquired into the matter. Moses responded by stressing the urgency of the acquisitions and argued that "quite a few complaints which have emanated from the St. Lawrence area have been motivated by the most dubious political and personal considerations by owners and their representatives who are primarily interested in speculative increases in value."[28] In an exchange the following month with the PASNY chairman, New York State Senator Robert C. McEwan, who represented a district bordering the St. Lawrence, wrote, "I can conservatively say that I have heard dozens of complaints over recent land acquisition policies and methods, and I can honestly say that I could not fairly label one of these complaints as a speculator."[29] The senator protested the need to take all riverside land, and criticized the acquisition agents' approach.[30] Moses retorted in characteristic fashion with a nasty letter, stating that McEwan's correspondence "consists almost entirely of garbled, rambling assertions unsupported by evidence."[31]

According to one of the few studies conducted, there was more dissatisfaction with the expropriation process in the United States than in Canada.[32] The public resistance in New York did seem more militant, and there appears to have been more incidents of physical resistance to land expropriations. HEPCO took a more nuanced approach to the

---

25. PASNY, Minutes of Trustee Meetings, July 13, 1955.

26. "Town Loses $4 Million Valuation," *Massena Observer*, August 8, 1955, 1.

27. Mabee, *The Seaway Story*, 210.

28. HEPCO, SPP Series, Moses to Kuykendall, July 26, 1955.

29. HEPCO, SPP Series, Meeting of the St. Lawrence Fruit Growers' Association with HEPCO, November 2, 1955.

30. HEPCO, SPP Series, Meeting of the St. Lawrence Fruit Growers' Association with HEPCO, November 2, 1955.

31. HEPCO, SPP Series, Moses to McEwen, August 25, 1955.

32. Cox et al., "Drowning Voices," 241–42.

acquisition of individual properties and valuations, indicating that PASNY's desire to adopt a blanket expropriation route was not as strictly necessary as claimed. Rather, it reflected logistical and economic factors, as well as the PASNY chairman's steamrolling nature and impatience. PASNY did little to assuage the fears of residents, and the power authority's land agents were perhaps even more despised than were their Ontario counterparts. In St. Lawrence County, bitterness toward PASNY is still palpable.

The St. Lawrence project had significant repercussions for the Akwesasne (St. Regis) community, a Mohawk group that was part of the Haudenosaunee Confederacy. Their lands stretched across the St. Lawrence, including islands and the mainland, with parts in Ontario, Quebec, and New York. They claimed Barnhart Island, the site of the Moses-Saunders Power Dam, as ancestral territory. This was not recognized, and in 1956 the Mohawks filed a $33.8 million suit against New York State for compensation for loss of the riverbed and water power. The case rose to the state's highest court of appeals, but failed to halt the project. Land seizures for bridge construction were major sources of grievance, as were the various borders, tolls, and customs issues resulting from the transborder placement of the reserve lands. The widening of the river channels, and New York's relocation of Highway Route 37, required the dislocation of several homes. Parts of the St. Regis Reserve were needed for sections of the Wiley-Dondero Canal and dredging below the power dam, and protracted discussions revolving around an eighty-six-acre section of Raquette Point were finally concluded in January 1957. Furthermore, their shorelines were significantly reshaped by construction, and the new project altered water flows and levels.

Moses controversially made a deal to bring Alcoa to the area, and Reynolds Metals and General Motors also built plants near Massena. These three industrial concerns contracted for over half of the U.S. power from the St. Lawrence development. They were also sited immediately upstream from Akwesasne, and the resulting toxins would plague the community. In 1981, the St. Regis Mohawks formally complained to the IJC that changed water levels resulting from the power project had a noticeable and deleterious long-term impact on the ecological health of the area.[33] The adverse effects were grouped into three main categories: those caused by higher water levels, those caused by changes in flow, and those caused by environmental change.[34] The wide range of changes identified in the St. Regis submission serve as a summary of the ecological damage done by the St. Lawrence project: decreased water quality; loss of land by various types of erosion and island drowning; marshland flooding; weed growth; redistribution of pollutants; scouring and silting;

---

33. Laurence M. Hauptman, *The Iroquois Struggle for Survival: World War II to Red Power* (Syracuse, NY: Syracuse University Press, 1986), 144; Kallen Martin, "Akwesasne Environments, 1999: Relicensing a Seaway after a Legacy of Destruction," *Native Americas* 16, 1 (1999): 24–27
34. International Joint Commission (IJC), Canadian Section, 68-5-6, St. Lawrence Power Application, General Memorandum 1955, a Report to the International Joint Commission on Concerns of the St. Regis Band Regarding Impacts from the St. Lawrence Seaway and Power Development, March 1982.

fish and eels killed by powerhouse turbines; impediments to fish movement and spawning; concentrated pollutants in fish; shoreline erosion; and adverse effects on the muskrat population.

This colonialism and ecological remaking had a tremendous social and cultural cost. The Native Americans were treated as expendable second-class citizens, but many showed less deference to authority than those from the "Lost Villages" on the Canadian side, and adopted more confrontational approaches. In August 1957, Mohawks occupied land on Schoharie Creek near Fort Hunter in New York to protest their treatment. The St. Lawrence and Niagara experiences together gave rise to a more radical nationalist movement that led to other Mohawk conflicts with the American and Canadian states.

Niagara Power

In 1950, after decades of diplomatic talks—often intertwined with St. Lawrence negotiations—and many previous Niagara hydropower developments and environmental modifications, the United States and Canada agreed to the Niagara Diversion Treaty. This accord set up a water diversion regime so that New York State and Ontario could supply their hydropower stations, and also called for remedial works to hide the visual impact of abstracting the majority of the Niagara River's water before it went over the falls. Among other modifications, this would involve carving out the lip of the Horseshoe Falls and shrinking it by 355 feet; excavation took place along the flanks of the Horseshoe Falls (64,000 cubic yards of rock on the Canadian flank; 24,000 cubic yards on the American flank) in order to create a better distribution of flow and an unbroken crest line at all times. A control dam with gates was installed above the falls. The treaty restricted the flow of water over Niagara Falls to no less than 100,000 cfs (cubic feet per second) during daylight hours of the tourist season and no less than 50,000 cfs during the night and all times from late fall to early spring. This meant that the two nations together take about half of the total flow over the falls during tourist hours, and three-quarters the majority of the year. As has been detailed in the book *Fixing Niagara Falls*, this "disguised design" approach transformed the waterfall into a hybrid infrastructure blending the natural and the artificial, and had a wide range of ecological impacts.[35]

To produce electricity with the diverted water, Ontario Hydro built a massive new generating station, Sir Adam Beck No. 2, near its other station at the top of the Niagara Escarpment. But on the U.S. side, politics and debates about public versus private power delayed the selection of the body that would have the right to develop the American share of the water diversions and build a new power station. Even though the Niagara treaty predated the St. Lawrence agreement by about four years, PASNY would not receive

---

35. For more detail on the remaking of Niagara Falls, see Daniel Macfarlane, *Fixing Niagara Falls: Environment, Energy, and Engineers at the World's Most Famous Waterfall* (Vancouver: University of British Columbia Press, 2020).

Robert Moses at a generating station. COURTESY OF NYPA.

permission to build a new Niagara generating station until the St. Lawrence Seaway and Power Project was almost finished.

During the congressional ratification of the 1950 Niagara Diversion Treaty, the Senate Foreign Relations Committee had attached a reservation that reserved to Congress the right to decide which entity would get the right to generate the power from the water volume that the United States received under the treaty. This was an attempt to put off opening the can of worms that would come with deciding whether Niagara power would be developed by federal, state, or private interests. PASNY spent the early 1950s making preliminary plans for a Niagara generating station, hoping to be tabbed as the agency to develop the new Niagara power. But private utilities such as Niagara Mohawk also sought this role. PASNY awaited the decision of the 84th Congress, which had to pass legislation to delegate authority to the Federal Power Commission to license the Niagara development. There were many competing bills, some of which promoted various forms of public development, but many others which were not so friendly to PASNY or public power. Some favoring private enterprise did so because of ideological or economic commitments, and others did not like the fact that public developments did not have to pay taxes and, according to some, gave preference to groups who also avoided taxes. This so-called preference clause was a sticking point for many.

Moses railed against the private utilities' record at Niagara, which "on our side have bedeviled the Niagara River for seventy-five years. In spite of a record of shameless exploitation, they still have the effrontery to claim that the only question here is that of making power. . . . The record shows that the private companies have never had any genuine interest in the preservation of these public assets."[36] Moses lauded the history of public development on the Canadian side, though whether he really cared about the public ownership principle, or the public, is debatable. After all, Moses was simultaneously being accused of giving too much St. Lawrence electricity to private companies at too low of a cost.

Then an "Act of God" intervened. On June 7, 1956, Niagara Mohawk's Schoellkopf generating station was crushed by a major rock fall.[37] Located in the gorge not far downstream from the falls, this was the major generator of American power at Niagara, accounting for one-twelfth of New York State's total electricity. The congressional impasse over the Niagara power license now had a new urgency. By the end of August, the FPC had issued a conditional license, including a "preference clause" designating some power for public bodies, to New York State, and thus PASNY, to develop Niagara power.[38]

PASNY envisioned a huge hydropower station, along with a reverse pumped storage plant, just south of the Niagara Escarpment in the Village of Lewiston, immediately north of the city limits of Niagara Falls, New York, and directly across from Ontario's new Beck generating station. This Lewiston station, which would be carved out of the gorge wall, would take the full American allotment of Niagara water under the 1950 treaty with its total generation capacity of 1,950,000 kw (2,190,000 kw counting the pumped storage plant). All the related infrastructure and changes—water conduits, roadways, parks, etc.—had an enormous footprint requiring far-reaching land acquisition.

However, until it received a final power license—not just "conditional"—PASNY was limited in how far it could proceed. For example, there was uncertainty about the type of conduit that would funnel water from above the falls to a new generating station (e.g., open canals vs. covered tunnels) as well as the shape, size, and location of the station's reservoir. It was difficult for PASNY to obtain bond financing without knowing what the final works, and thus the cost, would be. PASNY issued bids for equipment and letters of intent, but until bonds were subscribed, binding contracts could not be signed and construction could not formally start. At the end of January 1958, the FPC finally issued the license to PASNY. It called for two water tunnels that could carry 83,000 cfs; this was the preference of locals, and a minor defeat for Moses, who wanted open canals because of the lower costs.

---

36. PASNY, Meeting Minutes—December 21, 1954: Memorandum to the Members of the Authority, Niagara Report (by Chairman), December 20, 1954.

37. On the Schoellkopf disaster, see Craig A. Woodworth, "The Schoellkopf Disaster Aftermath in the Niagara River Gorge," *IEEE Energy and Power Magazine* 10, no. 6 (Nov.–Dec. 2012): 80–96; Macfarlane, *Fixing Niagara Falls*.

38. Library and Archives Canada (LAC), RG 25, Volume 6782, file 12680-K-40, pt. 10.2, Subject: St. Lawrence Niagara River Treaty Between Canada and the U.S.A. – Additional Diversion of Water at Niagara: Project No. 2216, Release No. 9397, August 29, 1957.

Robert Moses (far left) and PASNY officials. COURTESY OF NYPA.

PASNY immediately issued public bonds, which eventually raised the full cost ($720,000), and work started on all phases of the project in earnest.

Moses had previously adopted a "use value" approach to New York City slum clearance, believing that property acquired for the common good by public institutions (like PASNY) should not have to pay market value for land.[39] PASNY reached an agreement with Niagara University, at the sum of $50,000 an acre, for the school's land close to the new generating station and reservoir.[40] The power authority also had to acquire a range of privately owned properties, as well as big swaths of land from the utility Niagara Mohawk.[41]

For Niagara, PASNY largely continued the same land acquisition practices it had employed along the St. Lawrence, but sought to make it even easier to take property. PASNY had the state legislature pass a bill giving it the right to appropriate, without first condemning, lands needed for the project.[42] The power authority simply had to file a map with the secretary of state and deposit the market value of the land with the state comptroller.

39. Hilary Ballon, "Robert Moses and Urban Renewal: The Title I Program," in Ballon and Jackson, eds., *Robert Moses and the Modern City*.

40. PASNY, Meeting Minutes—August 9, 1957: House Moving and Relocation at Niagara, August 9, 1957.

41. PASNY, Meeting Minutes—September 18, 1961: Niagara Power Project, Acquisition of Remaining Niagara Mohawk Property, September 18, 1961.

42. Edmund Wilson, *Apologies to the Iroquois* (New York: Farrar, Straus, and Giroux, 1960), 143.

PASNY's director of land acquisition, along with Thorne Appraisal Service, was in charge of negotiating purchase agreements, and had the authority to close a settlement as long as it was within 10 percent of the appraised value (above 10 percent required approval of the authority's trustees). Condemnations would result if no agreement could be reached. In cases where an owner resisted condemnation, the power authority would need to file a petition in court. Those who held out for higher prices often succeeded since PASNY was on a tight time schedule and was keen to avoid protracted legal dealings for small properties. But many people felt pressured or bullied into giving up their property quickly. For Moses, the ends justified the means: "soon forgotten will be the inconvenience suffered by the few people discommoded by construction activities."[43]

In a glossy PASNY pamphlet, Moses noted the many local improvements his authority would make, and the wider benefits that cheaper electricity would bring in terms of attracting industry, creating jobs, and improving the standard of living. All of this would counteract any "small losses of taxable real estate occasioned by land acquisition by the Power Authority and, in the final analysis, will result in more taxes."[44] But the City of Niagara Falls was going to lose substantial tax revenue since the station would be in Lewiston, and thus outside of the city, unlike the Schoellkopf and Adams stations. Moses proposed a $2.5 million payment in lieu of taxes to the city, council, and school district of Niagara Falls.[45]

About 100 residences needed to be moved in the City of Niagara Falls, mostly from the "Alphabet Street" area, with the owners given the option of repurchasing their residence.[46] Another 110 homes would be constructed for the engineering staff. The new Veteran Heights Subdivision hosted 168 houses. The power authority hired Hartshorne housemovers to transport residences, which was just finishing up its St. Lawrence work for Ontario Hydro.[47]

Initially, PASNY had planned to take 1,684 acres from the Tuscarora Reservation, a little more than one-third of what was required for the reservoir. The FPC license reduced the size of the reservoir and the amount needed from the reservation to about 950 acres, but then PASNY announced it had to bump up the amount needed from the reservation to 1,250 acres, and then to 1,383 acres. The Tuscarora formally objected, arguing that it was feasible to redesign the reservoir so that it did not impinge on their land. Moses quickly became impatient and combative, fearing the impact on bond sales.

---

43. PASNY, *1961 PASNY Annual Report*, February 1962.

44. PASNY released for public consumption a glossy booklet titled "Niagara Power and Local Taxes." SUL, Robert Moses Papers, Box 6: PASNY, "Niagara Power and Local Taxes," December 2, 1957.

45. PASNY, Meeting Minutes—February 4, 1957: Niagara Taxes, February 4, 1957.

46. In the end, seventy-six houses were moved from the Alphabet Street area. PASNY, Meeting Minutes—August 3, 1960: Niagara Power Project – Niagara Power Project, Disposal of Surplus Lots and Houses in Veteran Heights Development, August 3, 1960.

47. LAC, RG 25, Volume 6782, file 12680-K-40, pt. 11, Subject: St. Lawrence Niagara River Treaty Between Canada and the U.S.A. – Additional Diversion of Water at Niagara: IJC Meeting, IJC Docket No. 62: Niagara Falls Reference, April 1957.

The Tuscarora were well aware of Moses's recent methods dealing with the Mohawks as part of the St. Lawrence project. The PASNY chairman was brusque, arrogant, and condescending, as were many of the delegates he sent to negotiate with the Tuscarora.[48] In the long run, PASNY would end up spending so much on legal fees, delays, and other costs that it probably would have been cheaper just to acquire nonreservation land. To illustrate, the contractor conglomerate that built the Niagara power station put in a claim for extra work caused by the delays, and PASNY ended up making a $2,793,000 lump sum payment.[49] For Moses, however, quashing opposition at any cost seemingly trumped other practical considerations. No type of land use was more valuable than the power and parkland he had in mind, and no one, particularly not seven hundred American Indians using the land for what Moses deemed nonproductive purposes, could be allowed to stand in the way. Moses himself wrote: "the bulk of the land is not used for any purpose at all."[50] Neither he, nor much of society, could conceive of a use for property beyond its commodity and economic value; the Tuscarora's cultural connection to their land was alien. For the Tuscarora, land was a link to the past, a guard against the erasure of their threatened heritage. At court hearings, PASNY went to great lengths to show that Tuscarora land was quite worthless and unmodern: such a small and insignificant group should not be able to stop the kind of progress that would benefit so many.

The Tuscarora took legal action, contending that PASNY could not take their land via eminent domain under state legislation or the FPC license since it was a sovereign Indian nation, part of the Iroquois Confederacy and covered by the confederacy's treaty rights.[51] Federal consent, via an act of Congress, as well as Tuscarora concurrence, is what they argued it would take to dispossess reservation land. PASNY countered that the Tuscarora land in question had been privately purchased, and thus could be taken like any other private property. A state court ruled in favor of the Tuscarora, followed by a series of legal appeals that would stretch for two and half years and reach all the way to the Supreme Court of the United States.

Considering the long history of mistreatment by the American state, there was internal tribal disagreement about whether to make a deal or fight a protracted legal battle. Moreover, the federal government was in the midst of its assimilationist "Termination Policy" and appropriating vast amounts of Indigenous land throughout the country, such as along the Missouri River through the Pick-Sloan Plan.[52] While some members called for

48. Hauptman, *The Iroquois Struggle for Survival*, 156–57.
49. PASNY, Meeting Minutes—February 9, 1961: Niagara Power Project – Increased Costs for Contract N-10 – Construction of Tuscarora Power Plant, February 9, 1961.
50. SUL, Robert Moses Papers, Box 8: Robert Moses, "Tuscarora Fiction and Fact: A Reply to the Author of Memoirs of Hecate County and to his Reviewers," 1960.
51. Anthony F. C. Wallace, *Tuscarora: A History* (Albany: State University of New York Press, 2012), 133.
52. See chapter 4 in Nick Estes, *Our History Is the Future: Standing Rock versus the Dakota Access Pipeline, and the Long Tradition of Indigenous Resistance* (London: Verso, 2019).

militant action, the Tuscarora buttressed their legal challenges with a campaign of passive resistance. At first, this included impeding PASNY surveyors and pulling up or burning survey markers, though the resistance would take other forms—often women and children were at the front lines of protests, since the men were at work.[53] PASNY showed up with police bearing riot gear, tear gas, and submachine guns.[54] Physical altercations occurred, and some Tuscarora were arrested. A judge issued a restraining order to stop the surveyors. The Tuscarora's phone lines were tapped, and there were many other forms of intimidation, bullying, and legal sleight of hand, such as not providing advance notification about court dates.

Moses tried to balance his many sticks with a few carrots: he offered to build a $250,000 community center, and upped the amount that the Tuscarora would receive for their collective property to $1.5 million—though that was just a fraction of what PASNY had paid to the nearby private university. By 1959 the offer had risen to $3 million, but was rejected. PASNY also dangled the potential for a land exchange on the other side of the power reservoir, but when the reservation expressed interest, speculators bought up the land and jacked up the price beyond what Moses was willing to pay.[55] Moses tried to turn the surrounding communities against the Tuscarora, implying that if the intransigent Indians did not budge, the reservoir would have to move further onto white property. Moreover, since Indian land was nontaxable, taking their territory would not entail a hit on local coffers, compared to removing other properties from the tax rolls.

The Tuscarora appealed to the media. A series of articles was published in the *New Yorker* by Edmund Wilson, which were then collected into a 1959 book titled *Apologies to the Iroquois*. The Tuscarora themselves thought the book flawed, though it did accurately reveal the "low tricks" Moses and PASNY employed.[56] Moses replied with publications of his own bearing titles such as "Niagara Desperately Needs more Power" and "Tuscarora: Fact or Fiction."[57] In these tracts, he made many claims to discredit them, and suggested that it was just a small group of recalcitrants blocking the reasonable majority. Public opinion, locally and around the country, exhibited some sympathy for the plight of the Native Americans. Many others could relate, indirectly or firsthand, to what it felt like to be shunted aside by the Moses machine.

Legal challenges went back and forth, each side scoring some victories. The Court of Appeals held that Tuscarora land was a "reservation" within the definition of the Power Act. In February 1959 the FPC found that the license it had granted to PASNY "will interfere

---

53. Clinton Rickard (Barbara Graymont, ed.), *Fighting Tuscarora: The Autobiography of Chief Clinton Rickard* (Syracuse, NY: Syracuse University Press, 1973), 139.
54. Rickard, *Fighting Tuscarora,* 142.
55. Moreover, PASNY would not give them the treaty land rights they desired if they swapped land. Rickard, *Fighting Tuscarora,* 148.
56. Rickard, *Fighting Tuscarora,* 145.
57. SUL, Robert Moses Papers, Box 7: PASNY – Niagara Desperately Needs More Power, June 9, 1958.

and will be inconsistent with the purpose for which such reservation was created" and the Tuscarora could not be compelled to sell it.[58] This decision was upheld by United States Court of Appeals for the District of Columbia Circuit, but the FPC appealed the ruling to the Supreme Court, hoping for either a final judicial decision or an out-of-court settlement.

In March 1960 the high court issued a 6–3 decision against the Tuscarora. The majority opinion held that it was not a reservation since the title to the land was vested in the Tuscarora and not the federal government. The dissenting opinion disagreed about this interpretation of the legal definition of an Indian reservation. One of the dissenting justices, Hugo Black, lamented that "[s]ome things are worth more than money and the costs of a new enterprise. . . . I regret that this Court is to be the governmental agency that breaks faith with this dependent people. Great nations, like great men, should keep their word." "A Niagara of fictional treacle of molasses has been poured on the Indians," Moses crowed, "a sticky flow finally stopped by the United States Supreme Court. We have never harmed the Indians. We have been more than generous in delaying with them." Now, he condescendingly and paternalistically chided, "we only hope that they will use the money we pay them for a fraction of their land wisely and in the interest of their children."[59]

While the court drama had been playing out, PASNY prepared contingency plans for the reservoir in case the courts ultimately ruled against them. Consequently, PASNY was able to build a 60,000 acre-feet reservoir that required less Tuscarora land than originally sought. PASNY took the southwest area of the reserve, about 550 acres (55 acres were for a transmission line) with eleven houses—a bit less than a square mile—for the reservoir that covered about 1,880 total acres. Technically, it was an easement, and the reserve retained ownership. The Tuscarora Council reluctantly consented, characterizing the payment as a damages settlement.[60] PASNY either moved the affected houses, provided a new one, or gave a cash settlement. The authority spent a total of $370,091 on Tuscarora relocations, about half of that on residences, which included a range of improvements such as heating, lighting, and landscaping. PASNY made a blanket payment of $850,000, or $1,100 per acre (far less than the $3 million offered in 1959), and every tribe member, regardless of whether or not their property was directly affected, received $800 as part of the final settlement.[61]

The new power facility had been named after the Tuscarora. But an editorial in the *Niagara Falls Gazette* now suggested that it be named after Moses. This was quickly

---

58. FPC Opinion No. 217, Opinion and Finding, Project No. 2217, Power Authority of the State of New York, February 2, 1959.
59. SUL, Robert Moses Papers, Box 8: Remarks of Robert Moses at a Luncheon of the New York State Society of Newspaper Editors, Treadway Inn, Niagara Falls, June 20, 1960.
60. Wallace, *Tuscarora*, 135.
61. The appendices of a PASNY memorandum list the eleven families and give a breakdown for each, as well as totals: $188,622 for Residence, Including Foundation; $28,573 for Utilities: Water Supply, Sewerage, Electric Service; $29,315 for Access: Roads and Driveways; $25,700 for Cash Advance; and $97,881 for Other: Outbuildings Grading, Garage, Moving personal items, etc. PASNY Meeting Minutes, June 20, 1960: Memorandum to Col. William S. Chapin, Relocation of Families – Reservoir Area, June 17, 1960.

Aerial view of Niagara Power Project. COURTESY OF NYPA.

implemented. With the stroke of a pen, the Tuscarora went from not only being physically displaced to being symbolically displaced as well. The Tuscarora lost any remaining faith in the U.S. government. In retrospect, the deck was surely stacked against them, and given Moses's stature and PASNY's importance, it was virtually inevitable that the legal apparatus of settler colonialism would be mobilized against the Tuscarora, for even if one court rebuffed PASNY, that proved merely to be a delay until other legal avenues could be found. This was the logical extension of several centuries of settler societies taking land to use for purposes that they perceived as providing a more important societal benefit.

In one of his propaganda pieces, Moses repeated a statement by one of the many judges who had dealt with the Tuscarora issue: "If the Indians are to enjoy equal protection of the laws and all the other benefits extended to each citizen it may well be that they should bear some of the burdens including that of being subjected to having their lands condemned for public purposes, beneficial to the State in which they live."[62] But it is environmental racism and injustice when it is repeatedly the same groups who have to shoulder disproportionately greater burdens while also receiving lesser benefits and legal protection.

In addition to the new generating station and related infrastructure, PASNY was also

---

62. SUL, Robert Moses Papers, Box 8: Robert Moses, "Tuscarora Fiction and Fact: A Reply to the author of Memoirs of Hecate County and to his Reviewers," 1960.

developing the surrounding area. The Robert Moses State Parkway, as it was christened, would run along the edge of the Niagara River. Thirteen million cubic yards of rock and earth were excavated from the trench for the dual tunnels taking water to the Moses station, and much of it was used to reclaim land along the American shoreline. The parkway ran over top of this extended shoreline, which gave drivers an excellent view of the water, but cut off nonvehicular access to the water in many locations. The parkway ran right through Prospect Park—allowing motorized tourists to see the American Falls without even getting out of their car, but forcing those approaching on foot to climb cumbersome pedestrian ramps within the Niagara Reservation just to get to the cataract. Motorists could also drive to Goat Island and leave their vehicles at the new parking lot, which had replaced a forested area in 1951. But the new parkway was not very popular, and parts near the falls were soon removed.[63]

Agreements were inked so that the Niagara Falls Bridge Commission could build a new international crossing between Lewiston and Queenston. In conjunction, New York State also constructed the Niagara Expressway and the Niagara Thruway. At Prospect Point, PASNY covered the cost of an observation tower, which featured an elevator down to the Maid of the Mist dock. PASNY built new water and sewer systems for the communities of Lewiston and Niagara Falls, eliminated railway grade crossings, installed playgrounds, and expanded Hyde Park by 140 acres, including a nine-hole addition to the golf course. PASNY funded improvements to the state park at the falls and Goat Island, and other parts of the Niagara Reservation, while creating the 132-acre Reservoir Park behind the new generating station (fishing was permitted in the artificial lake, though boating and swimming were not). New York State's entire Niagara project required over 39,000,000 cubic yards of excavation. Ten million yards of excess material was deposited at a spoil pile north of the Moses powerhouse, along the Niagara Escarpment, which later became Lewiston's Art Park.

Moses's eponymous generating station met the target date of February 10, 1961, when two units came into service. It would take until October 1962 before all twenty-five units were operational. First power was celebrated with an elaborate ceremony in February 1961. This three-day affair featured celebrities and VIPs, commemorative medallions, and the debut of a specially commissioned orchestral work.[64] The new power station was clearly intended to be a tourist draw beyond its opening: PASNY had installed a visitor's center with an observation deck atop the station's south end, and it attracted 300,000 people in its first year. The same sort of celebration and "hydro tourism" had also taken place at the Moses-Saunders generating station on the St. Lawrence.[65]

---

63. More recently, much of this divided highway has been reduced to one lane or abandoned, and it is no longer named after Moses.

64. Caro, *The Power Broker*, 825–26.

65. See Daniel Macfarlane, "Fluid Meanings: Hydro Tourism and the St. Lawrence and Niagara Megaprojects," *Histoire Sociale/Social History* 49, no. 99 (June 2016): 327–46.

Moses Station under construction. COURTESY OF NEW YORK FALLS PUBLIC LIBRARY.

It would take until 1963 before all other aspects of the project, including recreational facilities and clean-up, were completed. Over 1,231 parcels of land had been acquired by PASNY, but at the start of 1963 many cases remained unsettled.[66] At that point, ninety-one claims had been filed in the Court of Claims: thirty-eight cases were still pending, with ten awards under appeal. A number of condemnation cases had gone to the Supreme Court,

66. PASNY, *1962 PASNY Annual Report*, February 1963.

though about one-quarter were still pending a settlement or ruling.[67] Since it had to dispense with leftover property in a relatively depressed real estate market, the power authority ended up selling twenty-four houses and thirty-five vacant lots for $345,000 in one transaction, about $50,000 less than the appraised value.[68]

Conclusion

Robert Moses had been appointed to head PASNY while it built the Niagara and St. Lawrence power projects. With both complete at the end of 1962, after eight years as PASNY chairman, Moses resigned from this position as well as his other state posts. Moses had made a habit of threatening resignation, and with his popularity on the wane—no doubt influenced by his Tuscarora fight—this time Governor Nelson Rockefeller called his bluff. PASNY and HEPCO had requested permission from the International Joint Commission to extend the control dam above Niagara Falls and increase the amount of water diverted for power production. Faced with a public outcry against this, in 1962 Rockefeller compelled Moses to withdraw the request by refusing to fill two vacancies on the PASNY Board of Trustees. This contributed to the growing friction between the two.[69] Two years earlier, Moses had resigned or lost most of his New York City posts as well. Partly because of the lucrative salary, he took a new position as president of the 1964–65 World's Fair.[70]

Moses was, indeed, a man of his times, exhibiting many of the attitudes and prejudices of his background and station in life. But isn't the ability to transcend widespread mindsets precisely what defines "great" figures? Moses built his projects chiefly for the benefit of the white middle class, which he paternalistically viewed as an amorphous mass who needed to be told what was good for them. The St. Lawrence generating station would have been built regardless of whether Robert Moses was in charge of PASNY; whether PASNY would have secured the right to build the Niagara development sans Moses is less certain. To be sure, how both were built, where some of the related infrastructure was placed, and the character of relations with locals, were all chiefly determined by Moses. Under Moses's PASNY

---

67. PASNY, *1962 PASNY Annual Report*, February 1963.

68. Since many did not purchase back their houses, PASNY was left with ownership of thirty-one of the houses moved to Veteran Heights, as well as thirty-six vacant lots on this subdivision, and houses it had rented to engineers, which were now becoming vacant. Because of the depressed condition of the real estate market, PASNY was forced to sell much of this property at a loss. PASNY, Meeting Minutes—August 3, 1960—PASNY Minutes: Niagara Power Project, Disposal of surplus lots and houses in Veteran Heights Development: August 3, 1960; PASNY, Meeting Minutes—February 9, 1961: Niagara Power Project, Sale of Houses and Lots Owned by Authority in Veteran Heights Subdivision, February 9, 1961.

69. The control dam extension, however, was built. PASNY, Meeting Minutes—February 19, 1962: Niagara Power Project, Withdrawal of Request to International Joint Commission for Additional Summertime Water Diversion, February 19, 1962; IJC, Docket 74, Niagara River Reference, Box 114, 74-1-1: 1 Reference Dated 1961/05/05: Memorandum for File – Niagara Reference, March 1, 1962.

70. The Rockefeller-Moses story is recounted in Caro, *The Power Broker*, 1077–79.

leadership, the power generating stations were built well, on time, and on budget. The majority of the people across the state seemed to feel that the good (electricity) probably outweighed the bad when it came to these new power developments, though most probably did not realize that the new power was not distributed locally and the majority went to industry rather than consumers.

Moses frequently employed the saying that one had to break some eggs to make an omelet, and this attitude was apparent in his efforts in northern New York State. But the eggs-omelet metaphor elides the externalized cost to the chickens, who ultimately pay the biggest price; with the many projects Moses spearheaded, it was the nonhuman environment that paid the higher price. Both the Niagara and St. Lawrence megaprojects had enormous ecological consequences, as some of the largest rivers on the continent were replumbed and transformed into hybrid envirotechnical machines that blended the mechanical and the organic. The immediate ecological impacts of Moses's myriad efforts were legion: they destroyed habitat for many forms of aquatic life, extirpating or significantly reducing fish species such as sturgeon. Or consider that less than half of the Niagara River's water annually plunges over Niagara Falls, the rest siphoned off by power utilities. Furthermore, Moses's contributions to the built environment created many path dependencies— particularly by centering many plans on automobiles—that are now obstacles to a sustainable future.

Robert Moses's chairmanship of the Power Authority of the State of New York is a phase of his career that should not be overlooked. Under Moses, PASNY lost much of its commitment to public power beyond emphasizing industrial development.[71] The two megaprojects he oversaw on the Niagara and St. Lawrence Rivers changed waterscapes and famous landmarks on a spatial scale that arguably exceeded his many New York City undertakings. The years Moses spent with PASNY therefore provide a valuable perspective on his practices, techniques, and outlook. Furthermore, the opposition that Moses encountered downstate after 1950 should be understood in the context of his PASNY role. The Tuscarora did stand up to Moses and force alterations to his plans, which garnered a wide degree of media attention and public support. Considering that a number of Moses's schemes for more New York City expressways were successfully blocked around this time, perhaps the battle with the Tuscarora fits into a broader pattern of grassroots resistance to Moses's imperial projects in the postwar period.

---

71. Petersen, "Public Power and Private Planning," 15–17.

Dutch Reformed Congregationalism in New Netherland

The Case of Rev. Wilhelmus Grasmeer

Kenneth Shefsiek

In 1642, Kiliaen van Rensselaer, patroon of Rensselaerswijck, contracted with Rev. Johannes Megapolensis Jr. to serve the religious needs of the colonists of the patroonship for a term of six years.[1] At the time, Megapolensis was minister for the congregation at Schoorl in the Classis of Alkmaar, both of which had to formally dismiss him before he could take on a new charge.[2] The Classis of Amsterdam, the regional church council in the Netherlands that had assumed a dominant role in religious affairs in New Netherland, also needed to draft a call to the minister, in accordance with special policies it established in 1636 regarding the appointment of colonial ministers.[3] The classis penned such a call and instructed its deputies appointed to manage colonial affairs to assist Van Rensselaer and Megapolensis in expediting his dismissals.[4] After receiving dismissals from both his consistory and classis,[5] Megapolensis, his wife Machtelt, and their four children set sail in June 1642 for New Netherland, where he became only the third minister to serve in the colony. Megapolensis intended to serve in New Netherland only briefly, but he ultimately served there until his death in 1670, as the West India Company (WIC) hired him for the Manhattan congregation after his contract with the patroon expired.[6]

---

1. *ERSNY*, 143–46. For an overview of Megapolensis's life, see Gerald F. De Jong, "Dominie Johannes Megapolensis: Minister to New Netherland," *New-York Historical Society Quarterly* 52, no. 1 (January 1968): 7–47.
2. *ERSNY*, 145–46.
3. *ERSNY*, 91–94.
4. *ERSNY*, 146–48.
5. *ERSNY*, 149, 152.
6. *ERSNY*, 225, 230–31, 237–39, 242–44, 246, 249, 251–52, 261–63, 264–66, 271; Arnold J. F. Van Laer, ed. and trans., *Council Minutes: 1638–1649* (Baltimore: Genealogical Publishing Co., 1974), 611–12; Charles T. Gehring, ed. and trans., *Correspondence: 1647–1653* (Syracuse, NY: Syracuse University Press, 2000), 57, 71, 81.

The process by which Megapolensis came to serve in New Netherland reflected that which was followed in the Netherlands in accordance with the Church Order of Dort (DCO), the 1619 document that provided guidance for how ecclesiastical power within the Dutch Reformed church in the United Provinces should be defined and structured. This church order was grounded in an aversion to both ecclesiastical independence and hierarchy and therefore aimed to link church members, congregations, ministers, and governments in a tight-knit web of collaborative relationships. Slight adjustments were nevertheless made to account for the colonial situation, such as Megapolensis's appointment being only for a limited term and his being sent by the Classis of Amsterdam rather than being called directly by the congregation that he was to serve. Unfortunately, the calling of Dutch ministers in or for New Netherland did not always go so smoothly, particularly when ministers and colonial congregations acted independently of classical authority. This independence deeply troubled the Classis of Amsterdam, as it ran contrary to principles of Dutch Reformed church polity and had the potential to undermine the orderly development of the New Netherland church.

As a form of congregationalism was developing in North America, alternatives were nevertheless possible, as the history of other Dutch colonies reveals. That no formalized solutions to counter congregationalism were developed for New Netherland set the stage for conflict that lasted for more than a century after the English conquest. Many Dutch Reformed ministers in the eighteenth century on both sides of the Atlantic interpreted the ongoing struggles as being the fault of those who refused to adhere to the Church Order of Dort and the directives of the Classis of Amsterdam, and in doing so, challenged the way it had always been. As the Classis of Amsterdam noted in 1743 to three prestigious ministers serving in New York, the "subordination," of the American churches and ministers to the Classis of Amsterdam, "has already existed from early times. When the provinces, wherein your congregations are situate, belonged to the Honorable West India Company, this relationship came into existence as a matter of course; and it remained unaltered after they passed under the power of England."[7] Historians have generally interpreted the situation similarly.[8] The ministers' understanding of the ecclesiastical history of the Dutch

---

7. *ERSNY*, 2826.

8. Gerald F. De Jong, *The Dutch Reformed Church in the American Colonies* (Grand Rapids, MI: William B. Eerdmans, 1978); Dirk Mouw, "Moederkerk and Vaderland: Religion and Ethnic Identity in the Middle Colonies, 1690–1772" (PhD diss., University of Iowa, 2009). While Mouw argues that the eighteenth-century controversies in the American churches were complex, and that the Classis of Amsterdam's power in New Netherland was more expansive than the DCO allowed, he does note that "During the period of Dutch rule, colonial consistories were forced by the geographic, political, and economic realities of the colony to accept a significant diminution of the authority and the role afforded them by Dutch Reformed church order and custom" (188). As will be demonstrated, all certainly did not "accept" this dependent status. Earl Kennedy offers a bit more qualified interpretation of the Classis of Amsterdam's power over the colonial church, noting that it "never [had] fully uncontested authority" (Earl Wm. Kennedy, "Guiliam Bertholf (1656–1726): Irenic Dutch Pietist in New Jersey and New York," in *Transatlantic Pieties: Dutch*

Reformed church in America was nevertheless flawed. It was also built on what ministers rather than congregations did and thought, even though congregational power was integral to the Dutch Reformed church. Eighteenth-century ministers were not aware that New Netherland congregations had not always bowed to the power of the Classis of Amsterdam, nor that they had had legitimate grounds for not having done so. Those in the eighteenth century who therefore claimed that conflict arose because some American ministers and congregations challenged the status quo misunderstood what the status quo had actually been.

One situation that reveals the limits of classical power in New Netherland involved Megapolensis's stepson (son of his wife Machtelt from her first marriage), Rev. Wilhelmus Grasmeer, who boldly decided in 1650 to seek a call in New Netherland entirely on his own initiative. He did so after domestic troubles with his wife led to his suspension from the ministry and later his excommunication by the Classis of Alkmaar. Instead of accepting this imposition of ecclesiastical discipline and reconciling with his wife, he chose to flee his problems by seeking employment abroad. Much to the displeasure of the Classis of Amsterdam, Grasmeer found a position in New Netherland with his stepfather's former congregation in Rensselaerswijck, which hired Grasmeer without seeking classical approval. Even more alarming, the congregation continued to employ him even after it had learned of his excommunication. Amsterdam's classis worried that if other colonial congregations followed a similar independent path rather than seek qualified ministers through classical channels, the result would be chaos, but such independence was nevertheless possible. Amsterdam's classis therefore responded with both anger and fear, threatening Grasmeer and imploring his congregation to dismiss him. While historians have generally suggested that the Classis of Amsterdam reacted as it did because Grasmeer's personal inadequacies and his unwillingness to follow church order made him unsuitable for colonial service, the actual problem was that his choices made it possible for American congregations to act independently, independence which Amsterdam hoped to prevent.[9]

Clergy in Colonial America, edited by Leon van den Broeke, Hans Krabbendam, and Dirk Mouw (Grand Rapids, MI: William B. Eerdmans, 2012), 197–216, quote at 212). Randall Balmer's study of eighteenth-century conflict in the Dutch Reformed church in North America grounds the conflict in the growth of pietism and ecumenism, marginalizing the issue of church order, and is therefore not relevant to this discussion (Randall H. Balmer, *A Perfect Babel of Confusion: Dutch Religion and English Culture in the Middle Colonies* (New York: Oxford University Press, 1989)). Balmer's interpretation has also been successfully challenged by Mouw.

9. There is very little concerning Grasmeer in the existing literature on New Netherland. While historians have in general discussed both Grasmeer's marital problems and his unwillingness to adhere closely to the Church Order, they have generally treated Grasmeer himself as the problem, rather than suggesting, as I do, that the ultimate issue was colonial congregational independence, which his choices made possible. Albert Eekhof, *De Hervormde Kerk in Noord-Amerika* (Den Hage: Martinus Nijhoff, 1913), 126–39; Frederick J. Zwierlein, *Religion in New Netherland: A History of the Development of the Religious Condition in the Province of New Netherland, 1623–1664* (Rochester, NY: John P. Smith, 1910), 88–90; Janny Venema, *Beverwijck: A Dutch Village on the American Frontier, 1652–1664* (Albany: State University of New York Press, 2003), 140–41. Jaap

Grasmeer only served in New Netherland for about a year, as he soon returned home to resolve the problems with his wife and his classis. He hoped that doing so would enable him to secure a more prestigious position. However, his New Netherland congregation never succumbed to the Classis of Amsterdam's pressure campaign, as it considered its power and judgment as a Dutch Reformed congregation beyond the bounds of all Dutch classes sufficient to make decisions as to who would fill the pastoral role.[10] Although short-lived, the conflict reveals the difficulties colonists faced in securing ministerial leadership, as well as the challenges that arose in trying to apply the DCO in a colonial context. Almost out of necessity, the colonists of Rensselaerswijck began to abandon their presbyterial-synodal church order in favor of a form of congregationalism, establishing a controversial pattern that others in New Netherland, and later New York and New Jersey, would sometimes follow.

Dutch Colonies and the Church Order of Dort

When religious reformers such as John Calvin, Huldrych Zwingli, and Jan Łaski separated themselves from the Roman Catholic Church in part due to their theological critique of its ecclesiastical hierarchy, it was incumbent upon them to develop new church polities that both created and governed power relationships within their new churches. The new church orders institutionalized an array of relationships, including that between church members, their ministers, and their governing councils; between congregations; between individual ministers; and among ministers collectively. Although the various Reformed church polities were similar, particularly in establishing a more collaborative form of church governance that incorporated lay participation, Reformed church orders could take various forms, given that many Reformed leaders claimed that the Bible did not specify a precise order for the visible church. As a result, a variety of church orders were created following the perspectives and experiences of their framers, who were also influenced by the history and politics of the places where they labored. Nevertheless, those who created the

---

Jacobs, however, does not even count Grasmeer as a New Netherland minister, due to the fact that he served in the colony against Amsterdam's wishes (Jaap Jacobs, *The Colony of New Netherland: A Dutch Settlement in Seventeenth-Century America* (Ithaca, NY: Cornell University Press, 2009), n.8, 280). In another essay in which he briefly discusses religion in the patroonship, Jacobs does not even mention Grasmeer (Jaap Jacobs, "Dutch Proprietary Manors in America: The Patroonships in New Netherland," in *Constructing Early Modern Empires: Proprietary Ventures in the Atlantic World: 1500–1750*, edited by Louis H. Roper and Bertram van Ruymbeke (Leiden: Brill, 2007), 315). Danny Noorlander notes that the entire Grasmeer affair represents "the church's serious concern regarding the quality of colonial ministers and the lengths it would go to guard and control colonial religion." He also argues that the Dutch church establishment "wouldn't tolerate men who flouted hiring policies and escaped the vetting process" (D. L. Noorlander, *Heaven's Wrath: The Protestant Reformation and the Dutch West India Company in the Atlantic World* (Ithaca, NY: Cornell University Press, 2019), 205–06).

10. By "Dutch classis," I am referring to one of the classes within the United Provinces rather than simply a classis that considered itself Dutch Reformed, such as the one formed in Brazil, which will be discussed below.

church orders sometimes held beliefs that were inviolable relative to relationships within the church.[11] For the Dutch Reformed, this was an ecclesiastical egalitarianism, such that ministers and congregations individually could not hold any formal power over their peers. Early articulations of this principle were offered at the Convent of Wezel (1568) and the Synod of Emden (1571). This egalitarianism was also an essential element of the DCO, such that Article 84 forcefully holds that "No church shall in any way lord it over another church, no minister over other ministers, no elder or deacon over other elders or deacons."[12] This does not suggest that they all possessed the same level of informal authority, but simply that their formal power to act or coerce existed within decidedly circumscribed limits.

As much as the Dutch Reformed were committed to such an egalitarian church, they were also averse to congregational and ministerial independence, which endangered doctrinal unity and might permit unqualified or inappropriate ministers to serve in the church. They therefore adopted a presbyterial-synodal church order structured around a rising series of church councils that did possess formal power over their constituent members.[13] These church councils were the congregational consistory, the regional classis, the provincial (or particular) synod, and the national synod (at least in theory), with contiguous church councils of a similar type linked together to form each higher level of church council. Central to this governance structure was that the power of each church council was derived from the direct participation of ministers and congregations (or their representatives) subject to the council's power. As such, power rose both from above and below in ways that prevented both independence and hierarchy.[14]

These principles were inscribed into the DCO, although a number of issues involving the application of the DCO at home affected the development of the church in the colonies. The primary issue is that the DCO was never approved by the States General and was therefore not binding on the church throughout the United Provinces.[15] Rather, how the

---

11. Philip Benedict, *Christ's Churches Purely Reformed: A Social History of Calvinism* (New Haven, CT: Yale University Press, 2002). For a concise statement of Benedict's central thesis, see p. 546.
12. Pieter Coertzen, "Dordt and South Africa: Church and State Relations in the Netherlands and South Africa," in *Protestant Church Polity in Changing Contexts I: Ecclesiological and Historical Contributions*, edited by Allen J. Janssen and Leo Koffeman (Zurich: Lit Verlag GmbH & Co, 2014), 137–54 (see in particular 141).
13. Pieter Coertzen describes such a church polity as one in which "the responsibility for leadership in the church rests with the church councils: the local churches are the *presbyterium*, while the broader meetings are the expression of the synodical character of this form of church government" ("Dordt and South Africa: Church and State Relations," 140).
14. Benedict, *Christ's Churches Purely Reformed*, 135–36, 189; Mary-Anne Plaatjies van Huffel, "The Relevance of Reformed Church Polity Principles: Revisiting the Concept," in *Protestant Church Polity in Changing Contexts I: Ecclesiological and Historical Contributions*, edited by Allen J. Janssen and Leo Koffeman (Zurich: Lit Verlag GmbH & Co, 2014), 29–48.
15. Fred van Lieburg, "Re-understanding the Dordt Church Order in its Dutch Political, Ecclesiastical and Cultural Context," in *Protestant Church Polity in Changing Contexts I: Ecclesiological and Historical Contributions*, edited by Allen J. Janssen and Leo Koffeman (Zurich: Lit Verlag GmbH & Co, 2014), 117–36 (quote at 128); Benedict, *Christ's Churches Purely Reformed*, 193–94.

church was ordered was defined locally, such that "On the juridical level there were only provincial church orders."[16] Still, "they shared the essentials of Reformed church polity," as both the DCO as well as the provincial orders created before Dort were used as guides in establishing the various church orders.[17] While this lack of a uniform church order prevented a single approach to church governance, according to Fred van Lieburg, the DCO became "in practice a legislative framework that was able to accommodate continuous additional decisions in concrete situations in day-to-day church life," such that it "was the result of as well as the starting point for successive adaptations."[18] The fact that the DCO was never approved meant that both the internal structure of the church and the church-state relationship could be adapted for different situations, both at home and abroad. This gave the West and East India Companies, as the governing authorities in their respective colonies, considerable leeway in establishing for themselves both how the colonial churches would be ordered and how the church-state relationship would be structured.

Secondly, in the era of the Dutch Republic, the States General never permitted another meeting of a national synod after Dort, making it impossible for the Dutch Reformed to formally resolve any questions that affected the church as a whole. This had important ramifications for the development of the church in the colonies, since many provincial synods asserted that the development of the church in the colonies was indeed of interest to all Dutch Reformed. For more than two decades after New Netherland's founding, some provincial synods therefore argued that all synods, classes, and even congregations could involve themselves in overseas affairs.[19] In contrast, the Synod of North Holland feared that such decentralized power would impede the development of the church in the colonies. It therefore attempted to restrict colonial oversight and support to the provincial synods in those regions where chambers of the WIC and VOC (Dutch East India Company) were situated.[20] While all of the provincial synods did not necessarily want to have a direct role in colonial oversight and development, they were troubled by the Synod of North Holland's apparent arrogation of power, which seemed to challenge the church's formal egalitarianism. Even the Synod of South Holland, which was itself associated with a WIC chamber, expressed its concern that North Holland was attempting to gain power to which it was not entitled.[21] Still, by 1649, all of the provincial synods did conclude that it was unwise and impractical for all of them to oversee and support the colonial churches. However, the only restriction they were willing to place on synodal action during the New Netherland period was to limit oversight to those synods within provinces where there were company chambers, a policy for which the Synod of North Holland had advocated all along.[22]

---

16. Van Lieburg, "Re-understanding the Dordt Church Order," 128.
17. Van Lieburg, "Re-understanding the Dordt Church Order," 128.
18. Van Lieburg, "Re-understanding the Dordt Church Order," 130, 132.
19. *ERSNY*, 38–39, 123–26, 130–34, 138–39.
20. *ERSNY*, 38–39, 208.
21. *ERSNY*, 158.
22. *ERSNY*, 158–60, 211–12, 218, 232, 277–78.

Although this decision did not assign the oversight and guidance of the church in any of the colonies to any one particular synod, it did make practical sense for the Synod of North Holland to take a dominant role in the New Netherland church. This was so because Amsterdam was within the bounds of the Synod of North Holland, and the Amsterdam chamber of the WIC had assumed the greatest role in the development of New Netherland. It was therefore most convenient for the two to work together in support of the colony's church. Still, North Holland did not take direct action in New Netherland, and devolved any power it had to the Classis of Amsterdam.[23] It was also only logical that a classis rather than a synod would oversee the colonial church, given that classes had far more responsibilities than did synods in church governance. Classical responsibilities included the examination of ministerial candidates and oversight of ecclesiastical discipline, both of ministers and church members. Ordinations in the United Provinces were also subject to classical control and were performed by a minister of the local classis in the presence of the congregation the new minister was to serve. Classical approval was also required for all ministerial calls and dismissals. Finally, classes had the power to send ministers to establish new congregations, although once established, congregations were responsible for initiating ministerial calls and dismissals themselves. Many of these classical functions would be central in the establishment and continued support of the church in the colony, particularly in the calling of ministers, as it would be many years before the colonial congregations would develop the means to regularly recruit ministers on their own.[24]

It is important to note, however, that the control that a Dutch provincial synod, and by extension a Dutch classis, had over the colonial church was limited because the provincial church orders were for local use only and neither had they been constructed with the colonies in mind. This meant that no particular church order was operative in any of the colonies. Instead, Dutch Reformed ministers and congregations, as well as the companies, had to extrapolate from the basic principles of church governance that underpinned the DCO in order to decide how to govern the colonial churches, although the ultimate power rested with the companies as governing authorities. The provincial synods certainly could informally agree among themselves which would play a role in colonial affairs, and as long as the other provincial synods were comfortable deferring to the Synod of North Holland in its oversight of New Netherland, conflict could be avoided. The classes within the Synod of North Holland likewise had the right to defer to the Classis of Amsterdam in its support of the church in New Netherland. However, the ecclesiological principles of the DCO made it problematic for power over the colonial church to rest with a classis in the Netherlands. This was the case because classes were organized geographically and were by

---

23. De Jong, *The Dutch Reformed Church,* 170–71; Mouw, "Moederkerk and Vaderland," 163–66; Willem Frijhoff, *Fulfilling God's Mission: The Two Worlds of Domine Everardus Bogardus, 1607–1647,* translated by Myra Heerspink Scholz (Leiden: Brill, 2007); Noorlander, *Heaven's Wrath,* 21–22.
24. Mouw, "Moederkerk and Vaderland," 153–224.

definition participatory, as were all Dutch Reformed church councils, and colonial ministers and congregations strewn across the globe obviously could not participate in church
councils situated in the Netherlands. If any classis in the Netherlands attempted to wield
power over colonial ministers who and congregations which did not participate in classical governance, the egalitarianism of the church would be compromised. Danny Noorlander argues that this is exactly what happened, as agreements made in the Netherlands
produced "a uniquely subordinate, controlled position for the colonial clergy."[25] Again, if
colonial ministers and congregations accepted such a subordinate position, conflict would
not arise. However, if ministers or congregations in the colonies were unwilling to position
themselves in a hierarchy that challenged essential principles of Dutch Reformed church
governance, there was little any Dutch classis could offer to support the legitimacy of colonial subordination.

Without a doubt, the Classis of Amsterdam did become the Dutch classis with the
strongest position and greatest stake in the New Netherland church, and it was thoroughly
committed to controlling its development. Many New Netherland ministers were also willing to maintain a strong connection with the Classis of Amsterdam, primarily because it
had sent them to serve in the colonial sphere. But it must be remembered that no decision
was ever made by the Dutch Reformed provincial synods that assigned oversight of the
church in any colony to any Dutch classis, as only a national synod could make such a decision. However, such a decision would have required a rethinking of the very principles that
undergirded the Dutch Reformed church orders in use in the Netherlands, as it would have
created an ecclesiastical hierarchy that the Dutch Reformed inherently opposed. When it
came to colonial affairs, their simultaneous aversion to independence and hierarchy placed
them between a rock and a hard place.

Still, the role of the DCO and the limits of classical and synodal power in New Netherland were never clearly articulated and did not become a central topic of discussion in
North America until well into the eighteenth century. How the church was governed in
other Dutch colonies was sometimes more clearly explicated, such that a brief exploration
of those colonies can help to frame the North American experience. Without a doubt, such
an exploration reveals that the DCO was not controlling outside the geographic boundaries of the United Provinces—just as it was not in the United Provinces themselves—and
neither did any classis situated in the Netherlands have formal power in any of the colonies.

In Batavia, a colony of the East India Company (VOC), a local church order was
established in 1624 and later revised in 1643. The 1624 church order was drafted by ministers in the colony with permission from the Synods of North and South Holland, with
the participation, support, and approval of the VOC governor. Nevertheless, it is not clear
that permission was required nor that the two provincial synods even had the right to

---

25. Noorlander, *Heaven's Wrath*, 14.

grant it.[26] Though the basic substance of the Batavian Church Order was derived from the DCO, it required "significant modification to make the church order applicable to the daughter church in Java."[27] One modification was that the Batavian Church Order rendered ministers subordinate to the state rather than to any classis, with the only exception being that ministers serving in the East Indies still had to be appointed by a Dutch classis.[28] Importantly, the governor-general also had sole authority over the appointment of ministers to congregations—which made logical sense, since they were VOC employees—with the result being that they "were apt to be shifted at short notice from one place to another at the whim of the Governor-General and his council in Batavia."[29] In other words, the process of calling and dismissing ministers articulated in the DCO simply did not apply in Batavia, and neither did any Dutch classis have any administrative power within the colony itself. This adjustment had its logic, given the undeveloped state of the church in the east. However, according to C. R. Boxer, this realignment between the East India churches and the state came about because the VOC was "firmly resolved to subordinate the overseas Churches to their own authority."[30]

The colonial government's power was strengthened further when the Batavian governor-general unilaterally revised the 1624 church order in 1643 in ways "that limited even more strictly the independence of the church."[31] He did so without the support or approval of any ecclesiastical assemblies in the Netherlands. As Leon van den Broeke explains, this change was necessary due to the "different cultural, societal, political, and ecclesiastical context, [such that] the corpus of the Dort Church Order of 1619 was not entirely helpful to the East Indian churches."[32] The Classis of Amsterdam protested, but not because the church council believed a separate church order in Asia was inappropriate or unacceptable; rather, the classis was concerned that the governor allowed for baptisms by *zieck-entroosters* ("comforters of the sick"), a responsibility defined by the DCO as belonging strictly to ministers. The classis therefore requested that the new church order be abrogated. The company refused, maintaining that it would "do in the matter what the best order of the church and civil government there might require," even if doing so challenged

26. Yudha Thianto, "Elements of Calvin's Theology and Practice in the Establishment of Reformed Churches in Java in the Seventeenth Century," in *John Calvin, Myth and Reality: Images and Impact of Geneva's Reformer, Papers of the 2009 Calvin Studies Society Colloquium*, edited by Amy Nelson Burnett (Eugene, OR: Cascade Books, 2011), 91–106; Donald F. Lach and Edwin J. Van Kley, *Asia in the Making of Europe, Volume III: A Century of Advance, Book One; Trade, Missions, Literature* (Chicago: University of Chicago Press, 1993), 273.
27. Thianto, "Elements of Calvin's Theology and Practice," 93.
28. Thianto, "Elements of Calvin's Theology and Practice," 96.
29. C. R. Boxer, *The Dutch Seaborne Empire: 1600–1800* (New York: Knopf, 1965), 135.
30. Boxer, *The Dutch Seaborne Empire*, 134.
31. Lack and Van Kley, *Asia in the Making of Europe*, 274.
32. Leon van den Broeke, "The Composition of Reformed Church Orders: A Theological, Reformed and Juridical Perspective," *In die Skriflig/In Luce Verbi* 52, no. 2 (2018), https://doi.org/10.4102/ids.v52i2.2351.

something as central to the church as one of its two sacraments and provided the state with power normally held by classes.[33]

The DCO was also not applicable in the VOC's colony at the Cape of Good Hope, yet precisely how the church was governed there was never explicitly stated. What is clear, however, is that while "the Classis of Amsterdam, which was responsible for all the overseas churches, did follow the DCO," the company only allowed ministers in the colonies "to correspond with a classis if the classis were involved in a matter, but the classis served only as an advisory role."[34] In other words, the Classis of Amsterdam may have been the only Dutch classis looking out for the church in South Africa, but it nevertheless lacked the formal power to control it. These ambiguities did not immediately produce conflict, but they did lead in the early eighteenth century to the question as to whether any existing church order was operative in the South African colony. One Dutch minister even wondered if the Batavian Church Order of 1643 might apply to South Africa, which by extension suggests that the DCO might not. Another Dutch minister serving in South Africa in 1710 answered in the negative, arguing that "The Church Order can easily be found in the Acts and Post-Acts of the Synod of Dordt." Nevertheless, the colony's governing authority was not convinced that the Church Order of Batavia did not apply, so officials specifically inquired of the VOC whether the colonial church should follow the DCO or the 1643 Batavian Church Order. The answer was not self-evident, so the VOC took the question under advisement but ultimately never clarified the situation. This has led one historian of the church in South Africa to forcefully maintain that "It must... be clearly understood that the Church Order of Dordt was never officially accepted as a church order for the church at the Cape."[35] Neither did the DCO obtain in the colony by default. The Dutch at the Cape therefore determined for themselves how to apply the principles of Dort in a local context, even if that meant that they had no formal church order at all.

In Brazil, no separate church order was created, although the ministers did create their own broader church councils to better control the development of the church. They first established a classis, and, after splitting it in two, a synod. The Dutch church councils did not gainsay the Brazilian ministers the right to create their own classis, although they did dispute their right to create a synod without approval from patria. They may have suggested as such not primarily on principle but because they considered it impolitic to create a synod, since it might have given WIC officials a greater role in church governance than some Dutch Reformed ministers considered advisable. The Classis of Amsterdam nevertheless did dispute the full independence and legitimacy of the colonial classis, claiming that even if the classis existed, it lacked full classical rights, particularly the right to ordain.

33. *ERSNY*, 3380.
34. Coertzen, "Dordt and South Africa: Church and State Relations," 145, 144.
35. Pieter Coertzen, "Dordt and South Africa. The Nature and Challenges for Reformed Church Polity in South Africa," *Nederduitse Gereformeerde Teologiese Tydskrif* 53, nos. 3 & 4 (September/ December 2012): 82–83.

Although the Brazilian classis ultimately decided not to conduct ordinations except when absolutely necessary, the colonial ministers never conceded the point to Amsterdam. While Noorlander takes the position of Amsterdam by arguing that the Classis of Brazil "didn't enjoy the autonomy of other classes. It was an ecclesiastical curiosity, a classis by name but still subject to its Amsterdam and Walcheren counterparts,"[36] the historian of the Dutch Reformed in Brazil, Frans Schalkwijk, argues differently. Considering the situation from the Brazilian perspective, Schalkwijk forcefully maintains, "There can be no gainsaying about it; there functioned in Brazil an authentic classis of the Christian Reformed Church," one independently created by the Brazilian ministers without any approval from abroad.[37]

These divergent scenarios demonstrate that just as Reformed groups throughout Europe created a variety of church orders, Dutch ministers both in the fatherland and the colonies understood that distinct church orders could be created in Dutch colonies according to the political and social contexts of their time and place, even without approval from patria. Clearly, the DCO did not apply in Batavia, Brazil, or the Cape of Good Hope either by definition or default, and neither did any Dutch classis have formal power over the church in any of those colonies. This is not to say that Dutch ministers, classes, or synods in the Netherlands did not try to use their informal influence to affect colonial affairs, which they did with some success, but informal influence is not equivalent to formal ecclesiastical power. Although these governance issues were not explicitly addressed in New Netherland, the situation in North America was similar to those in other colonies, as is revealed in the events surrounding the Rev. Wilhelmus Grasmeer and his unwillingness to behave.

The Rise of the Congregation in New Netherland

Wilhelmus Grasmeer was born around 1621, the son of Machtelt Willemse Steengen, who became a widow after Grasmeer's father died when their only son was just a child.[38] Machtelt soon remarried Johannes Megapolensis Jr., nephew of Rev. Johannes Megapolensis

36. Noorlander, *Heaven's Wrath*, 116.

37. Frans Leonard Schalkwijk, *The Reformed Church in Dutch Brazil, 1630–1654* (Zoetermeer: Boekencentrum, 1998), 88.

38. The following discussion of Grasmeer's experience and that of his family in the Netherlands is based on Bert Koopman's excellent essay, "Wilhelmus Grasmeer (1621–1678) Probleempredikant en Boltonvertaler," *Documentatieblad nadere reformatie* 42-1, no. 1 (2018): 23–40; Cor Visser, "De Familie Megapolensis van Koedijk tot Nieuw-Amsterdam," unpublished manuscript, 2008, http://docplayer.nl/19880661-De-familie-megapolensis.html#show_full_text; Cor Visser and Jan Drewes, "Indianenverhalen in Alkmaar," *Oud Alkmaar* 33, no. 2 (2009): 29–37, https://tijdschriften.archiefalkmaar.nl/issue/OAL/2009-09-01/edition/0/page/3?query=megapolensis&sort=periodicalcode%20descending&f_issuedate%5B0%5D=2000-01-01T00:00:00Z--%2B100YEARS; and Dick Mantel, "Wilhelmus Grasmeer en de Beroering in de Kerk van Graft-dijk," *De Kroniek: Historisch Tijdschrift voor Graft-de Rijp en Schermer* 29, no. 2 (June 2012): 55–61, https://tijdschriften.archiefalkmaar.nl/issue/KRO/2012-06-01/edition/null/page/1?query=megapolensis&sort=periodicalcode%20descending&f_issuedate%5B0%5D=2000-01-01T00:00:00Z--%2B100YEARS. Further information is provided in *ERSNY,* as cited below.

Sr. Megapolensis Sr. was himself a widower who had married Machtelt's also-widowed mother—Grasmeer's grandmother—Hillegont. Grasmeer's stepfather began his career as a schoolteacher, but in 1633 was ordained to the ministry when Grasmeer was twelve. When Megapolensis Jr. relocated to Rensselaerswijck, Grasmeer remained behind. He began preaching in the village of Graftdijk in the Classis of Alkmaar, and the congregation called him as its minister the following year. In 1646, he married Ida Joose Twisch, but the marriage quickly became turbulent. Ida claimed that Grasmeer was verbally abusive, and rumors spread that he abused alcohol. By 1648, the two were living separately, a situation that "violat[ed] the matrimonial obligation to live under one roof."[39]

The Classis of Alkmaar learned of this separation in 1648 when Grasmeer sought its assistance in a dispute between himself and one of his elders, Willem Claessen, who had apparently commented disapprovingly about the minister's separation. Grasmeer did not take kindly to such criticism, and he shot back that Claessen was a liar and a hypocrite not worthy of the office of elder. Grasmeer approached his classis to gain support against Claessen, but his choice backfired. The classis deemed Grasmeer's refusal to live with his wife unacceptable and directed him to return to her side. The classis also ordered him to humble himself by publicly apologizing to Claessen from the pulpit. Grasmeer likely complied with the second directive. He did not return home.

The conflict escalated when Ida went before the classis in 1649, claiming that her husband had used very harsh words against her, while she had always been peaceful and accommodating. Ida hoped for classical intervention; Grasmeer hoped to steer any attempts to resolve his domestic disputes away from the already-disapproving classis, suggesting that it would be more appropriate for his consistory to address the issue. His consistory disagreed, leaving it in classical hands. Because a minister's marital separation was particularly worrisome, the classis convened a special committee of six ministers and an elder to address the situation. The committee met with Grasmeer and Ida, each with his or her own advocates; Grasmeer came to the meeting with Rev. Johannes Megapolensis Sr. (his step-grandfather), while Ida was accompanied by her parents. Grasmeer attempted to apologize; Ida rebuffed him. Not sensing that reconciliation was immanent, the committee recessed. When they returned, Ida remained unwilling to accept her husband's apologies, bemoaning that his words had cut too deeply. It is impossible to determine to what extent Ida was indeed a victim of spousal abuse. Even if her husband had been verbally abusive, she gave as good as she got. In the course of the hearings, she snidely remarked that a stint in the East Indies might change his behavior. Grasmeer took this to mean that his apologies had fallen on deaf ears.

---

39. Ariadne Schmidt and Manon van der Heijden note that while legal separation "from bed and board" was possible in the seventeenth century (requiring notarial and judicial involvement), divorce was only available if a spouse committed adultery or desertion. Nevertheless, "couples might decide to break up without judicial intervention—thereby violating the matrimonial obligation to live under one roof" (Ariadne Schmidt and Manon van der Heijden, "Women Alone in Early Dutch Towns," *Journal of Urban History* 42, no. 1 (January 2016): 32).

The classis could not let the separation continue and charged Grasmeer with resolving the conflict. The classis subjected him to church discipline, censuring him and barring him from communion, further declaring that until he publicly demonstrated his repentance and reconciled with his wife, he would be suspended from his ministerial duties. If he did not reconcile, he might even be deposed from his position permanently, leaving him without a livelihood. In short, the classis told Grasmeer to find a way to live with his wife—or else.

Although the classis condemned Grasmeer for the marital conflict, those closer to the couple were less quick to assume his guilt. Johannes Megapolensis Sr., a respected minister and teacher, stood by Grasmeer when he was called before the Alkmaar committee.[40] Later, Megapolensis Sr. violated the discipline imposed by the Classis of Alkmaar by allowing his step-grandson to preach in his own congregation. Grasmeer also had vigorous advocates in his grandmother Hillegont (wife of Megapolensis Sr.) and his mother Machtelt (wife of Megapolensis Jr.), who had returned to patria before her husband's contract with the Van Rensselaer family had expired. Machtelt composed and had printed a harsh critique of the Classis of Alkmaar for its treatment of her son, which the classis considered slanderous. Hillegont apparently agreed with her daughter Machtelt and distributed the pamphlet around the town of Alkmaar.

Grasmeer also found support in his congregation, which protested to the classis that its acts were unjustified, particularly its suspension of Grasmeer from the ministry, as they found no fault in his behavior or his doctrine. Annoyed that Grasmeer's congregation had challenged its authority, the classis told the congregation that its decision stood. Ironically, the classis vigorously punished Grasmeer for the supposedly poor example he set for his congregation, which nevertheless clearly respected and did not want to lose him. Still, the classis had to hold its ministers to very high behavioral standards. They simply would not countenance marital separation and attempted to use church discipline to motivate Grasmeer to alter his course. Much to the chagrin of the classis, Grasmeer refused to bend and left town without the required prior approval from his classis. He did receive a dismissal from his congregation, which was also required, but its validity was open to question.[41]

After the classis learned that Grasmeer had left his post, it summoned him on April 16, 1650, declaring that if he did not appear, he would be considered a "deserter who abandons his church in violation of proper order."[42] Grasmeer refused to attend a hearing, as he believed that the die had already been cast. He railed, "And what should I do before you? Already you show, by forbidding me to preach, what you mean to do, did I come. Therefore I propose not to appear before you. Do and act in such a way that you may be able

---

40. Megapolensis Sr. taught two ministers sent by the Classis of Amsterdam to the New World, his nephew Johannes Megapolensis Jr. and Johannes Backerus, who served first in Guiana and then briefly in New Amsterdam as a supply minister after Rev. Everardus Bogardus's death and before Megapolensis Jr. took over the Manhattan charge (Cor Visser, "De Familie Megapolensis").
41. *ERSNY*, 271–73, 275, 283.
42. *ERSNY*, 274.

to vindicate yourselves before God and unprejudiced parties. Farewell."[43] He nevertheless disputed the assertion that he had abandoned his charge, claiming that his consistory had provided a legitimate certificate of dismissal.[44] Still, he knew that a classical dismissal was also required, and the classis certainly would not have supplied one given his suspension. His choices left the classis with no option but to impose the ultimate punishments, officially removing him from office on April 26, 1650, and excommunicating him soon after, an act later approved by the Synod of North Holland.[45] While the Classis of Alkmaar had initially threatened to remove him for leaving his wife, the classis ultimately deposed and excommunicated him for willfully challenging church order by leaving his post without its approval.

While Grasmeer's consistorial dismissal was indeed invalid, given that it had not been approved by the Classis of Alkmaar, the classis was also infuriated by its tone. The document condemned the classis so harshly that they assumed that Grasmeer had dictated it and manipulated his consistory into signing it. According to the Classis of Amsterdam, which later reviewed the certificate, "The style of this, in exaltation of himself, is so extravagant, and so slanderous in reference to the entire Classis [of Alkmaar], that it is a very shame, and is loathsome in the judgment of all fairminded persons." Alkmaar further concluded that the consistory had given Grasmeer a certificate of dismissal "in simplicity," suggesting that he had tricked the church elders into providing it.[46] Alkmaar's conclusion was likely erroneous, as his consistory had supported their minister all along.

Even before Grasmeer's formal deposition, rumors spread that he planned to flee to New Netherland to seek a call there. Grasmeer later claimed that the idea to go to New Netherland was not originally his own but that of his mother, who suggested that he seek his stepfather's former position in Rensselaerswijck.[47] That position had been vacant for more than two years, as the new patroon (Kiliaen's eldest son Johan), his guardians, and the partners in the patroonship had not, for financial reasons, sent a replacement. By January 1650, the Classis of Amsterdam had finally convinced those involved in the patroonship to send another minister, but nothing further was accomplished because "They must now, first ascertain, however, where the salary for a pastor is to come from." The guardians planned to consult with the director of the patroonship, presumably to inquire whether the colonists themselves could provide a minister's salary.[48] In short, it would have appeared to both Machtelt and Grasmeer that the patroon and the Classis of Amsterdam were unlikely to send a new minister to the Rensselaerswijck congregation, leaving it bereft of pastoral care and presenting Grasmeer the opportunity to seek the position by circumventing formal channels.

---

43. *ERSNY*, 275.
44. *ERSNY*, 275.
45. *ERSNY*, 283–84.
46. *ERSNY*, 284, 286–87.
47. *ERSNY*, 301.
48. *ERSNY*, 225, 230–31, 237–39, 242–44, 246, 249, 251–52, 261–63, 264–66 (quote at 265).

Amsterdam quickly condemned Grasmeer's intentions, which countered its attempts to control the colonial church, and endeavored to thwart him in his path. In March 1650, the deputies of the Classis of Amsterdam noted that Grasmeer was intending to migrate to New Netherland, and asked "whether the Patroons of Rensselaerswyck, present in this city [of Amsterdam], and also the church of Manhattan in New Netherland ought not to be warned against him in that he will arrive there without an ecclesiastical certificate? Otherwise they may put too great confidence in him, and cause offence and disquietude in the church there."[49] The classis agreed and ordered the deputies to make it so.[50] They then contacted Wouter van Twiller, former director of New Netherland and guardian of the new patroon Johan, who wrote to Gerrit Vastrick, a member of the Council of New Netherland, who in turn transmitted a copy of a portion of the letter to the Court of Rensselaerswijck. On August 4, 1650, the secretary of the court entered that excerpt into its records, which stated that

> The son-in-law of Megapolensis, who has been a minister here and who was forbidden to preach by the Classis of Alkmaer, goes over with the same ship. In case he should attempt to perform any church service in the colony, we order Director [of the patroonship] Slichtenhorst not to employ him thereto or to tolerate him in the colony, about which we shall write him personally if time will permit it. And Whereas we have been requested by the Deputies of the Classis of Amsterdam to make this known here, we hereby order the director and commissioners of our colony to carry out our instructions in this matter.[51]

The classis sent a similar letter to the Manhattan consistory, "warn[ing] that you do not allow him to officiate in any of the duties of the ministerial office, if perchance he should so desire, until he shall have rendered satisfaction to the Classis of Alckmaer, and be lawfully called to such service," even though as an independent congregation, Manhattan had no power to restrain either Grasmeer or the Rensselaerswijck congregation.[52]

Grasmeer may not have known of these attempts to thwart his scheme, but knowing that the Rensselaerswijck congregation appeared to be on its own, the stepson of their former minister arrived on the congregation's stoop in late summer 1650. The congregation immediately called him to serve without consulting any classis, even though the DCO required classical approval of all calls. They apparently did not consider such approval

---

49. *ERSNY*, 271–72.
50. *ERSNY*, 272.
51. Arnold J. F. Van Laer, trans. and ed., *Minutes of the Court of Rensselaerswyck: 1648–1652* (Albany: State University of New York Press, 1922), 125. There is some question as to the authenticity of the original text, as Vastrick submitted only his own handwritten extract from the original letter and would not let the court compare his extract with the original. Nevertheless, this extract does seem to comport with the intent of the Classis of Amsterdam (Van Laer, *Minutes of the Court: 1648–1652*, 125–26).
52. *ERSNY*, 272–73.

necessary, possibly because their congregation was outside the geographic bounds of all Dutch classes. They also agreed to provide his salary directly, which was at variance with traditional practices; in the Netherlands, ministerial salaries were paid by the state, and in New Netherland, by the company or the patroon serving as the state (although both were hoping to shift that responsibility to the colonists in light of growing financial woes).[53] Importantly, no one in the colony did anything to restrain either the congregation or Grasmeer, not the Manhattan consistory, New Netherland Director-General Stuyvesant, nor Van Slichtenhorst, the on-site director of the patroonship.

It is unclear whether the congregation knew when they hired Grasmeer that he had been deposed and excommunicated, but they learned soon enough. Nonetheless, the congregation did nothing, possibly because of what they may have seen as conflicting information. Although Amsterdam informed the colonists that Grasmeer was "under censure" and had been "forbidden to preach," the minister came with two certificates that indirectly suggested that he could be lawfully called to serve another congregation. These included the previously mentioned certificate from his former consistory, which the classes incorrectly believed to have been fraudulent. He also had a letter from a minister from Alkmaar, which seems to have suggested that Grasmeer had been formally and honorably dismissed by the Classis of Alkmaar, which was nevertheless not the case.[54]

It is also possible that Grasmeer intentionally misled the colonists as to the meaning of these certificates, as he later offered a bald-faced lie to the Classis of Amsterdam as to why he thought they were sufficient. He later argued that he left Graftdijk "with the consent of his people but as no full Classis was going to be held there at that time, he had not been able to obtain a proper dismission from the same, nor to take with him a full certificate. He had therefore contented himself with private testimonials from his church and from one of the ministers of Alkmaer."[55] Why Grasmeer thought Amsterdam would accept such a falsehood is incomprehensible, as Amsterdam knew what had actually transpired. Still, whatever he told the Rensselaerswijck congregation initially, it did not dismiss him even after it received further information from Amsterdam, choosing instead to follow its own independent path.

Amsterdam not only asserted Grasmeer's ineligibility, the Dutch ministers also called his character into question by first informing the Manhattan congregation that he had separated from his wife, and later informing the Rensselaerswijck congregation directly.[56] It is hard to imagine that his separation would not have troubled the colonists and that they would not have questioned Grasmeer on this point. We do not know how he might have

---

53. *ERSNY*, 290; George L. Smith, *Religion and Trade in New Netherland: Dutch Origins and American Development* (Ithaca, NY: Cornell University Press, 1973), 44; Noorlander, *Heaven's Wrath*, 194–99, 209–10.

54. It is likely that the minister, Rev. Johannes Knyf, only provided the certificate because Grasmeer had suggested that he intended to make things right with his classis before he left for North America, which he decidedly did not do. *ERSNY*, 283–84, 286–87, 289–93.

55. *ERSNY*, 301.

56. *ERSNY*, 272–73, 289–93.

responded, but we can reasonably assume that the colonists in Rensselaerswijck were no fools. Every marital dispute has two sides, and obviously Grasmeer could provide only half of the story. Nevertheless, the classis's condemnation of his marital separation never motivated the congregation to dismiss him, as they chose to judge for themselves whether he was a worthy minister.

When the Classis of Amsterdam learned that the Rensselaerswijck congregation called Grasmeer in spite of its commands and warnings, the classis engaged in another round of character assassination. The classis wrote the congregation that Grasmeer was "guilty of domestic quarreling, abandonment of his wife, drunkenness, and, other great faults."[57] Because of his behavior, he "has not only been suspended by the Classis of Alkmaer from his ministry, but also, since he has treated said censure with contempt and disgraceful insult, and has continued without legal dismission from his church, that he has been deposed from all ecclesiastical functions."[58] In total, he is "a person so unworthy; for by his evil conduct he has unfitted himself for so hallowed a service."[59] As much as Amsterdam attacked Grasmeer, the Dutch ministers feigned to condemn the congregation, noting that "We perceive in your conduct, your zeal to establish the service of the divine word among you, and we rejoice in this. Indeed, it cannot well be otherwise, than that they, who have had a real taste of the preaching of the Holy Gospel, and the use of the Holy Ordinances of God, should retain the desire to be edified and strengthened by the same means, even by the service in their most holy faith."[60] The classis also absolved the congregation for having accepted Grasmeer's dismissals as authentic and sufficient, suggesting that the congregation "ha[d] been drawn into your course by some persons in a sinister way."[61] The classis therefore hoped that

> These matters being duly considered by you, will enable you to perceive that we have great reasons to urge, and which we do with the full approbation of the Patroon of the colony of Rensselaerswyck, the removal from your midst of so irregular a person from the holy service of the church; and we earnestly *request* [emphasis added] you herewith to separate yourselves immediately from such a minister. For he is deposed from the right to perform any church ministrations, and possesses no right whatever to preach God's word among you, or to administer the sacraments.[62]

To gain support, the classis sent a similar letter to the Manhattan consistory, even though it had no formal power to enforce its will on another congregation.[63] Importantly, the Classis of Amsterdam never ordered the Rensselaerswijck congregation to do anything; rather,

57. *ERSNY*, 290.
58. *ERSNY*, 290–91.
59. *ERSNY*, 290.
60. *ERSNY*, 290.
61. *ERSNY*, 290.
62. *ERSNY*, 291–92.
63. *ERSNY*, 293–95.

they simply requested that they set Grasmeer aside. Perhaps the classis believed a light touch would be more effective than a heavy-handed order, but the classis also understood the limits of its power.

Once again, the colonists of Rensselaerswijck ignored the Amsterdam ministers who sat in judgment three thousand miles away. Rather, they viewed Grasmeer in the same light as had his congregation in Graftdijk. Neither congregation perceived him as being "evil" or "unworthy," regardless of what the classes had said or done. Neither did Director Van Slichtenhorst, Director General Stuyvesant, nor the Manhattan congregation abandon him. In fact, Grasmeer later received "testimonials, both of the church of Rensselaerswyck as well as of New Amsterdam in New Netherland, which were praiseworthy."[64] Stuyvesant also later recommended Grasmeer to the directors of the WIC.[65]

We cannot know precisely why the Rensselaerswijck congregation ignored the classis's directives. Perhaps they knew that the classis had little power to control the congregation's actions, especially when neither Stuyvesant nor Van Slichtenhorst supported the classis's demands. They also probably realized that Grasmeer was likely their only choice, as it did not appear that the Classis of Amsterdam was ever going to be able to provide another minister. The classis did indicate in 1651 that the patroon had finally agreed to send a replacement, but because it was still unclear how a new minister's salary would be paid, this was less than a guarantee.[66] Still, whatever motivated the Rensselaerswijck congregation to ignore the classis, the important point is that the colonists ultimately believed that they had the independent right to do as they pleased.

While it is likely that Grasmeer did have character flaws, the heart of the classis's attempt to prevent him from seeking a colonial call was ultimately to prevent the colonial congregation from acting independently. To put this another way, the Classis of Amsterdam's only method to prevent congregations from acting independently was to control the ministers themselves, as its power over the colonial church was restricted both by the geographic organization of the church and the fact that the DCO was not operative in the colonies. And clearly, ecclesiastical order was Amsterdam's primary concern, a point they repeatedly made, as the classis deemed classical authority essential to the development of the American church. As the classis forcefully maintained to Grasmeer, "We can not, and we will not, allow all ecclesiastical order to be violated, by tolerating you in this service."[67] The classis used a softer tone with the Rensselaerswijck congregation, but the point was the same. After learning of Rensselaerswijck's calling Grasmeer, the classis noted that "We heartily wish that

---

64. *ERSNY*, 301–02.
65. *ERSNY*, 307–08.
66. *ERSNY*, 287, 292. The classis had indeed found another minister, Jacobus Beth van der Burg, although the classis was not so precise in their communications with Rensselaerswijck. However, Van der Burg never served in New Netherland; the minister who ultimately followed Grasmeer was Gideon Schaats.
67. *ERSNY*, 289.

our warnings, which we sent you in good conscience, and only to preserve sound order in God's Church, had been better heeded."[68] The classis further remarked upon the danger that arose from the congregation's choice to accept one who did not follow church order, urging them to "Act ye accordingly, so that all things may be done decently and in order in the house of God, that all confusion may be warded off from the churches, and good discipline may be exercised and maintained, in conformity to the word of God."[69] The classis also warned that "it would be nothing else than a notorious infraction of all lawful order, yea, an open violation of ecclesiastical discipline, should you determine to retain such a person among you in the holy service of the church."[70] The classis therefore informed the congregation that they would not countenance Grasmeer's defiance, and that they aimed to "use every means in our power, in case he does not willingly desist, to remove him. We will do this that God's holy name be not blasphemed, your church demoralized, and the good order and discipline of the church be trampled under foot."[71] Importantly, the classis indicated that Grasmeer—not the congregation—must desist. The classis spoke similarly to the Manhattan consistory, noting that if Grasmeer was to find a charge, it "would be in violation of the order of the Synod, and cause great offence here."[72] The classis explained, "Hence we could not remain inactive; but in order to secure the performance of everything decently and in order, in the house of God, and to prevent all confusion, and that good discipline, conformably to God's word, may be exercised and maintained, we have been obliged to secure the removal of Rev. Grasmeer from the sacred church service, until he return to the Fatherland and be properly released from his deposition."[73] The classis further remarked to the Manhattan consistory, "[We p]ra[y] that our mutual cooperation in the maintenance of the good order and discipline of our church may increase more and more."[74]

In spite of the classis's attempts to encourage the Rensselaerswijck congregation to take a different path, the congregation chose to act in a congregational rather than in a presbyterial-synodal way. This is not to say that the Rensselaerswijck congregation wanted to be independent—the record is silent on that point—but it nevertheless was, since it was not, nor could not be, a constituent member of the Classis of Amsterdam or any Dutch classis. Ultimately that is what made the Classis of Amsterdam so anxious for the future of the colonial church and so vigorous in its attempts to shut down Grasmeer's attempts to serve in the colony. If ministers and congregations acted and governed themselves in a congregational way, dismissing classical oversight and support, the future of the church itself was at stake. The Classis of Amsterdam was deeply troubled by this possibility, which they

---

68. *ERSNY*, 290.
69. *ERSNY*, 292.
70. *ERSNY*, 291.
71. *ERSNY*, 292.
72. *ERSNY*, 273.
73. *ERSNY*, 294.
74. *ERSNY*, 295.

believed placed the American church at grave risk. If they did not stop Grasmeer from de-fying church order, others might follow, giving American congregations the opportunity to act independently of higher ecclesiastical authority, which might leave the colonial church in tatters. The classis simply could not stand idly by and watch the church drift into chaos.

This is not to say that what had precipitated Grasmeer's choice to flee to New Nether-land was irrelevant to the Classis of Amsterdam. He had inappropriately separated from his wife. He had quarreled publicly. He had had been accused of drunkenness. According to Amsterdam, he had lied and manipulated his congregations and his fellow ministers. From such a perspective, Amsterdam claimed that he had lived "an evil and offensive life"[75] and was "unworthy" and "unfit" to be a minister.[76] Yet, the Classes of Amsterdam and Alkmaar did not indicate that he was too "evil" to return to the fold. If he returned home, reunited with his wife, and apologized to the Classis of Alkmaar, he would again be eligible to ac-cept a call. As the classis wrote to the New Amsterdam congregation, they had attempted "to secure the removal of Rev. Grasmeer from the sacred church service, *until* he return to the Fatherland and be properly released from his deposition" [emphasis added].[77] Am-sterdam even held out the possibility of Grasmeer's return to Rensselaerswijck, imploring the congregation to "Place the said Grasmeer [to] one side, and exhort him to return to the Fatherland by the first opportunity, that he may purge himself according to the Order of the Church."[78] His unworthiness was therefore only provisional. It is important to note, however, that proper order was not just a matter of principle, as Dutch Reformed church order both reflected and preserved God's will for His people, such that church order never existed simply for the sake of itself.

It is unknown whether the congregation encouraged Grasmeer to return to the Netherlands, yet neither did his congregation ever separate from him, such that the fun-damental independence of congregations in the colonies was never challenged. Still, the Classes of Amsterdam and Alkmaar did finally get their way, as Grasmeer returned home in late summer or early fall 1651 to resolve his situation, although doing so was ultimately his decision.[79] When he finally came before Alkmaar in November 1651, he acknowledged that he should not have sought a call in New Netherland given that he was under classical discipline. He nevertheless requested that his punishment be abrogated so that he could return to New Netherland, where he hoped to become the second minister in Manhat-tan alongside his stepfather. He further noted that he had received positive testimonials from the Rensselaerswijck congregation, as well as from the director and Council of New Netherland. Alkmaar agreed to remove the discipline only if he stipulated that it had been just, and if he made every effort to reunite with his wife. The classis also demanded that he

---

75. *ERSNY*, 283.
76. *ERSNY*, 290.
77. *ERSNY*, 294.
78. *ERSNY*, 292.
79. *ERSNY*, 301.

explain his contribution to his mother's libelous publication, if any. He refused to do the latter, but the classis gave him time to reconsider. By January 1652, he had become more contrite, such that he was finally willing to sign a confession of his guilt for all of which he was accused. The Classis of Alkmaar thereupon released him from discipline and recommended that he be sent to serve in New Netherland once again.[80] Amsterdam was surprised by Alkmaar's willingness to bring Grasmeer back within the fold so easily, but then again, Amsterdam was worried about more than just one difficult minister. For Amsterdam, the future of the colonial church itself was at stake.[81]

In order to effect his final reconciliation with the Dutch ecclesiastical establishment, Grasmeer had reconciled with his wife by April 1652 and presented himself to his synod in August 1652. Again, he was less than contrite. As the synod noted,

> He did in part, deny [the charges] in the face of all the facts; and as for the rest, he covered them up with groundless excuses, evasions, and glossings over; and on the whole made so meager and hesitating a confession, that the Rev. Synod resolved that he should have time for further reflection; with the admonition to confess his sins unfeignedly and without any reservation; and to promise in this Synod, and in the presence of the Lord, to conduct himself in the future as his Christian profession and the sacred ministry demands.[82]

With the possibility of a job in New Amsterdam in the balance, he "promised that he would always speak in honor of the Rev. Synod and the Rev. Classis of Alkmaer in reference to the procedures taken against him, and that henceforth he would conduct himself as becomes a pious and godly minister, walking worthy of the Gospel, and the sacred ministry." Even though he had so hesitatingly declared his wrongdoing and had needed much prompting to confess his guilt, the synod did remove his punishment, allowing him to seek a call.[83] Ultimately, Grasmeer did not return to New Netherland, due to the danger arising from war between the Netherlands and England. He instead accepted a call in 1653 from the congregation in Ursem, in the Classis of Hoorn, where he served until his death in 1678. Maybe Grasmeer had a harsh tongue, and maybe he drank too much. Maybe he was not sufficiently deferential to his ministerial peers. Still, as long as he followed church order and remained with his wife, he was worthy of serving as God's minister. And if colonial ministers followed the DCO as closely as they could and retained ties to a Dutch classis, then at least the independent congregations in North America would not have the opportunity to hire illegitimate or inappropriate ministers.

Historians have paid little attention to Grasmeer, presumably because he atypically

---

80. *ERSNY*, 301–02.
81. *ERSNY*, 302.
82. *ERSNY*, 312.
83. *ERSNY*, 313.

chose to act outside the DCO and because his service in New Netherland was so brief.[84] He was therefore an outlier who had no lasting effect on New Netherland. To some extent this is true. Yet the Grasmeer affair is significant because it reveals that the formal power of the Classis of Amsterdam, or any classis, did not unequivocally extend to the New Nether land congregations. The particular power of Amsterdam in relation to New Netherland was based only on informal agreements made in the Netherlands, and such power could not be formally imposed as it would have created an ecclesiastical hierarchy that was contrary to ecclesiastical egalitarianism, an essential principle of Dutch Reformed church polity. While a Dutch classis might legitimately aim to restrain a minister such as Grasmeer, who was formally barred from the ministry, it could not touch congregational independence in the colonies. All of the involved parties understood this, as no one—not the Classis of Amsterdam, the Synod of North Holland, the patroon, nor the director general and Council of New Netherland—ever even remotely suggested that the Rensselaerswijck congregation did not have the right to independently call its own minister.

While the particular actions of both the Rensselaerswijck congregation and Grasmeer were atypical, their choice to act independently was certainly not unique, neither before nor after the English conquest. In 1654, three Long Island congregations called the Rev. Johannes Polhemus without the formal approval of the Classis of Amsterdam after he had lost his charge in Brazil following its fall to Portugal.[85] The Acquackanonk congregation sent the tailor Guiliam Bertholf to Europe for ordination in 1693, where he was ordained not by Amsterdam but by the Classis of Walcheren in Zeeland, which also approved his call.[86] The Schenectady congregation similarly called Rev. Bernardus Freerman in 1700, who had been recently ordained by the Classis of Lingen in Westphalia for the church in Albany, even though a call to one congregation could not be simply transferred to another without classical approval. That approval was never even sought.[87] While both Bertholf and Freerman were pietistic artisans who lacked academic training and whom Amsterdam would likely have refused to ordain, American congregations and ministers viewed any classical ordination as sufficient for service in North America, even if that meant that some American ministers had no relationship with the Classis of Amsterdam.[88]

---

84. See n.10.

85. *ERSNY,* 87, 110, 330, 332, 334–39, 345–47, 350–51, 364–69, 416–17, 424, 441, 444; Charles T. Gehring, trans. and ed., *Council Minutes: 1652–1654* (Baltimore: Genealogical Publishing Co., 1983), 185; Charles T. Gehring, trans. and ed., *Council Minutes: 1655–1656* (Syracuse, NY: Syracuse University Press, 1995), 70, 285–86; Charles T. Gehring, trans. and ed., *Correspondence: 1654–1658,* (Syracuse, NY: Syracuse University Press, 2003), 52; Heywood Peck, "The Rev. Johannes Theodorus Polhemius and Some of His Descendants," *New York Genealogical and Biographical Records* 90, no. 3 (1959): 171–72.

86. *ERSNY,* 1067, 1072–73, 1100; Kennedy, "Guiliam Bertholf," 197–216.

87. *ERSNY,* 1371–73, 1384–85, 1469–72, 1532–37; Mouw, "Moederkerk and Vaderland," 220–25.

88. Bertholf and Freerman were some of the last uneducated individuals—known as "Dutch clerics"—ordained to the ministry in the Dutch Reformed church. Fred van Lieburg, "Preachers between Inspiration and Instruction: Dutch Reformed Ministers without Academic Education (Sixteenth–Eighteenth Centuries)," *Nederlands archief voor kerkgeschiedenis/Dutch Review of Church History* 83 (2003): 166–90.

Some eighteenth-century American congregations also continued to consider themselves fundamentally independent of all classical authority, as had both the Classis of Amsterdam and the Rensselaerswijck congregation during the Grasmeer affair. As such, they felt comfortable selecting their own ministers, even those who had not even been ordained in the Dutch Reformed church. For example, the Kinderhook and Claverack congregations called the Rev. Johannes van Driessen in 1727, who had been ordained by the Congregationallst ministers at Yale after having been denied ordination by the Classis of Amsterdam in part because he had submitted fraudulent documents concerning his education. Johannes van Driessen was later called by the Acquackanonk congregation in New Jersey in 1735.[89] Although the Classis of Amsterdam did not accept Johannes's ordination as legitimate, some American congregations certainly did, and perceived themselves competent to make their own decisions and act on them. Similarly, the Dutch Reformed congregation of Tappan called the Rev. Fredericus Muzelius, a German Reformed minister from Kroppach, Germany, in 1727, who did not develop a relationship with Amsterdam for another ten years.[90] Another German Reformed minister, George Wilhelmus Mancius, was called to serve Dutch congregations in Schraalenburg and Paramus, New Jersey (1730), and Kingston, New York (1732), without any involvement of the Classis of Amsterdam.[91]

There is also the case of Rev. Johannes Henricus Goestchius, who was ordained in 1748 and soon called by several Long Island congregations. The principal minister involved in his ordination was Rev. Petrus Dorsius, who had been sent by the Classis of Schieland in Rotterdam to serve a Dutch Reformed congregation in Pennsylvania. Dorsius claimed that the teachings of the extremely influential Dutch Reformed minister Rev. Gisbertus Voetius supported his power to ordain, as Voetius suggested that one minister might ordain another in areas outside of classical authority. Dorsius also suggested that he had been authorized to conduct ordinations by the Classis of Schieland, although that had not actually been the case. Nevertheless, a number of New York ministers considered it possible that he had indeed been given such authorization by a classis other than that of Amsterdam.[92] While the ordinations of Johannes van Driessen and Johannes Henricus Goetschius were contested by some colonial ministers and the Classis of Amsterdam, the point is that some American congregations and ministers claimed or simply proceeded as if the power of neither the DCO nor the Classis of Amsterdam extended to them. Each of these situations was far more complex than can be explored here. Each was also unique, yet together they reveal

---

89. *ERSNY*, 2176, 2389, 2564, 2571–73, 2580–81, 2606–08, 2610–12; Kenneth Shefsiek, *Set in Stone: Creating and Commemorating a Hudson Valley Culture* (Albany: State University of New York Press, 2017), 144–45.

90. Matthias Dahlhoff, *Geschichte der Grafschaft Sayn und der Bestandtheile derselben* (Dillenberg: E. Weidenbach, 1874), 265, http://ahnen.volkh.de/stammbaum/pafg18.htm#679; David Cole, *The History of the Reformed Church of Tappan, N.Y.* (New York: Stettiner, Lambert & Co., 1894), 21–23.

91. *ERSNY*, 2601–02, 2606–07; Mouw, "Moederkerk and Vaderland," 248.

92. Kenneth Shefsiek, "'Make an End to My Misery': Rev. Johannes Henricus Goetschius and the Negotiation of Authority in Eighteenth-Century Dutch New York," *de Halve Maen* 88, no. 2 (Summer 2015): 27–34. For the reference to Voetius, see *ERSNY*, 2782.

that the DCO as written did not clearly apply to any Dutch colony—not in Batavia, South Africa, nor New Netherland. By definition, neither did the Classis of Amsterdam unquestionably hold power in any colony.

The Grasmeer affair was only one of the many controversies involving church order that affected the American Dutch Reformed church in the seventeenth and eighteenth centuries. The fact that the DCO and classical power did not extend to New Netherland created an unstable environment in which the church would develop. This was understood during the New Netherland period, although the limits of the DCO and classical power in North America were forgotten following the English conquest. Still, there were those on both sides of the Atlantic who attempted to counter colonial American ecclesiastical independence, even if there was no formal way to prevent it. Such a situation ultimately became untenable, such that American ministers and congregations finally negotiated their functional independence from Amsterdam in 1772. Still, there were those who had always known, or at least argued, that that independence was not new; rather, it had existed from the very beginning.

Monuments, Legitimization Ceremonies, and Haudenosaunee Rejection of Sullivan-Clinton Markers

Andrea Lynn Smith and Nëhdöwes (Randy A. John)

As we reach the 250th anniversary of the Revolutionary War, states and civic organizations are seeking ways to commemorate the conflict. It is timely, then, to take a closer look at the granite monoliths established by New York's Education Department in 1929 to commemorate the Sullivan-Clinton Campaign of 1779. In the contemporary era, characterized by heated debates over the meaning of monuments to the Confederacy, many Americans now recognize that understandings of national historical events are not fixed but evolve over time, and that historical markers do not necessarily represent a national consensus or even a nationwide vetting, but rather more immediate local interests. As the sociologist James Loewen has argued, a full understanding of any historical marker involves two eras, that of the event being commemorated, certainly, as well as that of the marker's establishment. It is in this spirit that we explore how and why a New York agency decided to develop the Sullivan-Clinton markers in the 1920s.

The thirty-five Sullivan-Clinton monoliths identifying the paths taken by Sullivan's troops and the Native settlements they destroyed were developed as part of a multiyear celebration of the 150th anniversary (sesquicentennial) of the Revolutionary War.[1] Stylistically

Acknowledgments: A version of this article was presented by Smith at the Seneca-Iroquois National Museum on March 21, 2019, and at the Conference on Iroquois Research in Montreal, Canada, on October 5, 2019. We thank David George-Shongo, museum attendees, and conference participants, especially Jessica Dolan and Edward Countryman, for their many helpful suggestions. Devin Lander, Laurence Hauptman, Marian Leech, and an anonymous reader of this journal offered helpful suggestions on previous iterations. Smith's research has been funded by a postdoctoral grant from the Wenner-Gren Foundation for Anthropological Research, and a Richard King Mellon Fellowship, Lafayette College. James W. Loewen, *Lies Across America: What Our Historic Sites Get Wrong* (New York: New Press, 1999), 36.
1. The Haudenosaunee were known as the "Five Nations" to the English; they became the "Six Nations" with the inclusion of the Tuscaroras in the eighteenth century. The French called them the "Iroquois."

they resemble other historical markers of the era, and, moreover, as a marker series, were at the height of commemorative fashion reflecting a growth in automobile tourism. The same state committee commemorated the route Henry Knox had taken in transporting canons from Lake Champlain to Massachusetts with thirty stone markers in 1927.[2] Unlike most other Revolutionary War markers, however, the Sullivan-Clinton markers carry additional meaning, for they recognize an expedition against a Native American population. They also resemble other markers and place names across the United States that document the country's origins in violent warfare against the land's Indigenous inhabitants.

In this article, we consider the socially constructed nature of the 1929 Sullivan markers. In part due to their aura of permanence, stone markers can give a false sense of preordination, suggesting that the message they bear is the only one possible or the "correct" interpretation of the past. Passersby may assume that they reflect consensus when in fact it is usually a small group of people—wealthy benefactors or well-positioned elites—who make decisions regarding marker placement, wording, and appearance. The state-funded Sullivan-Clinton markers are no exception. We also consider this commemorative project within a wider context that includes the Haudenosaunee, exposing a relatively unknown meeting when Six Nations participation in the planned festivities was flatly refused. Finally, we introduce an often-unseen element of the wider context of the Education Department's program, a land claims case that threatened state sovereignty in much of the Haudenosaunee homeland.

New York's Invention of the Sullivan-Clinton Campaign

New York State's monuments recognizing the Sullivan-Clinton Campaign evolved almost by happenstance. In the early 1920s, while some cities like Philadelphia were gearing up for massive 150th anniversary celebrations, a similar movement did not emerge in New York until the question was raised by Utica industrialist and New York road advocate W. Pierrepont White (1857–1938).[3] In his role as president of the Mohawk Valley Historical Society, he passed a resolution in August 1922 calling on the state legislature to observe "New York State's magnificent Revolutionary record," promoting funding for an Oriskany battlefield

---

2. "Sesqui history," 139–139b. Manuscript, New York State Education Department, Division of Archives and History, General Files Relating to Observances of the 150th Anniversary of the American Revolution and other events, Series 13912-83, box 1, New York State Archives, Albany, New York (hereafter, NYSA). This paginated unpublished manuscript is stored as follows: pp. 1–139 are in 13912-83, box 1; pp. 140–290 are in 13912-00, box 2; and pp. 291 and above are in 13912-00, box 1. When possible, we include the relevant page number and "Sesqui history."

3. William Pierrepont White had made a name for himself at the turn of the century by energetically promoting New York State road construction. Albert Brigham, "Good Roads in the United States," *Bulletin of the American Geographical Society* 36, no. 12: 732–23; "Highway Pioneer Expires in Utica," *Daily Sentinel* (Rome, NY), July 11, 1938, 2.

park and celebrations of key events such as the Battle of Saratoga.[4] While it is unclear what prompted White to prepare the extensive proposal, he seemed motivated by competition with other states. He estimated other states' expenditures for their sesquicentennial ceremonies and tallied wartime battles to demonstrate that more conflicts occurred in what became New York (ninety-two) than any other state, arguing it was time the state received the recognition it deserved for its role in the nation's founding conflict.[5]

When Governor Alfred E. Smith signed a bill on May 24, 1923, granting funds ($5,000) to the New York State Historical Association (NYSHA) to report back on what a state sesquicentennial might entail, there was no consensus on which Revolutionary War-era events the state might celebrate.[6] The NYSHA committee communicated with hundreds of historical and patriotic societies across the state soliciting suggestions, and respondents proposed a remarkable 457 local historical events and sites as "worthy of recognition." By February 1924, this number had grown to 640.[7] Two years later, the Regents of the University of the State of New York formed the New York State Executive Committee of the 150th Anniversary of the American Revolution (hereafter, the "150th Committee") with the newly appointed state historian, Syracuse University European history professor, Alexander C. Flick, serving as chairman, and the supervisor of public records, Peter Nelson, serving as executive secretary, and sent it to work.[8] To assist communities in developing local programming, the state historian prepared and distributed 50,000 copies of a 371-page book, *The American Revolution in New York,* to schools, libraries, and organizations across the state, developed programming suggestions, and encouraged more than "1000 local and

---

4. "Memorial," No. 1381 to the Senate of the State of New York, February 14, 1923, Introduced by F. M. Davenport in "Sesqui history," NYSA, 3–8.
5. He pointed out that only fourteen conflicts occurred in Massachusetts over a two-year period while New York's ninety-two conflicts spanned eight years of the war. We are uncertain what constituted a conflict as the list of battles does not appear in the archival record, however, the high number may reflect the fact that much of the future state had been the stronghold of the Iroquois Confederacy. "Memorial," No. 1381, "Sesqui history," NYSA, 5.
6. "New York State, Chapter 687 of the Laws of 1923. An Act making an appropriation for a preliminary survey and report by the New York State Historical Association for the appropriate celebration of the one hundred and fiftieth anniversary of the important events of the revolutionary period." "Sesqui history," NYSA, 10.
7. Letter, July 20, 1923, from the New York State Historical Association. "Sesqui history," NYSA, 16–17.
8. The NYSHA committee first proposed an ambitious eight-year program involving the creation of a massive "Revolutionary Anniversaries Commission" with $9 million from state, federal, and local coffers. Governor Smith rejected it since it sought to create a *new* state commission at a time when the legislature had just passed a proposal to amend the state constitution to *reduce* the number of state bodies. To meet these objections, the committee regrouped and developed a much more modest, two-year plan working within existing state agencies ("Sesqui history," NYSA, 28–29). Memorandum filed with Assembly Bill, May 2, 1924, Introductory Number 1569, Printed Number 1787, signed by Alfred E. Smith ("Sesqui history," NYSA, 74). William Leland Thompson, "The Observance of the 150th Anniversary of the American Revolution in New York," *New York History* 15, no. 1 (1934): 59–65.

county historians" to play a "prominent part" in arranging local celebrations.[9] This was a massive exercise in public history making.

The Sullivan Expedition was not an initial or primary focus of the state's Revolutionary War programming. Only one paragraph of the state-published monograph was dedicated to the expedition, and it is summarized in five lines in the book's twenty-page "Chronology of New York in the Revolution."[10] As celebrations of the events of 1777 were coming to an end, however, state historian Flick began lobbying the state for funding to include the 1779 expedition in future programming, writing, "next to the Burgoyne campaign, the Sullivan expedition was the largest military operation within the Empire State during the Revolution."[11] The fact that the expedition covered so much land was significant; in his view, "both the magnitude and importance of the operation justify the observance of its sesquicentennial."[12] In his annual address to the legislature on January 4, 1928, Governor Smith repeated the geographical argument for the program, noting that previous sesquicentennial events were "restricted to the eastern, northern and central portions of the State," while "the people of the southern and western sections are interested in observing in 1929 the 150th anniversary of the Sullivan Campaign which was planned by Washington, authorized by Congress and carried out on New York soil."[13] The legislature approved $70,000 for the proposed Sullivan activities.[14]

Celebrating Washington's "Indian Expedition"

The expeditions Flick proposed to commemorate were part of General George Washington's multipronged "Indian Expedition" designed to address the increasingly devastating Indian-Tory attacks on frontier settlements.[15] After intense lobbying by Congress,

---

9. "Sesqui history," NYSA, 130; Letter to "local historian" by Alexander C. Flick, February 1, 1926, "Sesqui history," 101; Flick, "Sesqui history," 134.

10. Alexander Clarence Flick and The University of the State of New York, Division of Archives and History, *The American Revolution in New York: Its Political, Social and Economic Significance: For General Use as Part of the Program of the Executive Committee on the One Hundred and Fiftieth Anniversary of the American Revolution* (Albany: University of the State of New York, 1926), 169, 266.

11. Alexander Flick, "The Sullivan-Clinton Sesquicentennial, 1779–1929, General Significance of the Sullivan Campaign," Typed manuscript, New York Education Department, Division of Archives and History, General Files Relating to Observances of 150th Anniversary of American Revolution and other events, Series 13912-00, Box 2, Folder. "Sesqui history," NYSA, Part Two.

12. Flick, "The Sullivan-Clinton Sesquicentennial."

13. "Sesqui history," NYSA, 468.

14. Thompson, "The Observance of the 150th Anniversary," 64.

15. There are several good secondary accounts of the Sullivan Expedition. This summary is developed largely from Barbara Graymont, *The Iroquois in the American Revolution* (Syracuse, NY: Syracuse University Press, 1972), 192–93. See also Colin G. Calloway, *The American Revolution in Indian Country: Crisis and Diversity in Native American Communities* (Cambridge, UK: Cambridge University Press, 1995); Joseph Fischer, *A Well-Executed Failure: The Sullivan Campaign against the Iroquois, July–September 1779* (Columbia: University of South Carolina Press, 1997); Max M. Mintz, *Seeds of Empire: The American Revolutionary Conquest of the Iroquois* (New York:

Washington ordered the troops to destroy settlements, crops, and all stored food to force loyalist Native nations to rely on the British for their survival, ordering, "The immediate objects are the total destruction and devastation of their settlements and the capture of as many prisoners of every age and sex as possible. It will be essential to ruin their crops now in the ground and prevent their planting more."[16] Most of this destruction was carried out in the summer of 1779 by over four thousand troops under the command of General John Sullivan, who traveled into the homelands of the Iroquois Confederacy and destroyed approximately forty settlements. Classic battle strategy for the Haudenosaunee often included fleeing from their villages before attackers arrived and thus reducing human loss, as occurred in the response to Denonville's invasion of Seneca territory in 1687.[17] Because most residents fled in advance of Sullivan's armies, it is difficult to know how many Native people were killed by these expeditions. However, the destruction of dwellings, property, sustenance sources, and orchards, all carefully documented by Sullivan and in the soldiers' journals, was unfathomable.[18] Thousands of Six Nations members and their allies fled to British-held Fort Niagara where hundreds of Haudenosaunee and their allies died of famine and disease that winter, a grim, prolonged outcome of the attack designed by the future first president of the United States.[19]

It is difficult today to understand how and why one might commemorate such a complex, lengthy, and devastating mission, especially when survivors' descendants were state residents and potential audience members; this would be like celebrating the Fourth of July with the British. Iroquois nations do not celebrate this genocidal act upon their ancestors that by some accounts directly and indirectly killed roughly 50 percent of their entire population, a generalization that stands for all generations of Haudenosaunee people.[20]

New York University Press, 1999); Glenn F. Williams, *Year of the Hangman: George Washington's Campaign against the Iroquois* (Yardley, PA: Westholme Publishing, 2005).

16. Washington's full orders can be found in "From George Washington to Major General John Sullivan, 31 May 1779," *Founders Online*, National Archives, https://founders.archives.gov/documents/Washington/03-20-02-0661. Original source: Edward G. Lengel, ed., *The Papers of George Washington, Vol. 20, 8 April–31 May 1779* (Charlottesville: University of Virginia Press, 2010), 716–19. According to Article 2 of the Convention on the Prevention and Punishment of the Crime of Genocide, the Geneva Convention of 1948, genocide includes "deliberately inflicting on the group conditions of life calculated to bring about its physical destruction in whole or in part." By these standards, Washington was ordering his men to commit genocide.

17. Thomas S. Abler and Elisabeth Tooker, "Seneca," in *Handbook of North American Indians*, Vol. 15, Northeast, volume edited by Bruce G. Trigger, series edited by William C. Sturtevant, 505–17 (Washington, DC: Smithsonian Institution).

18. Soldiers' journals were published by Frederick Cook and George S. Conover, eds., *Journals of the Military Expedition of Major General John Sullivan against the Six Nations of Indians in 1779* (Auburn, NY: Knapp, Peck & Thomson, Printers, 1887).

19. Colin G. Calloway, *The Indian World of George Washington: The First President, the First Americans, and the Birth of the Nation* (New York: Oxford University Press, 2018), 53; Graymont, *The Iroquois in the American Revolution*, 242–44.

20. Kurt Jordan provides a useful table of the Seneca homes destroyed by the Sullivan Expedition in *The Seneca Restoration, 1715–1754: An Iroquois Local Political Economy* (Gainesville: University

Genocide is an explicit policy of wartime, and the atrocities are always heinous. Memories of the horror Sullivan's troops caused are found in later Haudenosaunee accounts. For instance, in 1794, the Seneca leader Cornplanter reprimanded surveyor John Adlum for making false accusations of Seneca wartime behavior, reminding him of some of the practices carried out by Sullivan's men fifteen years before:

> You in your books charge us with many things we never were guilty of—But if we were to or could write books we could tell you of things, that an Indian never practices and would be ashamed to be charged with. Whenever we treated with you at the end of a . war, there was always an article that all prisoners on both sides should be delivered up,—Did you ever deliver up any? Did you ever deliver up one? *I answer for you* NO.... Does your books tell you of Indian legs being skin[n]ed and tanned? Do your books tell you of parts of Indians being skinned, and those skins being dressed and made razor strops of? I know that all these things were done by the whites and I heard them boast of it. Does your books tell you, then an Indian ever did such a thing[?][21]

Washington's first priority was to starve the Six Nations by destroying their homes and crops, then to threaten their lives. A devaluation of human life is exemplified by the careful recording of the land and property destroyed while information on the deaths of Haudenosaunee remained unclear.

Building momentum for the 150th commemoration, Flick gave addresses across the state in 1928, and media accounts of these visits suggest he was trying to tackle some misgivings within the white community by reframing the events for public consumption.[22] One of his first tasks was the matter of branding. He wrote that although Washington and Congress had referred to the operation as the "Indian Expedition," after it was over, "it came to be known as the Sullivan Expedition," nomenclature that "endured for 150 years" (and which he had used in the 1926 state publication). He asserted that it is now "more correctly designated as the "Sullivan-Clinton Campaign"—"campaign" and not "expedition" due to its extensive geographical scope and multiple major and minor "operations."[23] General James Clinton's name was added as well, ostensibly because he was "second in

Press of Florida, 2008), Table 6.3, 189. For effort at quantifying the human and material losses, see Rhiannon Koehler, "Hostile Nations: Quantifying the Destruction of the Sullivan-Clinton Genocide of 1779," *American Indian Quarterly* 42, no. 4 (2018): 427–53.

21. Donald Kent and Merle H. Deardorff, "View of John Adlum on the Allegheny: Memoirs for the Year 1794," *Pennsylvania Magazine of History and Biography* 84, no. 4 (1960): 435–80, 459. These actions by Sullivan's soldiers have been corroborated in soldiers' journals; see Cook, *Journals of the Military Expedition*, 279. We would like to point out that they are as horrific as the Boyd and Parker tortures that are recognized by the State of New York.

22. As a head of a local Sullivan-Clinton committee reported, there was a "sobby notion I find quite prevalent ... that the Expedition represented a 'terrible thing to do to the poor Indians, etc.'" Richard Drummond to Peter Nelson, April 10, 1929, B0566 -77, NYSA.

23. "The Sullivan-Clinton Campaign in American History," 2 (typescript paper, "Sesqui history," 13912-83, NYSA).

command," personally conducting "one major and one minor movement."[24] The fact that General Clinton was the brother of the first governor of New York likely prompted this shift in nomenclature. This renaming, unique to New York, not only elevated Clinton above the other generals, but also minimized the roles played by troops from other states. Clinton led the New York brigade; leaders of the other three brigades were William Maxwell (New Jersey), Enoch Poor (New Hampshire and Massachusetts), and Edward Hand (Pennsylvania).[25] The expedition was fixed in stone as the "Sullivan-Clinton Campaign," and not the "Sullivan, Hand, Poor, Maxwell, Clinton Expedition," providing a New York-centric message. In contrast, markers established the same year in Pennsylvania commemorate a "Sullivan Expedition."

Turning a many-months-long mission of destruction into a set of "celebratory" events posed a challenge no matter what it was called. At the annual meeting of the Livingston County Historical Society in Geneseo in June 1928, Flick seemed to adopt a defensive posture. He explained that Sullivan's was of "more importance that it generally gets credit for," admitting that although Sullivan never reached Niagara as directed, he did "conquer the Indians and forever stopped their depredations" (a patently false assertion, as we address shortly). In case his audience found something distasteful about commemorating a mission of devastation, Flick told them that "next year's celebration is not to be for the commemoration of the military victory gained by Sullivan but more for the results of the campaign and its significance afterward."[26] Early news stories mistakenly reported that there was going to be a reenactment of the entire journey; at a meeting in February 1929, Flick was asked if he had abandoned his "original plan of forming an army and marching over the exact route of Sullivan's Expedition." Flick quickly responded, "We never had planned to march over the entire route. It was merely suggested. But it has been dropped, for we could not ask men to march from Tioga Point through the heart of New York." He added, suggesting that this had indeed been contemplated, "And if we used busses it would mar the effect."[27] In the end, the Regents committee developed seventeen components for public recognition, strategically spread out between the various counties, and encouraged communities to carry out commemorations as close to the actual dates as possible. A massive historical pageant reenacting the expedition, held in three locations in September 1929, was the centerpiece of the summer festivities.[28]

24. "The Sullivan-Clinton Campaign," 2 ("Sesqui history," 13912-83, NYSA).
25. Graymont, *The Iroquois in the American Revolution*, 206–07.
26. "Says Sullivan Expedition Had Far-Reaching Effects," *Democrat & Chronicle* (Rochester, NY), June 10, 1928, 4.
27. "Sullivan Army to March Again in Sesqui Celebration Pageant," *Star-Gazette* (Elmira, NY), February 22, 1929, 15.
28. Andrea Lynn Smith, "Settler Colonialism and the Revolutionary War: New York's 1929 'Pageant of Decision,'" *The Public Historian* 41, no. 4 (2020): 7–35.

Including the Iroquois

In order to be inclusive, the Sullivan-Clinton festivities would need to involve the state's Haudenosaunee residents. Members of the 150th Committee recognized this on some level and outlined the inclusion of "the Iroquois" in their initial proposal to the regents:

> The purpose of the memorialization of the 150th anniversary of the Sullivan-Clinton Campaign is to obtain an intelligent understanding of its meaning and results in the history of New York State and the American Republic, and not to revive old hatred or to gloat over defeated foes, consequently representatives of the Iroquois, of Canada, and Great Britain should be cordially welcomed to take part in the commemoration.[29]

Flick sought Haudenosaunee involvement throughout the months of his Sullivan-Clinton activity, as we discuss here, but these efforts seemed to fall on deaf ears.

The interpretation of Sullivan-Clinton that Flick presented for New Yorkers had many flaws that Haudenosaunee observers would have recognized immediately. Each of the three dozen state-sponsored markers included a plaque summarizing Flick's framing of the significance of Sullivan-Clinton to the evolution of New York, as also developed in his speeches that summer and in the script of the historical pageant presented to tens of thousands of New Yorkers that summer (see figure 1):[30]

ROUTES OF THE ARMIES OF

GENERAL JOHN SULLIVAN

AND

GENERAL JAMES CLINTON

1779

AN EXPEDITION AGAINST THE HOSTILE INDIAN

NATIONS WHICH CHECKED THE AGGRESSIONS OF

THE ENGLISH AND INDIANS ON THE FRONTIERS

OF NEW YORK AND PENNSYLVANIA, EXTENDING

WESTWARD THE DOMINION OF THE UNITED STATES.

This account suggests that the Sullivan-Clinton expeditions represented the end of conflict with Iroquois foes ("checked the aggressions"), and expanded New York State and the country more generally westward ("extending westward the dominion of the United States"). The pageant linked the expedition even more closely with white expansion by describing pioneers arriving en masse while cornfields still burned in the background.[31] The message here was

---

29. "Sullivan-Clinton Sesquicentennial, General Program." Sullivan-Clinton Folder 3, Onondaga Historical Association.
30. For a discussion of the ways the pageant text recounts this past while neglecting the state's role, see Smith, "Settler Colonialism and the Revolutionary War."
31. Smith, "Settler Colonialism and the Revolutionary War," 32.

Figure 1. Dedication of a Sullivan-Clinton marker at Elmira, NY, September 1929.
(PHOTOGRAPHS OF OBSERVANCES OF THE 150TH ANNIVERSARY OF THE AMERICAN REVOLUTION,
SERIES B0567-85, FOLDER 26, ELMIRA SCENES, NEW YORK STATE ARCHIVES).

simple: Sullivan-Clinton set the stage for the expansion of the Empire State. This is a gross simplification, if not an outright lie. For one, Iroquois attacks on frontier settlements after 1779 were even *more* devastating than before. In fact, to this day, historians debate whether the expedition achieved its wartime goals and are mixed in their assessment of its strategic consequences. Joseph Fischer has gone so far as to describe it as a "well-executed failure," praising the troops for meeting logistical challenges while emphasizing that it never achieved its long-term objectives of taking Niagara or stopping frontier warfare. Barbara Graymont has argued that while Washington's goals were to break the power of the Indian foe and make the frontier safe, the "expedition achieved neither of these aims." Instead, "the war now became very personal to the Iroquois. If they did not have a cause before, they now had one."[32] As the historian Colin Calloway has recently documented, the scorched earth campaigns "stunned the Iroquois but did not break their war effort. If anything, they stiffened their resolve." He recounts the Six Nations' response as follows:

> Come spring, they resumed their raids on the American frontier, looking for food and vengeance. According to John Butler fifty-nine parties totaling almost 2,300 men went

---

32. Graymont, *The Iroquois in the American Revolution*, 220.

out from Niagara between February and September 1780. They killed 142 Americans and took 161 captives, destroyed 2 churches, 157 houses, and 150 granaries, and drove off 247 horses and 922 cattle. In New York, the raids led by Brant, Butler, and the Seneca war chief Cornplanter... that spring destroyed 1,000 homes, 1,000 barns, and 600,000 bushels of grain. Pennsylvania fared little better. The Susquehanna Valley, through which Sullivan's army had marched before following the Chemung River into Seneca country, suffered at least thirty-five separate raids from 1780 to 1782. Washington's war on Iroquois homes and food generated more, not fewer raids on American settlers.[33]

Not only did the Haudenosaunee remain a formidable foe, but the 1929 markers and the associated historical pageant neglected to mention that aside from some two thousand Iroquois and allied Indians who moved to Canada, most Iroquois returned after Sullivan's devastation and on paper held vast amounts of land, including all of western New York, most of central New York, and much of northern and western Pennsylvania, land they lost years after 1779.[34] In her study of Haudenosaunee settlements near Buffalo Creek into the 1840s, Alyssa Mt. Pleasant reports on thriving communities with rich farmlands and a high standard of living.[35] Similarly, Beth Ryan found that every Euro-American traveler in the Finger Lakes region from 1780 to 1810 came across Native Americans on the road, concluding that "This was still Indian territory."[36] Even after villages were relocated, Haudenosaunee still used nearby land for hunting and gathering, or to visit resting places of the dead.[37]

The Haudenosaunee lost vast stretches of their homeland well after the Sullivan-Clinton raids and the Revolutionary War. The New York State legislature was trying to seize Iroquois territories for military bounty lands before the Treaty of Paris was signed in 1783, and state Indian commissioners evaded state law by concocting a private company that made fraudulent 999-year lease arrangements.[38] The federal government inserted its authority with important treaties with the Six Nations, including the Indian Trade and Intercourse Act in 1790, which mandated a federal agent, Indian consent, ratification by the Senate, and a presidential signature to purchase Indian land legally, and the federal Treaty of Canandaigua of 1794, also known as the Pickering Treaty, which recognized Haudenosaunee

33. Calloway, *The Indian World of George Washington*, 257.

34. Robert W. Venables, *The Six Nations of New York: The 1892 United States Extra Census Bulletin* (Ithaca, NY: Cornell University Press, 1995), xii; Barbara Graymont, "New York State Indian Policy after the Revolution," *New York History*, no. 4 (1997): 376.

35. Alyssa Mt. Pleasant, "After the Whirlwind: Maintaining a Haudenosaunee Place at Buffalo Creek, 1780–1825" (PhD diss., Cornell University, 2007), 89–103.

36. Beth Ryan, "Crowding the Banks: The Historical Archaeology of Ohagi and the Post-Revolutionary Haudenosaunee Confederacy, ca. 1780–1826" (PhD diss., Cornell University, 2017), 85, 91.

37. Ryan, "Crowding the Banks," 201, 247.

38. Laurence M. Hauptman, *Conspiracy of Interests: Iroquois Dispossession and the Rise of New York State*, (Syracuse, NY: Syracuse University Press, 1999), 62; Graymont, "New York State Indian Policy," 381.

sovereignty in two-thirds of the state. Haudenosaunee leaders and activists continue to recognize these treaties to this day.[39]

Despite these federal laws, New York State speculators and political leaders persisted in their pursuit of Haudenosaunee territory, making twelve separate land disposition agreements with distinct Haudenosaunee nations from 1785 to 1796.[40] Entrepreneurs and leading state politicians openly conspired to obtain lands held by Oneidas, Cayugas, Onondagas, and Senecas to benefit from transportation revolutions that transformed the state.[41] Politicians used the threat of further land loss to force Haudenosaunee leaders into exploitative land deals. As Laurence Hauptman and others have demonstrated, the rapid growth of the Empire State was only possible by the repeated seizure of Six Nations land.[42] By the mid-nineteenth century, Haudenosaunee nations had lost most of their homeland, and in the 1920s, Iroquois were living in scattered tiny reserves, or had moved to Canada, Wisconsin, or Oklahoma.[43]

In the 1920s, Haudenosaunee were fighting back. In 1922, the same year that W. Pierrepont White submitted his petition to the New York State Historical Association proposing the Revolutionary War sesquicentennial, the state was rocked with a land claims movement that put much of the territory's legal foundation into question.[44] "Is White Man's Title to More Than Six Million Acres of One-Time Indian Land in New York State Threatened?" asked the *Knickerbocker Press* in a dramatic full-page spread on April 30, 1922. This uncertainty was raised by the findings presented by a New York State Indian commission chaired by assemblyman Edward A. Everett from Potsdam.[45] Everett's Commission was created in 1919 in response to an Oneida land claims case that raised jurisdictional confusion (see

39. Graymont, "New York State Indian Policy," 386. For Native American perspectives, see G. Peter Jemison and Anna M. Schein, eds., *Treaty of Canandaigua 1794: 200 Years of Treaty Relations between the Iroquois Confederacy and the United States* (Santa Fe, NM: Clear Light Publishers, 2000).
40. Dorothy V. Jones, *License for Empire: Colonialism by Treaty in Early America* (Chicago: University of Chicago Press, 1982), 180–81. See also Deborah A. Rosen, *American Indians and State Law: Sovereignty, Race, and Citizenship, 1790–1880* (Lincoln: University of Nebraska Press, 2007), 33–49.
41. Hauptman, *Conspiracy of Interests.*
42. Hauptman, *Conspiracy of Interests.*
43. Threats of allotment and removal persisted for much of the nineteenth and twentieth centuries. See Hauptman, *Conspiracy of Interests,* 21819; Laurence M. Hauptman, *The Iroquois and the New Deal* (Syracuse, NY: Syracuse University Press, 1981), 4. The Cayugas had lost their land base, and many were living among Senecas on Cattaraugus Reservation or other reservations; many Mohawks moved to Canada, many Oneida moved to Wisconsin or to family at Onondaga, and other Oneida moved to Canada in 1849. Barbara Graymont, "New York State Indian Policy after the Revolution," 404–09. For the fate of the Oneida, see Karim M. Tiro, *The People of the Standing Stone: The Oneida Nation from the Revolution through the Era of Removal* (Amherst: University of Massachusetts Press, 2011), and Hauptman, *Conspiracy of Interests.*
44. Andrew Bard Epstein, "Unsettled New York: Land, Law, and Haudenosaunee Nationalism in the Early Twentieth Century" (Master's thesis, University of Georgia, 2012), 85.
45. Laurence M. Hauptman, *Coming Full Circle. The Seneca Nation of Indians, 1848–1934.* (Norman: Oklahoma University Press, 2019).

Figure 2. Edward A. Everett and his secretary, Lulu G. Stillman, with three Cayuga leaders on the steps of the capital building in Albany, NY. Left to right: Alexander John, Ernest Spring, Edward A. Everett, Edwin Spring, Lulu G. Stillman. This photograph was likely taken in February, 1922, when Everett presented his commission's findings to the legislature (Graymont, *Fighting Tuscarora*, 1973). IMAGE COURTESY OF SIX NATIONS INDIAN MUSEUM, ONCHIOTA, NY.

figure 2).[46] The New York State legislature created the New York State Indian Commission in May 1919 to determine once and for all whether the Six Nations of New York were under federal or state control.[47]

As Everett's commission looked into these details, holding hearings with each New York Haudenosaunee nation and with the Six Nations in Canada, it confronted the fact that the lines separating state and federal power were never clearly drawn, and multiple state treaties had not followed federal law.[48] Everett determined that the tenure of much of New York State, including whole cities such as Buffalo and Syracuse, large industrial centers,

---

46. A U.S. District Court voted to return land to an Oneida family, stating that New York courts could not remove the Oneida as they were a federally recognized tribe. Laurence M. Hauptman, *The Iroquois and the New Deal* (Syracuse, NY: Syracuse University Press, 1981), 11.
47. The Machold Bill (Chapter 590 of the Laws of New York) established the commission on May 12, 1919. Republican assemblyman Edward A. Everett was elected chairman, and it is often known as the "Everett Commission." The most detailed account of the commission's work is in Helen M. Upton, *The Everett Report in Historical Perspective: The Indians of New York* (Albany: New York State American Revolution Bicentennial Commission, 1980).
48. Epstein, "Unsettled New York," 17.

power plants, railroads, the Erie Canal, and more, was uncertain, asserting that the Six Nations in New York State "have title to lands estimated at 6,000,000 acres and valued at approximately $2,500,000,000."[49] When Everett presented these radical conclusions to the New York Assembly in February 1922, the other commission members refused to sign onto his report, and the only minority report submitted had been prepared before any of the hearings were conducted.[50] The report was never forwarded to the legislature. Everett had already released his findings to the Haudenosaunee, however.[51]

The Iroquois began to meet at the center of the metaphoric longhouse (Onondaga) to consider a response, and New York presses were noticing. "Six Nation Remnants Seek Return of Old Holdings," the Rochester *Democrat and Chronicle* announced on November 30, 1924, continuing, "The Six Nations are out on the war path. Not with tomahawk and sharp pointed arrows for the heart of an enemy, but with lawyers and ancient records." On February 22, 1925, the *Buffalo Courier* announced: "Land on Which Buffalo is Situated Sought by Tribes of Six Iroquois Nations." The story of the bringing together of disparate Haudenosaunee factions and nations often centers on the figure of Mrs. Laura (Minnie) Kellogg, a Wisconsin Oneida woman who collected funds from Haudenosaunee and is known as the "most controversial Iroquois leader of the twentieth century."[52] Despite the drama she fanned, Haudenosaunee leaders formed a coalition, hired a legal team, and brought a "momentous" land claims case to federal court on June 6, 1925, starting with a case against a power company that plaintiffs argued was occupying land that still belonged to the Mohawk Nation.[53] The New York attorney moved to dismiss the case on the grounds that the federal court had no jurisdiction due to the 1924 passage of the federal Indian Citizenship Act (ICA) that rendered Native Americans citizens. Appeals were soon filed. Although its outcome was eventually a negative one for the Six Nations, it was while the future of much of the state was in question that the state historian was planning the wider Revolutionary War events. In 1928, when Flick was traversing the state to garner interest in his Sullivan-Clinton programming, appeals and amended appeals were still in play. The land dispute case ended on May 7, 1929, a few months before the pageant was held, when claimants decided not to bring the case forward to the U.S. Supreme Court.

49. "Everett Believes Indian Claims Good," *Courier and Freeman*, February 15, 1922, in Epstein, "Unsettled New York," 74.

50. Upton, *The Everett Report*, 102.

51. Epstein, "Unsettled New York," 85; Hauptman, *The Iroquois and the New Land Deal*, 11–12.

52. Laurence M. Hauptman, *The Iroquois Struggle for Survival: World War II to Red Power* (Syracuse, NY: Syracuse University Press, 1986), 183. See also Laurence M Hauptman, "Designing Woman: Minnie Kellogg, Iroquois Leader," in *Indian Lives: Essays on Nineteenth- and Twentieth-Century Native American Leaders*, edited by L. G. Moses and Raymond Wilson (Albuquerque: University of Mexico Press, 1993), 159–88.

53. Hauptman, *The Iroquois Struggle for Survival*, 185.

A Six Nations Rebuff

For the state to promote public celebrations at the very site of destroyed villages on the very date of their destruction seems callous at best.[54] Flick and his executive secretary, Peter Nelson, were inviting Haudenosaunee members to take part in a celebration of a military victory over them, and an event framed to make it appear that their lands were lost in 1779 when Haudenosaunee leaders were arguing that they were never legally ceded. It is no surprise that Flick's solicitations were getting nowhere.[55] In February 1929, Peter Nelson made an official visit to Cornell University at the twenty-second annual Farms and Home Week to offer invitations to Six Nations leaders gathered there. Rather than a welcoming, Nelson encountered one of the clearest demonstrations of Six Nations opposition to the state's Sullivan-Clinton anniversary fanfare expressed thus far.

Nelson was meeting with the Cornell Indian Boards, an organization that had emerged out of the Indian Extension work established by Erl Augustus Caesar Bates (1889–1973), a doctor of obstetrics (see figure 3). Bates helped establish Cornell University's College of Agriculture Indian Extension program in 1920. New York's Indian Nation Councils selected representatives to travel to Cornell to assist in selecting Six Nations students for college courses, and these councilors became known as "Boards." The delegates or Cornell Indian Boards met each year at the annual Farms and Home Week (see figure 4).[56] Nelson was meeting sixteen men and women who were gathered for the meeting's concluding powwow, including Head Chief Andrew Gibson of the Six Nations.[57] The Boards' chair at the

---

54. Flick also sought Seneca Nation approval to place a Sullivan-Clinton marker on Seneca land. See Andrea Lynn Smith and Randy A. John, "A Misplaced Marker: Celebrating Brodhead on Seneca Territory," under review.

55. William B. Newell to Alexander Flick, January 9, 1929. Correspondence of the Supervisor of Public Records and the Secretary of the Advisory Committee on the Commemoration of the Sullivan Campaign, New York Education Department, Division of Archives and History, Series B0566, Box 16,"Indian" folder, NYSA. See also Frances Dorrance to Alexander Flick, February 9, 1929, Correspondence of the Supervisor of Public Records and the Secretary of the Advisory Committee on the Commemoration of the Sullivan Campaign, New York Education Department, Division of Archives and History, Series B0566, Box 16, Folder "Pennsylvania," NYSA.

56. "Founding of Indian Village," Erl Bates, Erl Bates papers, #21-24-790, Division of Rare and Manuscript Collections, Cornell University. Online at https://aiisp.cornell.edu/about-us/history /indian-village/; see also Laurence M. Hauptman, *An Oneida Indian in Foreign Waters: The Life of Chief Chapman Scanandoah, 1870–1953* (Syracuse, NY: Syracuse University Press, 2016), 88.

57. Attendees included Russell Hill, James Jonathan, Inez Blackchief, Aaron Poodry, Mrs. Rose and Mrs. Irene Poodry, and Miss Dorothy Moses (Tonawanda); Mrs. Eli Henry, Mrs. Harriet Pembleton, Mrs. Ella Printup, Miss Gladys Ganesworth, Louise Pendleton, Ray Ganesworth, Harry Patterson, Havemeyer Jack, and Joseph Woodbury (Tuscarora); Mr. and Mrs. Walter Kennedy, Sylvester C. Crouse, Jerome and Edison Crouse, Adelbert John, Hiram Watt, Frank John, Mrs. Joshua Pierce, and Miss Ruth Pierce (Allegany Seneca); Mr. and Mrs. John K. Button, Mr. and Mrs. Theodore Gordon, Mr. and Mrs. Ulysses Kennedy, Frank Logan, and James Jones (Cattaraugus Seneca). Leroy E. Fess, "Relic Hunters' Desecration of Cemeteries Stirs Indians," *Buffalo Evening News*, February 14, 1929.

Figure 3. Erl Augustus Caesar Bates
(1889-1973). ERL BATES PAPERS, #21-24-
790. DIVISION OF RARE AND MANUSCRIPT
COLLECTIONS, CORNELL UNIVERSITY LIBRARY.

time was Walter "Boots" Kennedy, a Seneca man from Killbuck, New York (Allegany Territory).[58] The *Cornell Daily Sun* described Kennedy as a "well-known orator and farmer."

According to the *Buffalo Evening News*, Kennedy gave Nelson "an earful of Indian griev-
ance."[59] He explained to Nelson, "the Six Nations of the Iroquois did not feel that conditions
warranted their participation in the [Sullivan-Clinton] program."[60] Why? Because "the white
man had broken his part of the agreement." As Kennedy put it, at the end of the Revolutionary War, "the Iroquois reserved for themselves certain pieces of land of two characters.
One was lands now embraced in their reservations in Niagara, Genesee, Erie, Allegany, and
Cattaraugus counties and the other pieces reserved were the burial places of their ancestors
in Chautauqua, Wyoming, Livingston, Orleans, Monroe, Wayne and Ontario counties." Kennedy explained that the Indians had "the solemn promise of George Washington himself that
these burial places would never be disturbed," adding, "When we made our treaties, George
Washington promised that the spade and plow of the white man would never molest the
sleeps of our fathers." This is not what happened. As Kennedy continued:

---

58. Kennedy succeeded former Boards chair and Seneca Nation of Indians president William C.
Hoag in 1927. *Cornell Daily Sun,* December 2, 1927, 2; *Ithaca Journal,* December 17, 1927, 7. See
Randy A. John, *Who Is Walter Kennedy?* (Allegany Territory, Seneca Nation: RAJ Publications,
2019).
59. Fess, "Relic Hunters' Desecration of Cemeteries Stirs Indians."
60. Fess, "Relic Hunters' Desecration of Cemeteries Stirs Indians."

INDIAN VISITORS AND WINTER COURSE STUDENTS AT CORNELL
A group of delegates from the reservations, including Chief Nicodemus Billy,
   Chief Yankee Spring, Chief Albert Shenandoah, and Chief Justice
   Walter S. Kennedy

Figure 4. Six Nations Delegates (Indian Board precursor) and Winter Course Students at Cornell
University during Farmers' Week. Source: *Extension Service News* (ITHACA, NY: THE NEW YORK
STATE COLLEGE OF AGRICULTURE AT CORNELL UNIVERSITY, 1921 VOL. 4 (5), MAY 1921, 23).

> Now in Chautauqua County and in other places the white men have thrown up the
> bones of our fathers and they are bleaching in the sun and snow at this moment. We
> understand that these white people send their collections of arrow heads and copper
> beads taken from the graves of our ancestors to the museum in your museum cases
> in Albany.[61]

The museum he was referring to, the New York State Museum, was also under the direction
of the Education Department overseeing the Revolutionary War programming. The Head
Chief Andrew Gibson and "16 others of his tribesmen who were seated in solemn council"
nodded in agreement.[62] According to the journalist Leroy Fess, an Onondaga man "told of
plans his people had to dig in white men's cemeteries and scatter the bones around unless

---

61. Fess, "Relic Hunters' Desecration of Cemeteries Stirs Indians."
62. Fess, "Relic Hunters' Desecration of Cemeteries Stirs Indians."

this careless practice is stopped." The next day, the Cornell Indian Boards went a step further to pass a resolution condemning the desecration of Indian graves and sent a copy to the New York legislature.[63] This resolution represents a clear articulation of Native concerns regarding the sanctity of the dead and the desecration and theft of mortuary remains, concerns that often fell on deaf ears until the passage of the Native American Graves Protection and Repatriation Act in 1990.[64] It is interesting that it was the invitation to participate in the public Sullivan-Clinton events that yielded this unanimous resolution and that Flick's extensive manuscript documenting the state's Revolutionary War sesquicentennial says nothing about the standoff. For their part, rather than directly challenge the boastful nature of the Sullivan-Clinton festivities, Haudenosaunee leaders used the opportunity presented to them by Nelson's invitation to turn the tables and raise a matter of great Six Nations concern to state officials' attention.

Dancing at Sullivan-Clinton Festivities

Despite this unusual collective rebuff, Flick and Nelson continued to seek Haudenosaunee involvement in the pageant and in marker dedications, to almost no avail. This was unusual for this time. Public events in New York in the 1920s such as outings of the Finger Lakes Association or the opening of Allegany State Park often included Haudenosaunee performers, and one might even argue that Haudenosaunee participation in such festivities dropped dramatically in 1929 in comparison with other years.[65]

One notable exception was the performance by several Cayugas at a Sullivan-Clinton marker dedication organized in September 1929. The Auburn lawyer Richard C. S. Drummond organized a marker unveiling at "Great Gully," the former site of the Cayuga Castle, and invited a group of Haudenosaunee to perform. While much of the performance was presented in a Native language and opaque to us today, Drummond framed the event as a ceremony of "lasting." In her masterpiece, *Firsting and Lasting*, on nineteenth-century New England historical accounts, Jean O'Brien discusses the development by New England antiquarians of "replacement narratives," historical accounts that explain how whites came to replace Native peoples on the land. She identifies the use of rhetorical formulas of "firsting" and "lasting" in these texts. Local histories relentlessly documented "firsts": the first (white) baby born, the first log cabin, the first store, and so forth, and in so doing presented themselves as the "first" people worthy of note. Along with this "firsting" practice, historians engaged in "lasting," an often-nostalgic recognition of the "last" of this or that great Native

63. Leroy Fess, "Indian Complaint Heeded," *Buffalo Evening News*, February 18, 1929, 3.

64. Native American Graves Protection and Repatriation Act, Public Law 101-601; 25 U.S. Congress, 3001–3013.

65. "Real Indian Braves Appear in Pageant," *Dunkirk Evening Observer*, June 4, 1927, 11. The other Haudenosaunee participant we identified was David R. Hill, Onondaga, who participated in an event recognizing Van Schaick's raids on the Onondaga in April 1779.

leader, tribe, or family—a kind of settler wishful fantasy that reflected the pervasive belief that Native Americans were bound to vanish.[66]

Drummond's Sullivan-Clinton marker dedication was an elaborate "lasting" cere-mony.[67] His own speech was an over-the-top ode to the Cayuga nation, starting, "O, People of the Long House! We come to you this day in friendship, with a message of good will." After "saluting" the Mohawks and the Onondaga, he turned to the "Cayugas" present:

> And you, Gah-Yo-Gwa-Oh! At the place where once your stronghold stood we greet you. In that former time you were a great nation, mighty in war, powerful in council. . . . But now for more than a hundred years their ancient domain has not seen the Cayugas. By grant we hold that land. Once numerous, compact and strong, the Cayugas are few and weak and scattered. As a nation soon will they have vanished from the earth. . . . Accept our tribute. Take back to the Cayugas our message. Tell them that your ears have heard our words, and that your eyes have seen the pledge we give of our sincer-ity: this monument of bronze and granite... upon which, to the end of time, shall be found emblazoned the name, Cayuga – Gah Yo-Gwar-Ohn'! Oon-eh![68]

Newspaper reports followed suit, describing the event as the "last Council fire of the Ca-yugas."[69] That Flick was eager for Haudenosaunee involvement of this type can be inferred from his gushing response to Drummond's event, stating, "the exercises at Great Gully were unusually impressive. The presence of the Indians and their participation added a note which, I regret to say, was *lacking in most of our dedication observances*."[70]

In order to carry out this performance, Drummond needed to be speaking to actual Cayugas, and it took him some time to locate people willing to play this role.[71] It is unclear how Drummond first connected with Shongo, but it was likely through Arthur C. Parker, Seneca director of the Rochester Museum.[72] The only Cayuga man identified by name was James Crowe; presses highlighted Dr. Wilbur Clifford Shongo instead, a well-known Sen-eca man from Buffalo. Son of Moses and Alice Ellen (Pierce) Shongo, Dr. Shongo served in

66. Brian W. Dippie, *The Vanishing American: White Attitudes and U.S. Indian Policy* (Middletown, CT: Wesleyan University Press, 1982).

67. Drummond to Chief Wilbur C. Shongo, September 27, 1929, Cayuga County Historical Society correspondence files, Cayuga Museum of History and Art and Case Research Library, Auburn, NY (hereafter, CCHSCF, CMHACRL).

68. "Original Manuscript of Richard C. S. Drummond. At Dedication of Monument at Great Gully. September 24, 1929," CCHSCF, CMHACRL.

69. "State Historian Delivers Presentation Address on Site of Ancient Iroquois Village," "Sesqui history," NYSA, 674.

70. "Dr. Flick Congratulates Cayuga County on Success of Its Sesqui Celebration," "Sesqui history," NYSA, 663 (emphasis added).

71. Letter to Drummond from Annie Laurie Davis, Washington, DC, September 11, 1929, CCH-SCF, CMHACRL.

72. According to Drummond, "the Indians reported promptly to Doctor Parker, at Rochester" after the event. Drummond to Flick, October 8, 1929, B0566, folder 7, NYSA.

the New York 74th Infantry National Guard (1902–07; 1907–12), and was described as the "only physician in New York state authorized to practice medicine without a state license."[73]

How might we interpret Shongo's decision to participate in this ceremony? Correspondence we discuss below suggests that this was partly a money-making venture. After an initial meeting, Drummond detailed Shongo's obligations, requesting that "the actual part to be performed by you and your people, as you outlined it to me yesterday, had better not be planned to exceed one half an hour," adding that he hoped that he would accomplish "the best and most dramatic result possible under the circumstance."[74] Shongo replied with a quick note:

> Dear Sir,
>
> I am pleased to hear from you and something definite, it means $255.00, 5 meals and lodging for 2 nights, for our party for services we render on the day of Sept. 24th Tuesday 1929. I am working along the lines we discussed, and have called a meeting for a rehearsal. Do not harbor any thots of disappointment. We are square shooters.[75]

There may have been more than financial compensation encouraging the Cayugas to perform in Auburn, however. After the events were over, Drummond and the local police chief took the men on a tour of the area, driving along the "old Indian trail" and to Great Gully where they observed mounds and said that "they are certain are the graves of their forefathers."[76] Four years later, central New York presses made much of the visit of three Cayuga men (David Cook and Chief Charles Fun of Buffalo, and Chief Robert Fishcarrier of the Six Nations Reservation near Brantford, Ontario) to Albany seeking information on parcels of land that they believed belonged to the Cayuga nation. "A yellowed copy of the Indian treaty of 1784 was brought out of the secretary of state's files early today at the request of three Cayuga Indians seeking to establish a claim to a large piece of land in Western New York," reported the *Jamestown Evening Journal* on Wednesday, September 24, 1934, adding, "Warrior Charles Funn of Buffalo said the land in question 'ought to be about 100 miles square.'" Were some of these men the same people who performed during the Auburn event? We do not know, however, Drummond's colleague, Mr. Searing, former president of the Cayuga County Historical Society, brought the matter to Drummond's attention.[77]

---

73. Harold Murphy and Bob Dunn, "Hard to Believe," n.d. We thank Terri John for this information.

74. Drummond to Chief Wilbur C. Shongo, September 6, 1929, CCHSCF, CMHACRL.

75. Chief Shongo, Buffalo, NY, to Richard Drummond, Auburn, NY, CCHSCF, CMHACRL.

76. "Indians Visit Logan Monument," *Auburn Citizen*, September 26, 1929.

77. Mr. Henry Allen of Auburn inquired about the land claim to Mr. M. K. Sniffen, secretary of the Indian Rights Association, who conducted research on the case and discussed it with George Decker. Sniffen to Henry Allen, Auburn, NY, October 4, 1934; Sniffen to Allen, October 31, 1934. Unsigned note to file dated November 19, 1934, states, "These papers were delivered to me by Mr. Searing (former president of the Cayuga County Historical Society) for perusal in November, 1934," CCHSCF, CMHACRL.

Synchronicity or Something More?

While the Haudenosaunee land claims were certainly of interest to Six Nations members in New York, were they equally visible to non-Native New York residents? More to the point, can we link these land claims in any way to the Sullivan-Clinton festivities? It is tempting to see the state's decision to celebrate the Sullivan-Clinton Expedition with historical markers as "ceremonies of possession," as a means of claiming territory or of responding to the threats underway to state sovereignty.[78] We have sought correspondence between the main actors on this matter, to no avail. However, it is worth noting that some people with close connections to the state's Revolutionary War commemorative programming were aware of potential Haudenosaunee claims. W. Pierrepont White, the man who initiated the proposal to mark the Revolutionary War, made them aware early on.

Just a few days after Governor Smith approved White's 1923 proposal, he began writing the trustees of the New York State Historical Association to bring their attention to the Haudenosaunee land claim. It is unclear why he decided to act then. Perhaps the euphoria associated with the success of his bill motivated him to try to take on the unthinkable? As president of the Mohawk Valley Historical Association, White wrote to Reverend Frederick Richards of Glen Falls transmitting an unknown article and stating the following:

> At the present moment, there is being held on the Onondaga Reservation, near Syracuse, a gathering of the Six nations, with representatives from Wisconsin and Brantford. The subject of their conference is the wrongs done them by our State and Nation, through breach of treaties. The Sioux Indians are now before the Court of Claims, asking for $700,000,000 from the U.S. for breach of treaties made with their Nation. It is not improbable that a similar uniting of the claims of the Six Nations will be accomplished. New York and MA dealt directly with the Indian tribes. Damages, not ouster from the land, are asked by the Sioux.
>
> New York State has a remarkable history, and our busy populace so engrossed in commercial enterprise can scarcely pause too often to consider the sources of its prosperity and the history of the movements and events that have made New York the Empire State. Let it be hoped that the native red man will have his part properly depicted and that his position as a constructive factor in the development of the state be emphasized at least as much as his acts of hostility. The time has come when our people can afford to understand the red man in other light than that of prejudice.[79]

---

78. Patricia Seed, *Ceremonies of Possession in Europe's Conquest of the New World, 1492–1640* (Cambridge, UK: Cambridge University Press, 1995). We thank Dr. Jessica Dolan for this insight.
79. W. Pierrepont White to Frederick B. Richards, Glen Falls, June 6, 1929, Cor. 1-469, William Pierrepont White Papers, Oneida County History Center, Utica, NY (hereafter, WPWP, OCHC).

One of his interlocutors wrote an extensive response to what we can assume was a similar letter. NYSHA trustee William O. Stillman, president of the American Humane Association, responded to White on June 7, 1923:

> Dear President White,
>
> Your very kind favor of June 6, 1923 is duly received; also the clipping which you enclose. I am heartily in sympathy with the proposition that the descendants of the native Indians in this State shall be dealt with justly and fairly by our State and National Government. Residents of the United States cannot afford to be unjust or unfair with those from whom land has been taken and important privileges secured.
>
> I earnestly hope that New York will go on record as doing the right thing to the Indians. The subject is being actively agitated at the present time. My friend, George Wharton James, of California, has been publishing some valuable discussions of this subject. There should be no legitimate ground for discussion of the questions as to whether we should be honest, whether we should be just, whether we should be decent. With kind Regards, . . . Stillman.[80]

Rewriting New York History

Dedication exercises for the Sullivan-Clinton monuments wound down in the fall of 1929, just weeks before the market crash of October 1929 that ushered in the Great Depression. Dozens of metal roadside signs were erected in the 1930s, further detailing the locations of the Native settlements and orchards destroyed by Sullivan and Clinton's men. The military expedition received heightened recognition at key anniversaries, such as the 175th anniversary in 1954 when newspapers sometimes presented lengthy weekly recounting of the expedition.

The bicentennial reaction in 1979 was more muted suggesting evolving attitudes. During the planning stages, Richard Allen, the program director of the New York State's Bicentennial Commission, argued that the emphasis should be on commemoration, not "celebration," adding, "Any ceremonies should be dignified and not offend modern sensibilities."[81] The Cayuga County Historical Society chairman wrote that "no-re-enactments of battles or disturbances will be scheduled. No emphasis upon the conflicts of the day will be re-cast. The theme of peace and brotherhood will take the place of conflict and bloodshed in the story represented."[82] Publications played it safe and reprinted Flick's 1929 statements.[83]

---

80. William O. Stillman to W. P. White, June 7, 1923, Cor. 1-470, WPWP, OCHC.

81. Minutes, "Sullivan-Clinton Expedition Bicentennial – 1979," Thomas Byrne, "Unofficio" Secretary," Chemung County Historical Society, November 4, 1977, Sullivan-Clinton folder (hereafter SCF), Cayuga County Historian Archives, Auburn, NY (hereafter, CCHA).

82. General letter of June 22, 1978, from Thomas Byrne, Chemung County Historian; Walter Long, "Sullivan-Clinton '79," unpublished memorandum, SCF, CCHA.

83. Thomas E. Byrne, ed., "A Bicentennial Remembrance of the Sullivan-Clinton Expedition 1779 in Pennsylvania and New York," Sullivan-Clinton '79, a group of County Historians from twelve counties, New York State Bicentennial Commission, Chemung County Historical Society. Sullivan Expedition folder, Bradford County Historical Society, Towanda, PA.

The muted nature of the 1979 commemorations may have stemmed from land claim issues that were returning to the fore. The Oneidas had long believed that the state had violated the Indian Trade and Intercourse Acts of 1790 and 1793 as there were no federal commissioners present at their 1795 "treaty," or at twenty-four of the twenty-six "treaties" made after 1798.[84] To the surprise of many, in January 1974, the Supreme Court agreed to hear their case, opening up the federal courts to the Oneidas, and the Cayugas followed with a case soon after. Land titles were hanging in the balance, fostering economic uncertainty and anti-Indian sentiment in central New York.[85]

This resurfacing of land claims seems to have taken many of New York's residents by surprise. Richard Allen's speech given on the anniversary of the destruction of Cayuga Castle on September 22, 1979, was not publicized widely because of the Indian land claims issue. As one member explained, "We didn't want any pickets."[86] In fact, there is evidence that Flick's reframing of the past as depicted on the 1929 Sullivan-Clinton markers may have contributed to some New York residents' surprise at renewed activism. When a leak occurred regarding negotiations underway with the Cayugas in August 1979, pandemonium ensued.[87] Over 1,500 people attended a public meeting held in Seneca Falls in September 11, 1979, and a Waterloo, New York, supervisor stated, "I thought when Clinton and his troops marched through here in the 1700s that the Indian problem was taken care of."[88]

Conclusion

Haudenosaunee resistance to the state's Sullivan-Clinton extravaganza took many forms. In 1929, only a few Native people agreed to perform at the dozens of Sullivan-Clinton marker dedications held across the state. Walter Kennedy led a strong rejection of the state's program, continuing the Haudenosaunee condemnation of the ways war tactics were reported—and silenced—in the written record. During the time of a pending land claim in the face of so many other challenges to Native sovereignty, Haudenosaunee may have had more important tasks ahead of themselves. Whether battling new separate land claims, citizenship, educational policies, hunting and fishing regulations, interstate travel, or draft regulations and compensation, New York's Haudenosaunee were pressing for their rights against formidable odds and against a formidable foe. We might read their noninvolvement in ceremonies commemorating the destruction of their homeland as rising above a relatively frivolous activity, especially when pressing matters such as allotment or termination

---

84. Laurence M. Hauptman, "Iroquois Land Issues: At Odds with the 'Family of New York,'" in *Iroquois Land Claims*, edited by Christopher Vecsey and William A. Starna (Syracuse, NY: Syracuse University Press, 1988), 67–86, 71.

85. A good review of this era can be found in Vecsey and Starna, *Iroquois Land Claims*.

86. Ed Rossman, "Sullivan-Clinton Campaign," n.d., Sullivan-Clinton folder, CCHSCF, CMHACRL.

87. Chris Lavin, "Responses to the Cayuga Land Claim," *Iroquois Land Claims*, 87–100, 92–93.

88. Lavin, "Responses," 94.

were threatening. We might also read noninvolvement as a kind of silent protest. However, when Six Nations leaders were confronted with an official invitation at a public celebratory powwow, they refused to participate and condemned the state with eloquent charges of hypocrisy.

Who was responding to whom? Perhaps we should not look for Haudenosaunee resistance to the Sullivan-Clinton extravaganza, but see the Sullivan-Clinton events as a reaction to Haudenosaunee activism. "See, this really is our land," the plaques seem to claim. "We really won this land fair and square in the Revolutionary War."

The success of Flick's mission led to New York State's formal programming for cyclical commemorations across the decades and a permanent recognition of Washington's "Indian Expedition" through monuments. In hindsight, should we view the state's exercise in public patriotism solely as a recognition of the heroic deeds of the past of the monuments' progenitors, or as an elaborate response to contemporary Haudenosaunee activism during the 1920s, and/or an attempt to sanitize the state's participation in George Washington's plan to exterminate the Cayugas, Mohawks, Oneidas, Onondaga, Senecas, and Tuscaroras and secure possession of their sovereign territories for the new nation, the United States?[89] The creation of these commemorations can indirectly serve to indoctrinate new generations of New Yorkers with their "heroic" deeds. Yet the Haudenosaunee will always remember the plan to wipe them out, as noted here in accounts spanning the centuries from Cornplanter in 1794 to Walter "Boots" Kennedy in the 1920s. What social reactions awaits new events surrounding the Sullivan-Clinton Campaign in the future?

---

89. The Oneidas and Tuscaroras supported the colonists in the Revolution yet were subject to hómeland destruction as well.

Artifact NY
The Spirit of 1776 Suffrage Wagon

Marguerite Kearns

Jane Van De Bogart raced into Woodstock town board meetings with her nose pointing in the direction of her council seat.[1] She balanced stacks of books, maps, and reports under each arm. The monthly session would have the usual budget line items to discuss, a zoning report to review, and one more town employee to advise about New York's Freedom of Information legislation.

Jane stopped, laid down her burden, and yanked a steno pad from the stack to check off another task completed. She added three more items. Jane Van De Bogart modeled multitasking before the rest of us ever heard the term. The town of Woodstock in the Hudson Valley teemed with vocal and visible individuals like Van De Bogart, those determined to "change the world" during the 1970s. Many locals were convinced the town of Woodstock should remain as it had always been—a laid-back retreat stirring from Memorial to Labor Day.

In the years after the Festival of 1969, Woodstock residents reluctantly came to terms with the transition from a part-time to a year-round town. Did the community need a conventional or a custom solution to take care of the disposal of municipal sewage? Town board members considered additions to a community master plan and circulated progress reports on the town's projected growth. Council members like Van De Bogart immersed themselves in detail. I survived hours of public deliberations by taking copious notes and then heading to the newspaper office to file my articles before the Tuesday deadline. Reporting for *Woodstock Times*, I believed, had to be one of the best jobs in town.

"What drives you to serve on the town board?" I asked Jane Van de Bogart.

"Among other things—my great aunt Elisabeth Freeman and what I heard about her pounding the pavements for the women's suffrage movement," she replied. "I owe my ability to represent the people of Woodstock to my great aunt, Elisabeth."

---

1. This excerpt has been adapted from the author's upcoming book, *An Unfinished Revolution: Edna Buckman Kearns and the Struggle for Women's Rights* (Albany: State University of New York Press, 2021).

"My grandmother Edna organized for votes for women, too," I told her.

We weren't aware then that Jane's great aunt, Elisabeth Freeman (1876–1942), not only knew Edna but they had worked together for what they called "The Cause." Both were wagon women, on-the-ground organizers who drove horse-drawn wagons to mobilize support for women's voting rights. New York's men, as voters, were in the position of approving these rights. But would they?

Novel organizing techniques such as horse-drawn wagons took the women activists to locations in rural areas where they might not otherwise have canvassed. Advocates on both sides of the voting issue flooded the state, from top to bottom, during the 1915 referendum campaign that failed, and then again in 1917 when New York's women celebrated a statewide voting victory. Elisabeth Freeman and Edna Kearns were in the forefront of these on-the-ground efforts.

The suffrage campaign wagons used by Edna Kearns, Elisabeth Freeman, and Rosalie Jones provided visibility and mobility. Edna drove the "Spirit of 1776" vehicle in New York City and on Long Island. Elisabeth and Rosalie traveled in another wagon within Long Island and around New York State. They also drove to Massachusetts, Ohio, and Washington, DC. Rosalie Jones was from an old Long Island family that had self-identified as Tories during the American Revolution. Except for Rosalie, her family members generations later were sympathetic to the "antis," those who opposed women voting.

Wagons on the suffrage campaign trail were popular attention getters. A woman driving one with freedom messages might not sound like a cutting-edge organizing tactic today. But during an era when horse-drawn vehicles hit the streets for the women's cause, the vehicles attracted publicity, and, best of all, crowds.

Wagons required skill in driving. Occasionally the women managed the wagons themselves. Often they hired someone to handle the horse so they could concentrate on public speaking. Wagons provided instant speakers' platforms. Pedestrians and others responded to the suffragists' impromptu demonstrations and rallies with curiosity, support, and heightened emotion. Jones, Kearns, and Freeman wrote articles for publication, agreed to interviews, and served as press agents for votes-for-women issues on the local, state, and national levels. They took advantage of the emerging presence of newspapers in the New York City metropolitan area at the turn of the twentieth century.

With jewels like these in Jane's and my background, we worked out a partnership with the Floating Foundation of Photography in High Falls, New York, for a 1986 exhibit in Ulster County featuring Edna and Elisabeth.[2] The exhibit justified moving the "Spirit of 1776" campaign wagon from Granddaddy's Philadelphia-area garage and placing it on

2. State University of New York New Paltz professor Amy Kesselman presented a program on New York's women's suffrage movement to accompany the 1986 exhibit. Hundreds of people attended the exhibition and programs about Edna Kearns and Elisabeth Freeman. Joel W. Culp, with the assistance of Thomas B. Culp, transported the "Spirit of 1776" wagon from Pennsylvania to New York State for the 1986 Mansion House exhibition in Kingston, New York.

Edna and Serena Kearns
(L-R) with Irene Davidson,
1913. COURTESY OF THE
AUTHOR.

exhibit for the first time in New York State. The large-format archival prints and wagon collages fashioned by Jone Miller guaranteed that after the exhibition, the wagon took on a life of its own.

Over the decades, the "Spirit of 1776" wagon became recognized as a prime artifact of women's struggle for the franchise, as well as symbolic of patriotic protest themes embedded in this and other twentieth-century American nonviolent social revolutions. After the wagon's inaugural Hudson Valley exhibition in 1986, the importance of building a support infrastructure prior to the centennial celebration of the ratification of the Nineteenth Amendment to the U.S. Constitution became clear to me.

Edna was well known for her community organizing and public speaking. Jane's great aunt Elisabeth, an organizer and lecturer, made a priority of sharing the anticipated benefits of voting rights with working women in cities. She supported peace efforts, women's trade unions, equal rights for African Americans, and Irish independence.

Elisabeth Freeman conducted a lecture tour to raise money for the NAACP antilynching fund. She also traveled to Washington, DC, in 1913 with Rosalie Jones and others on the

"Pilgrim's Hike" to join the suffrage parade organized by Alice Paul and Lucy Burns under the auspices of the National American Woman Suffrage Association. This was the same suffrage parade that Edna, Wilmer, and Serena marched in. The following year, in 1914, Freeman was arrested with writer Upton Sinclair for protesting the treatment of striking Colorado miners.

When chasing after accounts of Elisabeth and Edna, I uncovered several of their collaborations, including how Jane's great aunt, my grandparents, and my mother's older sister Serena showed up in New York City in early January of 1914 to join a march to Albany to speak to the governor. The appointment of poll watchers for the 1915 suffrage referendum was considered essential to prevent election fraud. Another purpose of the march, which some referred to as a "hike," was to educate citizens on the way north. Not every participant completed the over 150-mile trek from New York to Albany on foot. The Kearns family didn't. They returned home, but Elisabeth Freeman persisted, in addition to hike organizer Rosalie Jones and several others.

After the weary group reached the mid-Hudson Valley, they slept overnight at the Mansion House near the Rondout Creek in Kingston, then a popular hotel, before continuing on to the state capital. Shortly thereafter, the *Daily Freeman* in Kingston published an editorial calling the women "bedraggled and charmless" and criticized them for attempting to push their ways into spheres of action for which their own performance proved them to be "pre-eminently unfitted."

The suffrage marchers may not have won over the majority of male voters of the Hudson Valley, but the purpose of the march was accomplished when New York's Governor Martin Henry Glynn approved poll watchers for the 1915 referendum. The men of Ulster County and statewide voted down suffrage in 1915, but New York women finally won the right to vote in 1917. There were 5,800 affirmative votes for the suffrage referendum in Ulster County that year. A total of 9,300 voters were opposed. In New York City, 104,000 affirmative votes carried the state. When the women of New York won the right to vote in 1917, this was considered a major victory that tipped the balance of women's voting rights support across the nation.

Jane Van De Bogart and I continued sharing family suffrage tales with others long after the 1986 exhibit about Elisabeth and Edna closed in Ulster County.

"Elisabeth Freeman was my mother's aunt, a daring and dramatic single woman who dazzled my mother when she was a young child with a flamboyant green velvet dress, titian red hair, and wild stories," Jane Van De Bogart told a college audience at SUNY New Paltz. "I never met my great aunt. She died when I was six months old, but I know my mother and her sisters liked and admired her."

Jane Van De Bogart and I presented several voting rights programs at the state university in New Paltz, first in 1986 and through to 1990. Our respective mothers, Jeanette Wittman and Wilma Kearns Culp, participated. This added human interest to the program.

Jane and I dug even deeper into the past to uncover what both women believed about militant versus more conventional suffrage tactics and strategies. The Pankhurst family of suffragettes in England had trained Elisabeth. She served time in prison for voting rights activism there. Jane's great aunt Elisabeth referred to herself as a "militant suffragist." In an article explaining her position, Freeman wrote: "Six years of battle on English soil and two terms in the hideous Holloway jail have convinced me that militancy is the only way to suffrage for women in England."

"But what about militancy in the United States? Is it justified?" Edna Kearns asked in an undated copy of a speech I found buried in my grandmother's suffrage archive. In it, she wrote:

> I feel that Miss Freeman has taught me a great lesson in regard to passing judgment on others. For I had judged the militant women when I heard that they attacked the property of private merchants. I said, "They can break all the government windows they want to, but when they attack the property of private merchants, I am afraid I cannot sympathize with them." And then, being a believer in justice, and with the knowledge that had I lived in the time previous to the Revolutionary War, I too, regardless of the fact of whether it was lady-like or not, I too would have done anything in my power to help free my country from the tyranny of England. And because of this sense of justice, I am in sympathy with our brave English sisters. . . .[3]

Edna Kearns and her suffrage movement associates dressed in colonial costumes in July 1913 and hung banners on the "Spirit of 1776" wagon. With the pending approval of a federal income tax that year, they protested "taxation without representation." This reinforced a tradition of returning to the nation's founding principles to define and support dissent as an essential part of American history.

Frederick Douglass relied on arguments of patriotic protest in his writings and speeches to justify the abolition of slavery and the extension of freedom to those long denied. Dr. Martin Luther King Jr. grounded many of his arguments for equality and social justice in patriotic protest. Examine the speeches and journals of many U.S. women's suffrage leaders and organizers during the decades following the 1848 women's conference in Seneca Falls. Examples of patriotic protest can be found in references embedded in many sources, if not prominently displayed, in American protest art, speeches, and writings.[4]

It took until I reached age thirty when I lived in Woodstock to fully grasp the contributions of a generation of activists, many of them like my grandparents. Their spirit, vision,

---

3. Handwritten notes for a speech from the archival collection of Edna Buckman Kearns in the possession of the author.
4. Simon Hall, *American Patriotism, American Protest: Social Movements since the Sixties* (Philadelphia: University of Pennsylvania Press, 2011).

The New York State Museum acquired the "Spirit of 1776" suffrage wagon in 2007.
COURTESY OF THE NEW YORK STATE MUSEUM.

and impatience led to committed action. They understood the difficulty of organizing in their own communities and continued in the unflinching awareness of a tradition of patriotic protest. They never considered retreating from a social commitment. It became their duty, their mission, and reflected the burning fire in their hearts.

Community NY
Historic Sites Relating to Women's Suffrage in Central New York

Judith Wellman

The movement for women's right to vote—totally nonviolent—formed one of the largest campaigns for human rights in U.S. history. Central New York was nationally important in this movement. We all know something about famous woman suffragists from this region—from Susan B. Anthony to Elizabeth Cady Stanton, Hester Jeffrey, Matilda Joslyn Gage, and Frederick Douglass. But what do we know about the hundreds of thousands of ordinary and not-so-ordinary people who joined these national leaders? These women and men from farms, villages, and cities reflected a wide variety of ethnic, racial, cultural, and economic backgrounds.

Their numbers were astounding. Here are just three examples, from 1894, 1915, and 1917.

In 1894, suffragists organized a statewide petition campaign "to strike the word 'male' from Article II, Section 1, of the constitution, and thus secure to the women of the State the right to vote on equal terms with men." The Grange, labor unions, and Women's Christian Temperance Union joined the New York State Woman Suffrage Association to collect almost 600,000 signatures from men and women, upstate and downstate (almost one-quarter of New York State's adult population in 1890), on these petitions.

In 1915, about 40,000 marchers walked down Fifth Avenue in the largest suffrage parade ever organized. Suffragists printed 7,230,000 leaflets, 657,200 booklets, 149,533 posters, and a million suffrage buttons, urging New Yorkers to vote yes on women's suffrage in 1915. They lost.

Two years later, in 1917, suffragists repeated their campaign with even more energy. More than a million New Yorkers (about 25 percent of the total adult population in 1920) signed a petition for woman suffrage in 1917. Suffragists held 9,000 meetings upstate and more than 11,000 in New York City. This time they were successful. Although upstate New

Workshop participants, Wood Library, Canandaigua, October 2018. PHOTO BY AUTHOR.

York defeated the measure by 1,510 votes, New York City—buoyed by labor unions and immigrant districts—carried the amendment by 103,863 votes.[1]

Homes, churches, and meeting spaces that help tell the story of this immense movement still stand in neighborhoods all across New York State. In 2019, to help locate these historic sites, Preserve New York (a program of the New York State Council on the Arts and the Preservation League of New York State) funded a cultural resource survey focused on women's suffrage sites in central New York. The Ontario County Historical Society (with Ed Varno, director, and Wilma Townsend, curator) sponsored this survey and hired Judith Wellman, principal investigator, Historical New York Research Associates, to carry it out. Dana Teets, a student in the public history program at Nazareth College, was database manager.

By limiting this first attempt to central New York, we hoped to (a) identify historic suffrage sites that could be nominated to the National Register of Historic Places; (b) create a model project that might be expanded to the rest of New York State; and (c) identify sites that could be added to the National Votes for Women Trail (www.nvwt.org) with markers supplied by the William G. Pomeroy Foundation (https://www.wgpfoundation.org/).

We began with a workshop of local historians and other interested stakeholders from central New York. We ended with three main documents:

(1) an historic context statement, outlining the development of the suffrage movement in central New York;

(2) a database with names of 475 central New York suffragists, adding to Tom Dublin's suffrage biographies for Women and Social Movements (https://documents.alexander street.com/VOTESforWOMEN); and

(3) a database listing 209 women's suffrage sites in central New York.

---

1. "The Two State Campaigns," in *History of Woman Suffrage,* IV: 1883-1900, edited by Susan B. Anthony and Ida Husted Harper (Indianapolis, IN: Hollenbeck Press, 1902), 383; VI, 469–84. The estimate that 25 percent of New York State's adult population signed petitions in both 1894 and 1917 assumes that 40 percent of New York State's total population in both 1890 and 1920 were adults.

These results are online at https://www.ochs.org/womens-suffrage/. Three major possibilities emerged from this project. First, New York State's Historic Preservation Office determined that many of these suffrage sites are eligible for the National Register of Historic Places. Our work might also form the basis of a Multiple Property Document Form, so that suffrage sites can be nominated to the National Register under this general rubric, recognizing the importance of women's suffrage for state and national history.

Second, this central New York survey presents a model that will also work well for other sections of New York State, using similar sources and methods. Future surveys might focus either on specific regions (including western New York, the southern tier, northern New York, the Hudson Valley, New York City, and Long Island) or on the whole state. Sources and methods for all of New York State will be similar to those used for central New York.

Third, sites identified through this survey may also be eligible for historic markers from the National Votes for Women Trail, a program sponsored by the National Collaborative of Women's History Sites (www.ncwhs.org) and the William G. Pomeroy Foundation (www.wgpfoundation.org), with support from the federal Women's Suffrage Centennial Commission (https://www.womensvote100.org/). The first marker from New York State approved through this program was submitted by Karen Lago through the Depauville Free Library. It commemorates six women who signed a petition from Jefferson County for women's suffrage in 1846. Several other nominations are now being considered. We have a statewide committee, chaired by Debra Kolsrud of Johnston, to review possibilities for future markers and to recruit volunteers to work on these.

Women's suffrage marks one of New York State's largest grassroots movement for social change. Passage of the Nineteenth Amendment in 1920 brought more people into the electorate than any other single piece of legislation. Yet it did not lead to voting rights for everyone. African Americans, especially in the South, Asian Americans, Native Americans, Latinx people, and poor people all faced continued challenges to voting rights.

As the fight for women's suffrage showed us, we cannot take democratic institutions for granted. Generations of women and men worked for women's suffrage. For democracy to succeed in our own time, we can do no less.

If you know of historic sites relating to women's suffrage, or if you would like to nominate suffrage sites to the National Register or the National Votes for Women Trail, please contact Judith Wellman (historicalnewyork@me.com). And, don't forgot to vote.

Ontario County Historical Society, Canandaigua, 1914. In 1915, the Canandaigua Political Equality Club hosted the Ontario County Woman Suffrage Association's convention here, with Carrie Chapman Catt as guest speaker. COURTESY OF THE ONTARIO COUNTY HISTORICAL SOCIETY, CANANDAIGUA, 1914.

Methodist Episcopal Zion Church, Rochester, 1906. Hester Jeffreys, nationally known suffragist, organized the Susan B. Anthony Club in this church. Anthony gave her last public speech in this church, and Jeffrey gave a eulogy at Anthony's funeral. PHOTO BY AUTHOR.

Opendore in 2004. Opendore was the home of Isabel Howland, who worked with the
New York State Woman Suffrage Association, especially during their unsuccessful 1894
campaign. PHOTO BY AUTHOR

Opendore in 2016. Isabel Howland Home, now being renovated by the Howland Stone
Store Museum. PHOTO BY AUTHOR.

Teach NY

Exploring Haudenosaunee Influence on America's Suffrage Movement with Students

Kathryn Weller

At the beginning of the nineteenth century, women in American society, once married, ceased to exist in the eyes of the law. Following the precedent of English law, American women were considered minors or wards of their husbands and husbands had absolute control over their children. After the wedding, all assets a woman brought into a marriage or made while married were turned over to the husband. Women could not vote or exercise any official influence in the American political process. In essence, women were ruled by laws written by men, in which they had no say in creating or changing.

However, women in upstate New York experienced a different societal norm in their own backyards, that of the Haudenosaunee. Early women's rights advocates and leaders, including Matilda Joslyn Gage, Elizabeth Cady Stanton, and Lucretia Mott, witnessed first-hand Haudenosaunee communities where there was equality between the sexes. In these Native communities, women maintained custody of children when a relationship ended, held political power by choosing leaders, and controlled their family's property and wealth. Women's rights advocates interacted with Haudenosaunee women and saw how their lives and experiences differed from white women. These women's rights advocates tried to apply what they learned from the Haudenosaunee to American society.

As we celebrate and commemorate the long fight for women's suffrage in the United States, it is important for students to explore the indispensable contributions Haudenosaunee culture had on early feminists. Haudenosaunee society provided a successful model for a system of government built on gender equality. Early women's rights advocates had access to this example and acknowledged the benefits of learning from Haudenosaunee people when developing their strategy for improving women's rights in America. Exploring the strong connections between early suffragists and the Haudenosaunee allows students to create a deeper understanding of the early suffrage movement, the systemic sexism that

Savagery to "civilization" by Joseph Keppler, 1914. COURTESY OF THE LIBRARY
OF CONGRESS.

affected women in American society, and the willingness to look to Native communities for
inspiration in the fight for women's rights.

The New York State Museum's lesson "Haudenosaunee Influence on Early American Feminists" engages students with the guiding question, "How did the Haudenosaunee
inspire early women's rights advocates?" By exploring diverse forms of primary and secondary source material as evidence, students will work to answer the question and build
comfort and familiarity with a variety of sources. With three activities, students progress
toward independent inquiry through artifact analysis and comparing and contrasting different primary documents.

The image *Savagery to "civilization"* provides a visual form of primary evidence that
assists students to build comfort with the topic and using primary sources. Using Visual Thinking Strategies (VTS), students can explore the image discovering details that
introduce the importance of Haudenosaunee society in inspiring suffragists through a
non–text-based document. VTS, a "student-centered facilitation method to create inclusive
discussions," developed by the educators at the Museum of Modern Art, provides a way of
reading the image for information. Educators can engage students with the image through
the following simple guiding questions:

What is going on in this image?
What do you see that makes you think that?
What more can we find?

The questions invite students to participate in discussion through their observations
and state their supporting evidence. This will help students naturally begin to question and
justify their observations and the evidence they are using. When educators invite other

students to build on these observations or make their own observations, students will discuss different interpretations and build a communal experience of discovery that is inclusive, supportive, and student directed. Students will then create a deeper connection with the image *Savagery to "civilization"* through a shared inquiry experience.

This activity provides a way for students to work together when dissecting and interpreting a primary source. The use of a visual primary source is purposeful. Text-based archival documents can sometimes be daunting for students. The techniques needed are already new, but the language is often also unfamiliar. The foundation in the topic may not be strong enough to understand a primary source written for a very different time and place. Vocabulary can be difficult for younger audiences unfamiliar with historic texts. An image helps students hone the same observational skills needed to critically read a historic document but in a way that is more comfortable and removes the barriers to text-based resources. The image acts as a form of scaffolding for all students, especially those who might struggle with English language arts. By introducing the inquiry-based activity with *Savagery of "civilization"* students can contribute and begin to feel competent in their own interpretive skills before moving onto a combination of text-based and visual forms of evidence.

Savagery to "civilization" is a promotional propaganda piece created to celebrate the suffrage movement and its foundation in Haudenosaunee ("Iroquois" on the document) society, and the juxtaposition of racist beliefs about which society exhibits "savagery" and "civilization." The dialogue students have with the image will build comfort with the topic and a base of understanding to explore deeper into the ways Haudenosaunee women and society showed activists what they should demand to make their society more equitable.

To delve deeper into the evidence to answer the guiding question, "How did the Haudenosaunee inspire early women's rights advocates?" students next work together but in smaller groups to compare and contrast primary sources as evidence in four different categories of specific rights that were important to advocates:

1. A woman's right to her children

2. A woman's right to her property

3. A woman's right to equality in her employment

4. A woman's right to political voice in her community

Within these four groups, students work through representative primary sources from American (or English society, which acted as the model for American laws regarding women's rights) and Haudenosaunee society. After identifying their assigned right they learn how each society dealt with it for men and women. Using the evidence provided within the primary sources, students determine if women in each society had the right and how it was apparent in their lives. The evidence is then used to justify their statements and interpretation.

Primary sources include quotes from Haudenosaunee women (as recorded by eth-
nologist Alice Fletcher), observations by suffragists including Elizabeth Cady Stanton and
Matilda Joslyn Gage, newspaper articles, and the laws that Americans were subject to in the
nineteenth century. By comparing these different sources, students can create their own
ideas about how life differed between women in Haudenosaunee and American society.
They can observe how suffragists felt about these differences and the inequity inherent in
American laws. They can also learn how Haudenosaunee people reflected and observed
American law (through the lens of American ethnologists, suffragists, and researchers).

For example, looking at "A woman's right to political voice in her community," students read the quote from Elizabeth Cady Stanton about Haudenosaunee women: "The
women were the great power among the clan, as everywhere else. They did not hesitate,
when occasion required, 'to knock off the horns,' as it was technically called, from the head
of a chief and send him back to the ranks of the warriors. The original nomination of the
chiefs also always rested with the women." This quote shows the informal and formal role
of women in choosing leaders and in helping those leaders maintain power. This observation from a prominent suffragist demonstrates the "great power" that Stanton saw Haudenosaunee women hold in politics.

To compare, students read the "Susannah, Don't You Cry" newspaper article from the
New York Herald on June 20, 1873. The title quickly sets the tone in the article documenting
Susan B. Anthony's sentencing for voting. Anthony was fined $100 for voting. When asked
by the court, in what the article described as "A Superfluous Question," if she had anything
to say, Anthony responded, "she had a great many things to say, and declared that in her
trial every principle of justice had been violated; that every right had been denied; that she
had had no trial by her peers; that the Court and the jurors were her political superiors and
not her peers, and announced her determination to continue her labors until equality was
obtained."

In two documents students see the difference in power between women choosing
leaders in Haudenosaunee society and a woman not only being fined but also denied rights
for attempting to do the same things in American society.

Through self-directed and student-based inquiry, students discover the answer for
themselves instead of the simple acceptance of it as a fact told to them. Students will see
how important it was for early women's rights activists to see a model of the society they
hoped to create in their neighbors living in Haudenosaunee society. This galvanized them
in the belief that equality between the sexes was possible and sustainable. It also shows how
advocates had to question their own accepted norm and perceived dominance as a society
when looking to the advances already accomplished in Haudenosaunee society.

The importance of Haudenosaunee laws and societal norms in the development of
the women's rights movement in New York and American is instrumental in understanding
the suffrage movement for students. It provides a foundation into how the women's rights

owd, which
as, from the
rere at once
rested the

plied with,
d a charge,
to had been
among the
flat of their
see exactly
lves off in a
d. The sol-
pal occupa-
e President
to consider
abor an un-
uld only re-
eir country
ve employ-

arging, six
he hopes of
Brazilians
d got as far
oie.
TION.
was extra-
ng the side-
er near the
le incensed
ed as some-
ry tickets
ting he was
streets as
contusions
against a
getting out

ed in the
ue forward
"brutal act
issued an
and arms,
removed,
perfect re-

YBOAT.

evening as
as leaving
cet, New
red to be
t, suddenly
lity he was
Williams-
ict statien
sciousness,
ed that he
ut refused
elf-destruc-

will be taken to Court this morning,

"SUSANNAH, DON'T YOU CRY."

Miss Susan B. Anthony Fined $100 for Voting—A New Trial Demanded, but Denied—Harrowing Scene in Court—The Man Who Gave Out the Little Papers.

CANANDAIGUA, N. Y., June 19, 1873.

At two o'clock this afternoon Judge Selden made a motion in the case of Miss Susan B. Anthony for a new trial, upon the ground of a misdirection of the Judge in ordering a verdict of guilty without submitting the case to the jury. He maintained, in an elaborate argument, the right of every person charged with crime to have the question of guilt or innocence passed upon by a constitutional jury, and that there was no power in this Court to deprive her of it.

The District Attorney replied, when the Court, in a brief review of the argument of the counsel, denied the motion.

The District Attorney immediately moved that the judgment of the Court be pronounced upon the defendant.

A SUPERFLUOUS QUESTION.

The Court made the usual inquiry of Miss Anthony if she had anything to say why sentence should not be pronounced.

Miss Anthony answered and said she had a great many things to say, and declared that in her trial every principle of justice had been violated; that every right had been denied; that she had had no trial by her peers; that the Court and the jurors were her political superiors and not her peers, and announced her determination to continue her labors until equality was obtained, and was proceeding to discuss the question involved in the case when she was interrupted by the Court, with the remark that these questions could not be reviewed.

MARTYDOM COURTED.

Miss Anthony replied that she w shed it fully understood that she asked no clemency from the Court; that she desired and demanded the full rigor of the law.

Judge Hunt then said that the judgment of the Court is that you pay

A FINE OF ONE HUNDRED DOLLARS

and the costs of the prosecution, and immediately added, "There is no order that you stand committed until the fine is paid." And so the trial ended.

THE CASE OF THE INSPECTORS.

A motion for a new trial is to be made in the case of the inspectors to-morrow morning, on the ground that Hall, one of the defendants, was absent during the trial.

"'Susannah, Don't You Cry,' Miss Susan B. Anthony Fined $100 for Voting," The *New York Herald*, June 20, 1873.

movement moved toward the more focused suffrage movement and will help students understand the interconnectedness of themes seen throughout the nineteenth century.

For students and educators looking to learn further, Sally Roesch Wagner's book, *Sisters in Spirit: Haudenosaunee (Iroquois) Influence on Early American Feminists*, provides a clear resource into how the Haudenosaunee inspired suffragists Elizabeth Cady Stanton, Matilda Joslyn Gage, and Lucretia Mott, as well as how they challenged what was accepted in American society by the stark juxtaposition of the two cultures. The exhibit

"Hodinöhsö:ni' Women: From the Time of Creation" at Seneca Art & Culture Center at Ganondagan "examines the many ways in which Hodinöhsö:ni' women have acted as positive forces in our world, and provides a glimpse into their complex and sophisticated way of life," including the important role they had on the suffrage movement.

For more information on the New York State Museum's educational resources, please visit http://www.nysm.nysed.gov/education; for more information on New York's role in the women's suffrage movement, please visit the New York State Museum's online exhibit "Votes for Women: Celebrating New York's Suffrage Centennial," http://www.nysm.nysed .gov/votes-for-women.

BOOK REVIEWS

In the Heat of the Summer: The New York Riots of 1964 and the War on Crime

By Michael W. Flamm. Philadelphia: University of Pennsylvania Press, 2017.
368 pages, 6" x 9", 21 halftones. $34.95 cloth, $27.50 paper, $20.69 e-book.

Studies of 1960s racial discord in the United States often begin with the Watts uprising in Los Angeles that occurred mid-decade. A year earlier, however—in July and August 1964—eight major rebellions erupted in four states throughout the Northeast and Midwest. The historian Michael Flamm's well-researched and extremely readable narrative explores the first of that summer's unrest, which occurred in New York City's Harlem and Bedford-Stuyvesant neighborhoods. Placing the disturbances in the context of the underlying conditions and the immediate incidents that precipitated the violence and the destruction of property that

ensued, he also deftly lays out the political and social ramifications that followed with Lyndon Johnson's desperate attempt to assuage the American public's growing fear of widespread bloodshed with his War on Crime initiative. *In the Heat of the Summer* offers scholars and casual readers alike an interesting account of a critical time in New York, but also a pivotal moment in the history of the country. Indeed, 1964 proved to be a year in which the events that unfolded had political, economic, and social implications for decades to come. Flamm successfully conveys the gravity of this era and the important role that the first long, hot summer played. For these reasons and more, this book is a must read, particularly for anyone interested in race relations and racial violence in the United States.

As with many instances of racial unrest throughout American history, the events that led to it in New York in the summer of 1964 were disputed. Not in doubt, however, was the fact that on the morning of July 16, white off-duty police lieutenant Thomas Gilligan shot and killed fifteen-year-old black student James Powell across the street from his summer school in the Yorkville neighborhood on the Upper East Side of Manhattan. Some witnesses at the scene suggested Powell had charged Gilligan with a knife; others suggested Powell did not even have a knife. In the end, the specifics mattered little. Two days later, a livid crowd filled the streets of Harlem in protest. What had initially been envisioned as a peaceful gathering organized by the Congress of Racial Equality to acknowledge the disappearance of three civil rights workers in Mississippi had shifted to the matter of police brutality. Although some of the leaders of the march stood down after meeting with officials at Gilligan's regional precinct, the rest of the crowd remained agitated and soon acted on their frustrations. For the next six nights, hundreds of black residents looted and destroyed businesses in Harlem and then in the neighboring borough of Brooklyn. A few days later, Rochester—following a similar pattern of accusations of police brutality—would follow suit. A new era of racial violence had begun.

Flamm's analysis draws on a wide variety of sources, both primary and secondary. By relying predominantly on personal interviews, political archives, and contemporary newspaper accounts, he weaves together a riveting story of the events as they played out in 1964 New York. Moreover, he explores the political backdrop of the presidential race that year that stoked the flames of racial animosity, even as incumbent Lyndon Johnson and his main opponent Republican Barry Goldwater made a public display of taking race and civil rights issues out of their campaigns. The call for "law and order," however, continued to remain constant, and especially after the violence erupted in Harlem, Bedford-Stuyvesant, and Rochester. Flamm also covers such topics as allegations of Communist agitators stirring unrest among African Americans; disagreements between black moderates and radicals; economic and educational disparities creating the conditions that allowed the uprisings to occur; the disconnect between the police and the citizens they served; the tensions between federal and state powers in addressing the violence; and strife between white and Jewish shop owners and the black residents where the destruction occurred. Finally, he ends with Johnson focusing his first full term as president on the War on Crime and a brief overview of its iterations in subsequent presidencies.

In the Heat of the Summer has a lot to offer its readers. The book is well researched and very accessible. Moreover, it fills an important gap in civil rights, 1960s, and racial violence literature. Flamm not only does a good job of describing the events that developed in New York in July 1964, but also of examining the core economic, political, and social factors—both locally and nationally—that fostered the conditions for them to occur in the first place. His account, however, could have been strengthened in at least one way—by including more diverse perspectives. While his chronicle incorporates an assortment of sources, they consist of predominantly the white actors involved and, to a certain degree, mainstream black civil rights activists. Emphasis on some of the more radical elements would have added more depth to his analysis. In addition, although he offers some commentary from black editors and journalists, presenting more of their viewpoints would have enriched his work. A complete rendering of the 1964 New York uprisings remains unfinished. Overall, though, Flamm provides a gripping and solid account of a previously neglected but important chapter in United States history. *In the Heat of the Summer* is well worth the time to read.

Reviewed by Ann V. Collins. Collins is a professor of political science at McKendree University. She is author of The Dawn Broke Hot and Somber: U.S. Race Riots of 1964 *(Westport, CT: Praeger, 2018) and* All Hell Broke Loose: American Race Riots from the Progressive Era through World War II *(Westport, CT: Praeger, 2012).*

Who Should Rule at Home? Confronting the Elite in British New York City

By Joyce D. Goodfriend. Ithaca: Cornell University Press, 2017. 312 pages, 6" x 9". $39.95 cloth, $19.99 e-book.

In a March 19, 1909, letter to Frederick Jackson Turner, Carl L. Becker wrote, "I am immensely confirmed in my idea that the Revolution was only incidentally a matter of home rule, and primarily a matter of democratization of politics & society." "The history of revolutionary parties," Becker added, "must be rewritten on that line."[1] Becker famously followed through on his statement to Turner with his oft-cited *History of Political Parties*, in which he offered analyses of factionalism and class conflict in Manhattan during the 1760s and 1770s.[2] Many historians, of New York and the American Revolution, have used or challenged Becker's

work.[3] In *Who Should Rule at Home?* Joyce D. Goodfriend is the latest to use Becker's work, but rather than use his "home rule" thesis, she instead uses the "home rule" aphorism and Becker only appears once in the entire book: in the index, for the book's title.[4]

By examining the "microsociology of power," Goodfriend explores "the unexplored dimensions of power relations in eighteenth-century New York City by zeroing in on sites where the elite's cultural authority was brought into question" (2). To do so, *Who Should Rule at Home?* is neatly divided into three parts, each of which examine "major sites where the cultural authority of the elite came under siege" (6). Throughout, Goodfriend shows

---

1. Becker to Turner, March 19, 1909, *"What Is the Good of History?" Selected Letters of Carl L. Becker, 1900–1945*, edited by Michael Kammen (Ithaca, NY: Cornell University Press, 1973), 11.
2. Carl L. Becker, *The History of Political Parties in the Province of New York, 1760–1776* (Madison: University of Wisconsin Press 1909).
3. See, for instance, Patricia U. Bonomi, *A Factious People: Politics and Society in Colonial New York* (New York: Columbia University Press, 1971); Roger J. Champagne, *Alexander McDougall and the American Revolution* (Schenectady, NY: Union College Press, 1975); Staughton Lynd, "The Mechanics in New York City Politics, 1774–1785," *Labor History* 5 (1964): 215–46; Lynd, "Who Should Rule at Home? Dutchess County, New York, in the American Revolution," *William and Mary Quarterly* 18, no. 3 (1961): 330–59.
4. Becker, *History*, 5; Goodfriend, *Who Should Rule at Home?* vi, 288.

how Dutch New Yorkers retained their cultural heritage through wide-ranging "oppositional behavior" through linguistics, print, religion, and race (214). Goodfriend's argument that New Yorkers—women, enslaved Africans, servants, the Dutch—opposed the elite almost continually reveals the marginal but notable progress these individuals made in English and then British New York City. Of particular note is Goodfriend's engaging analyses of print, in which she demonstrates the importance of the media form, indicating the immense agency of print, in an era in which English-language publications were increasing in number, as well as the agency of printers and their readers. Together, they shaped the society in which they lived and influenced how people behaved in that society. For Goodfriend, agency took more than one form. She also emphasizes the importance of religion, demonstrating how nonelites' resistance opposed and sometimes changed church practices. For instance, in her lively chapter on George Whitefield, Goodfriend shows how white congregants demanded more evangelical ministries. "Commoners from all corners of society," Goodfriend writes in a short conclusion, "challenged the elite's prescriptions on multiple fronts and in doing so poked holes in the fabric of authority" (238). These "holes," Goodfriend argues, emboldened the "most robust forms of resistance" that New Yorkers were confronted with during the Revolutionary War (239).

There are, however, some issues with *Who Should Rule at Home?* First, Myles Cooper, the Anglican clergyman and president of King's College (now Columbia University), fled the city in May 1775, not August (108). Second, given the limitations of the sources available, Goodfriend's research, though thorough and varied, applies more significance to New Yorkers' actions than is, perhaps, warranted. Many of the people she examines left little, or nothing, behind, and just because some chose to get drunk or have fun, those actions do not necessarily represent a form of cultural resistance (213). Third, the index contains several production errors that should have been caught prior to publication, including the unnecessary inclusion of full titles when abbreviations were offered. In fact, all the abbreviations offered at the start of the index are unnecessarily printed in full at first mention.[5]

Furthermore, by invoking Becker's home rule thesis about the American Revolution but not engaging with it, or the fight for or destruction of Manhattan, or the British occupation, Goodfriend leaves some questions unanswered. How did the commoners she examines respond to the imperial crisis, especially in the early to mid-1770s? Did they sign loyalist petitions or declarations or take the oath of allegiance when it was administered? Did they fight on either side or remain in the city or state after 1783? John Milner, an Anglican clergyman, noted on September 1, 1775, that "neither the descendants of the dutch (the hollanders) in York, Long-Island, or Jersey will risqué their Estates in a doubtful Cause— They will Join the Strongest."[6]

---

5. Goodfriend, *Who Should Rule at Home?* 241, 242 ("*CNYHS*"; "*Doc. Rel.*"; "*Ecc. Rec.*"), 243 ("*MCC*"), 244 ("*DHNY*"), 246 ("*Iconography*"), 259 ("*Whitefield*").
6. Milner to Myles Cooper, September 1, 1775, *The Cause of Loyalty: The Revolutionary Worlds of Myles Cooper*, edited by Christopher F. Minty and Peter W. Walker (forthcoming).

Historians will nevertheless appreciate Goodfriend's deep analyses of colonial New York City, particularly its attention to religion, and hopefully *Who Should Rule at Home?* will spark further studies of Manhattan's eighteenth-century residents.

Reviewed by Christopher F. Minty, managing editor of The John Dickinson Writings Project. Minty is author of "American Demagogues": The Origins of Loyalism in Manhattan *(Cornell University Press, forthcoming).*

Crafting Dissent: Handicraft as Protest from the American Revolution to the Pussyhats

Edited by Hinda Mandell. New York: Rowman & Littlefield, American Association for State and Local History Book Series, 2019. 339 pages, 6" x 9". $55.00 cloth, $52.10 e-book.

Crafting Dissent: Handicraft as Protest from the American Revolution to the Pussyhats is a collection of essays highlighting and examining women's use of textile craft to express their views and protest injustice. The essays also explore the implications of their actions, both for their intended political, social, and economic outcomes and their place in history. The collection was edited by Hinda Mandell, an associate professor in the School of Communications at the University of Rochester and a crafter who uses yarn to "explore and commemorate the suffragist and abolitionist legacies in Rochester, New York."[1] Essayists include activists per-

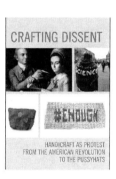

sonally engaged in using craft for protest, as well as scholars in a variety of fields who place these actions in the context of the past, examine their real social and political impacts, and explore ways of interpreting them.

The essays are divided into three parts. Part 1, "Crafting Histories," provides snapshots of the use of handiwork through history for activism and modern use of craft to commemorate history, as well as examinations of the interpretation of textiles as resistance. In part 2, "Politics of Craft," authors examine the actual impact of craft activism. Part 3, "Crafting Culture Conversations," focuses on recent craft activism activities that engage communities in conversation.

The essays in *Crafting Dissent* are primarily focused on the United States, although several have international focus (Great Britain, Australia, and India). For readers in New

---

1. http://www.omghinda.com/doing-yarn.

York State, there are three essays of particular interest. In "Finding Frederick and Anna Douglass's Parking Lot: Public Art's Role in Combating Historical Erasure and Urban Renewal," Hinda Mandell recounts her personal journey using public installations of crocheted work to spark interest in the former site of Frederick and Anna Douglass's home. Struck by the lack of a memorial at a parking lot for which the home was razed, Mandell began a process of historical research and interaction with the site through yarn installations. These actions led to formal recognition of the site and erection of a historical marker. This essay highlights craft as both a means for commemorating a place-based African American history, and as a way for enacting change to ensure that history is remembered long term.

Shannon Dehoff and Jill Swiencicki discuss a project with national focus, which was staged in New York, in "'Consent Trumps Everything': The Clothesline Art Project and the Election Politics of Sexual Assault." In traditional applications of the Clothesline Project (created in 1990), participants decorate shirts to address domestic violence, rape, and sexual assault, and the shirts are then mounted on clotheslines in public spaces. In this 2016 installation at St. John Fisher College in Rochester, New York, planners sought to "publicly condemn Donald Trump's sexual assault discourse" immediately before the 2016 presidential election.[2] In doing so, they tweaked a usual rule of the Clothesline Project, to not name an attacker or rapist not formally charged with a crime. The intended result of the clothesline, to spark thought and conversation about this form of misogyny, remained the same as more traditional iterations of the Clothesline Project.

Finally, "Stitching Dissent: From the Suffragists to Pussyhat Politics," by Anne Bruder, discusses both the embrace and rejection of textile arts by early women's rights reformers (many based in New York) and by contemporary women at the Women's March, and the many associations textiles carry within both movements.

While the content of the rest of the essays is not focused on New York specifically, our state's rich history of textile production and activism lends itself to many connections. For example, one can find a continuation in the timeline of struggle for fair labor practices and wages in the garment industry in both "The Entanglement of Consumption, Commerce, and Craft Activism," by Hannah Bush, and "How to Be a Craftivist: The Art of Gentle Protest and the Case of the 'Living Wage' for One of the Largest Retail Companies in the United Kingdom," by Sarah Corbett. With New York having served as a hotspot for garment industry-centered protests and union work, these essays provide useful contemporary context of the continuing struggle for equity in the production of textiles. While this fight has become more global, it continues to be an issue that disproportionately impacts women workers.

In "Reshaping the Narrative Around People of Color and Craftivism," Diane Ivey engaged crafting community members in conversation about the lack of representation

---

2. Hinda Mandell, ed., *Crafting Dissent: Handicraft as Protest from the American Revolution to the Pussyhats* (New York: Rowman & Littlefield, 2019), 202.

among big voices in the crafting world (i.e., major crafting magazines and producers of supplies), but also about the shift, especially after the 2016 election, toward more black and Indigenous people of color putting their work out into the world through alternate means, especially social media. This topic could have included even more voices and research, but ultimately, the essay in its present form is an important read for those of us who work on the history of craft, or curate craft-based collections. With the new resurgence and expansion of the Black Lives Matter movement, we see an even greater amplification of the voices and work of black artists and crafters, and the use of their work to support the movement.

On first impression, the essays of *Crafting Dissent* may seem to lack cohesion, and it is difficult to see why someone might wish to own this whole collection together. Upon more thorough review though, deeper themes emerge. For historians, the blend of the diverse essays is helpful in that it encourages linking past (and the history of crafts used for resistance and activism) to present (successful models of craft for political and economic engagement). This type of connection can only deepen our understanding of the history of craft for activism (or craftivism), and our representation of it in our museum collections and writing. For readers interested in engaging in craft for dissent, the lessons of activist crafting, both in the distant and more recent past, are valuable in making decisions about how to carry out craft-based actions.

Reviewed by Ashley Hopkins-Benton. Hopkins-Benton is senior historian for social history at the New York State Museum in Albany, New York. She is coauthor of Votes for Women: Celebrating New York's Suffrage Centennial *(Albany: State University of New York Press, 2017).*

America's First Freedom Rider: Elizabeth Jennings, Chester A. Arthur, and the Early Fight for Civil Rights

By Jerry Mikorenda. Guilford, CT: Lyons Press, 2020. 256 pages, 6" x 9". $24.95 cloth, $23.50 e-book.

Thirty years ago, African American historian John H. Hewitt's article about Elizabeth Jennings, an African American teacher who successfully sued the Third Avenue Railway Company for forcibly ejecting her from a streetcar in Manhattan in 1854 with Chester A. Arthur as her lawyer, was published in *New York History*. At the time, Hewitt lamented that a "thumbnail sketch" existed about Jennings in African American history narratives.[1] Three decades later, Jerry Mikorenda's *America's First Freedom Rider: Elizabeth Jennings, Chester A. Arthur, and the Early Fight for Civil Rights* fills this gap with this meticulously researched biography of Jennings and how her life diverged and intersected with Arthur's during nineteenth-century America.

America's First Freedom Rider is organized into fifteen chapters with an additional "Afterlife" chapter in which Mikorenda uses eloquent prose to illustrate how Jennings's and Arthur's lives reflected "the norms of a society that to this day values race and gender over all attributes."[2] Chapters 1 through 6 highlight the Jennings and Arthur family pedigrees, upbringings as children during the abolitionist movements of the nineteenth century, experiences in school, and training for their respective careers. Chapters 7 through 15 address the streetcar ejection, lawsuit, and Jennings's and Arthur's lives after the court case, noting the continuance of her teaching career and family life, and his rise from New York Customs House Collector to vice president and president of the United States.

This book possesses several strengths as an impactful teaching tool in the history and social science disciplines. Secondary or undergraduate students could examine *America's First Freedom Rider* as an example of how to conduct local history research. Mikorenda's use of newspapers served as invaluable primary sources that documented not only Jennings's case and Arthur's career, but also the context of nineteenth-century America that situated their lives in the racial climate of pre- and post-bellum New York. *America's First Freedom Rider* is an example of how important the efforts of universities, libraries, archives, professional organizations, and historical societies are to diversity their finding aids and digitize their collections. Such availability can lead professional and amateur researchers

1. John H. Hewitt, "The Search for Elizabeth Jennings, Heroine of a Sunday Afternoon in New York City," *New York History* 71, no. 4 (1990): 387.
2. Jerry Mikorenda, *America's First Freedom Rider: Elizabeth Jennings, Chester A. Arthur, and the Early Fight for Civil Rights* (Guilford, CT: Lyons Press, 2020), xii.

alike to uncover the voices of underrepresented people who left indelible marks on social justice and racial progress throughout United States history.[3]

Moreover, *America's First Freedom Rider* can be used as a case study tool in public history. Mikorenda states that the book "is intended for nonacademic readers interested in the subject matter," however, this research is entrenched in archival research that professional scholars and history buffs can both conduct.[4] According to Anna Green and Kathleen Troup, public histories "provide insight into the active processes of public engagement with the past."[5] For example, Mikorenda discusses how Miriam Sicherman's students at P.S. 361 successfully petitioned the New York City Council to erect a street sign in honor of Jennings in 2007.[6] He cites Dr. Katherine Perrotta, whose dissertation examined whether middle and secondary students' analysis of primary sources about Elizabeth Jennings could promote historical empathy.[7] Mikorenda also notes that a statue of Jennings will be erected at Manhattan's Grand Central Station as part of the "She Built NYC" initiative in 2022. These examples in *America's First Freedom Rider* demonstrate how public histories can be implemented as critical pedagogy to engage citizens in learning about "the usable past" with regard to examining which people are honored and included in curriculum, and how to take informed action in the present to address issues from the past.[8]

In light of the recent passing of John Lewis, expanded discussion of the parallels between the title of the book and the Freedom Riders of the 1960s would strengthen the historical contextualization of how Jennings's treatment and actions on the streetcar were not novel, but part of a long tradition of black women who endured violence when challenging Jim Crow segregation during the nineteenth and twentieth centuries. Overall, *America's*

---

3. Please see the faculty profile of Dr. Kenvi C. Phillips, who is the inaugural Curator of Race and Ethnicity at the Schlesinger Library on the History of Women in America, Radcliffe Institute for Advanced Study, Harvard University, https://projects.iq.harvard.edu/radworkshop2018/people/kenvi-phillips. Additionally, please refer to the keynote panel *Correcting the Archive: Historical Empathy and Inclusivity in the Social Studies Classroom Through the Lens of Woman Suffrage* from the June 23, 2020, National Coalition of Girls Schools virtual conference "Stand Up, Speak Up," where Dr. Phillips, Dr. Martha S. Jones, Dr. Allison K. Lange, and Dr. Katherine Perrotta discussed the issue of diversification of archives to represent women of color, https://www.ncgs.org/professional-development/2020-ncgs-conference/speakers/.

4. Mikorenda, *America's First Freedom Rider*, 223.

5. Anna Green and Kathleen Troup, *The Houses of History: A Critical Reader in History and Theory*, 2nd ed. (Manchester: Manchester University Press, 2016), 351.

6. Mikorenda, *America's First Freedom Rider*, 210. He also references Dr. Alan J. Singer of Hofstra University, who wrote *New York and Slavery: Time to Teach the Truth* (Albany, NY: State University of New York Press, 2005), in the chapter 3 bibliography.

7. Mikorenda, *America's First Freedom Rider*, 217. Also see Katherine Anne Assante Perrotta, "More than a Feeling: A Study on Conditions that Promote Historical Empathy in Middle and Secondary Social Studies Classes with 'The Elizabeth Jennings Project'" (PhD diss., Georgia State University, 2016, https://scholarworks.gsu.edu/mse_diss/41).

8. Green and Troup, *The Houses of History*, 351. Also see Katherine Perrotta and Chara H. Bohan, "Nineteenth Century Rosa Parks? Assessing Elizabeth Jennings' Legacy as a Teacher and Civil Rights Pioneer in Antebellum America," *Vitae Scholasticae: The Journal of Educational Biography* 30, no. 2 (2013): 5–23.

First Freedom Rider is a powerful piece of public history research on New York City, the antebellum North, and black freedom movement in U.S. history. Elizabeth Jennings and Chester A. Arthur led remarkable lives, and while fate may have brought them together under arduous circumstances, their actions in challenging long-standing racial discrimination in pre-Civil War New York blazed the path for future freedom riders and activists to fight for racial equity in the United States for years to come.

Reviewed by Katherine Perrotta. Perrotta is assistant professor of middle grades and secondary social studies education at Mercer University's Tift College of Education.

Communes in America, 1975–2000

By Timothy Miller. Syracuse, NY: Syracuse University Press, 2019. 280 pages, 6" x 9". $65.00 cloth, $29.95 paper.

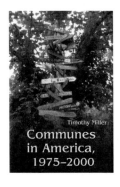

Timothy Miller, professor of religious studies at the University of Kansas, has done more important work on the history of intentional communities in the United States than any historian I can think of. *Communes in America, 1975–2000* is the third and final book in his series that examines the history and relevance of American communes from 1900 to 2000 and includes the previous volumes *The Quest for Utopia in Twentieth-Century America* (1998) and *The '60s Communes: Hippies and Beyond* (1999). Collectively they represent a groundbreaking approach to the subject by deeply mining the archival record, oral history, and quantitative methods.

According to the Foundation for Intentional Community's database, there are currently forty-seven "established" (including four or more adults in residence and in existence for at least two years) intentional communities in New York State, which is more than any other state except California, Washington, and Oregon.[1] New York has a long and varied history as the home of prominent intentional communities ranging from the Shakers settling in New Lebanon in the late eighteenth century, the Oneida Community's founding in 1848, and the establishment of the turn-of-the-century communal art colonies of Roycroft in East Aurora and Byrdcliffe near Woodstock, to the Gate Hill Cooperative avant-garde artists' commune cofounded by John Cage in 1954 near Stony Point and Timothy

---

1. "Communities by Country," Foundation for Intentional Community, https://www.ic.org /directory/intentional-communities-by-country/.

Leary's psychedelic commune residing on a 2,500-acre estate in the village of Millbrook, all of which are touched upon in Miller's series. His most recent work also notes the important communal Hindu ashrams Shree Muktananda Ashram in the Catskills and Shanti Mandir in Walden, as well as the Buddhist communes Dai Bosatsu Zendo and the Zen Mountain Monastery, also both in the Catskill mountains. The number and variety of intentional communities that called New York State home is truly amazing.

In the preface of *Communes in America, 1975–2000*, Miller outlines his criteria for inclusion in his study, which is consistent with the previous volumes and includes the following four "must haves" that a group must possess to be considered an intentional community:

1. The group must be gathered on the basis of some kind of purpose or vision and not simply just people living together by chance or family ties.

2. The group must live together on property that has some clear physical commonality.

3. The group must have some kind of financial or material sharing.

4. The group must consist of at least five adults who are not related by blood or marriage.

Miller adds that to be considered for the study, a group also must have "a sense of being withdrawn or set apart from conventional society," which is why he does not include Native American tribes, which he rightfully defines as being *of* the conventional society of their time and place, *not* outside it. Miller also does not include groups such as monasteries or convents belonging to traditional religious institutions.

Communes in America, 1975–2000 is broken down into seven thematic chapters and two appendices. Chapters 2 and 3 illustrate how intentional communities reacted and adapted to social and environmental challenges in the larger society through such innovations as cohousing communes and ecovillages. Chapters 4 and 5 are dedicated to intentional communities with a spiritual purpose, and chapter 6 outlines activist and social justice communities, including feminist and LGBTQ groups. Chapter 7 investigates the often negative public perception of intentional communities during the period of 1975–2000 as a result of tragedies such as the mass suicides at Jonestown and Heaven's Gate and the deadly assaults on MOVE and the Branch Davidian compounds. Miller cautions the reader not to paint all intentional communities with the same brush based on these horrifying (but rare) catastrophes.

The appendices provide excellent quantitative material drawn from the entire series as well as Miller's other works on the subject. Appendix A uses evidence going back to the 1600s to answer the question of whether or not intentional communities develop in waves as a direct result of what is happening in the larger society. Appendix B consists of a list of every intentional community that Miller has uncovered and that fits his criteria. Despite including over three thousand entries, Miller notes that this is but a fraction of the number of possible groups that have existed over time in America since the data that exists is spotty at best as many intentional communities kept few, if any, records.

Communes in America, 1975–2000 is an excellent final volume in Miller's series, which itself is the first attempt to comprehensively study the intentional community phenomenon from 1900 to 2000. Miller's work should lead to other such studies in other eras and geographical locations, and has the potential to build into a robust investigation of why people of various backgrounds and beliefs have continued throughout history to attempt to live communally and outside their dominant society. As Miller rightly notes, "For over four hundred years intentional communities have been in our midst, sometimes quietly, sometimes boisterously, and at centuries end they were still with us."

Reviewed by Devin R. Lander. Lander is the New York State Historian and coeditor of the journal *New York History.*

New York Recentered: Building the Metropolis from the Shore

By Kara Murphy Schlichting. Chicago: University of Chicago Press, 2019. 319 pages, 6" x 9". $40.00 cloth, $10.00 e-book.

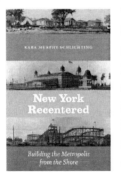

"If the skyscraper symbolizes Manhattan, the greater metropolis is captured by a more subtle yet nevertheless equally salient feature—its coast" (1). In this compelling new study of the growth of New York, Kara Murphy Schlichting offers a critical reorientation of scholarly focus, eschewing linear notions of city expansion in favor of a nuanced consideration of "the regional city as an evolving series of temporary environments with different users who had their own visions and practices" (6). Schlichting makes the case by engaging in environmental history at its most comprehensive—revealing "New York City's waterways and tides, islands, and estuary system" as "the parameters that shaped the form and function of the regional city" (12); and by presenting political history at its most dynamic—narrating "interaction between citizens, governments, and professional planners," that often proved most potent at the local level (7). This empowers the author to reframe "growth as a complex political process in part shaped by the litany of modest choices by local actors and filled with compromises, incremental accomplishments, and unanticipated consequences," and flowing from "the complexity of human interactions" with the natural world (8, 12). Schlichting deftly navigates those wonderful complexities, elegantly synthesizing the environmental with the economic, the political with the social. The result is a masterfully crafted revisionist exploration of the making of modern New York.

Schlichting challenges the traditional notion that "professional planners and the powerful administrative center that Manhattan represented" masterminded a "unidirectional" growth "radiating outwards from an urban core" to "transform" formerly "undifferentiated and unimportant" peripheral regions (2). Instead, the author reveals "the unpredictable dynamism of localism" that made "the periphery into a richly populated and politically contested territory rather than a space defined solely by official plans" (9). Modern New York was therefore "the civic heart of a great system of industrial and commercial centers and suburbs" representing "the culmination of a century's worth of regional projects" and unified by a shared environment into "a discernible geographic region best identified as the coastal metropolitan corridor" (1, 14).

While *New York Recentered* is a multifaceted revisionist work, the book never loses focus and does not get bogged down in arcane jargon. This is a credit to the author's skills as a writer and instincts as a historian. Theoretical terms are defined clearly and deployed seamlessly, and the writing is graceful and lively. Notwithstanding the analytical profundity of her work, Schlichting always elevates the human element—systematically demonstrating that generations of diverse local interests exacted a "cumulative influence" (9) that "made possible the realization of a modern regional city by the mid-twentieth century" (14). In telling those stories, as much as in her critical interventions, Schlichting makes significant contributions to New York history. Indeed, like the author's conceptualization of the regional metropolis itself, her monograph's powerful totality is the worthy sum of its fascinating parts.

The book presents a chronological series of case studies, interconnected through their protagonists' evolving economic aspirations for connection with Manhattan and their localities' dynamic ties to the unique coastal geography north and east of the city. The first is an absorbing consideration of nineteenth-century "benefactor planning" by P. T. Barnum in Bridgeport and William Steinway in Long Island City. Schlichting evokes the often ad hoc nature of Gilded Age growth: both Barnum and Steinway foresaw that their cities' advantageous position along New York's water and rail corridors could allow them to benefit from Gotham's growth (20), but they also recognized the dysfunction of inept local government and took matters into their own hands—turning "themselves into city builders by privately initiating public works" (19, 26, 33, 38). These entrepreneurial builders discerned that "the periphery was a unique place to experiment in urban form because it could be at once accessible to regional patterns of urbanization yet distinctive" (17). The author furnishes an important addendum to conceptions of business-minded urban planning dominated by the authoritarian paternalism of George Pullman or the isolated feudalism of mine and mill villages; alternatively, Barnum and Steinway intertwined private and public interests, engaged in civic boosterism, attracted diverse industries and population, and intentionally "created a manufacturing periphery for greater New York" (29, 43).

Simultaneously, local interests in lower Westchester were cultivating stronger bonds with the urban center. While planners in New York believed by the 1860s that "the city had outgrown Manhattan island" and sought to annex their northern periphery over environmental concerns, boosters beyond the Harlem River also encouraged urbanization, viewing "themselves as a part of a regional city" and eager to "tie core and periphery together politically" through annexation (48, 55–57). Significantly, annexing this trans-Harlem borderland "fundamentally shifted the meaning of New York City" by unmooring conceptions of the municipality from the physical borders of Manhattan: now "the material nature of greater New York became a framework with which to understand city boundaries" (58) and the Harlem River "was not a boundary line but a segment of an indissoluble natural system" (78). Therefore this "birth of the Bronx" in the late nineteenth century demonstrated that "nature set the stage for a unified city spanning the islands and peninsulas of the harbor" (78).

One result of this environmentally driven regionalism was the rise of a noncontiguous but interconnected "leisure corridor" stretching northeastward along the East River, and Schlichting explores how diverse New Yorkers developed those spaces, revealing working-class and recent-immigrant agency and correcting views of "suburbs as preserves of the affluent" (83). These urbanites sought the "benefits of the coastal environment" and "embraced the borderlands of the upper East River as common land, informal extensions of resorts where they could enjoy the nature of the beach and bay" (84, 91, 95). Such leisure-seekers differed from boosters and planners who had encouraged integration of the outlying districts because "they found distance and differences valuable," and some even developed "blue-collar suburbs," demonstrating that "the regional city developed through projects designed to unify districts but also at times through projects that marked the edge as distinct" (97, 99). The leisure corridor was marked by battles over access, and its boom led to the degradation of the very environmental features that had attracted city dwellers to begin with (117); yet this scattered peripheral suburbanization brought the metropolis "sewer and water systems, electrification, trolley and ferry lines, and roads to the city's remote corners . . . without conscious planning" (118).

Throughout this period, the interface of local interests with a shared coastal environment had encouraged regionalism. So, too, had a growing sense among planners that leisure was "a 'public problem' requiring government oversight" (123). Such attitudes informed Progressive Era notions of parks and parkways as "large-scale planning tools" (133). Yet at the very moment central planners were gaining institutional power with the creation of county and regional park commissions in the 1920s, the localism that had once enhanced metropolitan reach was increasingly hindering such integration. The strong local opposition to the designs of the Long Island State Parks Commission under Governor Alfred E. Smith and his parks czar Robert Moses is an infamous early example that is nicely contextualized in this account (142–49). Indeed, Schlichting's presentation of Moses throughout the book is perhaps the most balanced and nuanced I have encountered, characteristically grounded in assiduous archival research. Despite occasional setbacks for the planners, however, "new, powerful permanent park commissions structured the urban fringe with modern, public spaces," once again shifting initiative to the periphery: "landscape features often associated with New York's emergence as a modern city … the comprehensive highway network and quality large-scale public parks—originated in the hinterland projects of regional commissions," which, ironically "led to regional decentralization and the growth of suburbs in Nassau and Westchester" (155, 156).

By that time, decades of frenetic, disorderly growth on New York's periphery had transformed the city into a recognizably modern regional metropolis but had also revealed the environmental toll of "market-driven," "unplanned development" through catastrophes like the Queens sewer crisis (202). The forces of systematic regionalism, epitomized by Moses, could leverage the insalubrious results of administrative anarchy to gain traction for centralized master-planning thanks to a fortuitous confluence of events: preparation for Queens's 1939 World's Fair compelled investments in infrastructure (not only modern sewerage, but also the Bronx-Whitestone Bridge), while New Deal funds enabled Moses and others to commence transformative initiatives including the Triborough Bridge. Thus "regional projects funded by state and federal appropriations outpaced" but never quite overthrew localism (218).

Ultimately, Schlichting convincingly demonstrates how "the making of greater New York is an inherently regional story, a history of the periphery and center developing in tandem" (225). This book should command broad interest among readers of this journal and urban, political, and environmental historians. With her persuasively argued, gracefully constructed, and thoroughly fascinating study, Schlichting has produced a major contribution to the history of New York City and State.

Reviewed by Robert Chiles. Chiles is a senior lecturer at the University of Maryland with a focus on U.S. politics and society from the Gilded Age to World War II. He is coeditor of the journal New York History *and author of* The Revolution of '28: Al Smith, American Progressivism, and the Coming of the New Deal *(Cornell University Press, 2018).*

The Majestic Nature of the North: Thomas Kelah Wharton's Journeys in Antebellum America through the Hudson River Valley and New England

Edited by Steven A. Walton and Michael J. Armstrong. Albany, NY: State University of New York Press, 2019. 374 pages, illustrated, 7" x 10". $90.00 cloth, $34.95 paper, $69.30 e-book.

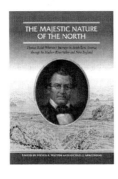

This extensive selection from the personal journals of Thomas Kelah Wharton offers rich rewards to anyone delving into its engaging pages. His fascinating entries, spanning the period May 1832 through October 1834, and June 25 through December 6, 1853, provide contrasting, vivid accounts of his youthful years in New York City and the Hudson River Valley, and his middle-aged journey from New Orleans to Boston nineteen years later. Wharton (1814–62), who over the course of a varied career combined his skills as artist, teacher, and architect-construction superintendent, deserves to be better known, a task that the editors of this volume set out to achieve. A young English immigrant to the United States, Wharton lived in the states of Ohio, New York, and Louisiana over the course of his life. His surviving manuscript journals, in the collections of the New York Public Library, comprise seven volumes dating from 1830 to 1862 (four illustrated with his drawings) in addition to a sketchbook.

Associate professor of history at Michigan Technological University, Steven A. Walton, along with retired senior vice president of operations for *U.S. News & World Report*, Michael J. Armstrong, united in their involvement with the restoration of a Wharton-designed chapel, edited these newly published portions of Wharton's journals. Also included are a selection of Wharton's sketches illustrating his skill as an artist and providing images of some of the scenes and places he mentions. Disappointingly, the small size with which these sketches are reproduced insufficiently conveys their fine detail and artistry.

Preparing this publication presented challenges to its editors. First, Wharton himself apparently edited and rewrote portions of his 1830s journals, deleting "several verses" which his "maturer [sic] judgement" suggested be "omitted" (2–3). Based on Wharton's own admission, the editors are right to wonder what else Wharton might have left out from his original notes, and they warn that surviving journal entries are "not an unfiltered composition" (3). Second, in their preface, the editors enumerate many individuals who over the last fifty years directly contributed to the research and transcription efforts culminating in the present work (xiv–xv). Much of this material was assimilated in their preparation of this book; not always as seamlessly as they hoped (xiii).

The resulting volume includes a short, explanatory paragraph on their transcription methodology, an introduction, three chapters comprising the body of Wharton's journal entries, Wharton family genealogical tables, a "Biographical Register" of many of the people mentioned in the journals, an appendix listing Wharton's known artistic and architectural works, endnotes, and an index. Of the three main chapters, the first is an autobiographical sketch penned by Wharton in June 3, 1854 (31). The sometimes confusing and repetitive introduction greatly expands the background of Wharton's life and career.

Chapter 2 covers the years 1832–1834 and offers an abundance of firsthand material about New York City and the lower Hudson River Valley in this period. Especially valuable are Wharton's recounted experiences of living in the Hudson River households of imminent physician, scholar, and botanist, Dr. David Hosack; Colonel Sylvanus Thayer, superintendent of West Point Military Academy; and Gouverneur Kemble, wealthy industrialist, patron of the arts, and a founder of the West Point Foundry in Cold Spring, New York. The societal and cultural interconnections among these individuals, in addition to prominent New York City architect, Martin Thompson, under whose direction Wharton studied, is revealed in remarkable detail. Recognizing his natural artistic talents, each of these men became important mentors to Wharton, shaped his career, and became lifelong friends. This portion of Wharton's journal includes descriptions of his introductions to many prominent New York artists, politicians, and writers of the period. Additionally, the reader gains valuable insights into the role of religious—especially Episcopalian—institutions in education. Through Thayer's connections, Wharton became an instructor in drawing and mathematics at William Muhlenberg's Flushing Institute, an occupation that he pursued in New York and eventually in Louisiana.

Chapter 3 includes Wharton's journal entries from June through early December 1853. Here he records a trip he undertook with his family from New Orleans to Boston. In contrast with his earlier entries, these reflect a mature adult whose architectural and artistic aptitude, along with a finely honed critical appreciation, are well developed. The reader is amply rewarded with engaging passages documenting myriad details of everyday family life and the communities he explores during long, almost daily walks. He writes descriptive accounts of steamboat and railroad travel, and of the lively Boston social, cultural, artistic, and architectural scene, which he appreciatively observes during his extended residence there. Each page reveals intriguing glimpses into the antebellum world through which Wharton travels and in which he lives.

The editors deserve great credit for having made this important source of historical information widely available. It is unfortunate that their accomplishment is marred by a series of errors peppering their preface, introduction, list of illustrations, and even extending to several notes. Many of these involve misidentifications of chapter and page numbers. One example must suffice here. In the preface, reference is made to "our chapter 3; *Journal* 1; 122–310" (xiv); it is actually chapter number 2, pages 37 through 128.

Those interested in reading more of Wharton's journals, can consult two previous publications. "From England to Ohio, 1830–1832: The Journal of Thomas K. Wharton," edited by James H. Rodabaugh, was published in *The Ohio Historical Society Quarterly* Volume 65, numbers 1 and 2, January and April 1956. *Queen of the South: New Orleans, 1853–1862, The Journal of Thomas K. Wharton,* edited by Samuel Wilson Jr., Patricia Brady, and Lynn D. Adams, was published by the Historic New Orleans Collection and the New York Public Library in 1999.

Reviewed by Paul G. Schneider Jr., independent historian. Schneider is a member of the National Coalition of Independent Scholars.

#MuseumFromHome

As I write this, five months have passed since the first COVID-19 case was recorded in New York State. Governor Cuomo declared a disaster emergency on March 7, 2020. On March 16, he announced restrictions on public gatherings. The NY on Pause Executive Order closing all nonessential businesses statewide was issued on March 20. The governor's NY Forward reopening plan designated museums as "attractive nuisances," unable to open until a region safely reached phase four. Recent upticks in the spread of the virus and the expansion of infection rates in densely populated areas has slowed the opening of museums. Although we are still gathering data, MANY's most recent COVID-19 impact study indicates that half of New York's museums have reopened, 40 percent plan to open in August or September, and 10 percent will not be opening in 2020. New York's museums have lost more than $500 million in earned income since closing their gallery doors.

Museum professionals creatively combine practice from business, art, tourism, academia, and cultural sectors to share the stories embodied in collections. The pace at which museum professionals leveraged these combined skills and refocused their work to deliver content digitally is astonishing. The economic and health care crisis caused by the insufficient response to this worldwide pandemic required a shift for which most were unprepared. Those museums who had resources prior to the pandemic to invest in robust websites, a library of digital images of their collections, and dedicated social media staff were well positioned to leverage their staff's creativity to reach beyond their walls with digital programming. Eighty-one percent of museums who responded to MANY's first COVID-19 Impact Survey (report issued May 27, 2020; https://nysmuseums.org/COVID19resources) increased their social media within the first month of NY on Pause. The Museum Computer Network (https://mcn.edu/a-guide-to-virtual-museum-resources/) has a comprehensive list of virtual museum resources. American Alliance of Museums has compiled a

section on their website about how museums have gone virtual (see https://www.aam-us
.org/category/covid-19/), and selected examples of best practices are available on the MANY
website (https://nysmuseums.org/COVID19resources#digitalengagement). This article is a
more personal perspective on how, under the pressure of a pandemic, museums combined
staff talent and creativity with virtual program delivery and digital images to extend their
reach beyond most of our imaginations.

I was fortunate to spend two days as part of a group of photography students at the
birth of MIT's Media Lab thirty-five years ago (see https://www.media.mit.edu/about
/history/). We stood around a room with a computer the size of five refrigerators at the
center and watched as the image on a Kodachrome slide was read by the computer, pix-
elated and projected on a small screen. The operator then changed the color and density of
the image pixel by pixel. What took hours, now takes seconds, formerly room-size equipment fits in our hands, and although the investment in professionally digitized images remains unachievable for many museums, few of us hesitate to take out our mobile devices
and capture what we see to create personal visual libraries shared across time and space.

As digital technologies became more accessible in the late 1990s, museums expanded
access to their collections through websites. Virtual galleries became substitute display
spaces for curators, homepages transformed into alternative visitor entranceways, and educators used virtual learning platforms to reach students in classes beyond the districts in
which the museums were located. At the time I was seeking support for greater funding
for digital initiatives, my mantra became "many more people will never walk through your
doors than will ever walk through your doors." I could not imagine the path we would
travel to reach the tipping point that defines our operational "new normal."

#MuseumFromHome blossomed in the cultural soil tilled by French author and art critic André Malraux (1901–76) who wrote of an "imaginary museum," a dislocated place where one could assemble a collection from the world's art to hang in a personally defined museum. In the first step away from the original object, photography in the nineteenth century made it possible to gather on printed pages objects that could never be physically assembled. The role of the photographer was eventually elevated in the museum hierarchy of the early twentieth century. As the cost of mass printing declined after World War II, objects became within the reach of those who could afford publications that re-formed narratives and built new connections between objects from around the world.

Illustrated art books, heavy volumes filling oversized shelves, served as the primary learning resource for generations of museum professionals like me who fall into the category of digital immigrants. I have been laughed at by a digital native (people born after 1980) who called up an image faster on their computer than I could locate it in the book I took from the shelf. Website collections and databases replaced books, and now smart phones have replaced websites as the primary tool to access images from museum collections.

For this article I wandered around Twitter, Facebook, LinkedIn, and Instagram looking at #MuseumFromHome and quickly concluded that there is no way to consume all of the content museums and followers created during quarantine. Google Analytics records the first use of the hashtag on March 15; their graph line continues to trend upward. Fifteen thousand people follow #MuseumFromHome on Facebook. A search on Instagram brings up 152,000 posts. On LinkedIn you can find 117,000 posts by museum professionals who share how they have delivered gallery-based content virtually. It is impossible to follow the threads on the hundreds of thousands of Tweets that use the hashtag.

As my searches branched off, collections that I had never hoped to see in person were at my fingertips. As expected, the backs of dresses, bottoms of vessels, details of wood carvings, glaze crazing on ceramics, and fingerprints on castings were not part of the experience. But as I scrolled through #MuseumFromHome on Instagram, my vision was washed with color, form, figure, light, and highly random adjacencies that created their own visual meaning. The hierarchy of architectural space in museums traditionally relegated the work of non-European cultures to lower-level galleries and less trafficked corners of display spaces. Those physical barriers dissolve in the virtual space into a new kind of consumption unfiltered by authoritative interpretation or a dominant curatorial narrative. By removing physical and temporal boundaries, #MuseumFromHome drew through lines across the globe, sparking hope that collections will be accessible to more than those who can afford the price of admission.

When reflecting upon how far museums have come in the digital space, it helped me to remember that we have traveled very far very quickly. Creative Commons began to change how museums think about copyright law in 2001. LinkedIn launched in 2002, Facebook in 2004, Twitter in 2006, Instagram in 2010, and Google Arts and Culture in 2011. Over the past five months I lingered at the edges of #MuseumFromHome when my eyes

#museumfromhome

156,215 posts

Following

Related Hashtags #museumathome #museums #arthistorian #virtualmuseum #artexhibit #artmuseum #museumvisit #virtualexhibition #collectart #contemporaryartists

Top posts

recovered from the blur of a seemingly endless schedule packed with meetings on Zoom. I dipped into art making lessons, took a writing class, listened to stories, drank cocktails with curators, watched digitally remastered archival films, asked questions in the chat box of virtual field trips, bid during online silent auctions, and took virtual tours of galleries that were closed to the public. My not-so-guilty pleasure was following Cowboy Tim from the National Cowboy Museum on Twitter who unwittingly redefined the tone of museum communications.

I miss visiting museums. In the past four years I have spent time in hundreds of museums, sometimes several in a day—as many as a dozen in a week. If you are reading this article, chances are you miss museums, too. The virtual museum experience will never replace my desire to examine original objects and experience a gallery's architectural space, but until we can all travel again, #MuseumFromHome creates a positive balance to doom-scrolling media headlines.

I did not address the tremendous loss of life and livelihood in these past five months, and how the cracks in our economic and health care systems revealed the deep roots of systemic racism in our nation and in our museums. Each time I look at the crowd-sourced Museum Staff COVID-19 Impact Chart (https://docs.google.com/spreadsheets/d/1acEaRss ONaAlFjThEFybfhBBIb3OIuOne-NHsghOMxg/edit#gid=0), I am crushed to see that so many colleagues have lost their jobs. As a field, we have lost the most racially and culturally diverse, digitally knowledgeable generation to enter the museum sector. I know that in some museums where educators and visitors services staff have been laid off, they could have been put to work taking collections, exhibitions, and programs into the digital realm. I also know that 30 percent of New York's museums closed 2018 in a deficit position, and the pandemic made hard economic choices and the loss of staff positions a necessity.

At this time, we know we will not be able to welcome large numbers of people into our museum galleries. We also know, especially in rural regions of our state and nation that internet access remains a real barrier to the ways in which museums can engage a wider audience. The pandemic has exposed the ways in which museums can and should conduct business differently in a post-COVID world, but social media metrics have allowed us to quantify the ways in which people value the role of museums in our society. I hope that funders will see the profound need for investment in technology to support digital infrastructure. It is time to think constructively about how we move forward in this new normal changing our primary relationship with our audiences and expanding our programs and policies to reflect the contributions of everyone who calls our nation their home.

Review by Erika Sanger. Sanger is the executive director of the Museum Association of New York (MANY) and has held positions at the International Center of Photography, the Jewish Museum, the New-York Historical Society, the Brooklyn Museum, the Asheville Art Museum (NC), and the Albany Institute of History & Art. She also served as director of development at Penland School of Crafts in western North Carolina. Sanger holds a BFA from Clark University and an MA from NYU's Steinhardt School of Culture, Education, and Human Development.

INSTITUTE FOR THOMAS PAINE STUDIES

Founded in 2011 to preserve and develop the rich archive of the Thomas Paine National Historical Association, the Institute for Thomas Paine Studies' expansive mission is to support the broader interdisciplinary research of early American studies. Building on the TPNHA collection, which includes writings, material objects and other items by and about Paine and his world, the ITPS focuses on archival studies, public history, and digital humanities efforts. This includes undergraduate research and internship programs, conferences, seminars, workshop series, and archival exhibits.

Highlights of ITPS initiatives, past and present, include the Gardiner Archival Fellowship program, the September 2020 virtual conference "Foundations of Independence," the Text Attribution Project, and the new podcast series "Public History, Public Heath" and "Public History in a Virtual Age." Collaborations include participation in the McNeil Center Consortium and undergraduate internship collaborations with Mount Vernon-Washington Library and the Thomas Paine Cottage. The ITPS is also developing a vibrant digital presence through its social media and brand-new research portal, theitps.org.

theitps.org
itps@iona.edu
🐦 @TheITPS

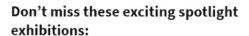

Museum Association of New York

The Power
of Partnership

April 10 - 13, 2021
Corning, NY

nysmuseums.org/annualconference

ART.
HISTORY.
AND MORE.

*because
history
matters*

NEW-YORK
HISTORICAL
SOCIETY
MUSEUM & LIBRARY

nyhistory.org
@nyhistory

SIENA COLLEGE'S MCCORMICK CENTER FOR THE STUDY OF THE AMERICAN REVOLUTION

The McCormick Center partners with nonprofits and the public sector to develop and share educational programming about the history of New York State and colonial and Revolutionary America. The Center provides Siena students with personally meaningful leadership and learning opportunities that advance history education and prepares them for life, work, and active citizenship.

SIENA

THE McCORMICK CENTER

For more information, contact
Jennifer Dorsey, Ph.D., Professor of History
mccormickcenter@siena.edu · 518-783-2319

MASTER DISCOVERY

DISCOVER MASTERY

M.A. in LIBERAL STUDIES
New York Studies

Choose from 20 interdisciplinary concentrations. *What will you master?*
http://bit.ly/32EqKul

THE GRADUATE CENTER
CITY UNIVERSITY OF NEW YORK

Looking for your New York family? Let us help you.

The New York Genealogical and Biographical Society is the most authoritative resource for research on families with New York connections.

NYG&B Members receive:

- Online access to exclusive digital resources
- Print and/or digital subscriptions to *The NYG&B Record* and the *New York Researcher*
- Discounts on programs, publications, and partner services

Join online at newyorkfamilyhistory.org or call 212-755-8532

State University of New York

C A H R
Center for Applied Historical Research

The mission of CAHR is to facilitate broad democratic access to historical resources and knowledge. CAHR accomplishes this by applying historical scholarship to projects outside the academy through partnerships and collaborations among public and academic historians, corporate and governmental agencies, and public and private historical institutions. CAHR fosters and preserves community and institutional historical memory; advocates the application of historical understanding in policy formation; expands the skills of historians; and utilizes information technology to make the fruits of historical research widely available to teachers, students, and the general public.

CAHR is seeking manuscript proposals for the SUNY Press series, "Public History in New York State." For this and other inquiries, contact: Ivan D. Steen (isteen@albany.edu).